AUGUSTINE

ALSO BY JAMES J. O'DONNELL

Cassiodorus (1979)

Boethius, *Consolatio Philosophiae*
(edition and commentary, 1984)

Augustine (1985)

Augustine, *Confessions*
(edition and commentary, 1992)

Scholarly Journals at the Crossroads (1995, with A. Okerson)

Avatars of the Word (1998)

LC21: A Digital Strategy for the Library of Congress
(editor and contributor, 2000)

AUGUSTINE

A New Biography

JAMES J. O'DONNELL

ecco

An Imprint of HarperCollinsPublishers

B
AUGUSTINE
14 DAY

HarperCollins books may be purchased for educational, business, or sales promotional use. For information, please write: Special Markets Department, HarperCollins Publishers Inc., 10 East 53rd Street, New York, NY 10022.

FIRST EDITION

Designed by Mia Risberg

Map by David Cain

Library of Congress Cataloging-in-Publication Data

O'Donnell, James Joseph, 1950–
    Augustine: a new biography / James J. O'Donnell.—1st ed.
        p.   cm.
    Includes bibliographical references and index.
    ISBN 0-06-053537-7
    1. Augustine, Saint, Bishop of Hippo.   2. Christian saints—Algeria—
Hippo (Extinct city)—Biography.   I. Title.

BR1720.A9O36   2005
270.2'092—dc22
[B]   2004058347

05   06   07   08   09   BVG/RRD   10   9   8   7   6   5   4   3   2   1

For Kezia and Nico Knauer
and
for Mama Lesia Shumelda

CONTENTS

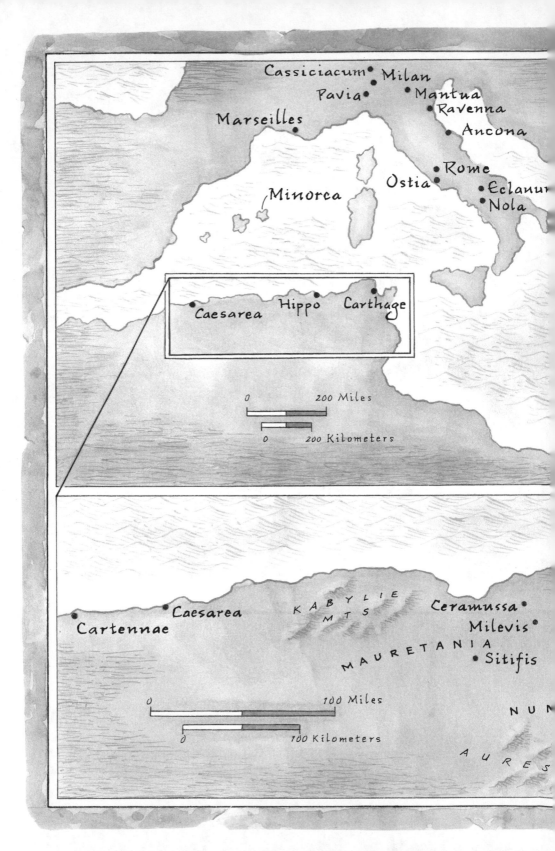

Cassiciacum
Milan
Pavia
Mantua
Ravenna
Marseilles
Ancona

Minorca

Ostia
Rome
Eclanum
Nola

Caesarea
Hippo
Carthage

0   200 Miles

0   200 Kilometers

Cartennae
Caesarea
KABYLIE MTS
Ceramussa
Milevis
MAURETANIA
Sitifis

0   100 Miles

0   100 Kilometers

NUM

AURES

The MEDITERRANEAN and NORTH AFRICA

- Sardica
- Constantinople
- Mopsuestia
- Antioch
- Beirut
- Diospolis
- Bethlehem
- Alexandria

Hippo Diarrhytus
- Uzalis
- Hippo Regius
- Carthage
- Mutugenna
DJEBEL EDOUGH MTS.
- Fussala
Medjerda R.
Seybouse R.
- Bulla Regia
AFRICA PROCONSULARIS
- Calama
- Constantine
- Tagaste
- Sicca
- Thubursicu
- Madauros
- Hadrumetum
...DIA
- Bagai
- Sufes
- Timgad
MOUNTAINS

CHRONOLOGY

311	Emperor Constantine publicly favors Christianity; Caecilianists and Donatists begin controversy that divides the African church
347ff	"The Times of Macarius": Roman commissioner sent to Africa to make peace between Caecilianists and Donatists; uses force to impose Caecilianist leaders on Donatist churches (including the church in Tagaste, where Augustine's parents married at about this time)
354	Augustine born in Tagaste (modern Souk Ahras, Algeria), 13 November, son of Patricius and Monnica
361–363	Emperor Julian ("the Apostate") withdraws support for Christianity; Donatism regains primacy in Africa
371/72	Augustine marries (wife's name not known); son Adeodatus born within a year
372/73	Reads Cicero's *Hortensius*—turns to philosophical studies
375–386	Teaching career (Tagaste, Carthage, Rome, Milan)
385/86	Sends wife back to Africa in order to make a better marriage (never consummated)
386/87	Religious crisis, culminating in baptism in March 387
388	Monnica dies in Ostia, Italy
388–391	Retires to Tagaste

390   Adeodatus dies

391   Emperor Theodosius bans public practice of tradi-
       tional religion

391   Augustine ordained presbyter at Hippo Regius (mod-
       ern Annaba, Algeria)

395/96 Ordained bishop at Hippo

399   Temple-busting and other anti-"pagan" initiatives by
       imperial government

397/401 Augustine writes *Confessions* (perhaps entirely com-
       pleted in 397)

405*ff* Anti-Donatist laws from emperor; mainly ineffective

410   Rome "sacked" by "Visigoths," 24–26 August

411   Conference at Carthage to adjudicate dispute between
       Caecilianists and Donatists, 1–6 June

412   Augustine writes first pamphlets against Pelagius

412–426 Writes *City of God*

430   Dies in Hippo, 28 August

431   Hippo captured by Vandals

AUGUSTINE

AUGUSTINE'S VOICE

I n this nothing town, the sun of the Maghreb outside the hall is relentless, but the shade between stone columns within is cool. Men stand on one side, women on the other, all hushed in concentration on the deliberate gestures of one man. He sits, dressed simply and plainly enough to attract attention, one step above the crowd at the end of the hall and listens attentively as a younger man reads a short account of two brothers competing for their father's attention, a contest the younger wins by trickery. Their names are Jacob and Esau.

When the reader finishes, the older man rises and begins to speak. The quiet deepens as his voice fills the space effortlessly. It shapes elegant and well-proportioned sentences and colors them with expression. He is a star performer in a room like this and few of these people have ever seen or heard anything to match him. In a world without mass media, his performance is the kind that gets talked about on other days in other towns. His voice has been the making of him.

The story of the two brothers, he tells his listeners, is part of a larger story. All these events happened long ago and in a very different world to people he calls "Judeans," and the story of the two brothers is one part of a larger story. The Judeans go into exile in Egypt and then escape through miraculous waters, for their god is powerful and favors them, up to a point.

The story, which most of us probably recognize, is still fresh for his audience and perhaps even unfamiliar to some. It has a contemporary message for the people standing before the speaker—"Christians" he calls them—and as he continues, persuasive and eloquent, he brings it home. They, too, have been through miraculous waters, and so the old story of the Judeans is somehow their story as well:

> Brothers, look and see: the Judeans were liberated in the sea, the Egyptians were destroyed in it. So Christians are liberated by the forgiveness of sins, and sins are destroyed in baptism. The Judeans go beyond the Red Sea and walk through the desert. It's the same way with Christians after baptism: they're not yet in the land of promise, but they live in hope. This world *is* a desert, but it becomes a real desert for the Christian after baptism if he understands what he has received. If he doesn't receive only the outward signs of the sacrament, but if these signs really take spiritual effect in his heart, then he understands how this world is a desert for him. He understands that he's living like a stranger here and that he sighs for his true homeland. But as long as he's sighing, he lives in hope. For in our hope we are saved.[1]

For the merchants and lawyers and officers and gentlemen in the audience, the alienation from the ordinary, comfortable social world around them, the saving and healing alienation that the speaker evokes, might not be obvious. He assumes that without him to tell them, they would go on about their business blithely at home in the world, thinking of nothing else. Is he speaking to an alienation he senses in them and shares with them, or is he creating it by his words? He tells them, at any rate, how they can and should read their own lives differently by reading, or hearing, the story of Jacob and Esau and their nation. He goes on:

> Temptations happen, so they happen to us even after baptism. The Egyptians who chased the Judeans out of Egypt weren't their only enemies—but they were their old enemies. In the same way, our past life and our past sins obey their prince, the devil, and continue to haunt us. There are enemies in the desert as well, trying to block our path. The Judeans fought with them and were victorious.

To call the pleasures of the world "temptation" is to put a moral cast on them. The audience this day keeps men and women separate as a symbol of a deeper suspicion of the relations that the sexes make when left to themselves. Thoughts and hands are to be under strict control, and the children of matrimony the only excuse for anything but the most austere avoidance of sexual contact.

But none present is free of stain. That devil, those past sins, and that past life follow every member of the assembly. No one there could think she or he has lived free and easy, at peace with the world. Hope, the inseparable twin brother of fear, is the best they can manage: hope for a better life, but a better life to be found only on the other side—of death.

Victory—over temptation, over the devil, over death—turns out to be a key word this day because almost an hour later, as the speaker is finishing, he reminds those assembled that today's gathering is meant to recall the virtues of a "witness" (he uses the relatively unfamiliar Greek word *martyr*) named Vincent ("the Winner" is how that name would have translated to a Latin-speaking audience) who had been killed some decades earlier by the Roman authorities. His story, a predictable tale of bright virtue resisting dark power, had probably been read aloud a little earlier and still lingered in the audience's mind.

Because he has shared this and other stories and tried to make them throw light on the contemporary life of this tedious North African town, the audience can go away thinking of themselves in ways that would puzzle many of their neighbors. The stories this man tells let the congregants rewrite themselves into other roles, with improbable hopes and unexpected responsibilities and pitfalls. If they can believe his interpretations of the stories, they would indeed be citizens of a great invisible city that differed in many ways from their ordinary condition.

When the speaker finishes, there is more stirring and speaking in front of the hall. A few minutes later, some in the audience are asked to leave, for they have not been fully admitted to membership in this fellowship. When they are gone, still more talking and doing and some singing follow, in which the speaker plays a central part. Eventually bread and wine are distributed, and after one last song the group finally disbands, having spent perhaps two hours together.

Within the walls of this place, the speaker is in command, uncontested. But as soon as his audience disbands, they enter a world where his authority is more problematic. Some of them have their doubts about what they have just heard, seen, and done. But for today, they made the choice to be there. As they scatter, some pass a similar hall not far down the street, where a larger audience has been doing similar things at the same hour. A few biting remarks are probably exchanged as the groups brush past one another, and the tension in the air marks a contest for authority between the two camps.

There are others in the town who are indifferent to both groups and who prefer their own ways of gathering and enacting community: another ceremonial meal, perhaps, different stories, different gods even. But twenty years earlier the authorities had made it clear that where Roman law held sway Christians and Christians alone would be allowed to celebrate such rituals. The man whose voice we have tried to hear is a master of using the public law and the emperor's authority to advance the cause of his community. For him, it is not enough that most of his rivals have been silenced. He insists that his way and his way alone shall prevail. In the end, he succeeds in this. And fails.

This book is about him. He was Aurelius Augustinus by birth, Augustinus Hipponensis (Augustine of Hippo) by profession.[2] If all we knew about him was that he was a powerful and eloquent leader and shaper of affairs in his own time, he would hold our attention easily enough. But he is also someone else—"Saint Augustine"[3]—and we know him not from what he did but from what he wrote. He died almost sixteen hundred years ago and there has been no decade in all that time in which he has not been read, admired, controverted, and read again. A few of his books have won their way into that body of literature that is continuously published in many languages and on all continents. More even than his books, his ideas (or stereotypes of a few of them) have become caricatures of themselves and leitmotifs for belief and controversy. "Just war," "original sin," "concupiscence"—we are right to attach these notions to him, yet we misrepresent him when we do.

The vignette with which I started already captures common themes of doctrine and conflict worth keeping in mind. On the one hand, Augustine makes it clear that, for him, divine power is absolute and above humankind, determining all that falls below. In later years he would speak of this as "predestination" and would engage in long wars with others of his own religious community who seemed to him to err by relying too much on human will and effort, and he would call them "Pelagians." At the same time, his tendency to divide the world into two great warring camps would be seen by many as a relic of his earlier religious enthusiasm for a new-age sect called Manicheism that spoke of cosmic warfare between the dual powers of good and evil, with outcome uncertain. And even as he spoke, there were still other Christians in the church down the street who reviled him and his flock as traitors and false Christians. He called them "Donatists" and fought a deadly war with them for two decades to wrest primacy among the Christians of Africa away from them. And then there were still many beyond the walls of any church, the ones he would call "pagans," who mistrusted him and all his like and hated them for the way they had gotten Roman armies to destroy old temples and force men into new religious ways. A quiet Sunday morning in church can conceal strong passions in surprising places.

Although there are many Augustines, some of whom were in church that Sunday, some of whom we will meet here, this book is about two in particular, the one who lived and died a long time ago and the one who lives to be remade by us and is known from his works. It's impossible to tell the story of the one without the other.

We will concentrate first on the Augustine who lived long ago. He is less well known than his undying alter ego but there is much to be known about him, and in telling his stories we will come in the end to a better sense of who he really was. Just as we've already seen him telling an old story with urgent present meaning, it will be impossible for us not to think of our *now* when we read about his *then*, and that's as it should be. But we should not jump to conclusions about him, or accept simple answers. I suspect most readers will find that he has more to offer our world, even as he becomes less simple to imagine or invoke in his own.

And throughout we will struggle to hear his voice. We know it filled theaters and churches for over half a century and dictated the five million words that survive today in his published works. Once it even stopped a riot. Yet we know almost nothing of how he looked—tall or short, dark or light, though he was probably thin, by ascetic choice. Even the very oldest image, from sixth-century Rome, only approximates his dress, but it cannot be an image of the man himself. Far more familiar are the medieval, Renaissance, and modern paintings that turn him into a great bishop of those later ages. In their time, they were at best edifying; today we should be amused by them and persist in imagining a man who held people's attention precisely by the way he seemed to eschew attention. So while we do know this of him, nothing that aspires to be a picture of the man has a prayer of being anything like him.

Of the books he dictated in his study, and that survived through arduous hand-copying for a thousand years and repeated printing for another five hundred, the one that is most often read today he called *Confessions*, a work of extraordinary artifice and power. If we use that book and his other books to imagine his life, we might then fall into the same trap his contemporaries did: of being overpowered by him, of being seduced by his art, of being driven to accept his words as he intended them, of taking his world his way. By writing these famous confessions, he wanted us to learn his story, wanted to make us think he was coming entirely clean. But no one ever comes entirely clean. No one tells the whole story. We cannot tell the whole of our own story, much less that of someone who lived and died sixteen hundred years ago. But we can tell more of the story than Augustine told us, more than he sometimes knew. If we read his words and those of his contemporaries with resistance and imagination, they will reveal him to us in many ways.

So we must struggle to hear his voice, and struggle at the same time not to be hypnotized by it. The balancing act is exhilarating and terrifying.

Let's start with these famous words:

Inquietum est cor nostrum, donec requiescat in te.

Our heart is restless, until it rests in you.[4]

They come from the first page of his *Confessions*. Another eighty thousand Latin words follow. Where do they come from? How did he speak them?

He spoke them aloud to his secretaries when he was forty-two years old. We mark the date as the year 397 of the common era (C.E.), but that familiar reckoning was constructed more than a century after his time by a monk named Dionysius from what is now Moldova and only became a standard of reckoning several hundred years after that. Augustine and his contemporaries knew the year 397 as the 1,150th since the founding of the city of Rome and the third year of the reign of the emperor Honorius in Milan and his brother Arcadius in Constantinople. Some people at the time noticed that 365 years, more or less, had elapsed since the crucifixion of Jesus and had various expectations of how that year might be marked. Would it bring the second coming? Augustine never seems to have thought so, but he knew the arguments and lived in a time when they found serious takers.

He spoke those words in the African city of Hippo Regius, now called Annaba in Algeria. A year or so before, Augustine had become the leader of a Christian congregation there, and he lived now at the center of a troubled community. His Christians were a small group, very much aware of the bigger, more prosperous Christian community that hated them and was headquartered just down the block, and his followers were in constant danger of being swallowed up by the larger group. Augustine's voice, and his connections in high places, ultimately would rescue his community and make it prevail over its rival, not only in Hippo but in all of Roman Africa. But no one, in 397, would have bet on such an outcome.

Augustine made the *Confessions* because he was afraid. Not just of defeat in local church politics, but of defeat in the eyes of an overpowering master to whom he owed absolute obedience and service, the "you" who will bring rest. That "master"—Augustine addressed him as *dominus*, a word we are used to hearing translated as "lord"—was as demanding as any Roman slaveowner, even if at the end of the day he might be more forgiving of his slaves' failures to live up to his expectations. To apply the word "god" to that master is to run a great risk, the commonest risk run by historians of this period, of assuming that we know just what Augustine meant. Augustine's world still knew lots of different kinds of gods, and ardent devotees of any one of them knew perfectly well what the competition was like and perhaps even sampled other religious products from time to time. Only the highest-minded had any idea of the identity of a single divine principle crossing all religions. Augustine was not so high-minded, at least not in the years when we know him best. (By leaving the word "god" in lowercase, I hope to remind readers of this danger throughout this book.)

The Augustine of the *Confessions* is a man who stands amid the political perils of his world—perils that almost took his life more than once—and the expectations of his slave driver. His god is too big to grasp, but he spent fifty years trying to do just that, the better to be an obedient slave. The story he tells is the one that made sense of his own experience, made sense in a way that others might understand and accept if they were of his own faction. At the same time, the act of telling his story sustained him and helped him shape the way he could lead his people and achieve his goals. From the first page of the *Confessions* to the last, we eavesdrop on a self-conscious and stylized performance. In that book, written a little more than halfway through his lifetime, but still more or less at the beginning of his public career as community leader, Augustine performed an interpretation of his own life. The man with the voice unlike any other was never more onstage than when he set out to reveal himself to us. Let's begin by looking for some of the things he chose not to mention.

THE VIEW
FROM AFRICA

HIPPO AND BEYOND

Augustine's Hippo Regius[5] was the center of the universe for some who lived there and the back of beyond for many who visited. A port city on the Mediterranean coast of Africa, where the river Seybouse came down from the mountains to the sea, it stood a distant second to Carthage in commerce and prestige. Augustine hadn't lived there all his life.

He had grown up between two Africas: the more Romanized coastal land with its port cities and settled society, and the up-country olive- and breadbasket of Numidia, a society less consciously dignified and Rome-oriented. Even at this date, the mid-350s, Numidia felt a little like western Canada before World War II.

Augustine never saw the sea as a child. He tells of imagining what it was like from a glass of water,[6] and then is enthralled by its colors,[7] but he's afraid to go out upon it again after his one trip to Italy and back, and he never saw the other sea to the south, the Sahara.[8] He was born in a green valley in the mountains, in the market town of Tagaste (the modern Souk Ahras), in a landscape reminiscent of Tuscany, his horizons bounded within a couple of miles on each side by hill crests and forests.

As a boy, he headed farther inland, to Madauros, climbing up out of his valley to find the beginnings of the broad expanse of high plain that lies between the coast and the desert of North Africa. From a closed-in valley, he entered vertiginous open spaces, where grasslands stretched to the horizons, interrupted only by the well-cultivated olive groves that brought this land its prosperity.

He was a nobody, the son of a minor landowner in a third-rate town, with no money to speak of and few connections. For such nobodies, proximity to power was the first step to eminence. A precise sense of the wealth and standing of his father, Patricius, eludes us, but the things we know are: (1) he belonged to the curial class, that is, the "senate" of landowners of Tagaste who were responsible for the community's governance, including collective responsibility for civic works (not surprisingly, membership on those councils was an honor many would just as soon avoid, and many, like Augustine, did so by joining the clergy[9]); (2) he owned a "few little acres" (*pauci agelluli*);[10] and (3) he relied on the friendship and support of Romanianus, a much richer landowner in the same town, to provide the financial resources to send Augustine off to university in Carthage (then the greatest port city of Africa). Augustine's important luck was in continuing to have Romanianus support him through his Milan days. (The patron fell in with Augustine's philosophical and religious enthusiasms up to a point, but in the end, he reverted to type, taking baptism only at death's door, recovering, and taking up in widowhood with mistresses. Augustine is last seen writing to Romanianus to rebuke him.[11])

Augustine succeeded three times in the public eye when still very young. It was an achievement when he was a young man that he got to teach in Carthage; an achievement again when he was crowned there by the proconsul Vindicianus, the man who lived in the palace on a hill, as winner in an oratorial contest (a very familiar and very "pagan" public scene in the old city);[12] and an achievement again when he went to Italy and won appointment to Milan as imperial professor of rhetoric through well-placed friends. When Augustine went to Milan, his family's ambitions pursuing him, he had hopes he later reconstructed[13] this way: "We have our powerful friends, and if nothing else (I say this in a rush), at least a governorship could come our way, and I could marry a wife with money (so she wouldn't be a burden on our outgoings)—that's the limit of my desires." Many provincials from backwaters like Tagaste would have shared this ambition, but it was remarkably within reach for Augustine. If he was not yet a "friend of the emperor," he was closing in on that status during his time in Milan.

Yet his worldly career came to an end, as we shall soon see, and when it did, he did as most others would do: he went home to make the best of things. Even with a worldly career of the sort we have just imagined, it's likely that he would still have ended, sooner or later, back where he started. In 388, he settled on his family property and lived there without visible hopes or plans for three years. Here is how his first biographer, Possidius, described his intention:

> And it pleased him, after he had been baptized, to take his friends and neighbors who had joined him in serving god, and go back to Africa, to his own house and lands. When he got there and settled down, for about three years he put aside worldly cares and with those who stayed with him he lived for god, with fasting, prayer, and good works, meditating on the law of god day and night. And whatever god revealed to him as he thought and prayed, he taught to others; with conversation and with books he taught one and all, near and far.[14]

Many writers have spoken of the Augustine of 388–91 as a monk, or at least a monk-in-all-but-name. That is an anachronism.[15] His retirement to the family property was entirely in character and entirely typical. That he chose philosophy over philandering would have puzzled only a few of his neighbors or relatives. In Tagaste, after his time in Italy, he was an oddity, to be sure. No one we can see in Africa of that time at all resembles the gentlemanly Augustine.[16] The closest contemporary comparison that presents itself is an unflattering one—to the fractious and obtuse Consentius of Minorca: amateur of theology, self-absorbed, and not much inclined to hear what anybody was saying to him. (We'll meet him later.) Consentius is in many ways the classical "idiot," the man living too much on his own and with his own ideas. If Augustine had really succeeded in finding isolation and retirement in Tagaste, he might very well have developed his own quirks and eccentricities. (As though there were not plenty of people to say that the Augustine of *Hippo* had his share of eccentricities!) But this Augustine is an easy one to imagine—beginning to age, obsessive, not quite in touch with the ideas and issues of his world, but ready to offer an opinion all the same.

Instead, he found himself back in the public eye.

He lived in a golden age in Africa, with wealth on display on all sides, even when surrounded by squalor, after five hundred years of Roman rule. No emperor had set foot in Africa in living memory, nor would any appear there again; they were busy with the army on Rome's northern frontiers. In Africa, the empire showed itself in the form of soldiers (some on frontier duty), tax collectors, and judges. People's fears were personal and local: sickness, death, drought, famine, brigandage in remote locations. The empire could take care of itself, or so it had seemed for a very long time.

When in 391 Augustine came to live in Hippo as a junior clergy member of the African church, the city was, while not great, at least busy. To an ancient visitor, it would have seemed noisy and "modern,"[17] with perhaps thirty to forty thousand residents (a tenth the size of Carthage at the time). The farmland that brought the metropolis its prosperity lay in an arc south of the city stretching twenty or so miles. On the city's northern and western approaches, the Djebel Edough mountains loomed large and shadowy, offering some cooling relief in the summer, when the sun fell behind the mountain ridge a good hour or so before natural sunset and left behind long twilights without the direct heat of the day. In winter, the mountains disappeared behind the rain clouds for days on end as Atlantic storms funneled through Gibraltar and hurtled across the inland sea. Hippo was much closer to Tagaste than to Carthage, but the mountains of the Medjerda lay between the two and offered no easy ascent or descent for man or donkey. Because Hippo was also the westernmost convenient port for travelers going to Numidia and the Mauretanias, the road from the city lay to the south and west inland to Cirta (modern Constantine), the next center of administration and prosperity.

Before Augustine, we know nothing of Hippo to suggest cultural or intellectual activity, apart from the anomaly of a statue of the historian Suetonius found there. It was a businessman's town, a small stage, and unlike today's cities in many ways. The stretch of class distinction was even wider than we see now, with abject slaves chained, sometimes literally, to their work, rich men and their grand retinues, and precious little egalitarian sentiment to counter such realities. Women were generally confined and excluded from public life. The greatest difference, however, probably lay in the comparative absence of the extraordinary overlay of *meaning* that marks modern communities. Today we see an urban street and know that every building is a conscious construction, with a sign on every door and every street and every parking place, and with explicit names and numbers that docket and control and define the space. The interpreter and the imagination have little to do but rebel. Ancient cities were naïve by comparison, with islands of overdetermined meaning proclaimed to the viewer in a limited number of public buildings, by inscriptions on stone designed to advertise the dignity of the donor who had them carved, and in the annual round of festivals and spectacles. Games in the circus and gossip in the forum could take people outside themselves, but not much else did, apart from church. Not long before Augustine's days there, a predictable round of public processions and ceremonies, often culminating in sacrifices in temples, had diverted the urban public. Augustine remembered those days with horror and spoke ill of them, but others must have recalled them fondly.

For in 391, the emperor Theodosius had forbidden all public sacrifice and "pagan" ritual. The ban had left empty spaces and times in every Roman city. The stench of butchery and barbecue that had regularly filled the public spaces of the cities faded away. The underlying order of the community came from the preverbal ties of family and community and belonging, an order invisible to a visitor but ineluctable to the resident. Christianity was the official religion and public practice, but Christians were divided and there were many in the city whose adherence to Christianity fell far short of what the bishop would like to have seen.

Since the 1950s, the visitor to modern Annaba has been able to see remains of what is called the Christian quarter of Hippo, and much of the rest of the ancient city besides. The site was excavated between the 1920s and the 1950s by a French naval officer and archaeologist, Erwan Marec. Much more could have been done and much is still unknown, but a visit to the site is nonetheless instructive. Two hillocks separated by a few hundred yards rise on either side of the remains of the ancient city. The forum lies directly between the hills, one of which must have been the citadel of the earliest city and the location of one or another god's temple over time.[18] The way from the forum to the Christian quarter lies near what was the seashore in antiquity (the sea has now retreated about half a mile). The Christian buildings uncovered in the 1950s lay very close to the water, separated from it apparently only by a row of opulent villas.

The centerpiece of the modern excavation is the grand basilica, the ground-level remains of a substantial church. The nave was about 120 feet by 60 feet, and at one end a semicircular apse about 30 feet across. The apse was surrounded by a low bench for the clergy, and at the center of the apse was the marble seat, now lost, of the presiding bishop. An altar table would have stood in front of where he sat. We can still walk around in this place, sit on the bench, and get a sense of the size and shape of the building. Too small to hold more than a tiny fraction of the city's population, but large enough to challenge the vocal capacity of any modern and most ancient voices, it was Augustine's familiar stage for at least a part of his career. Adjacent to the church is a smaller chapel, and next to it a small baptistry, with the font intact, waist-deep for an adult. The baptistry undoubtedly had a sacred quality about it, but the basilica itself would have felt remarkably secular to most ancients. Christians had modeled their meeting places on the open public spaces of the meeting halls around the forum, not on the closed and numinous temples.[19]

The basilica that survives was built sometime in the fourth century; we're not sure exactly when. It was not grand, and the ornamentation was probably never completed. We infer from inscriptions on graves in the church that in the fifth and sixth centuries it fell into the hands of Vandal conquerors and Arian clergy whom Augustine would have condemned. For some part of Augustine's life, this was surely his church. From his own works, we know of two churches in Hippo that Augustine used during his career: the *basilica Leontiana*, named after a bishop of Hippo who apparently was martyred in the late third century, and the *basilica maior*, or *basilica pacis* (greater basilica, or basilica of peace).

But there had to be a third substantial church in Hippo: that of the Donatists, whom Augustine hated. In Augustine's Africa, Donatism was an austere and well-established Christian community that looked back to great bishops of Carthage as guarantors of its authenticity. Cyprian, the martyred bishop of the third century, and Donatus, who led the church for thirty years in the early fourth century, were names to conjure with. Cyprian's annual feast day, celebrating the day of his martyrdom, was a high point of the Christian year.

Augustine chose a different community, one that followed the successors of Donatus's rival (from the early 300s), Caecilian. The divisions that separated Christians into angry and often violent factions were a characteristic and deeply rooted part of African life by now. The Caecilianist community had opposed the majority Donatist faction for almost all of the fourth century. Hostility and history separated the two communities, not doctrine. When pressed, they could find real disagreement only over the administration of baptism: Donatists found some sins so grave that only a fresh baptism could wash them away, while the Caecilianists thought baptism so high and powerful a rite that it could never be administered a second time. The two communities complicated and reinforced their enmity with obsessive historical argument and endless mutual recrimination. We will see how obsessively, and dangerously, Augustine fought to advance the cause of his sect against that of the majority.

The uncertainty of the dating of the extant basilica leaves open the strong possibility that it was constructed by the majority Donatists, probably during the time of respite from official harassment that came under the emperor Julian and his successors, after 362, thirty years before Augustine came to Hippo. That would explain how the ornamentation was left incomplete, likely reflecting some crackdown by the government against the sect. Was the original Caecilianist basilica somewhere nearby? Augustine tells us in one letter that the sounds of celebration from the Donatist basilica could be heard in his own church's precincts.[20]

If the church we can see was originally the Donatist basilica, the building would have come into Augustine's hands, but only in 411 or so, when edicts took effect dissolving the Donatist church, confiscating its property, and regularizing its clergy into the ranks of the official church. The capture of the majority church's property and people was a dramatic event in the life of the church of Hippo and Augustine's greatest personal victory, yet he never describes it. The story of that revolution will be central to our exploration of him and his world.

THE WIDER WORLD

Augustine stayed on dry land in Hippo, but his adoptive home lived on shipping and used its position to communicate quickly and well with the great world on the other side of the water, a world of which Augustine was always more conscious than most other Africans. In large part what made him independent and powerful were the comings and goings of his letter-bearers, who kept him in touch with the world beyond the mountains and the sea.

Our name for it, Mediterranean, recognizes that the water lies at the center of a circle of lands. The idea that all the seas from Gibraltar and Marseilles to Alexandria and Constantinople are one is an idea with its own history.[21] Fishermen in small boats in antiquity knew their own neighborhoods, rarely ventured out of sight of land, and told awe-inspiring and awful tales of what happened to those mad enough to sail far from home. The oldest of such tales that we read is the *Odyssey*: the Laestrygonians, the Lotus-Eaters, Circe, and Calypso all lay over the horizon for those readers, and they knew nothing of a "Mediterranean" yet.

Herodotus knew of lands beyond his ken, a little more accurately than Homer did. But it was the conquests of Alexander in Greece and Asia Minor and the Levant and Egypt that began to bind together a community of peoples, whose elite members spoke and wrote mainly in Greek, around the eastern end of the great sea. Romans and Carthaginians, meanwhile, fought it out for domination of the western seas between Italy and Spain and Africa. The Romans triumphed, took their conquests east again, and made what Julius Caesar was the first to call "our sea," *mare nostrum*, their own.

The Mediterranean was the superhighway of that world, and the cities that faced it could communicate with one another often more rapidly than with people nearer but separated by arduous overland journeys. Greek was often the international language of commerce, Latin that of government, and proud people took offense now and then at the influx of foreigners: Greek-speakers in Rome or Latin-speakers in the east. "The Orontes flows into the Tiber" was the satirist Juvenal's complaint at the influx into supposedly pristine Rome of people from distant Syria who spoke the wrong language and showed too little deference to their hosts.

There was one government for all these lands by the first century of the common era, and it persisted then for another five hundred years among most of the Latin-speakers and another fifteen hundred years among the Greeks. At its summit was the emperor, a title of military command first of all, but bringing with it civic authority to legislate, tax, and punish. The fourth century of the common era was a time on the upswing for the Roman regime. The reforming emperors Diocletian and Constantine (whose reigns together extended from 284 to 337, punctuated by a spasm of civil war between their times of ascendancy) had made the local authority of Roman government real and effective after a time of some disarray, and they restored military discipline and effectiveness. Two and sometimes three emperors split authority among themselves by military regions, with usually one to be found somewhere along the Rhine or Danube frontiers (or wintering at headquarters at Trier, in Germany, or Milan, in Italy) and the other most often in Constantinople but sometimes venturing out toward Mesopotamia to fight the Persians. Theodosius, who died in 395, was the last emperor to lead armies and the last to exercise authority in both eastern and western lands; his successors tended to stay home and let the generals do the venturing.

Africa lay at the geographic heart of this Mediterranean world, yet was happy to be politically marginalized. Its produce was brought down to the harbors at Hippo and Carthage and shipped from there across the water, some of it requisitioned by the government to support the army and the teeming population of the city of Rome. But there was ordinary commerce in these African ports as well, and large and small fortunes to be made and lost.

The local power and authority in such places was held by a senate, not unlike a modern chamber of commerce except that membership was like a form of taxation. If you had the money you had to join. The members of this senate (such as the one Patricius and Romanianus belonged to in Tagaste) were then obligated to provide for the public works of the community, and so would be compelled to contribute funds—for example, to the local forum and its decoration. Sometimes they did so reluctantly, other times the members vied with one another to see who could spend the most to best self-advertising effect. It had always been like this in the Hellenistic and Roman Mediterranean, and the genius of Roman government was to make ostentation compulsory and use it as the backbone of local rule.

One way in which civic pride flourished in olden times was in the expenditure of local wealth on temples, ceremonies, and shows. Those traditions had begun to fade in the half-century before Augustine's life. In his time and, to some extent, through his work, they lost out decisively to new practices and traditions. For three hundred years, followers of the teachings of Jesus had collected in smaller and larger bands around the Greek and Latin worlds, forming and dissolving over time, but gradually becoming familiar in more and more places. Traditional Romans could be forgiven for failing to distinguish Christians from Jews during those years.

Augustine shows us a world in which the lines between religious communities are clear and unmistakable, but he speaks as preacher rather than sociologist. In reality, the boundary between one group and another was often porous and the distinction between a religious ritual and a "secular" ceremony was often negligible. It was, as one recent writer has called it, a world full of gods, with a long history of eclectic toleration. Augustine's most vivid picture of that more-than-Christian world is his recollection of that god-filled world:

> When I was a young man, I used to go to their spectacles of sacrilege and their "pagan" games, to watch the priests in their frenzies and listen to the music. I got a thrill out of the disgusting shows enacted in honor of their gods: of Caelestis, their virgin god, and Berecynthia, the mother of the gods. Their lewd actors sang songs in front of Berecynthia's proces-

sional litter on the day of her solemn purification that were unfit for the ears of the mother of a senator—no, really, unfit for the ears of the actors' mothers, to say nothing of the mother of the gods! . . . But they sang them before a teeming crowd of both sexes. . . . I don't know where the worshipers of Caelestis got their ideas about chastity, but when they set her image up in her shrine, people thronged in from all sides, and we watched the sketches they played out there, looking back and forth from the virgin goddess to the crowd of whores, worshiping the one and reveling in the filthiness of the other. . . . They knew how to please the virgin goddess and displayed publicly things for the thoughtful married lady to take home with her.[22]

Some were too embarrassed to watch, but still they peeked.

The Jewish and Christian gods were not especially remarkable. Their followers were occasionally found to be hardheaded and offensive in proclaiming the excellence of their gods, and the Christians in particular ran afoul of authority for refusing to show appropriate respect to the few common rites of reverence for the emperor in his divine persona that anybody took seriously. Christian writers spoke of these occasional outbursts in the days before the emperor Constantine as "persecution" and complained of systematic judicial terror. Those in authority wouldn't have found the complaints particularly interesting or persuasive.

But the time came when an emperor fell in with the Christians. The story told of Constantine isn't necessarily true: he sees a vision of the cross in the sky, encourages his soldiers to mark their weapons with it the next day, wins his battle, and follows the new god ever after. It's certainly a very old-fashioned ancient god-story, but, however taken, it marks his turning toward Christian rites and ways. He wouldn't be baptized himself until on his deathbed in 337, a full twenty-five years after his supposed vision, but he had already begun taking public money away from the traditional cults and giving it to the Christians and their bishops, who flourished. When they fell to bickering among themselves, Constantine sometimes intervened, and he weighed in on their theological debates with a thorough lack of appropriate education.

Constantine's successors followed his new religious enthusiasm for the most part. The one real exception was the emperor Julian, the so-called apostate, reigning briefly (from 361 to 363) and dying in a battle (perhaps at the hands of one of his own men) of a misguided assault with too few troops on Persian territories near what is now Baghdad. The enthusiasm shown by other fourth-century emperors for Christianity varied, however, as did their choice of allegiance among the various competing forms of Christianity then in play.

In practical terms, back in places like Hippo, the coming of state-sponsored Christianity meant the emergence of new forms of power and patronage. The local Christian leader, bearing the Greek title *episcopus* ("overseer," carried over into Latin and then Anglo-Saxon, and contracted eventually to "bishop"), would emerge in many places as a figure of authority in his own right. Especially if he had powerful and wealthy friends, he could be someone to reckon with, and even in unprepossessing places where he had few connections, his claim to connection with the best new god in the world (enforced by the state) made him attractive to a variety of followers, some of them devout believers. The diversity of Christian beliefs and practices meant that in many places around the Mediterranean world, Christian rivals competed for the same local attention. There was nothing unusual about that. Augustine's own story is largely about the working out of the new role of bishop in his town and in his country. But by his time, even the locals who had no interest in such things had to pay attention.

WHY AUGUSTINE CAME TO HIPPO— AND WHY HE STAYED THERE

Hippo was Augustine's home from his late thirties until his death, almost forty years later. In his early seventies, prudently anticipating his end, he set out to clean house. He named a successor, took the privilege of semi-retirement by delegating some of his responsibilities to that successor, and then found himself pressed by embarrassing revelations about his clergy to make a public accounting of them, their finances, and their family affairs.

In the course of that account, spread out over two sermons given in the late 420s, Augustine told the story of his own coming to Hippo:[23]

> I came to this city a young man, as many of you know. I was looking for a place to set up a monastery and dwell with my brothers. I had left behind all worldly hopes and did not want to be the thing I could be [a country gentleman], but neither did I imagine being what I am [a bishop]. I chose to be lowly in the house of my god, rather than to dwell

in the tents of sinners. I set myself apart from those who love the world, but I didn't think myself the equal of those who govern others. Nor did I choose a better seat at the master's banquet for myself, but a worse and a lowly one. And it pleased him to say to me, "Go up higher." I was so afraid of the bishop's job that, because my reputation had begun to be of some weight among god's servants, I didn't go anyplace where I knew there was no bishop. I took care about this and did whatever I could to make sure I could be saved in a humble setting, not endangered on high. But, as I said, the slave should not contradict his master.

I came to this city to see a friend I thought I could win for god, to get him to be with us in the monastery.[24] I was careless, because the place had a bishop. They grabbed me and made me a priest,[25] and from there a bishop.[26] I didn't bring anything with me and I didn't come to this church with anything but the clothes on my back. And because I had set my mind on being in a monastery with my brothers, when he found out my intention and my wish, the aged bishop Valerius of happy memory gave me the garden where the monastery is now. I began to gather brothers of sound purpose, my peers, who had nothing, just as I had nothing, and who were just like me. Just as I had sold off my poor little bit of property and given it to the poor, they would do likewise if they wanted to live with me, so we would live in a community. The great and fertile property that was common to us was god himself.

So I became a bishop. I saw it was necessary for a bishop to show attentive hospitality to all who came or passed by. If a bishop didn't do that, he would be thought inhumane. But it would have been unseemly to allow this in a monastery. So I decided to have a monastic community of clerics with me here in the bishop's house.

The sermon goes on to sort through the touchy issues of wealth and poverty that are glanced at in these last words. The clergy's self-inflicted poverty originated with Jesus and his associates in first-century Palestine, people who had relatively little to sacrifice. But even the poverty they imagined, the result of "selling all that you have," was still a good distance from destitution and starvation. The first monks, who went out to the desert in the fourth century in Egypt and Palestine and Syria, came closer to that edge than most ascetics, and some of them seem to have lived in genuine misery, alone or nearly alone in the true desert. Poverty in the Latin world was harder to come by, especially because those we see looking for it, like Augustine, started out so well advantaged. Once an aristocrat, even a petty provincial one, always an aristocrat in those days; once wealthy, always shielded, protected, and comfortable.[27] True wealth was the privilege of the very few, who carried the burden off with a particular style. Augustine knew one such man in his early days: "I must confess that he has a certain grandeur of soul, lying dormant. . . . From this there springs his way of keeping open house, the charming wit that enlivens his social gatherings, his elegance, his grand manner, his impeccable good taste."[28] Augustine accepted that not all good Christians would divest themselves of wealth,[29] but he was careful to mark himself off by his behavior and dress and his studied lack of care for his appearance. He still worried, in his early forties, that the temptation of "worldly ambition" was the one that might most easily ensnare him as a bishop before his congregation.[30] His thoughts in this vein are so consistent and so understandable that we might easily grant him the benefit of the doubt, while observing the persistence of the theme. But we should not let him draw us in too easily. By making the issue an internal one—how one handles the fact of eminence—Augustine distracts us from the genuine social achievement and trappings of his life.

Even as a lowly priest, he never had to go hungry. His meals were prepared for him and served by others. There was wine. He had a well-built domicile in which to sleep. When he became bishop of Hippo, his residence was probably located in the Christian quarter near the water and the villas of the rich, where the air was healthier. There was olive oil enough to burn in lamps in the evening to allow reading and other activities by artificial light. He could travel to and from distant cities in comfort and safety, and did so regularly. (When resident there, he was the guest of others with facilities at least as comfortable as those he enjoyed at home.) He was surrounded by people who deferred to his social position. His role made him the center of attention for the hundreds of people who crowded his basilica in Hippo or came to hear him as guest preacher in Carthage.[31] He cautions one cleric that after the last judgment, he should not expect to be standing prominently in the apse of a great building, with a lavishly upholstered marble chair at the center of all attention, surrounded by flocks of devout virgins singing in processions.[32] Such a caution at the same time reminded his colleague of the perquisites of office short of that last judgment. (If Augustine's own church seems less than abundantly ornamented, that was a choice, for the lavishness of churches was proverbial in this period.[33])

Beyond the church building and from the outset of his residence in

Hippo, he was one of a handful of individuals of most senior standing in his community. (Unlike secular dignitaries, moreover, he took his direct power from a lifetime appointment.) Within five years, he had become the chief executive officer of a substantial enterprise, director of its considerable staff, with authority to disburse and manage the resources of the establishment. Among other duties, he sat in his audience hall each week listening to legal cases that were brought to him by citizens impatient with the civil law's delays, and in that capacity he decided cases and influenced the economic fate of the wider community. Plaintiffs and respondents pled before him, without lawyers, all manner of cases and requests. Some were direct legal cases for him to decide; he would go away in private after hearing the parties and then return with a written decision to be read out. He was caustic about those who came to him only because they thought him the best way to advance their worldly interests, while he would try to turn their attention to higher things,[34] so he made sure to preserve a set of letters showing him intervening in such a case on behalf of a man who has offended an unnamed big shot.[35] In addition to the usual legal immunities of membership in the upper class, moreover, his clerical status granted him several additional privileges. His visibility meant that many more pleaders came to him, looking for help in tax cases or seeking his intervention to protect defendants in criminal cases.[36] He was certainly one of those relatively few residents of the Roman empire who could be reasonably sure he would never be beaten or tortured by a judge. Like any rich man, he could expect to be suspected of pecuniary motives, as when people observed that laws against the Donatist Christians allowed, among other things, for the bishop to scoop up property for the church, and he has to remonstrate: "You know, these aren't *Augustine's* villas!"[37] Some hearers probably were not so sure.

The establishment included not just clergy and monks, but others besides. From Possidius[38] we hear of a *praepositus domus ecclesiae*, something like "steward," or even "chief financial officer." There was an accountant (*calculator notarius*[39]), and he could call on the services of a lawyer when tricky questions arose.[40] There must have been other people there. We have no count of the shorthand scribes (*notarii*), for example, who waited on him day and night, but at least a handful were there, taking turns at dictation and then at transcription, as well as other more conventional scribes backing them up. In other words, quite a household.

But were there slaves?[41] Slaves have been called the electricity of ancient domestic life, indispensably labor-saving, rarely mentioned by those who used and abused them. In the awkward and embarrassed account he gave of his clergy's lives in 425–26, a clergy that had been assuming that it would live the life of propertied gentlemen and understood Augustine's "monastic" ideals only imperfectly, Augustine acknowledges that several of them owned slaves.[42] One deacon was hustled into church on that day to manumit slaves he had bought before he became a cleric,[43] and others were hastily cleaning up their affairs at the same time. Augustine seems to have been unaware of these holdings and genuinely ashamed not to have known.

So Augustine himself as priest and bishop probably did not own slaves personally. But would the household of the bishop, the collective enterprise, have owned any? Every urban household of any pretensions had several, some had very many, and stories about people being sold into slavery against their will were heard on all sides.[44] Augustine offered a way to manumit slaves in church,[45] but he was never inclined to insist on anything remotely resembling an abolitionist position. A staff of free men and women, dependents in the ecclesiastical household, would have been possible, but it would have been, and seemed, unusual. The status of such individuals, while technically free, would have differed very little from that of slaves. Late in Augustine's life, an imperial law[46] explicitly exempted the bishops of the proconsular province of Africa (Carthage and its hinterlands) from having to supply recruits to the army, but for the issue to arise, some bishops at least must have been in the position of wealthy landowners.

Augustine could still call himself poor. Even if he left *something* behind in coming to Hippo, however, what he could not and did not leave behind was the class and culture in which he had been brought up. As bishop of Hippo, Augustine was very much a local potentate, a dignitary. In his lifetime, others like him were remaking the Christian bishopric in the image of classical gentlemanliness, bringing with them to the church the expectations, the habits, and the skills of their background.[47] Augustine himself distinguishes those bishops who take up the office for good reasons from those who do so to enjoy the secular honors and worldly benefits of the job,[48] and a church council of his time forbids sons of clerics from hosting the usual public games, at their fathers' expense, on entering into public life—a meaningless prohibition, were some not violating it.[49] The profile of bishop that they established is one with a very long history stretching out after it, keeping bishops of the Latin church in particular relatively independent both of civil government and of ecclesiastical order. Monk-bishops, more common in the eastern church at all periods, still owed something to the status of monk and to the community to which they notionally belonged. Augustine's bishopric was and remained independent of such control, and in his lifetime grew more autonomous, more powerful, and indeed more wealthy.

It was a natural enough progression. At home in Tagaste, he had to discharge all the responsibilities of his station, including membership in the town council and the management of Patricius's land. His natural son and heir, Adeodatus, child of the wife Augustine sent away when he was clearing the path for his ambitions in Italy, was with him and was the presumptive beneficiary of his father's stewardship of the land.[50]

But then at age nineteen Adeodatus died and a prime reason for continuing stewardship of the family property evaporated. *Now* we hear of Augustine thinking about a monastery, whatever he meant by that word, and looking for a place to settle. Readers of the Augustinian passage quoted above (pages 19–20) often seem to assume that he came to Hippo looking for monastic real estate, as it were, but the passage does not say any such thing. He sought to leave behind his family property, to sell it and give the proceeds to the poor, to be sure, though this probably hadn't happened before the moment when he came to Hippo.[51] The trip to Hippo was more precisely focused on the Roman bureaucrat he hoped to win for god. Where and how Augustine might have lived the monastic life he was imagining at that time, we cannot know. Then ordination intervened.

What happened next is slightly odd. Augustine preserved a letter in which he writes to his new bishop, Valerius, to profess his unworthiness for his new office.[52] He explains the tears he shed when he was forcibly ordained and seizes on the possibility of hope in the study of scripture, a study on which he had already set his heart. (The intellectual new cleric finds, that is, an intellectual mode of clerical existence for himself, far from the most obvious way to live the ordained life in that period.) So he pleads now for a little time off, immediately after his ordination: "For this business, I wanted to impose upon your transparent and venerable kindness for a little time, just till Easter. I sent a message through my brothers and now I ask you myself."

On the surface this is unremarkable and makes perfect sense, and is always read that way, as though Augustine were requesting a short research sabbatical. But what are we to make of the sending of the message, once through interlocutors and again in a letter? Why does Augustine need to communicate with his bishop twice, at second hand both times? The geography of the Christian quarter of Hippo (no building was more than two minutes' walk from another) would have facilitated face-to-face conversation. And Augustine admits in another letter of the same period that his absence from Hippo was causing comment.[53]

The answer can be surmised, I believe, if we recall another passage where Augustine speaks of how he found this churchly future for himself. Late in book 10 of the *Confessions*, he says, "I was terrified by the weight of my sins and the mass of my misery, and I had thought about fleeing into the solitary life, but you stopped me and comforted me, saying, 'Christ died for all so that we live now not for ourselves but for the one who died for us.' "[54] The same themes of fear of service and divine command occur. But that thought of flight creeps in. What if Augustine were writing to his bishop from Tagaste? What if, on the morning after his ordination, he had really fled Hippo, gone back home, and shuddered at the thought of what had happened? If he then decided that he had no choice but to accept what had been laid on him, messages like the letter he sent to Valerius would be just the reassurance, to say nothing of the cover, that the situation required. It gave him time to settle his affairs in Tagaste and prepare for the move. As a devout landowner, he had not thought highly of clergy (most of whom came from well below him on the social ladder).

Ascetic solitude was what was in fashion and what a reasonable person would say Augustine of the late 380s was heading toward. The urban distractions of unimpressive Hippo and the responsibilities of the clerical life played no detectible part in his intentions.

The parallel case a few years earlier of Ambrose of Milan, the man who finally inspired Augustine to join the church, is instructive. Paulinus of Milan, in his life of Ambrose,[55] tells of Ambrose's similarly involuntary election and his resistance. As Ambrose was the governor of Milan's province at the time of his election, his first move on being ordained was to seek to disqualify himself. He left the church and called a session of his gubernatorial court, ordering that the accused brought before him be tortured. This was against his habit, but he expected that by thus bloodying his hands publicly, he would be seen to be unworthy of the bishopric. But the crowd cried out in reply, "Let your sin be on *our* heads!" Ambrose's *second* resistance was to seek to "profess philosophy," by which he meant to escape into private life and devotion, but he was checked in this as well. Still, he made a third attempt: he ordered that prostitutes be brought to him openly, but the same ecclesiastical crowd had the same response: "Let your sin be on *our* heads!" Faced with that promise of forgiveness, his resistance collapsed.[56] In one of his first books written as bishop, Ambrose emphasizes his unreadiness and unripeness in a way that Augustine's own letter to Valerius echoes: "I was torn away from the bench and the signs of high office to the priesthood and began to teach you things I hadn't yet learned myself. And so it came to pass that I should begin to teach before I began to learn. So I had to learn and teach at the same time, since I had no time beforehand to learn."[57] (Augustine would likely have taken those protestations at face value, although we might be as suspicious as I suggest we should be in the case of Augustine.) Ambrose would often recur in Augustine's life as a model, for example as the heroic defender of the orthodox community against a rival church in his own city (in Ambrose's case, Arianism in Milan), but he seems eventually to have relished the job of bishop in a way Augustine never did.

Augustine submitted. In Milan a few years earlier, he had accepted the divine intervention for which he had been longing. When Hippo came calling, he accepted what he interpreted as a divine intervention that was in many ways unwelcome and unexpected. His famous Milan experience (which we will examine in the next chapter) created a conversion that was gentle and easy to pursue. If we grant him the difficulty of swearing off sex, we must also recognize that he had been thinking and hoping and fearing to do just that for many years, ever since taking up with a fashionable new-age sect at age eighteen.

Hippo made more of a difference in his life and his future than Milan ever did. In returning to Africa he had perhaps abandoned a future in public life, but that future, of public office and wealth, had never been entirely his to control, and its loss was no more than he might have faced in the ordinary course of things. A career in the clergy, on the other hand, changed Augustine's life dramatically. If we must put a moment of conversion somewhere in his story line, this is it. It would take a good while before he fully acclimated himself to the new life that had found him.

397: AUGUSTINE COMES OUT

A few years after he came to Hippo and found himself bishop in his own right he wrote his *Confessions*. To approach that book to best effect, let us dwell a bit on the Augustine of 397, the forty-two-year-old getting ready to tell his story in the form destined to become famous. For him, "youth" (*iuventus*) ended at forty-five, to be succeeded by "maturity" (*gravitas*) and then by "old age" (*senectus*) at sixty. In the account he gave of his life that year in the *Confessions*, he observes and makes much of similar boundaries at ages seven (between infancy and boyhood), fifteen (boyhood and adolescence), and thirty (adolescence—as the Romans defined it—and youth). The two defining moments in his life after the time narrated in the *Confessions* almost coincided with but anticipated the threshold ages of forty-five and sixty. The *Confessions* themselves and the associated revolutions in his thought fell in his forty-third or forty-fourth year, while victory over Donatism, the undertaking of *City of God*, and the birth of his anti-Pelagian zealotry caught him in his late fifties.

For now, consider the year 397. Augustine had been in Hippo as priest since 391. His talent for preaching and controversy was undeniable, but he was not socially prepossessing and, though he fancied himself a writer, he had yet to distinguish himself in that regard. What books he had written had been brief, scrappy, and unsatisfying, and his larger efforts had failed to come off.

Then, late in 395 and early in 396, his life changed. Augustine had not traveled much in his early years at Hippo (perhaps only one carefully stage-managed trip to Carthage to introduce him to the higher clergy of Africa), probably because of a desire not to be drawn into some other town's need for a leader. Possidius many years later tells us that bishop Valerius had spirited Augustine away and concealed him in a secret location when he suspected that devout visitors would attempt to carry him off to a bishopric elsewhere.[58] Then Valerius decided to ordain Augustine as bishop while he himself was still alive. Ordination was irrevocable and untransferable, so Valerius's laying hands on Augustine would assure that he would remain Hippo's for the rest of his life. Making a man bishop with a predecessor still alive was technically irregular but understandable as a way for Valerius to secure the younger man in Hippo. The visiting bishop who ordained Augustine was the senior bishop (or primate) of Numidia, Megalius, from Calama just south of Hippo, who had earlier written at least one letter critical of Augustine that the Donatists would later quote with relish,[59] and Megalius eventually said he regretted the irregularity of the ordination into which he had been pushed. He may have been influenced by the Donatist critics or may just have found the man he ordained a bit of a handful. Though episcopal election was the prerogative of the clergy and people, an old bishop could be forgiven for seeking to assure a desired succession, and the practice was far from unknown in Africa, where some bishoprics were even passed down from one generation to the next in the same family. (Augustine stage-managed his own succession thirty years later with Eraclius, though, likely remembering his own sticky ascent to bishopric, he prudently withheld actual ordination.)

A bishop's responsibilities and the assurance (or obligation) of a lifetime in Hippo were soon followed by the death of Valerius, leaving Augustine at the head of his congregation. No longer the sideman and attack dog, Augustine took on new responsibilities and opportunities. He had made several trips to neighboring cities in Africa shortly after the ordination, so now he must have felt safe to move about freely.[60] At the same time, to be a bishop in Africa was no great thing. Every town and some farmsteads had at least one, and by 411, when we have a good count, there were more than seven hundred men in Africa who could lay claim to the title in one of the two Christian churches. Augustine would work hard to make much of the role, but he had little enough to start with.

We can only surmise how things went in Hippo with his own flock. Now the pulpit and the regular sermons were his prerogative, now the reception hall where pleas and complaints could be heard was his. Controlling the property of the church, he became a leading local landowner, very much like a son succeeding to a father's estate. (Augustine and his father figures are a leitmotif in this story that we will refer to later, but he never speaks of his relationship with Valerius.) Late-antique dignitaries were expected to appear as soloists like this, centers of attention in their world, occasionally moving out to face their peers or rivals in a careful ballet of precedence, but living for the most part alone. The pulpit, above all, was a lonely eminence, where all eyes turned to the orator as monologist. Power and influence were tested every time the preacher took to his stage, but more than rhetorical and political authority were at stake.

The bishop was preeminently the man in contact with the divine forces that lay behind and around all that the eye could see. Late-antique men could debate the nature of divinity and quarrel over the precise techniques for assuaging and manipulating divine crankiness, but none doubted the authority and presence of *some* divinity, and all surely felt that presence more vividly than moderns can. To a visitor from Mars, the sight of people coming together regularly for these rituals of no obvious value would be very striking and puzzling. But the closing of the doors after the sermon and the exclusion of all save the baptized faithful left all still inside face-to-face with divine power brandished and appeased by the bishop. None else could do what he did, touch what he touched, or say what he said. The power elevated Augustine and made him the axis around which his little community revolved. At the same time, it made Augustine even more isolated and alone.

We have no frank acknowledgment of his ambitions at this moment and he wrote no strategic plans, submitted no annual performance reviews. Three things he did in his first year as bishop perhaps reveal his intentions.

First, he tried yet again to write a book. As a priest he had concentrated on studying and writing about books of Christian scripture, where the years of unemployment at Tagaste had seen him concentrate more on philosophy and polemic. Genesis, the Psalms, the Sermon on the Mount, and Paul's letters to the Romans, Ephesians, and Galatians all attracted his attention during the early Hippo years. Those efforts had all variously run out of steam by the time of Augustine's ordination. We still have the unfinished books. In particular, his engagement with Paul had been frustrating and incomplete, sign of an unresolved struggle with Paul's rebarbative ideas. With difficulty and some lapse of time, he managed to finish his *Free Choice of the Will* (*De libero arbitrio voluntatis*), a work whose insistence on human liberty, and thus human responsibility for sin, would square only with the greatest difficulty with his later views on grace and predestination. It became an embarrassing monument to the thought of the young Augustine on just the topics where the thought of the mature Augustine changed the most.

So the first book he tried to write shortly after his ordination was a manual prescribing how to do the thing that he was doing but finding difficult: scriptural interpretation. *Christian Doctrine* (*De doctrina christiana*) was the title he chose for a work he would eventually complete in four books. The title is less revealing than the model Augustine chose to copy.

Just as Ambrose had taken Cicero as a model for moral teaching in writing a book called *The Duties of Ministers* (*De officiis ministrorum*) with formal and substantial resemblances to Cicero's *Duties* (*De officiis*, written for his son in the last year of Cicero's life), Augustine picked Cicero's *Orator* as his model. The choice embodies rivalry and anxiety, rebellion and dependence. "Magnum opus et arduum," Cicero had called his book. "A big tough job" we might be inclined to render it, though traditional translation will insist on something more pious, like "a great work and a challenging one." The first page of Augustine's imitation turns that phrase with a wry grimace: "Magnum onus et arduum"—"a great burden" now instead of a great work. One part of the burdensome book outlines the ideological program rooted in the core doctrines of the Christian creed, and two more parts suggest interpretive techniques to use in harmonizing developed ideology with received and often resistant scriptural texts to satisfy the taste and curiosity of a sensitive late-antique audience. Before Augustine could finish the work, he broke it off. We don't know why. The last part of the third section and the whole of the fourth, where he finally came to practical direction for constructing and delivering Christian oratory, he completed only thirty years later.

Imitation like this struggles to declare independence, and often fails. *The Christians can do anything the Romans could do, only better, because we are rooted in a truer doctrine*—that's the argument, one other Christians as early as Clement of Alexandria, c. 200 C.E., had used. But to declare yourself better than someone is to acknowledge that the opposite opinion might be held. No one who could appreciate Augustine's act of mimesis was a stranger to the textual and performance rivalries of cultural styles in his time. Were Vergil and Cicero still the masters? Could the new Christian style rival and supplant them? A compelling performance in the new style could persuade some waverers. (Christian families continued to send their sons to schools of the old style, reading the old texts, well into the sixth century and stopped only when those schools disappeared.)

Even if Augustine is judged to have established his model of oratory worthily alongside that of Cicero, the act of modeling itself comes with a cost. The orator, the "good man skilled at speaking" (*vir bonus peritus dicendi*) that old Roman Cato had praised, was a prestigious but increasingly hollow model through Roman imperial times. Three hundred years before Augustine, Tacitus in his *Dialogue on Orators* had acknowledged that the forensic power of oratory had been vitiated by changing political times. Senate house and courtroom might both still honor the oratorical performance, and the orator might become a platform star to a wider public, but the performance itself would no longer be decisive in public affairs. Performance is what oratory had become in both Greek and Latin salons and audience halls: still a way of making a reputation but not a way of influencing politics. The young Augustine in Milan, awash in flop sweat in his stretch limousine en route to praise the emperor or his latest favorite, had made his way in the world as a prize-winning stage performer of just this sort.[61]

To win applause is one thing for an orator. To move men in ways that matter is another, and inevitably more alluring, achievement. In choosing to revive classical oratory, Augustine expresses ambition for himself and his peers and is more an innovator than he might seem.[62] What he says and does in the pulpit will be as powerful and effective as (and more public than) what he does behind closed doors in the liturgy. As a consequence, Augustine as bishop in his church becomes a communal focal point the way the orator in the forum used to be.

It's hard to know whether lives were or are actually changed by preaching. But if we are willing to leave the question open, we can surmise that the real function of preaching activity is measured in other ways than by persuasion and changes of mind.

The performer's achievement is to embody the opinions of some, flout the opinions of others, and demonstrate the *possibility* of persuasion and conversion. The greatest oratorical success leaves unbelievers thinking that the thing they don't believe has been too powerfully advocated for them to oppose it, and even perhaps suspecting that they are unworthy for thinking their recalcitrant thoughts. For every congregant who took Augustine's words to heart on a given Sunday and went away determined to mend his ways, dozens more found the oratory itself sufficient evidence of the cohesiveness and truth of the community for whom it was performed. Even if this community existed under one roof for only two hours a week, such speech could have implanted a sense of belonging to sustain the community through all the hours between services.

Christian preachers had always known and enacted this role. What was different about Augustine, Ambrose, and their contemporary in Constantinople, John, called Chrysostom ("golden mouth"), and other polished performers of that age is that they saw themselves in the tradition of the ancient orators as well. Membership in the church of Hippo, Augustine's style of self-presentation implicitly argued, made one not only a Christian but a person of taste. He had himself first gone to hear Ambrose on just those terms, not interested in the content of the preaching, but pleasantly judging the performance. Even when the content did matter and was found satisfactory, the pleasure could abide. Augustine in his church on Sunday gave that pleasure hundreds of times in his life.

But great orators need great audiences. The pulpit at Hippo was always too small for Augustine's ambitions, though perhaps small by choice. An interesting recent study impishly posed the question, just who could attend and hear sermons and church services in late antiquity, and pursued the answer in part by looking at the sizes of churches. Augustine's own largest church in Hippo at its greatest extent was about 120 feet by 60 feet inside. Even if we make allowances for standing-room-only crowds, it scarcely could have held more than a tiny fraction of the population of the city. Who attended? The argument that presents itself most obviously is that the congregation was made up of the upper classes of landowners, merchants, and officers, and that the bulk of the Christian population made do without the weekly inoculation of ritual.[63]

No sooner had Augustine been ordained than he was whisked away for his debut in the big city. In January 397 he would rather have been attending a Numidian bishops' conference in the city of Constantine, where the bishop was an old Tagastan friend, Fortunatus, but the call of his other friend and close collaborator, bishop Aurelius of Carthage, proved overpowering.[64] And so in January, and probably again from April to September of that year, he was in Carthage, making his society debut. We have always known that there was a significant concentration of sermons in our surviving texts from his time in Carthage that year, and in the last decade another fascinating sheaf of them has emerged from medieval manuscripts in which they lay undetected for centuries. The effect these sermons make is striking. They show us the new bishop at the peak of his physical powers, on display in the metropolitan center of the richest of Latin provinces of the Roman world. Augustine was welcome here because his friend was bishop, and he would be welcomed there again many times. For thirty years, he would remain the star performer of the church to which he belonged, a church that had, in Africa, rather suffered for want of such star performers.

The pattern set in 397 recurred regularly. He was back in Carthage for all or part of the summer in 399, 401, 403, 404, 405, 406 (perhaps), 407, 409 (perhaps), 410, a climactic season in 411, an unusual winter visit in 412–13, and then again in the summer of 413. We know of these trips because the scribes taking down his sermons would often enough make note of the place and date of delivery. Age and discouragement intervened and visits afterwards were fewer, but he still made the three hundred–mile round-trip in 416, 417, 418, and 419. After that we are less sure, but 421 and 424 may have seen him there again. This makes at least fifteen visits in thirty years, many of them taking him away from his duties, his congregation, and the respectful attention of his townsmen for months at a time. He mentions briefly in one place that the citizens of Hippo were restless at the thought of these absences, but he does not otherwise explain them or comment on them. These were not holidays or speaking tours, but times for direct engagement in the affairs of the African church. Late in his life, enmeshed in the tangles his anti-Pelagian enthusiasms had made for him, he was able to say that he was always busier at Carthage than anywhere else.[65] He remembered without apology being served pheasant at dinner there, at a socially prominent table, though at home the fare was more austere.[66]

He often stayed in Carthage until September for the great feast of the African church, the memorial of the martyrdom of the third-century bishop Cyprian that fell each year on September 14. In 397 he set this pattern, journeying home in the early autumn while the weather and the roads were still favorable. (In the ancient Mediterranean, the winter's rains and the sea's storms kept most people homebound in their towns for as much as half the year.)

Then we happen to know, from a letter, an odd fact. He fell ill, taking to his bed with an acute attack of hemorrhoids.[67]

At this point, we must pause. As recently as 1999, I could have written blithely about Augustine's debut year of 397, but scholarship marches on, and in 2000, Pierre-Marie Hombert published a massive study, *Nouvelles recherches de chronologie augustinienne* ("New Investigations in Augustinian Chronology"), and threw much that we thought we knew into doubt.

His starting point is the publication in the 1990s of more than two dozen sermons by Augustine that had lain unread for centuries in medieval manuscripts. These sermons, discovered, dated, and edited by François Dolbeau, have been the object of close study and lively discussion.[68] To sort through the thousands of surviving manuscripts of Augustine, identifying every short text written in whatever script, separating the ones that are really by Augustine from the ones that were inadvertently or deliberately assigned to his name along the way, and winnowing all that mass of material down to an agreed chronology of composition—these are huge jobs, jobs that have absorbed the energies of hundreds of scholars for hundreds of years. In the last two decades, two remarkable finds, one of letters discovered by Johannes Divjak, the other the Dolbeau sermons, have shaken up what we know about Augustine.

Dolbeau's assignment to the year 397 of many of the sermons he discovered encouraged me to write as strongly as I did about Augustine's debut year in Carthage. But Hombert digs deeper and finds that the foundations of Augustinian chronology are rotten, badly rotten. The most abundant texts, the sermons, were assigned a timeline generations ago by devout but relatively amateurish scholars. Much has changed, but the assumption of validity of those old datings has been unchallenged in the main till now. Hombert challenges all.

The upshot for the student of Augustine is threefold: first, Hombert leaves us with an awareness of the tenuousness of all that we say about the ordering of Augustine's work, especially for the very heart of his career, the years 395–411. It remains an oddity that for precisely the years of Augustine's greatest productivity and political achievement we are the least well-informed as to his doings and whereabouts. Second, he makes us consider that a lot of what we date to the first part of that period may in fact fall much later, and, in particular, Hombert stretches out the chronology of the composition of the *Confessions* over six years, from 397 to 403. Third, he thus suggests a complete rereading of the central part of Augustine's career.

The last point is most important. We have traditionally assumed that on becoming bishop in 397 and beginning to write his major books, Augustine quickly became a significant and recognized figure in the African church and beyond, first wielding his influence against the Donatists and Manichees, then against others as the years went by. What Hombert suggests is that it was really only after 410 that Augustine "the great man" emerged. The imperial legate Marcellinus, who came to Africa to make Augustine's party victorious and became his friend and co-conspirator, was a vital contributor to that emergence, and the completion of old projects (*The Trinity; Genesis Taken Literally;* the sermons on John's gospel and the sermons on the Psalms) and the opening of new ones (*City of God* and the anti-Pelagian campaign) become the steps by which this still provincial and obscure bishop became a figure of international celebrity, if not always acclaim. The period between 395 and 411 becomes, then, an extension of the hidden years, the years of struggling to make a name for himself and to rescue his church from obscurity.

It will take decades of meticulous work to assess Hombert's arguments and reach firmer ground. His book is rich and complex and designedly only opens a series of debates and investigations. But he needs to be heeded on the central point: that the study of Augustinian chronology, and thus of all of Augustine's life, is built on shaky ground. I will go on now to write the chapters I intend and want to write, but I write them, and you should read them, with a sense of suspended confidence, a recognition that the framework into which we fit all these pieces is one of our own making, not something handed down with confidence by ancient history, and that the life of Augustine thus continues—and should continue, and it is delightful and exciting that it continues—to evolve and change. History is never something carved in stone, but more like something saved to a temporary cache file on a computer disk vulnerable to the imperfections of memory and always ready to be revised.

The *Confessions* are Augustine's own first draft of history.

AUGUSTINE CONFESSES

Huck Finn's words are worth heeding:

> You don't know about me without you have read a book by the name of *The Adventures of Tom Sawyer*; but that ain't no matter. That book was made by Mr. Mark Twain, and he told the truth, mainly. There was things which he stretched, but mainly he told the truth. That is nothing. I never seen anybody but lied one time or another, without it was Aunt Polly, or the widow, or maybe Mary. Aunt Polly—Tom's Aunt Polly, she is—and Mary, and the Widow Douglas is all told about in that book, which is mostly a true book, with some stretchers, as I said before.

You probably don't know about Augustine without you having read, or at least heard about, the book called his *Confessions*. Perhaps, like me, you purchased a copy in a high school bookshop long ago because you had heard it had some salacious things in it. (If they're there, I haven't found them yet.) Since our first page, we've been preventing Augustine from getting on with his *Confessions*, taking time to look around at who he was and where he was and how he lived there. Now it's time to let him have his say and see what we make of it.

MAKING THE CONFESSIONS[69]

Augustine never practiced the humility of the man who would escape attention. In prostrating himself before the divine in the *Confessions*, Augustine performs an astonishing act of self-presentation and self-justification and, paradoxically, self-aggrandizement. Though friends and family get carefully scripted parts to play in the *Confessions*, the book as a whole is a one-man show, and a virtuoso performance at that. And for all that it is a testimony of faith and confidence, it is permeated with anxiety.

Two threads mix, one light and one dark. The light and obvious thread is the description of a life's career meant to impress its readers. No one could read the account of education and advancement without realizing that the youth Augustine had left behind had been a golden one: riding provincial ambition to a place on the fringes of the imperial retinue. He could write of this the more easily because he could dismiss it, but we get a good view of the future glory before Augustine casts it aside. As bishop and Christian, he was always the man who used to have a very different future, and made sure that you remembered it.

The darker thread is harder to see. Much of it lies buried in the repellent and frustrating text of book 10, where bright mystical vision, culminating in luminous and often-quoted words ("I was late in loving you, beauty so old and so new, I was late in loving you!"[70]), is suddenly derailed by an obsessive and meticulous examination of conscience that sifts through the ashes of regret and anxiety for the possibility of past and future sin.

The sins of the flesh have mostly left him behind. The intellectual arrogance that marked his youth had, he believed, also left him. (That argument is perhaps the most self-serving of this section, and some of his contemporaries would have found it hard to take.) What he sees still with him is the vein of worldly ambition that had driven him from Africa to Italy and which he thought he had abandoned with his career. But episcopacy has its glories, and the lonely eminence of the bishop attracted attention that can be hard to deflect. If there's one thing still to worry about, writes the new bishop, it's what he calls "pride of life."

He was making his peace with his new office. The debutant of Carthage, the prolific writer, the political schemer that Augustine was in the way of becoming: all these were roles that he had sought and accepted with open eyes. Involuntary recruit, Augustine was teaching himself how to be something his neighbors had never seen before: the humble teacher and minister as public figure, almost a celebrity, expressing the new while unmistakably resembling the old. The risk he does not see is that of his own future authoritarianism.

Was the book written in the exhilaration of Carthage or the quiet of a Hippo winter or somehow otherwise? To answer that question, given the limits of what we really know, is to make a declaration of taste and inclination about how to read this man and his ambitions, and I answer in favor of Hippo, while remembering we must also imagine lonely and fretful vigils in Carthage. The book is marked by a mannered self-revelation, almost self-betrayal, that comes from the Augustine who would continually return to, and often carefully display, anxiety and self-mistrust in the midst of his most self-assertive and overbearing of public displays. Wherever he wrote, the people who saw him day by day very likely suspected little of the subterranean seething that bubbles through on these pages.

WHAT AUGUSTINE *DID* CONFESS

So what did he say? To understand Augustine's life we need to be cunning in evading the snares he has laid for his biographers, but still we need to respect him and his own version of the story. If we will wring a real confession or two from him against his will, we must first listen to the story he wants to tell us. The reader, moreover, who does not have the narrative of the *Confessions* ready to mind might reasonably feel cheated by a book like this that tried to tell Augustine's story but left out the authorized version of his life. To that extent he has succeeded in making his self-making inescapable.

So in these next few pages I propose to set out in the simplest possible terms the story Augustine *did* tell in the first nine books of the *Confessions*. I will tell that story without comment, as a point of reference for the other stories I will tell, and as one of the points of view that must be taken along with the others. Later pages of this book will be more meaningful because these pages are here.

Augustine claims not to remember his infancy, but infers his own story from that of other infants he has seen and makes a point of including the inferred story at the outset of the remembered one. He does not quite remember learning to speak, but remembers the frustrations of schooldays and the beatings he received. His first specific anecdote is religious:

when ill in childhood, having heard the name of Christ, he begged for baptism, only to be denied what he wished because he recovered health and evaded danger too quickly. He disliked school and really couldn't stomach his Greek lessons, but at least he wept over the death of Dido in the *Aeneid*.

Childhood yielded to adolescence and sexual temptation, described with great circumlocution. His pious and solicitous mother, Monnica, told him to stay away from married women; his philandering and status-conscious father, Patricius, saw him pubescent in the public baths and went home rejoicing that a first grandchild could not be far off. (He was right.) Schooling had taken Augustine from home (Tagaste, which he does not name in the story) to Madauros (which he does name), then home for a year of impecunious idleness, then off to study in Carthage, supported by the generosity of a rich friend of his father's. An episode of adolescent self-assertion—the theft of some pears from a neighbor's orchard by Augustine, in the company of a band of his mates—is recounted at puzzling length.

At Carthage he studied, lived in a way he blushed to recall later, and went to the theater. He talks of going to church to pursue his sexual conquests.[71] Moderns with the slightest possible familiarity with Augustine's name often think of him obscurely as a paragon of promiscuity. "Oh, Master, make me chaste and celibate—but not yet!" He did write those words, to parody his commonplace adolescent dithering between libido and restraint.[72] The *Confessions* are intended to underscore the middle-aged bishop's sense that his youth had been dissolute and sexually unrestrained, but nothing suggests he was unusual, and indeed among the privileged young of his time he was probably more rather than less restrained than most. We know of the woman he made his wife and we hear of another woman with whom he lived for a few months in Milan after sending the first away, but he does not tell us anything of either, not even their names. Back in Carthage in earlier days, he could attest, as we have seen, to having gone to church to find what might now be called "hookups," but we have no hope of measuring their number and every reason to suspect that the bishop rather overdid the accusations against his younger self. In the end nothing indicates that his conduct in adolescence could have called attention to itself in any way, save possibly for modesty and discretion. But at least a few women knew him in a way we cannot hope to recover.

Somewhere in his days in Carthage, he took up with the woman who would be his wife for over a decade. She was his wife in the Roman sense, appropriate for a woman of lower social status who could be dismissed when a better marriage came along. (It helps to think of American slave-owners who took women from their households to bed, sometimes re-specting them for a lifetime, sometimes disposing of them callously when convenience or libido suggested it.) For more than a decade, Augustine lived in conjugal fidelity with this woman who looked after his household and bore and raised him a son. They parted company when Augustine's mother was seeking a better society marriage for him. Augustine's wife was probably a free woman, but she may have begun as a slave or come from slave parents. She gets short shrift from him, except for a muted pang of guilt expressed years later that still conceals her from our sight,[73] but we would love to know what she made of him. The Norwegian nov-elist Jostein Gaarder gave her a voice not long ago in a cheeky novel that does not always stay close to the facts or the probabilities but is at least a vivid thought experiment in a nonobvious way to read Augustine.[74] Garry Wills whimsically twisted a line of the *Confessions* to give her a name—Una—and emphasized her continuing role in Augustine's life by specu-lating that when back in Africa with their son, Adeodatus, Augustine must have had at least some social dealings with her.

The study of philosophy obtruded and led to religious zealotry. Cicero led him to Christian books that repelled him, and so he fell among the new-age Manichees and joined their sect. His mother was distressed, but found reassurance from a Christian bishop who had once been a Manichee himself. Manicheism had a bad rap with right-thinking people in the fourth century, and hasn't recovered much since.[75] They were out-laws to Christians, but Christian in some sense they certainly were. They shared ideas that have been attributed variously to the Gnostics of Egypt, the Zoroastrians of Persia, and to Mani's native Mesopotamia itself. Mani had lived and died a hundred years and more before Augustine fell in with his followers, and they wooed him with social polish, intellectual pizzazz, potent ritual, and doctrines about the power of evil in the world that both roused and allayed deep anxieties. Their good god lay imprisoned in a material world, held hostage by the devil, and only those who joined in the struggle to liberate that god would themselves be liberated. Some few would be the "elect," while most followers of the cult would be only "hearers," imperfect and impure. In daily ritual meals, the hearers brought offerings of vegetarian food and drink to the elect, whose diges-tive tracts transmuted the gross carnality of food into spiritual light and so released fragments of the light from fleshly imprisonment. It was heady and, in the Christian Roman empire, illegal stuff.

Augustine's school days led to teaching days back home and the small successes of a blossoming career: public performances, applause, vainglory. He added the study of astrology to his Manicheism, until a sober and eminent older friend dissuaded him. The unexpected death of a friend whose name he never tells us shook him, and he left his home town again for Carthage. There he read and wrote, wearied of his Manichee friends (but did not break with them), and sent off his first book dedicated to a famous orator at Rome. Shortly after, he followed the book to Italy, leaving his distraught mother behind. At Rome he fell ill, recovered, lived among Manichees, taught, grew impatient with his career, and finally used the Manichees to gain an audition with the city prefect for a better job—professor of rhetoric—at the imperial court at Milan.

He got the job and moved to Milan. There his mother, brother, and cousins caught up with him, sure that his advancement would profit them all. (He was the one with education and prospects, while his cousins Lartidianus and the aptly named Rusticus had never even been to grammar school; his brother Navigius always lags in the debates Augustine recounts.) He fell in with the local Christians, read philosophical books, and worked himself up into a crisis in the secluded garden of the house where he was living. The resolution of the crisis felt to him like a turning of the will to god, but looked to friends and colleagues like loss of will. He went off to the country, a place called Cassiciacum, for a holiday, resigned his position (by letter) while he was there, and came back to town only for a few weeks in the spring of 387 to have himself and his friends baptized in the church. Shortly after, the whole entourage left for Africa. Temporarily delayed on their journey home by the wake of a minor civil war, they were in the Mediterranean port city of Ostia when his mother died.

So there the narrative of the *Confessions* concludes, with the narrator age thirty-four and his "public life" at an end. He has died and been reborn in baptism, and that is that. The book's narrator is unmistakably a serving bishop, and that fact offers an implicit conclusion to the story. Service as bishop stretches out before him indefinitely, beyond narrative and event, leaving him on a threshold where he awaits what he hopes will be the end of his story, eternal life in heaven.

Told in that way, the story is curious but perhaps unexceptional: careerism and idealism at odds, with idealism prevailing. The story has taken on much more meaning for three reasons: first, the later success of Augustine's religious community in dominating the cultures of Europe for nearly fifteen hundred years; second, his success in swathing his narrative in intense reflection and impressionistic emotional reconstruction the like of which is not seen again until the Romantics, and not seen with such persuasive self-criticism until Proust and Joyce; and, third, the enthusiasm with which readers have entered into the spirit of that reflection and reconstruction, continuing to build on Augustine's narrative foundation.

But stories are what we have to show for our lives, and stories are malleable. In John Le Carré's *Smiley's People*, the plot's pretext is the suspicion aroused when a Soviet spymaster is reported to be "making a legend for a girl." In a Swiss institution, a young woman is acquiring a new story about her past, for it emerges that she is the spymaster's daughter and a new story is her guarantee of security if her father is at risk. Augustine provided his own legend as a guarantee of security in the *Confessions*, from his debut year of 397.

THE NARRATOR NARRATES HIMSELF

The *Confessions* are the work of a big frog in a small pond, determined to seize his moment of opportunity. The church he'd joined in Milan had been languishing for a century in Africa, as its better-established rival, that of the Donatists, flourished. Augustine believed with a zealot's conviction that his church was the true church and with a snob's commitment to his cosmopolitanism he was determined to make the church's success his success (and vice versa). He was talented, well connected, and driven, and his church would indeed prevail—a future that must have seemed highly improbable to most observers in 397.

But Augustine was a man with a past. Coming to such a place as Hippo as he did, a stranger with no friends and no family (his sister and her community of religious women only later took up residence there), inevitably drew speculative gazes. He was defined by who he was elsewhere. To be his father's son from Tagaste was no great distinction, but he was also a young man who had had a disconcertingly flashy career in Italy that ended rather abruptly. For him to turn up as priest in the smaller of two local Christian factions set tongues wagging. His ordination as bishop had been somewhat irregular, but he professed not to have known that. And he was rumored to be sending love tokens to a married lady, but he explained that it was all a misunderstanding of something perfectly innocent.

Furthermore, Augustine's very public early Manicheism could not be ignored. The aggressively orthodox churchman of Hippo had spent a decade of his life, from about the time he was first noticed in Carthage as a promising student until he sailed away to Italy in pursuit of fame and glory, in a proscribed sect. After four years in Milan he returned with neither fame nor glory to show for his time away and settled quietly at his family home in Tagaste. His son Adeodatus was with him, but he had sent away his common-law wife, Adeodatus's mother, at his own mother's insistence. He ostentatiously avoided the natural prerogative of the landowner, the sexual use of female slaves.[76] To some eyes, he was enacting the continence that Manicheism preached at least as enthusiastically as other Christians did. When Augustine appeared on the public scene again, in Hippo as priest, he was professing to have been baptized a catholic Christian while in Italy, by no less a figure than Ambrose of Milan.

Just how persuasive his story was is impossible to tell at this distance.[77] His own community seems not to have expressed doubts, but his opponents never accepted it. The suspicions the Donatists professed in the 390s would recur, better argued, in the 420s in the writings of a young rival we will come to know later—Julian, bishop of Eclanum in southern Italy. Perhaps these polemicists were merely using whatever weapons came to hand, but at least some of their followers will have believed what they heard: that Augustine had never given up his suspect behavior, that he had left Africa one step ahead of the law and crept back when it was safe to do so, and that his idiosyncrasies of doctrine and practice could be explained as a continuation of his earlier subversive and illegal ways.

Augustine had faced these suspicions when he came to Hippo. There he had to explain himself and persuade his new bishop of his orthodoxy. Only a year after he arrived, a public debate in 392 with a Manichee priest named Fortunatus provided a lucky chance for him to be seen in public attacking his old friends. The transcript Augustine published begins as he says these words: "What I used to think was true, I now think is wrong."[78] He made a point of conducting the debate not in his own church but in the city baths, where Christians and non-Christians of all parties could hear him, see him, and appreciate his triumph. The crowd is recorded (by Augustine's secretaries) to have broken up the first day of the debate in an imbroglio with Fortunatus, outraged by his interpretation of Paul's epistles. When Fortunatus left the debate the next day, thoughtful and not loudly disagreeing with Augustine (rather as he had arrived), Augustine crowed with success and made sure the transcript was published. Perhaps he really did impress the crowd that day, and that was probably his real goal. But gradually as he moved to prominence in the African church, high-minded and ferociously celibate, he attracted attention and the old whispers floated again.

How, when, and where Augustine began telling the story of his past we do not know, but we can see him rehearsing it in a passage of his *Free Choice of the Will*, probably finished while he was still only a priest. He tries a thought experiment on us there: *What if* a man were found, he speculates, who went through something like this:

> You don't think it's a small penalty, do you, when lust overpowers the mind and drags it about, impoverished and stripped of the riches of virtue? The mind takes false things for true, sometimes going so far as to make a great show of defending such falsehoods; then it casts aside what it has earlier believed and falls headlong into believing other lies. Next it withholds its assent from any truth at all and shudders at the sight of the plainest and clearest arguments. Finally, despairing of ever being able to find the truth it plunges wholly into foolish darkness. When it then tries to rise up to the light it falls back again, easily fatigued. All the while the tyranny of lust rules savagely over him and sends its storms raging all through his life and soul. He is torn by fear and desire, by anxiety and then by a show of good cheer, tormented by the thought of losing what he has loved and equally by the desire to acquire what he hasn't had. . . .[79]

The tale of this nameless, pitiable wretch, told as moral melodrama, parallels exactly the sequence of events Augustine tells of himself in the *Confessions*. Written as little as two or three years before the *Confessions*, it rehearses the theme the larger work will elaborate.[80] If this passage is taken soberly, it tells a simple story and then makes a tendentious association. The story is of a man who gives his passionate allegiance to one ideology after another, culminating in assent to an ideology of doubt. This descent—though serious people then and now would argue that the suspension of imprudent belief represents an ascent rather than a descent— is associated with the power of *libido*. But the matrix for determining what is *correct* thinking lies outside the frame of this narrative. As practiced readers of Augustine, or at least of Christian texts, we know where to look for it and we are happy to be right. But that leap of interpretation should not keep us from reading through the story to see what other narratives might lie hidden inside it.

The most obvious is simply that intellectual variousness associated with sexual irregularity among young men is a common story. The syndrome for which this is the symptom is called youth, or rather that particular form of privileged youth packaged with prosperity, leisure time, education emphasizing verbal skills, and a sense of self-importance. Augustine's variation on this story lies in the Christian framework he puts around it. His father, Patricius, would have framed it differently. Seeing Augustine in the baths long years before, he had made a correct diagnosis and chose to be pleased rather than censorious at the typical frivolity of youth, to be indulged for its intellectual as much as for its sexual divagations, and likely to settle over time into a predictable pattern and to be marked by whatever economic and social compromises (e.g., marriage) that society demanded. Augustine's friend and first patron, Romanianus, seems perfectly normal by these standards, having taken to Manicheism in early years, then dabbled in other allegiances along with Augustine, only to subside to his estates, marriage, and eventually, as we have seen, the company of slave girls.

This early version of the story also suppresses the importance of the Manichee phase of Augustine's life. Manicheism is here by implication only one species of *error*, error to which the younger self is shown giving its allegiance. And error has no continuity with truth: error is simply error. But Manicheism does not lend itself to such a simple description. Manicheism was the particularly Christian form of life to which Augustine gave himself when young, and much of what he knew and practiced then had resonance with his later Christian practice. One would never know it from the way he tells his story.

Even in the short compass of this first draft, Augustine's story-making is telling. When expanded in 397 into the *Confessions*, it retained all the features of the shorter form and developed new ones. It now gave names and places and dates, selectively, to Augustine's own experience, but it used all the resources of Augustine's art to show that the center of the narrative was not the youth recalled but the middle age presently lived. The story is told in relation to an ending that was invisible to Augustine and his contemporaries as he lived it, and even invisible to himself for some years after he'd lived the central events. In that story, the Manichee phase naturally recedes into the background, becoming merely a phase. Augustine minimizes the intensity of his association with the group, and he repeatedly states a length of time that is not quite in accord with the facts we can elicit from his other statements. "Nine years" he says he spent with them, but from his nineteenth year to his thirtieth birthday, dating

from the point of his first falling in with them until the point when he finally breaks off association with the Manichee community in Rome to go
to Milan, the minimum tally stands at eleven years of his life. And for all
his suggestions that he had his doubts about the group from some time
much earlier, and that the coming of an unpersuasive Manichee teacher
named Faustus confirmed his skepticism, it was only, in the end, when he
left Rome to go to a city where there was apparently no community of
Manichees to take up with, that he made a decisive break.

As he fades from the narrative, Augustine the Manichee is worth a
thoughtful look. We happen to know a lot about a man named Secundinus,
who was one of the other Manichean "auditors" with whom Augustine
passed time at Rome in 384, and he provides us our best contemporary
picture of the young zealot. Twenty years or more later, Secundinus came
upon Augustine's anti-Manichean writings (and probably the *Confessions*)
and was shocked that his old acquaintance had gone so far astray. He
wanted to reconvert Augustine, but Augustine wrote back peremptorily
and polemically. Years later, Augustine would say the reply was his best
work against the Manichees, though it reads to us as something slight and
insubstantial, a pamphlet of ten thousand words or so.[81]

The letter Secundinus wrote to Augustine survives more or less intact.
Not without charm, it breathes the same atmosphere of scriptural texts
and exhortation as the works of Augustine himself. Gentle and inviting, it
surprises the reader to see Augustine the object of such adversarial benev-
olence, such high-minded disdain.

> Change your mind, I beseech you, rid yourself of the faithlessness that
> marks the Punic race, and turn back from your fearful retreat from truth.
> Don't try to cover yourself in lies. My talent is slight for a Roman, but
> I've read some of your reverence's writings, in which you are as angry at
> truth as Hortensius was at philosophy.[87] I read these things over and over
> breathlessly and with darting eyes, and I found everywhere in them a
> wonderful orator—a veritable god of all eloquence! But I didn't find in
> them anywhere a Christian. I found somebody who took up arms against
> every other opinion and affirmed none of his own. You ought to display
> learning in matters of substance, not just of style. But I can't keep from
> speaking of this to your most patient holiness: for it seems to me, and it's
> quite true, that you never really were a Manichee. You couldn't have
> known their hidden secrets, and you're attacking—I don't know—Han-
> nibal and Mithridates perhaps, and calling them Mani! For I have to ad-

mit that the lofty marble halls of the Anicii don't gleam with so much fine care and work as shines in your eloquence. If you had just wanted to make it all accord with the truth, you would have been a splendid ornament to us all.

No, stop, I ask you, don't go against your nature, don't be the spear with which error strikes the side of the savior! For you see that he stands crucified in the whole world and in every soul though he never knew how to be angry himself. You are descended from that soul—give up, I ask you now, the hollow accusations, abandon the pointless arguments. . . . You were a chaste man, pure and poor, but you went over to the barbarous tribes of the Jews and you fill your teaching with their silly fables.[83]

Vincentius was another of Augustine's old friends from his Carthage days. He became in later years the bishop of a small sectarian community in Cartennae (modern Ténès), in the far west of Roman Africa, four hundred miles as the crow flies from Hippo. His group had broken off from the majority (Donatist) community around 370 under its own bishop, Rogatus. We can only guess at their motive: perhaps indignation at relying on the secular arm in support of church policy, a charge the Donatists faced when they took advantage of the emperor Julian's toleration to regain their footing. This was the issue that drove Vincentius, around 407–10, to write to his old friend from school days.

Vincentius had gone back to Cartennae and there become Rogatus's successor. The argument he has with Augustine is a predictable one, but Augustine quotes Vincentius's recollections of the young Augustine himself: "When I knew you, you were far from being a Christian. Given over to your literary studies, you were steadfast in your pursuit of good behavior and high principles. As I hear it, when you converted to the Christian faith later on, you gave yourself over to lawyer-style polemics."[84] *This* Augustine was certainly no libidinous hell-raiser in youth, on the one hand, but also no serene and pious bishop in middle age. By the time rumor brings Augustine's name to Vincentius, Augustine the self-righteous troublemaker is the one he hears of.

The echoes of Augustine's words that we hear in the words of Secundinus and Vincentius take us back to Augustine's early life by a path other than that of the *Confessions*. Once baptized by Ambrose, Augustine chose to privilege one of his lives, the one lived as a baptized member of the Caecilianist church in Africa, as the authentic religious experience of his life, but not all who knew him shared that view. Manicheism was with him early and late, and was the one truly impassioned religious experience of his life. He was the sort of person who has a great love affair when young, sees that it just won't work, breaks it off, then settles down in a far more sober and sensible marriage. What he says and does for the rest of his life will be marked by firm allegiance and commitment to the late-blooming relationship, but the mark of the first never goes away, and some who knew him early will be unable to credit the marriage because they remember the passion.

Manicheism is far better known to us now than ever before. The discovery of new materials, the continued interpretation of old materials, and a scholarly sense of conscience and opportunity in doing justice to an extraordinary movement have all come together to give us a fresh picture. On the one hand *The Cologne Mani Codex*,[05] a magically beautiful tiny book, not much larger than a pack of cigarettes, minutely written in a perfect Greek hand, has revealed how much more deeply Mani (the third-century founder of the movement, put to death on February 26, 277, giving rise to an annual feast called the Bema, which the young Augustine knew well) was marked more by Jewish and Christian influences in his Mesopotamian origins than by the Persian ones that had long been thought to lie behind his thought. Manicheism had already by Augustine's time, like Christianity, run well beyond anything the founders of the movement could have imagined and was at the peak of its fame and prestige in the Mediterranean world. Ambitious works of interpretation[86] have lately sketched a history that stretches from the western Mediterranean, where the fashion faded while Augustine was still alive, to the South China Sea, and continues to the present day.[87] The oases of the silk route of central Asia have offered up some of the most remarkable texts of the movement at just the physical point where it leaped the divide from the ancient western lands to the remote east.

There has been fresh emphasis as well on the practice and experience of Manichean community in the delicate etiquette that brought elect and hearers together for the ritual meals. "Manicheism" has come to us in Augustine's caricature as a thing of abstract doctrine, but few serious religious movements could survive such partiality of appearance.[88] The day-to-day life of Manicheism has emerged more clearly in recent research, making it easier to see how it seemed reasonable and prudent to sober ancients to participate in their rites. The movement offered its members a set of texts that gave an explanation of the human predicament, it staged impressive ritual meals at the center of a supportive community, and it held aloft the hope of a future life purged of the ills and evils of the present. The elect lived lives of special holiness that inspired the hearers who made up the bulk of the community and received their willing service.

Augustine fell among the Manichees because they were there with their questions when he had been reading the Christian scriptures, to which he had turned when inspired by reading Cicero in the course of his studies. This series of maneuvers seemed perfectly reasonable at the time and could be taken so. Manicheism was a new-age religion in its time, fashionable, exotic, with an up-to-date brand of humbug. Augustine, falling in with that crowd in Carthage, had the feeling of being just a little ahead of his time and among the true elite of his world. Orthodox Christianity had become the state religion, but what Augustine knew best was the very lightly Caecilianized native African Christianity of Tagaste. Against that background, the devout and slightly priggish Manichee (and we have to know Augustine's capacity for priggishness) could sniff persuasively at the orthodox tolerance for the "Old Testament." The church that should be the bride of Christ was like, for the Manichee, a shameless hussy, cherishing the letters and love tokens of another woman's husband—the god of the Jews.[89] When they say that, we have to hear the specific sneer of ancient Christian anti-Jewish polemic, attacking the old-fashioned god and old-fashioned religion that Christianity had left behind.

Augustine's affair with Manicheism took him from his early university days to the time of his first great professional success. His narrative in the *Confessions* would have us believe that he quickly saw through the intellectual shallowness of the cult and lingered passively and curiously, finally drifting away to wait for something else to turn up. He admits to sticking it out for nine years before breaking with them,[90] even if he fudges the count. He wants us to imagine the long, slow falling-away from the enthusiasm of the moment just short of age nineteen, when he fell in with the sect, until the time when, rising twenty-nine, he met the Manichee leader Faustus and found him unable to answer some probing questions. But until at least about age thirty Augustine lived among and participated with the Manichees in their rituals, and it was only after almost a dozen years, in 384–85, on his appointment to the imperial chair in Milan, that he finally broke with them and fell back into the habit of going to church with the catholic Christians he found there.

Augustine took his Manicheism seriously. He wrote and debated in defense of the sect and surely (though he nowhere brings himself to say this) participated in their daily liturgies. Augustine himself never became a member of the elect, but he must have considered the possibility and yet cannot bring himself to talk about it. He presents his detachment from the sect as a matter of his own choice, but religious advancement in late antiquity was more often a question of being invited to advance rather than merely choosing to do so. Augustine, living with his common-law wife and their child, was very likely too much a man of the flesh for the Manichees to take seriously. His later ditherings in Milan over how to live the life of philosophical retirement while maintaining a domestic sexual attachment suggest a recurrent pattern the Manichees had seen as well. When rumors went about later that Augustine had been sending love tokens to a married woman, some were entirely unsurprised, and a few insiders regarded him as a washed-up Manichee, the one who couldn't cut it.

Augustine in 397, telling the story of his Manichee years, had reason to minimize. He had left Africa a Manichee (and a polemical and outspoken one), returning four years later a belligerent Caecilianist, telling one and all that he had been baptized an orthodox Christian while away. On his return, he took up with and was accepted by a minority sect in Africa, the Caecilianists, and it was with them that he advanced to clerical office. For the rest of his life, Augustine would be surrounded by suspicions that he was still more or less a Manichee. The Augustine we should miss the most, of all the Augustines who never were, is the one who never left the Manichees, who threw all his talent and energy into defending and defining the most extreme of his causes. The Manichee Faustus, originally from Milevis, was what Augustine could have become; a well-educated man who fell among the Manichees and knew success among them and scorn everywhere else. Augustine found Faustus less profound than he had hoped, but the extensive work he wrote years later, *Against Faustus*, reveals a figure of considerable substance. If Augustine had tried to take the step of becoming one of the elect and not merely an auditor, he might have stayed in that community. Perhaps he stayed in the outer circles because his sexual appetites were too recalcitrant, or even because he found the Manichee elite inadequately devoted to their austerities.[91] His zeal as a celibate Manichee would surely have equaled his zeal as a celibate catholic, with the added reinforcement that Manichees would even more readily support and understand his hostility to sensuality and thus aid him in the sublimation or derailment of his energies. The risk is that we would know very little of this Augustine, his work and even his existence perhaps suppressed by the orthodoxy that prevailed.

At the end of Augustine's life, his last bitter foe, Julian of Eclanum, found it easy and persuasive to level against him the charge that his hostile view toward bodies and sexuality, so foreign to Julian's notion of orthodox Christianity, were the legacy of a Manicheism never fully abjured. When Julian could quote a Manichean commentary on Paul that argued that *concupiscentia* (Augustine's favorite word for the hankerings of the flesh that survive the purifying bath of baptism) is a permanent evil force, he was sure he had Augustine dead to rights as a Manichee. The embarrassment to Augustine was palpable.[92] But the very last words of Augustine's last book, the *Unfinished Work Against Julian*, are directed to turning the accusation back on Julian. You're the *real* Manichee, Augustine is saying, a tactic as familiar as it is ineffective.[93]

The portrait easiest to paint of Augustine the Manichee is of a failed enthusiast, and the enthusiasm is as important to see as the failure. The theological question asked in Augustine's lifetime about the lingering effect of Manicheism on his thought has persisted to this day, constantly readdressed. Augustine was smart enough to know what it took to disavow the doctrines and practices of Manicheism—that much is beyond question.

The enthusiasm of youth can be insidiously persistent. He tells us, for example, that the Manichees drove home to him the question of "evil": "Unde malum?" they asked. "Where does evil come from?" When he heard them ask it, he was baffled. The answer they offered was a flattering one to a guilty conscience (evil is so materially present that sin is only to be expected, and redemption requires hard heroic struggle against the powers of darkness), but that answer in the long run failed to satisfy him. The question never went away. To come to orthodox Christianity as a man who has been deeply bothered by that question and then to find (with the help of Plotinus) an answer to that question as the essential step in moving closer to the orthodox Christianity he had once left behind is to return home a changed man. Other Christians of Augustine's time had no such obsession with his question, and they were the ones who found his answers unsettling and unnecessary. As an orthodox Christian, Augustine differed from many of his contemporaries precisely because he had been a Manichee and couldn't quite let go. Ex-Stalinist neoconservatives are just as exciting among their new coreligionists, and just as out of place. The points where Augustine could and did most ardently insist that he could prove that he was not a Manichee were the ones that most continued to mark him as one who had been in their number and been marked by them for life. The many Christians who disagreed with Augustine's mature views on sin and grace did so not because of some idealized dialogue of reasonable men determined to find the truth of Christianity. If that dialogue has ever occurred in history, it has gone unrecorded. Rather, their own preoccupations and concerns were addressed in other ways by Christianity, and they found Augustine's questions as much the problem as his answers.

Manicheism itself as a formal movement faded from the African scene in Augustine's lifetime, to live on in lands far to the east. The increasingly vigorous state sponsorship for one brand of Christianity and the effective uprooting of other competing brands of religiosity eventually so chilled the climate of Africa and its cities that cosmopolitan fashions faded. Augustine the Manichee is easy to forget.

Augustine had broken now with the Manichees, but not in favor of any positive association. Like Dickens's Mr. Micawber, he is always waiting for something to turn up:

> So I decided to be a catechumen in the catholic church handed on to me by my parents so long as I was waiting for some certainty to show up by which I might guide my steps.[94]

What might another narrative have been? Let us try this experiment, in the voice of an imagined Donatist from Hippo:

> Augustine was born to a rakehell father and a conventionally pious mother who had been brought up in the African church but was forced in early adolescence, along with the rest of her family, to give up the practice of the true faith in favor of the puppet church imposed by Roman persecutors.[95] A woman of little substance, she maintained her Christian fidelity as best she could, but she was at most a mild influence on her son, warning him away from the most dangerous of sexual entanglements and placing her true hopes in his public career. The boy himself had been brought up in this milquetoast Christianity, deliberately putting off baptism on the sour example of his father (who waited until he was on his deathbed) until there were enough sins on his soul to make it a necessary and effective bath.
>
> He soon left home for the corrupting metropolis of Carthage, where he fell in among bad company in several ways. The least of his failings were his sexual ones, for he also fell in among the wicked and illegal

Manichee cultists. Under a pretended show of austerity and virtue, they maligned god and praised the devil. Their fashionable excesses included a contempt for marriage, and thus they put themselves outside the pale of civil society, while most of them (Augustine emphatically included) continued to practice irregular sexual lives, spawning bastards when they were not seeking out magic potions to abort the evidence of their incontinence.

Augustine may have hankered after the status of "elect" among the Manichees, but his sexual predilections meant he would never be more than a hearer in that crowd. His fashionable connections inside and outside the Manichee community looked after him, and so of course his career prospered. All his friends and associates were drawn into the sphere of Manicheism, and he spent his life among them, waiting on the elect at their daily banquets. Eventually they suggested he go off with them to Rome to advance his career still further, and once there they intervened to send him on to Milan and the imperial court. His timing was excellent, inasmuch as he escaped the great purge of 386 that decimated the Manichean community in Africa and left it ever after a tiny and pathetic fragment.

In Milan his talent failed him, his career came apart in his hands, and he slunk back to Africa, where he saw well which way the wind was blowing and made no profession of Manicheism again. Whether he had actually been baptized in any branch of Christianity in Italy is unclear, but when he did finally declare an allegiance in Africa, it was not to the true church, but to the small, pretentious fragment of church that kowtowed to the empire and its powers of persecution. He had been a Christian all his life, but never spent a day of it in the true church: which brand of heresy, or which mixture of brands, he chose to indulge was of little interest. He was thoroughly a bad sort.

The weakest link in that narrative is instructive. It makes light of the books Augustine wrote against the Manichees on his return to Africa. But the making of books was not an art in that world that would make the author's views widely known. Few members of the Donatist church would have access to copies of Augustine's books or know their contents, and they could be easily dismissed or even suspected as deliberate disinformation.

Whatever its merits, a version of *that* competing narrative lies behind the story of the *Confessions*. Whatever we come away believing, we must be made to forget the hostile counternarrative. We do not understand Augustine at this crucial point in his life unless we see that the central pre-occupations of the *Confessions* are the Manichees, whom he seeks to dismiss before the work is one-third complete—and the Donatists, whom he never mentions. Between them he sets his own performance, an artful confession, exculpatory in the way public confession exculpates and justifies at the same time.

Modern studies of the *Confessions* are all at pains to say and show how the text goes beyond what we think of as *confession*. We explain carefully the triple sense Augustine in his sermons often explains of "confession of sin" (the conventional notion of confession), "confession of faith" (a phrase still familiar to us), and "confession of praise" (the form least understood in his own time and ours, the form of confession that consists not of blaming the self but praising god, not of lowering the river but of raising the bridge, so to speak).[96] While everything we say is quite true, it is also slightly irrelevant.

In a vital sense, vital to Augustine's life and future in the African church, the *Confessions* are indeed his full public confession of his past, dramatically meant to mislead his readers. *Here is my past,* he says; *see how it justifies my present. The power of god has swept me to the place I am. Here I stand* (to anticipate Luther), *I can no other.*

To achieve this narrative a price had to be paid. First, his Manicheism had to be minimized, belittled as a youthful indiscretion, and associated with precisely the sexual profligacy that a real Manichee teacher would have rebuked. Second, all the intimations and inklings of Christianity in earlier life had to be minimized. Infant enrollment as a catechumen, childhood yearnings for religion, adolescent exploration, and an apparent lifetime of regular association with Christian institutions (Augustine probably never missed church on Sunday in his life, gliding from his childhood church to Manicheism in Carthage, then to the Christianity he joined in Milan, without ever missing a beat) were as nothing. On his reading, he had not been a *faithful* Christian until he entered the baptismal font in Milan on Easter eve in 387.

That is where the narrative of Augustine's life breaks off in the *Confessions*. But what we have already seen suggests that the narrative is questionable on multiple levels. One additional source of the reader's unease should be evoked. If the story of the *Confessions* is to stand, then the year and a few months at Milan must be the moment at which light overcomes darkness. But how does Augustine tell that story?

One might think that conversion to a new religion would take the form of disposing of old ideas and acquiring new ones. With Augustine and orthodoxy, the story is rather different. Repeatedly, he tells us that his conversion took the form of discovering that Christianity was not what he had thought it was. In matters of practice and doctrine, he does not so much change his view as discover that the view he had imputed snob-bishly to Christianity, as he had seen it practiced in Africa, was incorrect and that Christianity could be rehabilitated if practiced the way it was done in fashionable Milan. Ambrose was as prudish as the Manichees when considering the many wives and children of the old patriarchs, so he did not defend them outright, and Augustine was relieved. But where Manicheism condemned the patriarchs and their god as beyond hope, Milan's Ambrosian allegorism spiritualized it. Under the teachings of Ambrose, Christ's anomalous metaphysical nature was not either utterly materialist or utterly idealist, but a philosophically defensible transmuta-tion of both. Augustine had shopped long enough to find a Christianity he could buy.

Only in Milan would Augustine have found, in Latin Christendom, so helpfully engaging a version of the faith he had scorned. Ambrose, himself a gentleman of the highest classes (and before the conversion of Paulinus of Nola, whom we will meet soon, probably the most aristocratic bishop of Latin Christendom), had forged on short notice his own syncretism of Christianity and traditional philosophy. He had been a rising star and provincial governor when he was shanghaied into the church at Milan. (He was so unready, he needed baptism before he could be ordained.) He was well schooled in Greek and Latin. Philo of Alexandria in the first cen-tury had proposed allegorical readings of Jewish scripture, and Plotinus in the third century (a Greek-speaking Egyptian who taught philosophy to the elite in Rome) had rewritten Plato in "modern" spiritual dress; and Ambrose devoured and pillaged both as a basis for his own sermons.

For Augustine, the appeal of the exotic in Ambrose was great and not unlike the appeal that the Manichees had had, especially when the exotic served, as it did with Ambrose, the multiple orthodoxies of his time: not just one brand of Christianity[97] (and in Ambrose's Milan, that brand was as endangered and tendentious a thing as it would be in Augustine's Hippo, oppressed by an emperor's widow no less), but orthodox Roman upper-classness. It was from Ambrose that Augustine learned how to act the part of the gentleman bishop of a discreet minority church and how to turn that minority into a majority.

Ambrose's tool for unifying those traditions lay in exploiting the idea of the "philosopher." His vision was based on one part traditional Greco-

Roman reading of classical Greek ideas, one part neo-Platonic reinterpretation of Platonic notions, and one part Christian scripture, selectively read, and in particular with the Jewish scriptures reread as a story about a philosopher's preparation to receive wisdom, the wisdom embodied in Christ. To all this was added a far from insignificant spirit of rivalry: whatever the late-antique (un-Christian) philosopher could claim, Ambrose argued that the Christian philosopher could and should claim that much and more besides. If neo-Platonism had the theurgic power to make its god present in ritual, Christianity had its liturgics to do the same. In two treatises, *The Sacraments* and *The Mysteries*, Ambrose wrote more explicitly than any other Christian of his time about the claims and functioning of Christian sacramentality. We will see shortly how this rivalry with philosophy is the key to understanding the oddest thing about Augustine's "conversion," that is, his need to forswear his sexuality forever.

Augustine went to Ambrose in the first place because of his reputation as an orator. When Augustine encountered there this Ambrosian mélange and the full Ambrosian charm, he tells us he was bowled over. When his mother came to Milan and fell as well under the spell of the local guru, Augustine's fate was all but sealed. If we can simplify his youthful conflicts into paternal and maternal influences, then in Ambrose he found a future that promised to unite the class and culture of his father—the spirit of the Roman gentleman—with the religious commitments and practices of his mother.

And so we come to Monnica. No bit player in the history of autobiography plays quite the role that she plays in Augustine's. One must go to fiction to find the like, perhaps in Proust's mother and grandmother, or Sherlock Holmes's "*the* woman," Irene Adler: powerful, undeniably erotically charged, but at the same time unmistakably taboo and distant. A century ago Augustine's life and story readily lent itself to the novelty of Freudian interpretation. A very interesting and serious early essay in psychobiography, more serious than many that have since pursued Augustine, emphasized "inversion" and mother fixation in ways that were radical and unsettling then but seem conventional and obvious today.[98] One modern writer indeed speaks of the family machinations that Monnica engineers as a Balzac novel before its time. The most remarkable scene, as she weeps on the shore at Carthage while her son sails off, abandoning her for Italy, is dramatically inscribed into the literary tradition, with Augustine suddenly becoming Aeneas abandoning Dido. We can all connect the dots of that story.

The scenes Monnica plays in Augustine's life story are vivid and memorable: the solicitous mother concerned by her son's sexual maturation and encouraging him to avoid married women (thus in effect telling him to keep to women of lower social status, which he did); the pious mother hoping to win him for her creed; the solicitous mother again looking to make a good *and* pious marriage to assure the prosperity and social status of her whole family (and consequently hard-heartedly precipitating the dismissal of his lower-status common-law wife); and, finally, the pious and solicitous mother happy to leave this world once her son had been won for her god.

Quite apart from any trenchant psychological interpretation, the genuinely puzzling thing about Monnica's presence in Augustine's story is that she looms so large in the telling. Augustine was scarcely intending to offer us raw material for psychobiography, and indeed, nothing of what he gives us should be thought of as "raw" material for anything. In both the *Confessions* and his early dialogues at Cassiciacum, Monnica plays a large and striking part. At Cassiciacum, she ventures into the most exalted philosophical dialogues, a role that ancient writers gave to women only very rarely. Plato's Diotima in the *Symposium* may be the only truly comparable example. Whatever unconscious factors influenced Augustine's portrayal, the overt and conscious factors deserve attention too.

The key to Monnica's presence lies in her religious history and its capacity to embarrass Augustine. Her past was shaded by a childhood and adolescence played out in a church that Augustine found embarrassing and which he rejected. "Monnica the Donatist" is almost never mentioned by moderns, but she always haunts Augustine's presentation. She grew up in the majority Donatist church, then found her whole community hustled into allegiance, or nearly so, to the minority Roman-sanctioned sect when she was married. When she passed into that Caecilianist community, doubtless scarcely understanding the issues at stake, she retained the characteristic piety of the conventional African Christian community in which she had grown up. For example, she would take a picnic basket to a graveyard to honor the blessed dead, a habit she was surprised to find forbidden when she came to Italy. Even after giving his allegiance to the Caecilianist church, Augustine still spoke years later of the Christianity that he saw in his childhood and under his mother's influence as "superstition"—already a disdainful word for religious behavior deemed light on credibility and heavy on mumbo-jumbo.

But when Augustine *shows* us Monnica and her religion, we see nothing of a Donatist past and no direct censure. The most Augustine says comes early in the *Confessions*, when he suggests that concern for his worldly career trumped her religious ambitions for him, at least in his student days. That whisper of criticism is counterbalanced and erased in most readers' memories by all the other displays of her virtue and piety.

A few weeks after the moment in the Milan garden, in which a mysterious semi-divine voice tells Augustine to pick up his book and read what it says, a process that leads to his crisis of faith and eventual rebirth, Augustine, Monnica, his friend Alypius, and the rest of the family went up to a borrowed country villa at Cassiciacum.[99] The delights of philosophical retreat were surely appealing there,[100] but its distance from big-city temptation also probably made it a fine place in which a recovering libidinist could test his resolve.

So at the end of a long afternoon's philosophizing by the menfolk at Cassiciacum, Monnica hears a definition of the divine trinity and exclaims the first line of one of Ambrose's hymns: "Nurture those who pray to you, O Trinity!"[101] The explicit message is the consonance of philosophy and religion, but the implicit message is that Monnica's religion is itself part and parcel of the intellectually respectable religion Augustine created for himself under Ambrose's influence, and that her adherence to the right brand of religion is genuine.

Augustine's psychological makeup grows more evident. The urgency in his texts focuses on demonstrating his mother's religious *authenticity*. The exact word he would use for that authenticity is the adjective *fidelis* ("faithful"), which in ancient and modern usage alike applies both to religious authenticity and to marital behavior.

The more important family relationship in Augustine's life is the paternal one. We can have no doubt who Augustine's mother is, but Patricius remains a remarkably elusive figure for his son: stern, ambitious in a petty way, family-proud but casually unfaithful to his wife, distant. In the narrative of the *Confessions*, he vanishes early on, and we find out only dozens of pages later that he had died while Augustine was still young. When he disappears, Monnica goes off to Italy, there to attach herself to Ambrose with the same subservience she brought her husband and which ends in Augustine accepting Ambrose as a "father in grace."[102] And Ambrose is only a surrogate father invoking the image of god the true and final father, the one Augustine would notionally accept, even as he struggled to understand and finally to enact a fatherly role for himself as bishop, an Ambrose role, while recovering from the disappointment of his fatherly ambitions for his dead son Adeodatus. Suddenly the religion of his mother and the ambitions, the culture, and the masculine power of a surrogate father came together before his eyes.

The little that we know of Augustine's son, that is, of Augustine's own experience of fatherhood, throws some light here. Adeodatus ("God-send"[103]), the son of Augustine's flesh, was the pride of his eyes, the unspoken great loss of his life. The child was born around 372 and died sometime around 390, just reaching the age at which his father had begotten him. Few have seen the eerie parallels across generations and the way Augustine's relationship with his son echoes his own relationship with his father. Both find their sons to be promising and signs of great hope—Patricius looking to earthly propagation, Augustine impressed with intellectual precocity. Death allowed both to satisfy their fathers completely—Augustine by letting him hold off rebellion until long after his father's death, Adeodatus by dying young before he could run afoul of his father's strictures and temper. But Adeodatus, I fear, is too hidden for us to read, to know more than that he was there, that he meant something, and that he disappeared. (We glimpse the possibility for a poignant instant a few pages from the end of the last of Augustine's works, when the old bishop recalls an obscure line Cicero addressed to his own son: "You're the only man in the world that I would want to outdo me in everything."[104]) The father placed a heavy weight of expectation on the son (as his own father had done on him), drawing him into his philosophical dialogues at Cassiciacum as a junior but impressive partner, and then in the pamphlet *The Teacher* (*De magistro*) giving him the part of full interlocutor. The idealized version of the son we see there tells us nothing about the real boy. The best parallel we know of to this relationship in Augustine's world is the handing on of talent, authority, and quarrelsomeness from the bishop Memor of Beneventum to his own son (and Augustine's eventual bugbear), Julian of Eclanum.

As long as Adeodatus was alive Augustine was no cleric, and showed no signs of clerical ambitions for his son. The contemporary letters make no mention of him and the *Confessions* are silent on what his future might have been. Just at the age when Augustine was making his way into a wider world of learning, Adeodatus went home to Tagaste with his father and vanished from public view. What would have become of him? We have absolutely no way of knowing, but bear in mind that as long as Adeodatus was alive Augustine showed no sign of giving up his property or his social station. Of all the Augustines who might have been, though, Augustine the aging father (and doting grandfather?) is the most remote from our gaze. Imagine, for example, what the stern Augustine would have made of a scapegrace and dissolute Adeodatus, siring children by different women, a typical Roman gentleman. But if he was, as he must have been, a demanding and overpowering friend, he can only have been a looming and imposing figure as a father.

Not all of either culture could be taken up whole, and so Augustine had his chance to rebel against both Monnica and Ambrose in time. The banning of the festive excesses of African Christianity was Augustine's first campaign as cleric back in Africa, to purify religious practice of those parts of his mother's religion that were still too African (Augustine would have said too Donatist) for a real gentleman. Years later, Augustine would discover that the Platonism that Ambrose studied included far more specific anti-Christian content than he had suspected, and so books 8, 9, and 10 of his *City of God* (written by 417) represent his careful retreat from the full Ambrosian enthusiasm.

Not by accident, the culmination of Augustine's narrative in the *Confessions* is for most readers not the ninth book, where he brings the threads of his story to a decorous theological end, but the eighth: the garden scene at Milan, which has been marked since at least the sixth century as the dramatic turning point of the text. But it is very hard, if instructive, to try to say just what is happening in those pages.

To take the narrative at face value, we have a story of a religiously confused man who has been reading Paul's epistles. He hears multiple stories of dramatic conversions: that of the Roman orator Marius Victorinus, a distinguished rhetorician and student of Platonic philosophy (Augustine had to recognize a lot of himself in Victorinus), who accepted baptism at Rome a few years before Augustine did; of Anthony, the reputed founder of Egyptian monasticism who, upon hearing the gospel, did as Jesus had recommended, selling all he had and giving it to the poor; and of two courtiers at contemporary Trier who were inspired by the story of Anthony to give up their worldly lives and soon-to-be wives and convert. So Augustine has a dramatic conversion of his own. But from what to what?

In the seventh book of the *Confessions*, he describes how he had already given his intellectual allegiance to the Christianity that Ambrose represents. "I chattered about it like an expert" is his candid report of his reaction to *that* conversion,[105] and doubtless some ear-weary contemporaries in Milan could remember that phase.

Baptism would wait. The story recounted in book 8 is set in August 386, but for baptism he delayed until after a long winter in the country for the Easter vigil service in Milan on April 25, 387. In the narrative of the *Confessions* it will be mentioned discreetly only in the middle of book 9.[106] He had apparently thought about putting himself up for baptism in the spring of 386 but lost his nerve at the last moment. What happened? If his mind was changed by early 386 but baptism followed a year later, what was there that needed doing in between?

What happened is what book 8 of the *Confessions* wants to tell us. Augustine, like many ancients, and unlike many or most moderns, saw baptism as a step to be taken when and only when the candidate was morally (and, we would say, psychologically) prepared to accept the new responsibilities of Christian life. It was not that he sat in judgment of the new religion, deciding whether it was worthy of him (Augustine had been through that phase in the time recounted in the sixth book of the *Confessions*); rather, the church and its god challenged the candidate to make himself new. Most baptismal candidates were satisfied to present themselves when they had acquired the good intention at moral reform that marks New Year's resolutions or a decision to quit smoking or go on a diet. As long as there was no dramatic relapse, a relatively normal future life was quite in order.

But Augustine was more competitive than most. He does not so much tell us as show us how he decided that, for him, Christian baptism was only possible when he had decided to transform himself into the Christian philosopher, and for him that transformation necessarily entailed a life of absolute sexual continence.

So we see Augustine in book 8 of the *Confessions* wrestling with his intentions, unsure of himself, knowing what the challenge is and getting up his nerve to face it. The climactic moment in the garden is the moment in which he decides that he can indeed swear off sex forever. His mother, on hearing the news, is delighted. (Her delight was perhaps mixed with some anxiety that the good society marriage she had just arranged for him would probably require some serious negotiations and perhaps money to escape. In this case the bride-to-be was not, apparently, invited to join her betrothed in a life of Christian continence, as often happened in other zealous households of this generation.)

Modern scholarship has long worried about the lack of contemporary record for the garden scene but in a way has worried about the wrong thing.[107] The decision of August 386 took on meaning only when the intention formed then proved sustainable. The career change that Augustine undertook at that moment—abandoning Milan for Tagaste—was an ordinary sort of failure and retirement. Though Anthony of Egypt's example was before his eyes, Augustine did not sell all he had, give to the poor, and follow Jesus. He quit his job, went home, and lived very comfortably. Very little really changed, apart from Augustine's sleeping arrangements and the venue of his quite ordinary rustication. Some have argued that he only really became a Christian in 391, with ordination, or in the years following as the impact of ordination made itself felt. To think in those terms is to think too literally, but it was the change in Augustine's life in 391, ordination and the move to Hippo, that was dramatic and permanent. To have spoken of that crucial change in the *Confessions* might require him to go into details of his hesitations that were best glossed over and would blur the fundamental story of the text again. Choosing to emphasize what happened in Italy placed Augustine's story in a purely catholic milieu, far from African disorders, and left Manicheism at the margins and Donatism quite out of the picture. And that was the story, true in the details, if quite false in impact, that Augustine needed to tell in 397.

"And then we were baptized."[108] With those words, long hidden away not only in mid-book and mid-paragraph but mid-sentence by most editions of the *Confessions*, Augustine's story ends. That choice of ending tells a story of its own. The moment deserves to be emphasized not only for its personal significance to Augustine but for the link it provides to all the quarrels of his life. As a mature man, he projected its importance back to the childhood sickness when he begged for baptism but was denied it by his mother. The ritual would be the centerpiece of the liturgical year at Hippo, the focus of the liturgy of Easter, for which he tried always to be in Hippo, and at the same time it offered the point of division between him and all the imagined and real opponents of his mature life. The Donatists had their own baptism and insisted on overriding (and thus negating) the baptism that Augustine handed out; the "pagans" were the men who refused any form of baptism; the Pelagians were the ones who could not understand the urgent need to baptize infants; and even the Arians who began eddying onto African shores in Augustine's last decade of life were men separated from his community by the form and words of their baptism. Baptism was what made a person "faithful" in Augustine's eyes; but baptism, like orthodox doctrine, was terribly difficult to get right.

But if baptism was the culmination of the narrative, it is not the culmination of the book we read today.

A MODERN CLASSIC

The *Confessions* aren't about Augustine, they're about his god. Everything he wrote comes back to that obsession, even (or rather especially) this triumph of self-absorption. There's a character in Dickens who was writing to the crown for redress of grievances, only King Charles's head kept coming into the petition and he had to quit and start over, repeatedly. Augustine never quit and started over.

Augustine's readers, however, have made the *Confessions* into the first modern autobiography, and it is a classic of *modern* literature.[109] Indeed, Augustine's early medieval audience seems to have paid this book relatively little attention, preferring his more prosaic biblical commentaries and theological treatises. It began to come into its own in the twelfth century and after, but it's equally possible to argue that moderns have made far more of it than any earlier age. As Augustine's doctrinal eminence has faded with passing years, his prestige as self-narrator has grown stronger.

One book, two readings, theological and autobiographical. To sketch that duality will be one way of trying to do justice to the many-sidedness of the book, of making it harder to forget that books are often a good deal more complicated than their authors imagine. Curiously and appropriately enough, the fault line that separates the *Confessions*-about-god and the *Confessions*-about-Augustine runs right through the most vividly remembered scene of the book, the one in the garden in Milan, where he hears a voice and takes it as an instruction to read a book and thereupon to change his life.

The first page of the *Confessions* should throw a reasonable reader into confusion. Who is talking, please? To whom is he talking?

> You are great, Master, and worthy of every praise. Your power is great and your wisdom—well, the mind boggles at the thought of measuring it.[110]

That's not quite how you'll find those lines translated in any published text of the *Confessions*, because every translator knows the score. This is *Saint* Augustine, for crying out loud, and he's talking to *God*, right? The footnote at this point in a printed translation will even probably tell me that these words are not Augustine's exactly so much as a near-perfect quotation from one of the Psalms.

Of course. But pick the book up cold, leave aside what you know or might know, and throw yourself into it. What is it about these words that tells you all this? Nothing. You had to bring it with you. As it happens, you were right to bring it, but many of Augustine's earliest readers would find the style and the opening almost as brusque and confusing as my translation makes them. This intimate, indiscreet effusion, the fawning flattery, pouring out words to "god"—this is prayer, not literature. If we find things like this written down ordinarily, we read them in certain ritually defined kinds of ways and spaces. But the *Confessions* will always have looked like a literary book, though a very odd one. The book does not behave like well-mannered ancient prose. To do that, it should have a preface, it should tell us what it is about, it should tell us where it is going, and it does none of these things. But it is not written in verse, for all that it has some verselike qualities, opening with invocation of the divine and deploying language with rare intensity to convey subjective experience.

Take a text of the *Confessions* and start reading. On what page does it begin to dawn on you, if you don't know it already, that this is an autobiography? How is it signaled? The signaling is in the doing: Augustine merely turns abruptly in mid-sentence a few pages after the first and starts talking about his infancy.

> For what am I trying to say, Master, except that I don't know how I got here, here in this mortal life or living death? I don't know the answer to that. The kindness of your pity comforted me, as I heard later from the parents of my flesh, the ones from whom and in whom you gave me my

earthly shape. The kindness of human milk comforted me and it wasn't my mother or my nurses who filled their breasts by themselves, but you, who through them gave me the nourishment meant for infants, according to the way you have arranged the world and set out its riches right down to the foundation of things.[111]

This is a very abstract and philosophical infancy narrative, continuing in a slightly more matter-of-fact tone for most of the first book. By then, the reader is conditioned to be less surprised when the life-telling narrative continues in the second book. (It's another question how the first reader, unsuspecting, dealt with the ending of the narrative in the ninth book with, quite evidently, a mass of pages left to read.[112]) That the narrative is spotty and overembroidered with meditation and reflection should be a sign, often missed, that narrative isn't the whole purpose.

So what is going on? Here is one line of interpretation that can be stoutly defended and is probably the most historically grounded reading of what the text is in its complexity. It may disorient.

In the beginning, god was triple: not three *gods*, but three *somethings* in one god.

Small interruption: Some of us may be familiar with speaking of the divine "three persons," but it's worth knowing that when that word "person" was applied to the "three-ishness" of god, it had a long history that didn't have much to do with our notion of "person." The word originally meant "mask," the thing you wore in a drama (probably hiding a speaking tube to help you project your voice) to represent the character you *weren't*, but few now would try to represent Christian theology, as being about the three masks of god or the three stage roles he plays, although it might be a fresh approach to a difficult subject.

So, three somethings constituted Augustine's god. Father, Son, and Spirit are the commonest ways of naming the somethings, and once they are named in this way, they spawn a whole subsidiary pattern of triplets for Augustine. Each person has its own way of being: the father *is*, the son *knows*, and the spirit *loves*. Augustine loves to play with triplets, not least because for him humankind exists in the image and likeness of god, and whatever is three-ish about god is accordingly three-ish about humankind, with being, knowing, and loving similarly at the core of human reality.

But the image of god in man has gone bad. It needs to be fixed. Whatever is rare and strange and precious and unique about a given individual is probably an indication of the things that have gone wrong. Whatever is like god indicates what's gone right. And it all dances in threes.

To me, this belief is the most poignant thing about Augustine. He is criticized by many for undervaluing the human body, but in a profound way he undervalues the human personality, as we might understand it, in favor of a lifeless and unengaging notion of the soul. So take this text from Augustine's scripture:

> Everything there is in the world consists of the hankerings of the flesh and the hankerings of the eyes and worldly ambition.[113]

That's a pretty sobering way of talking about "everything there is in the world," but Augustine is happy to take that text on its own terms. He's looked around enough to have his own reading of what it means, and he is very explicit about this in the tenth book of the *Confessions*.[114] Hankerings of the flesh are hankerings of the flesh: hunger and thirst and passion for fine music and a drifting pleasure in lovely smells, and especially sexual desire.[115] "Hankerings of the eyes," on the other hand, means for Augustine *curiosity*, the desire to know things you're not supposed to know, especially in matters of religion and magic. Wanting to know about demons and false gods and ways of working wonders—that is what will get you into trouble. "Worldly ambition" is pretty straightforward: wanting the position in the world that makes you the envy of other men.

Three temptations: the pattern should look familiar. The three masks of god are here again, each betrayed in a distinctive way. For "hankerings of the flesh" have to do with love—the wrong love, charity gone haywire, spiritual life turned fleshly, ethereal love turned sexual. "Hankerings of the eyes" have to do with knowing—wanting to know what you shouldn't, not wanting to know what you should. And "worldly ambition" is about setting yourself up to rival your betters, to *be* what they cannot be. What were temptations to Augustine become life goals when moderns think of them as self-esteem, education, and sexual fulfillment.

For Augustine, the scriptures offered exactly the most vivid image of this triple temptation: the temptation of Jesus by the devil in the fourth chapter of Matthew's gospel.[116] The devil comes upon Jesus in the desert and finds him fasting and hungry. He says, take these stones and make them bread and eat: that's for the hankerings of the flesh, Augustine will say. When Jesus resists, the devil suggests he go up on a rock and throw himself down and see if the angels will catch him: hankering of the eyes, curiosity, desire to see if hidden powers can be controlled by special knowledge, says Augustine. So then, still trying, the devil takes Jesus up on a mountaintop and shows him the kingdoms of the earth laid out at his feet and offers them to Jesus in return for devil worship: worldly ambition, to be sure, and disloyalty to the divine father. If the devil took that approach with Jesus, then it was probably the best (or worst) he could do, and he will approach ordinary mortals the same way.

So if we take that piece of theory out of the middle of the *Confessions* and apply it to the beginnings of Augustine's story, what happens to him?

The infant Augustine is indiscriminately malicious and self-centered, but that is only a token of what is to come. By the end of the first book, Augustine is uncharacteristically accentuating the positive, the way in which three-ishnesses suggest that there was much good in the boy.

> For I existed then, I lived, and I was conscious. . . . I sinned in this, that I sought pleasure, exaltation, and truth not in god but in his creatures, and so I fell into pain, depression, and error. Thanks to you, my sweetness, my honor, my confidence: my god, thanks to you for your gifts.[117]

Then he discovers sex: book 2 is the book of the temptation of the flesh, and with it the primordial sin, the perplexing theft of fruit in the garden. A good biographer might worry about whether Augustine's adolescent sex life was much to speak of, and whether he and his friends really did steal those pears, but he would miss the point of the narrative. Augustine's strategy needs him to cave in to the hankerings of the flesh here, to lose the divine spirit and start down a bad slope. So the story tells us in the abstract that he was awash in sexual temptation, refracts this through the attitudes of his parents (paternal pride, maternal anxiety), and then settles on the story of the pear theft as an image of primordial sin with sexual overtones—quite in the same spirit as Augustine's interpretation of the story of Adam and Eve.

The third book takes Augustine to Carthage.

> To Carthage I came and there crackled around me on all sides the sizzling frying pan of sinful loves. I was not yet in love but I was in love with love. . . .[118]

This Carthage is represented by Augustine as a world of spectacles and shows—things to look at greedily—and of Manichees—people with secret hidden knowledge about god to share with him, to use to lead him astray. Curiosity is everywhere at this stage in his fall.[119]

So the last step downwards is ambition. The fourth book depicts a sensual and ideologically cocky Augustine, full of what he knows, living his life in his senses. Shaken by the death of a friend (and the friend's eerily effective baptism), Augustine falls back on his old pastimes—sex, drugs, and rock 'n' roll, so to speak:

> My soul found no rest in pleasant parklands, not in play and song, not in sweet-smelling places and elaborate banquets, not in the pleasures of the bedroom, not even in books and poems.[120]

Not *even* in books? That feels to us like an anticlimax, but for him "not even books" because the books are the place where, when sensuality fails, curiosity prevails. But even the books don't work for him, and so he flees, to Carthage and then to Rome, to pursue his worldly career. The two temptations to which he has yielded, carnality and curiosity, leave him miserable, and so he capitulates to the third—ambition.

In sum, the fall of Augustine in these early books of the *Confessions* is the fall Jesus shunned: one temptation at a time, in the same order as those faced by Jesus, with Augustine arrogantly succumbing, proudly falling, to one after another, betraying each divine person in turn, the father last.

How does he rise again? By reversing his path.

The fifth book is depressed and depressive. The wheels have come off Augustine's chariot. His career doesn't satisfy him, the Manichees disappoint him: we don't hear much of his sex life at this point, but nothing suggests that the flesh's various hankerings had much with which to console him. Indeed, the flesh betrayed him, for his flight from Africa took him to Rome, where he fell dangerously ill. Teaching there afterwards was disappointing, even though it led to a great opportunity, to move to Milan and teach in the shadow of the imperial court there.

Milan had become a major imperial city in the fourth century as the emperors spent more and more of their time in active military command on the northern frontiers of the Rhine and Danube. The flowering of the capital was short-lived, for in 402 the emperor felt overexposed on the Lombard plain and moved his headquarters to swamp-defended Ravenna on the Adriatic coast, which remained the headquarters of government in Italy for the next two centuries. For the moment, however, Milan was all bright lights and big city. There Augustine met Ambrose, the well-born bishop who pulled every string he could at court and played the crowds with great skill to support his aims. As we have said, Ambrose was famous as an orator, a man whom Augustine's ear-curiosity wanted him to go hear, to find out what sort of speaker he was. And with that choice, taken for the most worldly, sensual, curious of reasons, Augustine's spiritual ascent began, unexpected.

Still, the mist of intellectual confusion darkened his eyes (no surprise, by this point). He makes a show of his naïve and untutored ideas about god (is the world like a sponge that soaks up god like a liquid?) and the Platonists make their appearance, almost magically brought to Augustine by a man swollen with pride (these Platonists display that particular vice, but Augustine has learned something about abandoning worldly pride by now and is immune to that side of them), and when he reads their works, what does he find? An encouragement to take seriously what the Christian scripture says about the eternity of the divine word. Just how this happens is something we will return to below, but ten years afterwards, writing the *Confessions*, Augustine would remember mainly that the Platonists taught him about the abstract eternal word, not the "word-made-flesh" experience in Jesus, and he would regard that as a critical omission.

But the Platonic teaching defeats Augustine's curiosity forever by presenting him with the image of the divine word, eternal and unchanging, the source of all truth.

So he has one temptation left to surmount, the hankerings of the flesh. We come, then, at last to the eighth book, the book that ends with the scene in the garden where Augustine "takes up and reads."[121] In the course of book 8, he and his friend and sidekick, Alypius, who had followed Augustine from Africa and Rome and who would be politically at his side for the rest of their lives, as we will see, are depicted listening to conversion story after conversion story, and so Augustine went off to one side to enact one himself. Reasonable skepticism can observe that the scene he describes closely resembles a gospel scene and is too well constructed to be quite believable. Augustine made no mention of any such event in the things he wrote at the time or for the ten years after until the *Confessions*. But the book is unambiguous in insisting on the scene and its placement.

Much can be, should be, and has been said about that scene, but note for now one fact only: that the issue on the table, so to speak, is sex. Can Augustine swear to a life of complete sexual continence from this moment forward? Yes: that's what he learns—or *decides*—at the crucial moment, facing Paul's text in Romans: "no orgies and drunkenness, nothing about bedrooms and horniness, no wrangling and rivalry—just put on the master Jesus Christ and don't go on looking after the flesh and its hanker-ings."[122] Reading that is what makes his doubts fly away, and that's what they go and tell his mother a few minutes later, he and Alypius. Just why this decision should have been crucial for him at the time is one question, but within the shape of the *Confessions*, it looms large because it completes a neat (some would say too neat) pattern.

To summarize, then: Augustine fell because he lost control of the im-age of god in himself: spirit first, son/word second, father third. He rose because he recovered that image in reverse order: father, son, and, finally, spirit.

And then he died: not literally, but the interesting part of his life was over, and so he was ready for baptism. In the course of the ninth book of the *Confessions*, his mother's death is narrated, his father's is mentioned, his other friends, Nebridius and Verecundus, slip away to die in odd mo-ments of the narrative, and Augustine himself and Alypius, Adeodatus, and a new friend, Evodius, undertake the special form of death that is Christian baptism.[123] Adeodatus's bodily death is foretold in that context, and that's it. Story over.

But the Christian story doesn't end with death and rebirth: it holds that one must die and be reborn twice, once spiritually and once physi-cally. The time between the two is of indeterminate length and little in-terest, according to Augustine, both in the *Confessions* and in *City of God*, which applies the same narrative principles on a world-historical scale. Falling and rising facilitate narrative: the earthly afterlife, that time be-tween, what he calls in one place "this time between times,"[124] is without plot and order.

So, without plot, storytelling stops and a new model of existence re-places it, filling books 10 through 13 of the *Confessions*. Augustine the be-liever—the object of the narrative, seen at a distance—now has faith but not vision, believes but doesn't really know and see, and so lives in a per-petual state of longing and a new restless alienation, loving in a new way but still imperfectly. Anxiety is joined by its sibling, hope. Wisdom—so the Augustine of the *Confessions* will say and believe and enact, though other Augustines we encounter may say and think other things—consists of pining for the divine, hankering after it, and struggling to get momen-tary glimpses and tastes of it. The language of hankering carries over from sexual love to divine love:

I was late in loving you, beauty so old and so new, I was late in loving you. You were inside me and I was outside myself, and I was looking for you out there and went rushing headlong among all the beautiful things you had made, me in my self-made ugliness. You were there for me and I was not with you. All sorts of things distracted me from you, things that wouldn't have had any meaning without you giving it to them. So you called out to me and shouted and broke through my deafness! You flashed, you gleamed, you chased away my blindness! Your odor flooded me and I took a deep breath and sucked you in! I took a taste, and I hungered and thirsted the more! And then you touched me, and I was all on fire for your peace![125]

That's how the first attempt in the *Confessions* to show the new life in action ends—enraptured, orgasmic. The next page shows a collapse back into alienation. The rest of the tenth book is the mind-numbing analysis of temptation and its lingering effects, where the bishop shows us himself as far from god as he gets in these postconversion books, very nearly alone, faced with the temptations he might *yet* submit to. There's no Calvinist doctrine of assurance here.

And so he starts over. If we compare the juncture between the tenth and eleventh books of the *Confessions* with the first page of the whole book, we are back where we started, even to seeing some of the same words and biblical echoes. The bishop has completed his review of the past and is now ready to live in the present, and a bishop does that by looking after his flock (which he can't do while writing his book, and vice versa) and by studying scripture, which is something he *can* do while writing his book.[126]

For a long time now, I have been on fire to meditate on your law and in doing so to confess to you what I know and what I don't, the beginnings of my enlightenment and the remnants of my darkness, until my weakness can be swallowed up in your strength. I don't want my time to slip away on any other task, the time I can find free from refreshing body and mind with food and sleep and free from the service that I owe to my fellow man, and the service that I don't owe but give them anyway.[127]

The three books remaining should make the reader who has seen the patterns I have been outlining here suspicious. They profess to be a study of the first chapter of scripture, that is, the opening of the book of Genesis. If we are reading the *Confessions* as an autobiography, it takes some considerable stretching to make this part fit. The general bafflement has gone so far as to lead one scholar to compile in a dissertation nineteen

theories to explain the presence of these last books. At the furthest extreme, one of the most original and sensitive readers of the *Confessions*
dropped the biggest interpretative clanger: perhaps, opined Pierre Courcelle, Augustine meant to write a commentary on *all* of scripture as a pen-
dant to the *Confessions*, but when he saw how much space the first chapter
of Genesis was taking up, he gave up in despair.[128]

But if we look at what goes on in those books, pieces begin to fall into
place. The eleventh book starts the Genesis account, but it gets side-
tracked with a conversation about the nature of time and its difference
from eternity, and eternity is a quality of the first divine mask, the paternal one. The twelfth book starts in again purposefully, but gets its own
distraction: on the rules for scriptural interpretation, that is, on how you
get from the multiple words of the scriptural text to the one divine word
that stands behind it—the second mask. And the thirteenth book? Augustine rushes forward through the narrative of the first chapter of Genesis
to show how it recapitulates the history of the church on earth, the church
that represents (since the first Pentecost, in Acts 2) the presence of the
spirit—the last of the masks.

Each of the last three books shows us Augustine the bishop, now re-
formed in the image and likeness of god and well on his way into the bor-
ing interim stage of his life, fending off alienation and temptation, with
hope of the world to come, contemplating in turns both the divine nature
(one mask at a time) and human nature (that is, his own nature in its triple
reflection of the divine). And the two draw closer together. The last pages
of the text reach the seventh day of Genesis, which is (in Augustine's interpretation) a figure for the eternal rest of the blessed, the time when all
alienation and temptation pass away, all separation is erased, and humankind is reunited with god.

That's the story. We've followed it as Augustine wrote it, with the main
lines of its theological preoccupations, and it turns out to be what I said:
not about Augustine, who keeps fading away like the Cheshire cat (leaving behind not his smile but his preacherly voice), but about god. The human story is gradually erased, with all its confusion and mystery and
perplexities and contradictions; and the divine story, serene and bland and
bright, emerges behind it. Every story, in this way of reading, turns out to
be the same story.

Most likely that's how Augustine wanted his book to be read; and if
that were how it *had* been read for all the centuries since, I dare say it
would have few readers, mainly obsessive ones. How has the book survived and thrived, especially in modern times?

Let's go back to the garden scene in the eighth book. No book about Augustine's life is complete without the author taking the liberty of telling that story again. When Augustine's best biographer, for example, gets to that point in his narrative of Augustine's life, he just steps aside and gives us a little over two solid pages of quotation, slightly abridged but otherwise uncommented on, giving the story exactly as Augustine told it.[129] Let me try to describe it a little differently, in order to show how the scene *works*.

Take the whole eighth book of the *Confessions* first for two salient features, one obvious, one not so obvious. On the surface, the book is a compilation of conversion stories. Every story is the same: troubled indifference giving way to serene acceptance under the influence of a gesture, a word, or a moment of encounter. What is Augustine's reaction? In the narrative as we have it, he went away to seek his own conversion. There the "miracle" occurs. A mysterious voice, of divine origin, tells him to "take up and read." At that instant, Augustine has thrown himself down under a fig tree to weep (and he probably expects his Christian readers to think of the fig tree under which Jesus saw Nathanael in John's gospel[130]); but Augustine gets up and goes back to where he left Alypius and picks up a codex book of Paul's letters that was lying there from before. He opened it and read the first text he came upon, the one I translated above (pages 69–70). In the context, neither he nor we have any claim to be surprised.

What is not so obvious about the eighth book is that it has been setting up this Pauline reading all along. At the end of the seventh book, puzzled and inquisitive after a disappointing experience with "mysticism" under the guidance of the Platonists, Augustine had turned to reading Paul, whose vision of heaven made him a *Christian* expert on mysticism.[131] If we look back over the chapters of the eighth book of the *Confessions*, we can see that Paul has been instructing him all along.[132] Every few pages in the eighth book, we've had quotations from Paul's letter to the Romans, each one from a little further on in the Pauline text. He quotes chapters 1, 4, 7, 7 again, and 7 again. So when he now picks up the book and quotes the thirteenth chapter, one thing he's saying is that Paul is having his effect on him in more than just a random way. (Paul's relevance at the time of writing is something we'll come back to in a few pages.)

And so "the light of tranquility is poured into my heart and all the clouds of doubt fly away."[133] Why? What has happened?

If we let Augustine control his story, he probably doesn't want us to slow down at this point. For him, the culmination of his narrative will not come until the next book, when he leads us to the decisive moment of his baptism and a foretaste of heavenly bliss. Augustine the writer most likely thought that the ninth book would be the dramatic culmination to his narrative books. But as early as the sixth century, readers were taken by the *eighth* book, by this story. The drama is too good, the satisfaction of release too blatant—and the issue is sex.

LUSTING FOR CELIBACY

Why? Why did Augustine make the renunciation of sex central to his conversion? Why did he think he had to?

Lifelong celibacy was emphatically not a requirement of Christianity in the fourth century. Only higher clergy were expected (with quite variable results, it must be said) to practice such continence, though they could do so while remaining with wives they had already married. Yet Augustine, even at this moment in the garden, had no intention of joining the clergy.

But Ambrose had his own ideas. It's long been conventional to lament that Augustine and Ambrose never quite seem to have had what Bertie Wooster would call "a bit of the old heart to heart." For such an inveterate letter-writer, Augustine surprisingly appears never to have corresponded with Ambrose during or after the time he spent in Milan, though the older man lived until 397. Yet they were anything but two ships that passed in the night, and after the bishop died, Augustine was in touch with Ambrose's priest and successor, Simplicianus. Augustine later encouraged Paulinus of Milan to write the first biography of Ambrose. One reason Augustine is careful to insist that he never sat at Ambrose's feet is to make a theological point, that what Ambrose had to say was indeed not some secret inner doctrine (such things were suspect in orthodox Christianity) but his plain public message.

That message had several parts. Intellectually, it showed Augustine, the imperfectly self-taught philosopher, how to reconcile his rhetorical culture with the doctrines of Christianity. The Hebrew scriptures could be rescued from their scandalous portrayal of libidinous patriarchs and a vengeful god by allegorical interpretation, while Platonic philosophy could support a more rational understanding of basic doctrines. And what the bishop was preaching in those years was something quite special: not just Christianity, but Christianity as the true philosophy.[134] For him, the old classical ideal of the philosopher remained true and valid, something to be enhanced rather than overthrown by the Christian religion. Reading Platonic books, Ambrose found much to approve, much to learn from, and much to pass on, adapted to Christianity. The difference between philosopher and Christian, Ambrose argued, was not a great doctrinal chasm (it could be bridged easily enough) but a practical one: where and how to worship the divine. Ambrose had no doubt that his church was the right place and—this is his most Christian doctrine—the only place. He would live to see the emperor he supported and chastised ban all non-Christian public religious practice in the empire and thus force a huge population into the churches of Ambrose and his fellow bishops. Historians would remember this as the spontaneous conversion of a vast people.[135]

In that mob, there would be a few Christian philosophers, just as there had been a very few philosophers in the olden days. Those philosophers would be every bit as wise, sedate, elegant, and refined as the classical ones had been. Anything the old-timers could do—this was Ambrose's position—the Christians could do better. He made this explicit in books like his *Duties of Ministers* (*De officiis ministrorum*), in which he rewrote Cicero's own *De officiis* in a Christian key. In a lost treatise with the striking title, *On Philosophy, That Is to Say, on Baptism* (*De philosophia sive de sacramento regenerationis*), Ambrose made the claim that the path to true philosophy led through the purgative and healing waters of baptism. The few quotations we have from this treatise come from Augustine's later writings, and one that he uses repeatedly emphasizes the role of sexual continence: "Continence is the pedestal of piety, for it gives people slipping and sliding in the pitfalls of this world a firm place to stand."[136] Without this encouragement, it would have been easy for Augustine to accept a good society marriage and pursue his philosophical life with the support of his wife's financial resources. We know he was heading in that direction for a time at least.[137] Augustine with a pious and continent wife, like his contemporary and friend-by-letters Paulinus of Nola—there's an alternative that's hard to imagine!

In saying all this, Ambrose was playing his own part in what we will discuss later, the contest that raged in the Latin west from the 380s to the 420s over the nature and focus of Christian asceticism. He had inherited the idea that there would be Christian ascetics, and in this rather eccentric view of the Christian as true philosopher he found his own particular rationalization.[138]

So to follow his newfound, if aloof and distant, father, Augustine would become a philosopher in the new style. To do that, he needed to make up his mind about sex. It was not as if the issue had not been on the brain for a long time. The Manichees had preached continence, and Augustine had probably practiced some form of birth control in order that his relationship with his common-law wife might appear seemly in Manichee circles.[139] The challenge was one Augustine was expecting and was ready for, and Ambrose gave him a way and a reason to meet it.

Augustine made it hard on himself. Renunciation of sex was the condition he set for his "conversion." Then, when in the spring of 387 he sought baptism in Milan, he showed his hand by spending some time writing treatises on the "liberal arts." The liberal arts of late antiquity were not preparation for a worldly career, as they are often marketed to be nowadays, but preparation for philosophical retirement.[140] The sequence of disciplines (grammar, rhetoric, logic, arithmetic, geometry, music, and astronomy) was meant to take the mind away from the world of cacophonous appearances and see it through the medium of well-made discourse and numerical order. The sequence was important, ending with astronomy, which lifted the mind to the stars and to what lay beyond the stars. To work your way through the liberal arts was to prepare yourself for the mystical ascent to the divine unity that Augustine thought true philosophy would bring. His one treatise on the liberal arts to survive in substantial form, the *De musica*, bears out this interpretation by the way it culminates in its sixth book with consideration of the mystical number patterns of true music.

And true philosophy was what, in the *Confessions*, Augustine shows himself finding, and with it the commitment to a sexless life. What he did not and could not yet see in those days was the long stretch of years of disappointment, alienation, and temptation that he was bargaining for in return for the fleeting pleasures of mystical ascent.[141]

That failure, that disappointment, makes the *Confessions* a powerful work of art. The atmosphere and the anxiety that speak against the doctrine the book serves is what gives it staying power. The poignancy of the narrative, the fragility of the triumphs it achieves, and the anxiety that lingers in the wake of the storytelling are unmistakable. The outward form is a book of triumph and gain . . . and it is a book about losses. The last books of the narrative section, with the deaths of his family members and friends and the farewell to the life he had chosen and to his openness to sexual experience, are books of loss, and the garden scene at Milan represents exactly the culmination of that process, the thing that seals Augustine's fate.

We do well to ask of an author, precisely at the moment when he is most in control of his material and our attention, what he is afraid of. His fears, even more than his loves, fuel the urgency for what he has to say. If, say, a person writes passionately against religion and all its works and pomps, what are we to think? Is it not at least reasonable to ask that person what frightens him about religion? Very often the most ferocious assertions we encounter are the ones that seem to have the least basis in fact, because they are the ones that have the greatest basis in fear. If I do not say *this*, the polemicist implicitly says, then somebody else might reasonably say *not this*. The most powerful force is not so much the attraction of *this* as the fear of *not this*. Of the *Confessions* we should ask the same question.

Augustine needs to tell us his conversion story. He needs it so badly that we do him, I believe, a great favor if we allow ourselves to entertain the possibility that his conversion story is off the rails, that it consists of assertion after assertion that are not so much true as necessary, that are not so much what Augustine knows to be the case as they are what he has to *say* is the case in order not to face what might be otherwise. I do not mean to say that at age forty-five Augustine saw the long years of increasing loneliness, polemical isolation, and immersion in the ruthless politics of the time stretching out ahead of him. Far from it: he seems instead to have imagined that the life of the bishop could still be one of mystical contemplation of the truths of scripture, and he set about various literary projects (notably the works *The Trinity* and *Genesis Taken Literally*) to make that real.

But his text speaks, when read this way, more eloquently about his future than it does about his past. Readers who sense this—and these will be readers at some remove from his religious experience—will find the real power of this text coming to the surface just as the hegemony of its author's ideas and his church's ideas begins to fade from memory.

Who were his first readers? We will meet a few of them as we go on, and most of them were unconvinced by the book. But it shouldn't be missed that the book's most pervasive bit of artifice makes mortal readers irrelevant. The whole book is addressed to god, written in the second-person singular, Augustine "gossiping," as one skeptic put it, with his god. Human readers are not only disregarded, but seated in the balcony and ignored by the performer on stage. For no human reader was capable (Augustine thought) of telling whether he spoke true or not.[142] Only if the divine all-knower intervened to place the same *caritas* in the hearts of author and reader could a book like this ever persuade. God always comes between Augustine and his fellow humans, even in this, his most intimate work. Few have expressed so well, though perhaps not consciously, the loss as well as the gain of the chosen celibate.

AFTERMATH OF A CLASSIC

The *Confessions* mark a turning point in Augustine's life that cannot be mistaken. But the subtlest and most important turn often evades notice.

The theoretical pretext for the *Confessions*, as scholars have long seen, was the upheaval in Augustine's reading of Paul that occurred in the months that followed his ordination as bishop. His old mentor Simplicianus wrote to him from Milan with a few questions, leading questions, doubtless designed to provoke a reaction. They led Augustine into consideration of fundamental questions of Pauline interpretation, and his old optimism fell apart as he wrote his replies.[143] Whatever you may think of Paul, when you read him as Augustine did, he does not point to a post-conversion life of revolution and exaltation, but rather to a long, dark struggle in the soul itself. The life of the Christian is not immanent happiness but intensified promise. Promise, however, is not possession.

The sense of loss and deferral that such a reading of Paul can beget was well matched to Augustine's mood in his early days as bishop. His sense of his own unworthiness, his distaste for much of what his new job entailed, and the inability of his old version of Christianity to cope with the challenge of Donatism were all pressing him to accept the idea that the mystic peace that a Plotinus, or a newly baptized Augustine of 387, could hope for was slipping further and further away, never out of reach, but never within his grasp.

The amphibious quality of the *Confessions* makes sense in just that context. The book has three main forces running through it: first, the will to affirm the idealized, spiritual religion that he had discovered a decade earlier; second, the need to confront the ambiguities and frustrations of his episcopal position; third, his longing for an appropriate literary and spiritual agenda, for a personal life to accompany his public one. So the book presents different faces: the Plotinian narrative of the ascent of the soul to god from the first page to the middle of the tenth book, a jarringly melancholy assessment of his present status (in the tenth book and the beginning of the eleventh), and then a contemplative *effort* in books 11, 12, and 13. The result has often baffled scholars seeking a literary unity in it, and though a surface structure can be outlined (as I have done above), the underlying tensions must be recognized and dealt with.

One Augustine who emerged, then, was a man who thought he had succeeded in giving order to his life with the writing of his great book. He felt a new literary energy and he had a program. Polemical books flowed easily in the years after 397 against both Manichees and Donatists. First there was a plodding, literal refutation of the doctrines of his old Manichee teacher Faustus, the one who had disappointed him years before. Against the Donatists he produced an equally heavy-footed attempt (*Baptism* [*De baptismo*]) to prove the unprovable, that the great martyr bishop Cyprian's teaching about baptism was more in line with Augustinian than with Donatist teaching. Two ambitious projects carried forward specific lines of meditation opened by the *Confessions*. The scriptural exegesis of books 11 through 13 turned into an extended meditation on Genesis (*Taking Genesis Literally*) and the trinitarian images that had preoccupied his quest for his god turned into the project to write an extended work of dogmatic theology (*The Trinity*).

Those two books cost Augustine more pain and struggle than all the other books he wrote combined. The two projects went on for perhaps as many as twenty years apiece and were brought to completion only with the greatest difficulty, and not without pieces of at least one of them getting abroad without his consent. Whether those books succeed or not on their own merits is an open question, but considering their importance in Augustine's life and work, they are far too little known. The struggle they embody and their relative opacity to our eyes is the evidence of the failure of the effort of will that the *Confessions* represent. The idealized Platonic Christianity of Milan and after expresses itself in the great book and is broken in the effort, and the pieces begin to fall away. What had still seemed vibrantly possible in 391, when Augustine wrote an optimistic book called *True Religion*, now fades from view. That he seems to have discovered, or at least noticed, not long afterwards that Porphyry, the greatest disciple of the philosopher Plotinus, was a virulent anti-Christian at least gave pretext for the disavowal of neo-Platonism that fills the eighth, ninth, and tenth books of *City of God* in the 410s.

The man who lived in Africa and who had written the *Confessions*, in other words, was no longer the man *of* the *Confessions*, and that was Augustine's tragedy. To understand the man whose story is told in that book, we must understand the man who told it. The crabbed turmoil of Augustine's later years is only the externalization of the conflicts that he had chosen for himself. Conversion, which Peter Brown once memorably spoke of as a process of "hardening the will,"[144] was just that for Augustine. He had made his change, once and for all, and though he changed and changed again throughout his life, he could not admit or recognize those further changes. He had to insist that he had become in 387 the man he was in all the later years of his life, an evident untruth, but one he was perfectly sincere in uttering.

WHAT IF . . .

We should not turn away from the story contained in the *Confessions* without trying to do justice one more time to the extraordinary power of this book to shape our sense of Augustine. Everything we know and say and think about him, I believe, is shaped by this one book and its story. The Augustine who would most transform our thinking about Augustine is the one who didn't write the *Confessions*, or whose *Confessions* did not survive and therefore escaped our attention. We ourselves would be different in that case, because we would study him much more for his ideas, much less for his person, his psyche, and his adolescent development. The power of that narrative to shape all our thinking about the man is beyond reckoning, but it must be reckoned with. What would the story we told be like if we didn't have that book? Perhaps it would be something like this:

> Augustine was bishop of Hippo Regius from 396 to 430. A vast collection of his polemical and pastoral writing survives, including a muddled set of controversially attributed and dated materials that go back to his pre-episcopal days, when he seems to have been under the influence of a Platonism that did not understand either Plato or Plotinus any too clearly. Augustine's background was shabby genteel African, and he never surmounted the limitations of his type. Brought up Christian, he aspired first to worldly success, which eluded him, and he eventually drifted into the Christian clergy, where he gradually became an effective force in ecclesiastical controversy. Though some pages of his sermons have a discreet mystical charm, and though his *City of God* is a surprisingly effective *tour de force* defense of a rather forced Christian view of history, the vast bulk of his endlessly and tediously polemical writings against his many enemies weighs down our impression of him beyond recall. He is too like Jerome in his readiness to hate, and too unlike Jerome in his somber,

plodding style and his superficial learning. He has verbal facility, but he cannot bring it alive for more than brief flashes, and for the most part he is as dull as his "pagan" counterpart Symmachus, though perhaps more intelligently and thoughtfully read. He succeeded in destroying the morale and the organization of the native African Christian church, the so-called Donatists, and left it a prey to the combined forces of Arians and Vandals who arrived in Africa just as he was dying. He did his church few favors, and he had few friends—some of those few intensely loyal to be sure, but their number dwindled with the years. He set a style for ambitious churchmen aligned with state authority that had hitherto been seen mainly in the Greek east. His transfer of that model to the west is perhaps the most baleful of his achievements.

Do I exaggerate or misread? Many readers will probably conclude that I do, but the gravitational force of that immense and powerful book that is the *Confessions* compels us to struggle in exaggerated ways if we are to resist its pull and understand its effects.

AUGUSTINE'S SOUL

Modern writing on Augustine takes shape haunted by a huge absence. If we take him entirely seriously, if anyone can ever take another person entirely seriously, we would follow the line of thought of his *Confessions* to contemplate and discuss, not the pear thief or the Manichee, but the regenerate Augustine, the Augustine whose baptism was a mark of his assimilation to the divine. That Augustine would be interesting not for the deeds of his body but for the imputed purity and exaltation of his soul.

We come closest to taking him seriously in this way when we think and talk about his mystical discourses. In the *Confessions* those may be found in the ninth and tenth books, but his story assures us he had been looking for such exaltation for a long time.

In the first case, we have what might seem a matter-of-fact account of an experience that Augustine and his mother shared not long before her death, while they were staying in Rome's port city of Ostia, waiting for a ship home to Africa.[145] Mother and son are conversing by a window looking out over an enclosed garden in the wealthy house where they are guests. Their conversation falls to speculation on the nature of the afterlife, starting with echoes of Plotinus and ending with echoes of Christian scripture. A world in which truth lies hidden behind baffling appearances will give way to a world that proclaims its truth and its joy unambiguously. For a heartbeat's moment, they seem to reach that better world, then slip back into everyday reality. Monnica dies, at peace, a few days later.

In the second case, half of the tenth book is devoted to a textual account of mystical ascent that springs from the author's *present* experience as bishop and is probably meant to be shared by his readers as they read the *Confessions*. Philosophers read these pages and others like them in the eleventh book because they contain Augustine's most fluent and attractive meditations on the interlocking themes of memory and time, where memory is what happens to existence that slips away and time is the name humans give to the process of slippage itself. A deep discontent with the world as it is, anxious and evanescent as it can be in even the happiest moments, evoked from Augustine memorable statement of belief in a better (more permanent and unchanging and thus unanxious) world beyond. Death, of which he speaks little in the *Confessions*, becomes a liberating rather than a destructive force.

Those mystical Augustines, the Augustines who for a moment come close to union with the divine, for whom assertion of a wish could be more real than a grasp of present reality, are Augustines beyond the body, Augustines almost entirely turned into soul. In fairness to Augustine, and to help us understand how he understands himself, his soul deserves some attention. What was it like?

It was a spirit. That is to say, it was without shape, form, color, size, or substance or any material extension. Spirit exists, devoid of every usual sign of existence.[146] But Augustine's was an *imperfect* spirit. The sin of Adam and Eve had in some way determined that his soul, like those of all his fellow human beings, would be marked at the outset with sin and, even when that mark of sin was removed, a lingering inclination or hankering toward sin would remain. Only after death could the bearer of a soul like Augustine's hope that the final taint and its tugs would be removed. The taint, moreover, was not merely retrospective but prospective: once a sinner, surely a sinner again. Augustine is reluctant to go as far as the Platonists in thinking that any contact with a body was itself polluting, but he often uses (particularly in his earlier career) language that points in that direction, and he never fully rejects the style. He certainly shares with them throughout a preference for a perfect un-world over this imperfect one, for the unseen over the seen.

Augustine's soul, moreover, was the seat of his mental and intellectual activity: brainless consciousness and cogitation. The imperfection of that activity (forgetfulness and error) was itself a mark of the continuing disorder in the soul, a disorder that could be removed only in the afterlife. The soul rules the domain of the senses: "The inner sense is like an emperor to whom all the other senses go as messengers, telling of what they find outside."[147]

There was no guarantee about the afterlife, he argued. The soul was immortal in possibility, but it may live forever in misery or in bliss—and nowhere in between. The great question about human life, for Augustine, was whether his soul would triumph or fail. No one can know in this life which of the two will obtain. Even if a man were secure in virtue and ecclesiastical standing late in life, the possibility of a fall at the latest possible moment was always present, and one lapse could destroy a life's virtue.

One could go further, and Augustine did, in exploring the twists and turns and intellectual implications of such ideas about the soul. If we are thinking not as philosophers but instead as interrogators of Augustine and his life and the ways that life has been represented, we should pause to recognize, with perhaps a slight shock, how much of what Augustine thinks is both entirely without evidence and entirely familiar. Even in a post-Christian, postmodern, post-everything world, the discourse of "soul" fills conversation and bookstore shelves. Freudian thought has notoriously confirmed moderns in their habit of speaking of the invisible, insubstantial, indetectible twin who follows us through life and departs at death. Freud even found his own reflection of Augustine's divine trinity in his "I," "it," and "over-I" of the psyche (usually known in English by the Latinisms ego, id, superego).

At an even deeper level, we still possess an inheritance (most often unconscious) of Augustine and late antiquity's view of the soul. His narrative of himself is archetypal for humankind. His other works, most notably *City of God* and *Genesis Taken Literally*, bear this out. In the latter, an original unity and serenity is disrupted somehow, to leave humankind entering conscious life torn between impulses and thoughts, imperfect of memory, mixing virtue and vice in ways that yield to conscious control only with difficulty. But in a successful life, they do yield, and a happy human being is one who has reconciled the multiple impulses and sides of a personality into a coherent entity. Moderns may not think of the image and likeness of god as readily as Augustine does, but they nevertheless share notions of the integration of the personality that are fundamentally the same as Augustine's.

The story of a life, then, is a familiar story. Fragmentation moves toward integration, and if that happens, the story is a happy one. Or fragmentation triumphs, and if that happens, the story is tragic. Or perhaps, in more contemporary works, an apparent move from fragmentation to reintegration is found to be factitious, and the happy subject of biography is revealed to have been deeply troubled. Whichever of those stories gets told, the framework is Augustinian, or at least late antique. Breaking up that framework in order to see pieces of the man himself is a central task for this book.

DARK ORIGINS

I left to one side in an earlier chapter the meticulous commentary on the opening chapters of Genesis that fills the last three books of the *Confessions*, though it is the most surprising feature of that book for many readers. It's specially important because it was in his long wrestling with the stories of Genesis that Augustine worked out his sense of humankind's place in the world with all its imperfections. The version of his views of Genesis that we get in the *Confessions*, moreover, comes at just the point when he's beginning to rehearse his mature ideas about the fall of humankind and its consequences for everyday life.

To see how the pieces fit together, we should first feel the looming power of that scriptural text over him through many years. The book of Genesis was with Augustine early and late in his life. He worried about it and argued about it in his Manichee days, he wrote about it not long after his baptism, and then again and again: in the last three books of the *Confessions*, in a twelve-book commentary that took him from his fifties into his sixties, and in books 11 through 16 of *City of God*. Creation, sin, and revelation were his themes. There was no literal six days for him but his own set of textual puzzles threatening to obscure a philosophically rich and mysteriously meaningful process. Matter formless and void and darkness on the abyss spoke to Augustine of humiliation of material being, while the spirit of god upon the waters began the long struggle to exalt, transform, and bring order. "Let there be light" stood for the intelligibility and order that betrayed god's hand throughout creation.

And what to make of evil? The harm men do, the ills that befall them, the death that awaits us all: Augustine needs a god, but not one that can be faulted for bringing such misery. Like Milton, justifying the ways of god to man was his task, but Augustine had the Manichees running through his head all the time. They found the world a battlefield where god and devil fought for the lives of humankind. Augustine tried to share their optimism but failed, and found their version of god too weak and unappealing. The god he eventually surmised was remote, omnipotent, omniscient, immutable, irresistible. Genesis was that god's real biography. But Augustine still cannot explain evil, and the tortuous inquiry leads him to a virtuoso evasion:

> No one should ask what acts to cause an evil will—for it's not an effect-ing but a defection.[148] To defect from the highest of beings in favor of something lesser: that's the beginning of an evil will. But if you want to figure out what acts to affect such a will—when there's no acting but only defecting, as I said—that's like wanting to see darkness or hear si-lence. We know both those things—darkness only through our eyes, si-lence only through our ears, but not in perception but in the absence of perception. So don't go asking me what I know I don't know unless you want to learn how not to know. Whatever we know not in perception but in the absence of perception is known because we don't know it and be-comes unknown just in the act of knowing. When the eyes skim over material images, they never see darkness except when they begin not to see. Silence likewise affects no other sense than that of hearing, but it is sensed only when we don't hear it. So indeed our mind perceives things that make sense in its understanding, but when they begin to fall apart, it knows them by not knowing them. "For who has understood mis-deeds?"[149]

By quoting scripture to conclude that chapter, Augustine means to trump our puzzlement. You *can't* make sense of sin: the god's book says so.

REST ETERNAL

The last words of the *Confessions*:[150]

> We see the things that you made because they exist, but they exist be-cause *you* see them. And we see on the outside that they exist and on the inside that they are good, but you see that they are made the moment you imagine them makeable. And we are moved at some point to do

good, after our heart has become pregnant with your spirit—but at an earlier time we were moved to do ill in abandoning you. But you, one god and good, never cease from doing good. And our good works come to us by your gift, but they do not last forever. When they are gone, we hope that we will find rest in your huge scheme for holiness. But you are good and need no other good and so you are always at rest, for you are your own repose.

And what man can give another man to understand this? What angel can give it to an angel? We ask it of you, we seek it in you, we come knocking to you for it: and so we receive it, so we find it, and so the door is opened for us. . . .

That door opening onto eternity is the real goal of the overarching narrative of the *Confessions*, the narrative of the life of the bishop who remembers and narrates his past. Many readers don't make it that far with him.

AUGUSTINE UNVARNISHED

Moderns know Augustine from the *Confessions*, but Augustine's contemporaries came to know him in other ways. If the Mediterranean was the Roman world's superhighway, carrying commerce and governors and tax collectors, it was also a virtual world in which fame could run far beyond traditional locales. Hellenistic and Roman times see the emergence of the celebrity, the man known for being known, applauded by people who didn't know him. Augustine's near-annual visits to Carthage gave him a visible stage on which to perform, while his correspondence and authorship carried his name beyond Africa and beyond his lifetime. In the years after he wrote his *Confessions*, he found the renown he always wanted. Many seek fame, few are prepared for it. Augustine was no exception.

The story of his life should have been one of fame sought, then lost, and then forgotten. The first ambitions and first career of Augustine took him from his provincial home to the biggest city in Africa, then to the biggest city in the world, then to the center of all political power at that time. Just then real power and celebrity seemed within his grasp. But he gave up. Or failed. He left all the big cities and went back to the small town, to go native and to pray. After five years there, he went down to Hippo and became a churchman and stayed there for forty years. He would have been nobody to us, without the ambition and without the fame that came from that ambition.

AUGUSTINE THE SELF-PROMOTER

Many Christians like Augustine deliberately sought obscurity and fled from the bright lights of civilization to wall themselves up in a cloister or to isolate themselves in a desert. The stories of those so-called monks are so easy to read that we forget that something is not quite right in the stories themselves. The legend of the earliest of the Egyptian fathers, Anthony, who is said to have gone into the desert in the third century, emphasized how he had to keep moving farther and farther up-country, like some late-antique Daniel Boone, to stay ahead of the crowds coming to venerate his ascetic piety. Those early obscurity-seekers have a neglectedly important place in the history of publicity.[151]

The ideal self-effacing ascetic is the one we never hear of. She[152] or he would vanish into the faceless crowd of the city or disappear over the horizon into the desert, never to be heard from again. But for all the stories we don't know, it's surprising how many we know in detail, and in Augustine's time these stories were the ones most in circulation.

Augustine was never a wonderworker, never fled into the solitary life, and meets us in the authorized biography by his friend Possidius in muted terms, a model of restraint. To be sure, he chose to arrange his life in the clerical house at Hippo as a "monastery," but his contemporaries thought of such a thing with less structure and on a smaller scale than we might. Everything we know of him and his everyday life suggests old-fashioned dignity and reserve, the life of the leading citizen in a prosperous city.

What Augustine shared with the more flamboyant of his ascetic contemporaries was the instinct, not to say the deliberate purpose, of self-promotion and self-presentation. In strictest church rule, his business lay in Hippo and Hippo only. There he was assiduous in his earliest years at making his name. If Augustine's legitimate business did run beyond Hippo, it took him into the church province of Numidia, to which Hippo belonged, and the affairs of the proconsular province of Africa, led by Aurelius, bishop of Carthage. Augustine never became the primate (senior churchman) of Numidia (there was always someone senior to him), and he deferred, as was proper, to his friend and colleague in Carthage. But he made sure he was a force to be reckoned with throughout Africa, spending as much time as he could in Carthage and not infrequently traveling to other critical locations to intervene in local disputes.

His reputation did not stop at the water's edge. Though he never left Africa after returning from Italy in his mid-thirties, his fame reached broadly across the Christian Mediterranean, though he became famous in Italy only years after he left there. And for all the time we can hear his voice, he lived at the center of this expanding pool of fame, and he worked very hard to make it grow.

Every word he wrote (that is, usually, dictated) was written down on some organic material (either papyrus or animal skin) and bound together in stacks: large, expensive (for the materials and for the labor consumed in making them) luxury objects. Those books do not survive.[153] Instead, the texts survive because they were recopied by hand for centuries in libraries, often monastery libraries in medieval Europe. Such copies were themselves expensive and the abundance of manuscripts (thousands on thousands survive) are a sign of the prestige and power of Augustine's posthumous voice. Surviving in such abundance to the age of print, they have now been edited and reedited to the point where we have a high confidence that we know what he said, at least in these books. The last generation saw, to be sure, the rediscovery of two manuscripts—one of letters, one of sermons—that had gone unnoticed for centuries and so now could give us new light into his world. More such discoveries are possible, though the likelihood fades with time. We make sense of him out of the materials we have, for all their bulk only a fraction of what he wrote and said over a long and endlessly articulate career.

AUGUSTINE THE SOCIAL CLIMBER

He was always on the make, and had learned the tricks at home. His father ingratiated himself with Romanianus to get the money to send his son away to school, and Romanianus remained interested in Augustine's career for as long as it showed worldly promise. At Carthage, thinking of wider horizons, Augustine sent off his first book with a dedication to Hierius, a famous orator at Rome whom he had never met. Years afterwards, he remembered the endless round of calls he paid in Rome and Milan, seeking advancement, with notable success. He would not have gotten to Milan had not the great Roman senator Symmachus pulled strings for him. Symmachus—Quintus Aurelius Symmachus signo Eusebius, to give him his full name—triumphant in his self-esteem, leading citizen of Rome, defender of old prerogatives against upstart emperors, left eight hundred or so letters showing us the practice of patronage at that time. Two gentlemen of Hippo, for example, Quintus and Felix, who belonged to the same marginally prosperous class as Augustine's father, won the trophy of a letter from Symmachus at Rome introducing them to another man of whom we know nothing but who presumably could help the provincials. Quintus and Felix had never met Symmachus, but they had found intermediaries, "highly placed gentlemen" (*summates viri*), who intervened with Symmachus; since the senator respected the intermediaries, he was happy to write on behalf of the nobodies from Africa.[154] Symmachus advanced Augustine's own career crucially from Rome to Milan, responding to who knows what such intervention himself.[155] (Augustine's Milan friend Ponticianus, who has a critical role in the *Confessions* story of conversion, was another protégé of Symmachus.)

From the moment of Augustine's conversion to ostentatious Christianity, however, his tendency to curry favor upwards was if anything intensified, and that might be mildly surprising. The books he wrote in the winter of 386–87, while he was bracing himself for baptism and what it might lead to, were each equipped with dedicatory letters to gentlemen of higher rank than himself, potential patrons on some level or another. He embraced humility in good company.

From that time onward, Augustine never let up. His targets may have shifted, but the fusillade of approaches to those who stood above him and who could help him never wavered. Some of the targets were a little shady. The immensely wealthy lady Proba, for example, one of the highest placed Christian *grandes dames* in Italy, accepted at least two letters from Augustine,[156] and he tried to teach her how to pray. But one historian tells us the shabby story of her advance through rapine to riches, and another of a haughty selfishness that aggravated the miseries of others at Rome at the time of the city's sack in 410.[157] When Proba's granddaughter, Demetrias, became the most celebrated young woman to "take the veil" in Augustine's time, Augustine wrote again to Proba and Juliana (Demetrias's mother and Proba's daughter) to congratulate them,[158] as did other ascetics, competing for the attention of the powerful. One of Augustine's competitors was the same Pelagius who would come to haunt him later.

As time passed, the great ones he sought out (as we shall see) were of a different sort. As one generalissimo succeeded another at the imperial court, Augustine addressed the most recent with a direct request for sup-

port in a lawsuit between bishops.[159] In the late 410s, concern for winning the day in the doctrinal battles of Italy has him currying epistolary
favor from two future popes,[160] a great courtier who could intervene at
Ravenna,[161] and one particularly odious potentate in Gaul named Dardanus.[162] Dardanus was a retired prefect and a man of great prestige. He
had supported the emperor against a usurper named Constantine in Gaul,
murdered another usurper with his own hands, and probably accepted
Augustine's suggestions on matters theological because they were directed in Gaul against men who had been Dardanus's political opponents.
Even Sidonius Apollinaris, a grand Christian gentleman of Gaul of the
next generation, spoke ill of him, though Sidonius hardly ever spoke ill of
anyone.[163] But such men could be ostentatious Christians, and Dardanus
had founded along with others in his family a city he called Theopolis
("Godville") that some have seen as a clumsy attempt to take seriously the
ideas of a "city of god" received somehow from Augustine.

And we shall see how in his last years, Augustine was still currying
favor with generals and governors, seeing in them the protection he and
his flock now needed, sometimes from invaders, sometimes from other
generals.

AUGUSTINE THE CORRESPONDENT

Letter-writing was one of the tools with which Augustine shaped his social world. In old age, mulling over his books and letters and putting them
in shape for preservation, Augustine was at pains to include letters going
back to the year 386, the year of his dramatic conversion, but nothing
from before. In doing so, he reinforced the story he had told of himself in
the *Confessions* and the before-and-after division of his life. He had sought
in those "before" days a different fame, but he wanted his contemporaries
(and us) to think he had left all that behind. At the moment of conversion,
the old habit was still with him and he addressed some well-placed Christian gentlemen in Milan with his books, but those relationships didn't
lead to useful connections or social advancement.

Instead, for the first years of his post-Milan life, his letters show us a
man who never traveled and lived a life distinctly private and local. The
one real exception is an exchange with Maximus, a traditionalist teacher
at Madauros, whom Augustine taunted for his backward religious ways
and who replied in measured but firm words. That was a localized per-

formance that would not have attracted attention in any large city, but it was probably meant to stir up a little attention in Madauros and Tagaste.

On ordination, the reasonable pressures of office and the ambitions of an eager new cleric sent some letters moving in different directions, notably to Aurelius and Carthage. But letters went in other directions in the 390s, now across the water: to Nola in southern Italy (shrine of Saint Felix and home of the lately converted Paulinus), and to Bethlehem in Palestine, already for years the home of the master of Christian textual self-promotion, Jerome.

Paulinus probably settled in Nola in 395[164] and then a flurry of letters between Augustine, Alypius, and Paulinus began, not long before Augustine's advancement to his bishopric, a surely foreseeable elevation. Paulinus began the correspondence, prospecting for either a patron or a client—we can't tell which. Meanwhile, Augustine had begun sussing out Jerome as a correspondent a couple of years earlier.

Jerome was a tough case.[165] Augustine first wrote to him around 394 in a move to attract attention. Settled at Bethlehem, presenting himself to the world as the Latin reincarnation of the Greek polymath exegete Origen of 150 years earlier,[166] Jerome had already made himself famous in matters of biblical scholarship and was careful to build that fame on his reputation for deep learning in Greek and Hebrew. When Augustine first wrote to him, moreover, both were coequal in the rank of priest, though by the time Jerome took notice of Augustine, the younger man had come to outrank him by virtue of episcopal ordination. There had never been a town in which Jerome couldn't make himself unwelcome, but at least he had rendered himself immune to expulsion from Bethlehem. His stories of how he had won the patronage of the larger-than-life Roman bishop Damasus (a Renaissance prince-cleric before his time, whose election led to riots between his followers and those of a rival candidate that left 137 corpses in a basilica),[167] his record of publications, his trumpeted knowledge of Hebrew, and his reputed access to Origen's own manuscripts gave him the authority to set himself up as judge and jury in all matters of Christian Latin biblical scholarship. He was less eager to tell how he had had to leave Rome in the company of the lady with whom he was suspected of having inappropriate relations and settling with her in haughty isolation in Bethlehem. No later figure dares suspect Jerome of unchastity, to this day.

When Augustine wrote to Jerome, he had to know that challenging him was imprudent. He questioned the advisability of Jerome's translation enterprise and disputed him on a critical point of scriptural exegesis.

Were Peter and Paul, when they quarrel in Galatians over the mission to the gentiles, really arguing or was it all a didactic show? Jerome needed both men to be on the right side, but Augustine needed the written text to be truthful, and neither was willing to compromise on the question.

If the letter had made its way directly to Jerome, it would doubtless have set off an eruption. But the argument went unresolved, as mischievous fortune intruded and the letter did not find its way to Bethlehem for a long time. Years later, when the confusions were sorted out, Jerome finally received the letter and responded to it, but by this time Augustine was a bishop and well thought of in some of Jerome's Italian circles, so his response was more discreet than it would have been earlier. The comedy of the series of events lies in the fact that though the letter didn't make it to Bethlehem on the first try, it did get into circulation in Italy. Jerome heard of it, indeed, as a pamphlet *against* Jerome that Augustine was circulating, thus an open letter, as it were. (Such, at least, is Jerome's version of events.) Augustine protested keenly that he had no such intention and that the letter was sincerely sent to reach Jerome. We should probably accept his protestations (while perhaps pausing to wonder why scholars have been *so* ready to accept them), but observe two points: (1) Augustine may have been distressed that his letter did not make it directly to Jerome, but he was surely delighted that it had gone into circulation otherwise. (We'll read Jerome's miffed reply shortly.) One of the purposes of such correspondence was precisely to present him as a figure in correspondence with the great Jerome, and to get a letter back from Jerome would be a mark of approval and acceptance into circles that Augustine had otherwise not entered. Just to be read widely was worth the effort. (2) Nothing Augustine says rules out the possibility that the rogue copy in circulation in Italy was not the original gone astray but rather a separate copy somehow put into play by Augustine himself.

Jerome and Augustine remained in communication on and off almost until Jerome's death in 419 or 420. The initial jousting was a draw, but eventually the two found themselves on the same side in the controversies over Pelagius and his teaching and would settle into an uneasy, never intimate, but still functional epistolary relationship, all without ever setting eyes on one another, each the reluctant guarantor of a part of the other's reputation for holiness and learning.

On the surface, Jerome is very polite—but the surface is an inch deep.[168]

1. You send me letter after letter and you keep pushing me to reply to a letter of yours that came to me only as a copy in the hands of brother

Sysinnius the deacon (as I already told you). What got here had no signature. You said you had sent it first by way of brother Profuturus, then by someone else; but first Profuturus was called back, made a bishop, and shortly afterwards died. The next messenger, whose name you don't mention, was frightened by the thought of a sea journey and changed his plans. With all that, I just can't help but be amazed that this letter is widely spoken of at Rome and elsewhere in Italy. I was the only one who didn't get it—and it was meant just for me! And brother Sysinnius said he found it not in Africa, where you live, but on an island in the Adriatic five years ago, in a collection of your other books.

2. Suspicion and friendship can have nothing to do with each other, and you should speak to a friend as if to another self. Some of my colleagues, vessels of Christ, many of whom are in Jerusalem and the holy places, are saying that you did not act sincerely in this, but you were looking for praise and wanted the little flutters of reputation and celebrity from the people—that you're trying to make yourself famous at our expense.[169] You want many people to know that you are challenging me and that I am too timid to respond, that you write like a scholar and I sit quiet like a novice and have finally found someone who can shut me up. To tell the simple truth, I didn't want to reply to your letter at first, because I just didn't believe it was yours and (as the saying goes) you don't find honey on a sword. And then I was wary of seeming to reply arrogantly to a bishop of my communion and to quarrel with a quarreler, especially when I thought some of what was in the letter was heresy.

3. So to get to it: I don't want you going around saying, "So what? You saw my letter, you recognized the signature—and you so easily wound a friend and turn somebody else's malice into an insult to me?" Well, as I said, either send me a copy of the same letter with your signature or stop attacking an old man lying low in his cell. If you want to show off your intellectual prowess, look for younger men, learned and high-born—they say there are plenty of them at Rome—who are willing and able to fight with you about holy scripture, to take up the yoke and quarrel with a bishop. I'm just an old soldier, retired from the service, and I ought to be praising your victories over others, not going into battle with this weary old body again. If you keep pushing me to reply, I'll be forced to tell the old story about how Fabius Maximus

used patience and delay to break the power of Hannibal on his youthful rampage.

> *Age carries away all things, even the mind. I*
> *remember how, as a boy, I used to sing the sun down the*
> *sky on the long afternoons, but now I've forgotten*
> *all those songs. Even Moeris has lost his singing voice.*
>
> [Vergil, Eclogues 9]

To cite an example from scriptures, it was Berzellai of Galaad, handing over all the gifts of King David to a young man [2 Kings 19.32–27], who showed that old age shouldn't seek things like this or accept them when offered.

4. But if you swear you didn't write a treatise attacking me, and if you didn't send the book you didn't write to Rome, you still admit there are some things you've written that disagree with what I say, even if you're not attacking me, but just writing what seemed right to you—well, just listen to me patiently. You didn't write a book: so how did these criticisms of me come into my possession? Why does Italy have what you didn't write? How can you insist I reply to things you deny you wrote? I'm not so thick that I'm going to feel offended if you think your own thoughts. But if you parse my words closely and you ask for explanations and demand I change what I've written, and challenge me to recant, then I see things with fresh eyes. This is how friendship is harmed and the laws of relationship are violated. Let's not be seen fighting like boys and give our fans and detractors stuff to fight over.

I write this because I want to love you with a pure Christian love and not hold back anything in my mind that I can't bring to my lips. It's not right that somebody like me should dare to write against a bishop of my own communion when I've spent most of my life, from adolescence to this advanced age, toiling away with my brothers in this little monastery. Especially when it's a bishop whom I began to love before I knew him, who challenged me first to friendship and whom I rejoice to see rising up to come after me in scriptural learning. So either say it's not your book—if it isn't—and stop insisting I reply to what you didn't write; or if it is yours, admit it openly so that if I write something back in defense, the fault will be yours for challenging me, not mine for being forced to reply.

5. And then you add that you're ready to take it in a brotherly spirit if there's something in what you've written that bothers me or that I want to correct, and you really hope I will do this and let you take pleasure in my kindness. I'll just say again what I think: you challenge an old man, you poke at me when I keep quiet, and you seem to want to make a show of your learning. It's not for an old man like me to be thought malicious toward somebody to whose kindness I am indebted. And if twisted minds can find things to criticize in the Gospels and the Prophets, are you surprised if in your own books, especially when you expound complicated passages in scripture, you seem to go off the straight line sometimes? And I don't say this because I've ever found anything to criticize in your works! I've never gone to the trouble of reading them, and I don't have access to copies of them here: just your *Soliloquies* and some commentaries on Psalms.[170] If I *wanted* to talk about them, I wouldn't say they say anything that disagrees with what I've said—I'm nothing—but they disagree with the interpretations of the Greeks who have gone before us.

Farewell, my friend, dearest one, my son as far as age goes, my father when it comes to rank: just do me this one favor, that whenever you send me a letter, make sure it gets to *me* first.

Augustine could never get it quite right with Jerome. In addition to his natural defensiveness, Jerome in these years had to fear that he could be attacked at any moment for "Origenism";[171] it may have been Augustine's unsureness in dealing with those particular doctrinal issues that spared them falling out in that particular way. When Jerome tried for the light touch ("let's play together in the fields of scriptures without offending each other"[172]) Augustine sniffed in reply that scripture study is not a matter of play for him but a breathless struggle up a mountainside, all serious business.[173]

Paulinus of Nola proved to be the intermediary Augustine needed. Augustine and Paulinus fell into correspondence in 395 when Augustine's sidekick Alypius took the step of sending some of Augustine's books to Paulinus as an ice-breaker. Their reception was warm and the conversation that ensued would remain so for many years. Paulinus was a polished diplomat of the church, friends with everyone, hostile to almost no one. Though many times he found himself between warring parties, he remained a Teflon ascetic all his life. So smooth was Paulinus's approach that he and Augustine quickly found themselves in an epistolary style reminiscent of two polished jazz musicians meeting and playing for the first time.[174] Quickly they learned how to cap each other's quotations from scripture, to defer and pontificate simultaneously. (Paulinus, who wouldn't become bishop at Nola for another fifteen years, correctly intuited that the new bishop was better at being deferred to than at deferring.) Augustine's own mature style, rich with biblical language repurposed within his own syntax, owes much to this moment of mutual discovery and improvisation. Paulinus remained a friend and counselor, though relations appear to have quieted a bit in the 410s (we do not know if this is a real lull or just a period from which no documents survived[175]), and it was through Paulinus that Augustine's name and works became known in Christian aristocratic circles in Italy. Some of the leading aristocrats at Rome also had property in Africa not far from Hippo, and they heard of Augustine this way as well, but it was Paulinus who could supply context, sponsorship, and the books.

The reception was not always positive. Some years after the correspondence with Paulinus began, an unnamed Italian bishop (very likely Paulinus himself) arranged a reading of the *Confessions*. The monk Pelagius, not yet then a byword but already a fashionable society chaplain in Rome, was outraged by something he heard and stomped out of the room. The soirées of Anna Pavlovna Scherer in *War and Peace*, or of Proust's Madame Verdurin, offer a sense of the frisson of voyeuristic disapproval such a scene would cause.[176]

Here is only one paragraph (of five) from Paulinus's first "fan letter" to Augustine. We pick up in midstream a passage that resembles both a love poem and a sermon:[177]

> O brother of one spirit with me, you who are so admirable and so welcome in Christ our master, see how intimately I know you, how I admire you with open-mouthed amazement, how I embrace you with great love, how I enjoy everyday the conversation of our letters and feed on the breath of your mouth. For I should rightly call your mouth a pipeline of living water and a spring of the eternal fountain, because Christ has been made in you the fount of water leaping up to eternal life. [John 4.14] My soul has thirsted for you with the desire for this water, and my land yearned to be flooded with the abundance of your flow. So now that you have armed me with your "Pentateuch" against the Manicheans,[178] if you have constructed armaments against any other enemies of the catholic faith (because our enemy, who has a thousand ways to harm us, has to be fought with weapons as various as the ambushes with which he opposes

us), please supply them for me from your arsenal and do not disdain to bestow upon me the arms of justice. I am weary and now a sinner under great burdens, a veteran only in the number of my sins, but a new recruit in the soldiery of the eternal king. Wretch that I am, I have until now admired the wisdom of this world, and with my useless literary work and wicked wisdom I have been a fool before god, mute for all my words. After I had grown old among my enemies and vain in my thoughts, I lifted up my eyes to the mountains, gazing upon the precepts of the law and the gifts of grace—whence there came to me help from the master, who did not pay me back for my iniquities but enlightened me in my blindness, set me free from my fetters, humbled me when I had raised myself up wickedly so he might raise me up faithfully when I had been humbled.

Augustine had to be pleased when he read that.

Letter-writing is a complex social business, a way of making texts that pretend to be like speech. People may naïvely think they write letters to tell each other things, just as Augustine wrote (in his book *The Teacher*) that people use language to convey information. What we learn in the world of e-mail ought to be alerting us that the whole business of letter-writing and letter-reading is far more interesting and complicated than most people assume. Letters like these made Augustine's name where his voice could not reach.

In late antiquity, letter-writing flourished as a way for gentlemen to stay in touch with gentlemen.[179] Letter exchange offered a set of agreeable literary pastimes and conventions for exchanging pleasantries, insinuating requests, and commending worthy young people to the attention of other possible patrons. Prominent men were also in the habit of collecting and publishing their letters on an unprecedented scale.[180] Letters by now, moreover, let people establish and maintain friendships that were never supplemented by face-to-face introduction. In Cicero's age, correspondents knew one another "personally" and used letter-writing to maintain and manipulate relationships when presence was impossible. Though the conventions and, if one may call it so, the ideology of letter-writing remained constant in late antiquity, in practice many correspondents learned how to initiate, maintain, and occasionally destroy friendships with people they had never met. This was a fresh departure.

Many letters in those days were far more nearly public than private. When one gentleman wrote to another, it would be the exception rather than the rule for the recipient to mull the secret words of the text privately in his chamber. Far more often, the letter, carried by a trusted courier, would arrive as a social event, to be read aloud in the presence of friends and household, discussed with the courier, who often was charged with reporting more fully on what had been written about, then copied to share with friends.[181] An imperial letter stood at the acme of the pyramid of epistolary prestige, and on the one occasion in his life when we know Augustine received such a letter, we can be sure that it was a source of wonder and approval for the community at Hippo that associated with him. He held on to it carefully.[182]

We have in all about three hundred surviving letters to and from Augustine, including the ones rediscovered twenty-five years ago. Without having a complete record of his correspondence, we see patterns nonetheless, though we are never sure how they have been shaped by the accidents of survival and loss of evidence. Before and after 411, the year Augustine finally found real fame and power, two main pictures emerge. Until 411, his preferred correspondents were wealthy and well placed, people from the great world he said he'd left behind, the world into which he would have had a more direct path had he stayed with his youthful plans to pursue a provincial governorship or two. After 411, he settled for Africa, and his epistolary partners were increasingly the military governors of Africa. We might call this political realism on Augustine's part, for he had come up in a world in which he believed that wealth and social status were what mattered, but in the early 410s had himself rudely reminded, especially with the judicial murder of Marcellinus (of which we will hear below), that real power lay elsewhere.

Augustine shows himself to us in his letters overwhelmingly as a figure of authority. Others come to him with their questions and problems and he offers replies. The only real exception is Jerome, to whom Augustine takes exegetical problems, not truly to seek guidance. Otherwise, Jerome would have dryly suggested, there would have been at the very least much more Augustine would have had to ask. The missing partners in his letters are the other bishops in the church in north Africa. A few of Augustine's own friends (Aurelius, Alypius, Possidius, Evodius, Severus) appear, and there are isolated texts from a very few others, but the hundreds of bishops we will see trooping in and out of the baths at Carthage on the opening day of the great conference of 411 never appear among Augustine's correspondents. Most of them were of a class that did not practice the fine letter, were not Augustine's social equals, and very likely found the whole business of letter-writing a bit beyond them. If Augustine was a nobody in the great world in which he sought acceptance, to the provincial African world he was somebody who had gone away to Italy and learned to put on airs. The coming and going of couriers with letters, the reading and discussion of what they took and brought, and the careful docketing and preservation of the texts were all things that Augustine did to set himself apart.

Such effort was both utilitarian and ostentatious. The society of letter-writers in the late-antique world was rather like the community of e-mailers circa 1990. Employing a textual practice largely unseen, or at least disregarded, by the majority of their contemporaries, such participants in a small self-creating elite have the power to influence events at a distance denied their contemporaries. The early e-mailer perhaps only had the advantage of a few days' speed, but Augustine and his fellow letter-writers had the advantage of influence at a distance without the inconvenience of personal travel. The ability of Augustine's particular community of African Christians to win over imperial support for their various initiatives, for example, was to a large extent facilitated by the easy flow of information to and from the capital city of Ravenna in Italy.

In this way and others, Augustine was at the cutting edge of what may be called the high-tech religion of late antiquity.[183] The most successful forms of Christianity had always been adept at using the written word in old and new forms to extend influence at a distance. Paul's dominance in shaping later Christianity had less to do with his real travels in the Mediterranean world and more to do with the dissemination of his texts, in his own lifetime, but especially after. In his lifetime, they allowed him to continue to exercise an influence over newly founded congregations long after he had left them behind. Of all the early apostles, he had far and away the most powerful and long-heard voice, though he had never met Jesus and became an "apostle" by virtue of his encounter with Jesus's god on the road to Damascus. The Christian consciousness of a unity and an identity that transcended locality and bound Christians together was a powerful force in rallying Christians to defy opposition, not only when they were a minority (often persecuted, to hear them tell it), but when they fell by good luck into the state-supported majority status of the fourth century and after. The codex book that replaced the old papyrus scroll, first in Christian employ and then generally, was the symbol of their adroit use of the best information technology of their day.[184] Augustine, ever a traditionalist with an eye for the main chance, succeeded in his letters at shaping not only the affairs of his time but the representation of himself in those affairs to his contemporaries far and near and to all ages since.

AUGUSTINE THE FRIEND—AND HIS FRIENDS

Friendship in Augustine's pages lies hidden, as often as not, behind formulaic politeness. And then we have one letter to Augustine from an old and close friend, Severus, bishop of Milevis.[185] Severus had probably fallen in with Augustine in the late 380s at Tagaste, perhaps followed him to Hippo and monastic life, then gone on to his own bishopric. Augustine speaks of him with affection and longing at one point in a letter to another bishop: "As much as kinship affects you, it cannot be stronger than the bond of friendship by which my brother Severus and I cling to each other, but you know how rarely I get to see him. It's not my will or his that causes this, but the needs of mother church, and so we prefer the world to come, where we will live together inseparably, to the needs of this life."[186] To read this makes less surprising Severus's letter to Augustine (written perhaps in the late 390s or early 400s), in which the hyperbole of late-antique male friendship takes vivid form, plunging into a surprising terrain of metaphor. Augustine the high and abstract thinker is also the man who inspires this affection and this intensity:

> Severus, to the venerable and desirable bishop Augustine, whom I would embrace wholly in the bosom of love . . .
> . . . You know best how greedy I am for you: but still I do not grumble because I cannot do as much as I want, since I do no less than I can. Thanks be to god, sweetest brother, things are good for me when I am close to you, indeed clinging to you as tightly as possible, my one and only. I take in the abundance of your breasts and grow stronger, if I can just grasp and squeeze those breasts, so that whatever they protect and shut up secretly within—well, if I just take away the skin they give to the suckling to suck on, then maybe they can pour out their innermost essence to me. I want that essence poured out to me, I say: your innermost essence, your essence fat with heavenly stuffing and flavored with every spiritual sweetness; your essence, pure innermost essence, essence simple but crowned by the twofold bond of double love; *your* essence, innermost essence drenched in the light of truth and making the truth

shine back from within. I place myself under what drips from them, what comes back from them, so that my darkness may grow weak in the presence of your light, so we can both walk together in the brightness of day. O truly cunning honeybee of god, building honeycombs filled with divine nectar, dripping with mercy and truth, through which my soul runs with delight, and whatever it finds it lacks or wherever it feels weak, it struggles to fortify and support itself with your life-giving food.[187]

And at one point, in the *Confessions*, Augustine remembers for a moment what it was like to laugh, in a passage where he grieves for a dead friend:

There were other things about friends that captivated us: talking and laughing and doing each other kindnesses, reading together sweet-speaking books, being silly together and being serious together. Sometimes we could quarrel without any hostility, the way you argue with yourself, and that rare disagreement was the spice to all our many hours of harmony. We'd teach each other and learn from each other, miss each other with a little sadness and greet one another on return with pleasure. It was a thousand little signs like this, our expressions, our words, the look in our eyes, our gestures, that spread a single flame among our minds and in the blaze that followed made us feel as though we were all one.[188]

Beautifully and memorably put: and he leaves that way of life behind. Nebridius, the studious and eventually pious friend of very good family who joined Augustine's circle in Milan and then went home to his own family's place in Africa to write wistful letters about longing and illumination, died young. Augustine never quite made it to visit Nebridius at his home not far from Carthage. If he had, it should have been rather like Charles Ryder's first visit to Sebastian Flyte at Brideshead in Evelyn Waugh's novel. Augustine remembered his friend fondly long after:

When I read and reread your letter, thinking it over as much as time permitted, I recalled my friend Nebridius, who was a keen and assiduous student of everything dealing with the dark questions surrounding religious doctrine and really hated a short answer to a big question. Whoever had asked a question in such a spirit, he took it badly and (if the status of the interlocutor allowed) checked him with indignant expression and words, thinking it inappropriate to ask about such things without knowing just how much could and should be said about something so important.[189]

As late as his early years in Hippo, Augustine still had friends around him, real friends like Alypius and Possidius and Evodius (even if Augustine was always a little irked by Evodius's correspondence, and pleaded that he was too busy to respond properly[190]) and Severus—but, well, that's the list, and they all slip away to posts elsewhere within a very few years: Severus to Milevis, Evodius to Uzalis, Possidius to Calama, Alypius to Tagaste.

And then no more: no new friends, no new faces glimpsed through the rhetoric of his letters and other texts. Friendship remained valuable to him and in a new key, but it is painful to find his praise of friendship and its consolations in a letter to Jerome, the man who never could quite become a friend.[191]

Perhaps something warmer could be found in the face-to-face community of the monastery at Hippo, but it's hard to believe that when we come to the sober and dispiriting account of that community in a sermon we shall hear shortly, where Augustine has to explain all the little financial peccadilloes and family history his brothers had to account for. No warmth there, not even much sense that he really knew as people the clerics who lived with him. They were disciples, not friends.

When Possidius comes to the end of his short biography, he acknowledges the power of Augustine's writing and the vivid impression it makes of the man, but then adds:

> But I think we benefited more from him, we who could hear and see him present and speaking in church, and especially the ones who were privy to his ordinary behavior around people. He was not only a learned scribe in the kingdom of the skies, bringing forth new and old from his treasurehouse, or one of those businessmen who found a pearl of great price and sold everything they had to buy it. He was also one of those to whom it was said "speak this way and act the same way" and of whom the savior said, "If you act and teach men in this way, you will be called great in the kingdom of the skies."

Notice how Possidius is driven, in perhaps the most intimate part of this text, away from his own words into scriptural words to describe his friend and mentor. We grasp after the power of the relationship, even as Augustine himself fades into hieratic abstraction.

There was, to be sure, one friend above all others: Alypius. Alypius deserves his own volume, or his own play. He is Horatio to Augustine's Hamlet. In Shakespeare, though, we see Hamlet so often through Horatio's eyes that we grow used to his skin and his personality and fail to notice our ignorance of his heart. Alypius is different. We know a great deal about him from Augustine himself, and we see him and Augustine repeatedly on the same stage throughout Augustine's career. But Alypius still escapes us to an astonishing degree. Did he think of himself as a trusty sidekick to Augustine's heroic gunslinger, or did he see a stage on which he was himself the star player?

The pious narrative of Alypius's earlier life that we get in the sixth book of the *Confessions* is mostly irrelevant. It tells us only that he came of a good family, better than Augustine's, and had the prospects of a good career in public life through the law. He made his way up the ladder as an attorney at Carthage, Rome, and Milan. Like Augustine, he abandoned a promising career in the world while he and Augustine were in Italy; he, too, voyaged back to Africa in 388; and he spent the rest of his life living in Tagaste. When Augustine went away to Hippo and was ordained, Alypius stayed on, and, though younger than Augustine, became bishop of Tagaste while Augustine was still a junior cleric at Hippo. At the crucial conference with the Donatists in 411 he was always the legal eagle, the man of procedure and accuracy, never rising to Augustine's theological level but watching fact and process carefully. While Augustine confined his travels to Africa, and mainly to the route back and forth from Hippo to Carthage, Alypius was more adventurous. His business took him to meet people Augustine only shared letters with, including Jerome in the Holy Land and many in Italy. Particularly in the fraught years of 418–23, Alypius was the man on the case for the African church, going back and forth to the court at Ravenna, making sure that post-Donatist and anti-Pelagian initiatives did not misfire. Hostile contemporaries accused him of going beyond what was proper as well, delivering eighty horses to highly placed dignitaries at the court at Ravenna in order to assure their favor to his causes.[192] In an earlier time, in 397 or a little before, when he and Augustine found themselves in a public debate up-country in Numidian Thubursicu, the Donatist bishop of that place, Fortunius, whipped out a book to prove that overseas bishops had written friendly letters to the African Donatus, a telling sign of "communion" with the rest of the world if true. Alypius was the one to notice that the book favored the Arian heretics and was thus suspect.[193] We hear of Alypius last in 428, and do not know whether he outlived Augustine. He was not seen at his friend's deathbed (if Possidius has not simply forgotten to mention him).

So far, so good. But a few odd things strike us about Alypius.

First, the tensions between Augustine and his friend. A quarrel in 411 over the visit of two wealthy and devout Italians pushed them apart. We will see how threatened Alypius felt as he stood that day in Augustine's church, and Augustine's letter to Alypius afterwards shows the resentment and unhappiness Alypius felt.[194] Strikingly absent is the warmth and freshness, even if stylized, of the letters exchanged with Severus.

Second, Alypius had a decidedly untheological approach to his Christianity. This is hard to see behind the veils of piety Augustine and Augustine's readers are always ready to cover him with, but already in the *Confessions* Alypius's religion has a different flavor.[195] At the defining moment of conversion in the Milan garden, *his* verse from Romans was "but accept the one whose faith is shaky" (13.14), not a text about the strengthening of faith but about the place of the shaky-footed one inside the community. When he and Augustine and their household left Milan for Cassiciacum and plunged into the two intense weeks of dialogue that got recorded in the early books of that winter, Alypius slipped away to go back to Milan for ten days, missing much of the debate. When he *was* there, his contributions were measured and reserved. His one marked act of piety is of the body rather than the soul: in late winter 386–87, when they headed back to Milan to prepare for baptism at Eastertime, Alypius showed the greatest austerity, walking barefoot on the icy ground. That he fought the fight for the Caecilianist church forever after in Africa and Italy and that he lived the life of that church should still leave us room to consider how much was acquired social role, how much was the physical practice of religion, and how much or little was passion and belief.

One more thing about Alypius astonishes us: his textual silence. We can hear his voice in the transcript of the great public confrontation with the Donatists at Carthage in 411, and he is quoted and referred to otherwise. He seems to have written a letter to Paulinus of Nola that we *almost* know about, but for a long time we had only one tiny fragment of text from his hand. He wrote no books, though few bishops ventured that far. The only letters we have are ones he cowrote with Augustine for diplomatic or tactical purposes. He traveled far, on business of urgent interest to Augustine, but wrote no long informative letters home that we know of. If we did not have Augustine to compare him to, he would seem indeed a typical African bishop, pragmatic and unliterary. A single businesslike memo, recorded in a letter of Augustine's to another correspondent, has recently come to light.[196] Otherwise, he is the silent partner.

The one fragment we've long had is tantalizing. It comes from an undated letter that is mainly from Augustine to someone called Sebastianus, full of the mildest, if semidepressive, moral reassurance. The evil are always with us, a distressing fact, but divine promises accompany us as well. At the end of that letter, we have two appendages. First, with the notation *alia manu* ("in another hand," usually the marker of an authorial addition to a text otherwise written by scribes taking dictation), we get the encouragement: "Pray for us in good health, beloved and holy brethren!" Then this:

> I, Alypius, most devotedly greet your holiness, and all those joined to you in the master. I hope you will treat this letter as if it came from me as well. Though I might have written one myself, I preferred to add my name to this one, so that the single page could testify to the unity of our hearts.

And then his voice fades away, a voice that accompanied Augustine longer through his life than any other, from teaching days in Tagaste in the mid-370s until their last days, half a century later. Augustine we know so well, his best friend, so faintly.

AUGUSTINE THE PRIVATE PERSON

Was there an Augustine behind all these social façades, the ones that might have been and the ones that were? Rich, famous, socially successful, wielder of sacramental power in church and of a more ordinary power in his audience hall or in the courts of other powerful men, what did Augustine have left to himself? If we look for an unguarded, natural Augustine in his works, we will never find him. Do we catch glimpses? I notice the one who admits that he struggles to be high-minded and focus his mind on the things of his god, but his mind wanders at the curious sights of the world—a dog chasing a rabbit, a lizard catching flies, or a spider trapping them in its web—till he shakes his head and returns to his higher things.

Privacy is a modern invention and depends on conditions of life and an understanding of selfhood that were inaccessible to ancient people. To be "noble" (*nobilis*) in classical Rome meant literally to be "known," to be a figure under observation. Urban life centered on the activities and doings of the small elite group at the top of the social pyramid. The growth of cities and the emergence of a de facto bourgeoisie, people who could achieve wealth without achieving fully coordinate social standing, gave rise to the possibility of creating a disparity between social standing and visibility, which is the essence of privacy.

Privacy is cherished when a shadow falls over areas of a person's life that might otherwise be expected to be on more public display. The possibility of privacy begins for an elite, but (as we see in our own time) has the potential of reaching broadly in a mass society. And because privacy is a desirable good, its scope gradually expands for those who can manage it. But privacy and obscurity are not identical: in a way obscurity is privacy's reverse, the mark of a shadow that covers more, rather than less, than the individual might want. Privacy expresses the ability to control what is known about oneself.

A slave- or servant-based society, moreover, can never be entirely private. Royalty always live under the eyes of their retainers. To the end of antiquity, the dependence of elites on a slave society and the upward attraction exercised on the bourgeois by the nobility played strongly against any tendency to separation and privacy. Even without slaves, Augustine was rarely alone at home in Hippo. His choice to invite a community to live in the bishop's house with him created a household with some differences from that familiar to upper-class Romans, but it was still an open and public space nonetheless, not unlike the home of an extended kinship family. Much that a modern politician might reasonably hope to conceal from others would have been unavoidably public for Augustine. (We would love to know whether Augustine continued to frequent the public baths: unlikely but not impossible, not least because it was a good place to see and be seen and to meet others on neutral ground.) We see glimpses of Augustine's inmost bodily and emotional life, but only glimpses drawn from Augustine's self-presentation in his texts, gathered and rearranged here into a mosaic he did not design. We know that his body served him for seventy-five years, eight months, and fifteen days. Body and mind were in collaborative unison until the very end. By the standards of any generation, he must be regarded as a man of robust good health. Thus since the dawn of the twentieth century's psychological age, it has been regularly observed that Augustine's body had a tendency to subvert him at emotionally convenient moments. As a small boy, he was near enough death's door to plead for baptism, but his mother thought he was not sick enough to need that form of life insurance.[197] When he landed in Italy, escaping from his life, he fell deathly ill in the house of his Manichee host. Escaping his life, he almost left it.[198] When he fled from Milan to the countryside to test his newly celibate resolve, he pleaded an illness of the "chest" that made it impossible for him to go on as "salesman of words." And then while in the country, he was felled by an acute toothache, miraculously cured, but he seems unsurprised by the miracle.[199] In both cases, the physical disorder attacked the very center of his social personality, his capacity as a speaker of well-formed words. In 397, his grand debut at Carthage is followed by an acute attack of hemorrhoids that pulled him back from the public stage and left him unable to stand or sit; he may have begun dictating the *Confessions* thus prone, in pain, and the object of smiling pity.[200] In 410, on the eve of his great triumphs (and downfalls) of 411, he fell ill and left Hippo just as a wave of powerful and even competing individuals were arriving, and so was *hors de combat* at a moment when his carefully nurtured epistolary relationships of the last fifteen years could have begun turning into face-to-face friendship or rivalries.[201]

All that by the time he was fifty-six. For the next twenty years, we do not hear of disqualifying illness, until his last days or weeks, when he sensed the end was near, took to his bed, and prayed tearfully alone. Proving psychosomatic illness in a living patient inspected by qualified physicians is hard enough, but it's impossible not to suspect it, repeatedly, in every case in which we know Augustine was pulled away from the stage by his body.

From as early as we know anything about him, that body was a problem to him. We need not take overseriously (as most people do) his condemnation of infant greediness at the breast, but by the time he fell in with the Manichees, at age eighteen, he had put himself in for a lifetime of association with powerful forces, to which he gave a succession of allegiances, some unwavering, some not, that told him that the body is a problem. Not that it will get too fat, not that it will fall ill, not that it will break down: those ills of the body he takes for granted and shrugs off, as it were. The body rather will be for him a source of distraction and defilement: food, drink, sleep (and dreams), sex (even in dreams), and, most seductive of all, the wandering of the eyes. All these things are for him not part of himself, not his core inner self, the real Augustine, but are rather instruments of the bodily Augustine, the imperfectly spiritual Augustine, and vehicles by which temptation—and worse—penetrate the person. Augustine's "curiosity" never seems in truth to project itself beyond his absorption in the body and its processes. The disciplines of his life are designed to protect the soul from the body, to leave the soul free to wander and roam, a ghost before its time, running through the universe where it will, if only body will keep from pulling it back.

This should seem odd. At the heart of Augustine's religion was the firm belief in the triumph of the body in resurrection. But Augustine is hardly the only Christian who has been able to believe firmly in bodily resurrection and even to worry at length about the physical facts of resurrectedness without doing more than leap across the chasm that separates fallen bodilyness from risen.[202] Perhaps he does us a favor at this point. For the two apparent ideas about bodies, that they are threatening and that they are perfectible, both of which are at variance with modern attitudes, compel us to think how they might both coexist in the same mind, and when they do we can grasp the sense of unreality that Augustine lived with. The perfectible body and the tempted body are really the same: unreal bodies, bodies at a distance, bodies not quite made peace with, madonna and whore with no middle ground. If he did not believe in the resurrection, it would be hard to understand how he could be so distressed about sexuality.

AUGUSTINE THE TROUBLEMAKER

Augustine's fame is that of a beleaguered and heroic figure, unwilling warrior and faithful servant. Moderns commonly say of Augustine, perhaps parenthetically, somewhere early in a shorter or longer study of his work and thought, that much of what he produced was written for controversial purposes, to confute one or another heresy or error of his time. In a generous reading of Augustine's major writings, only the *Confessions* and the *Trinity* do not have their origin in immediate controversy.

The implicit view of Augustine that gives rise to those parentheses and *obiter dicta* runs something like this: it was natural and reasonable that orthodox Christianity found itself surrounded by error and opposition, and thus *not* surprising that a well-trained rhetorician like Augustine, who had begun public life as apologist for one embattled sect and came to ecclesiastical prominence in another, would find his time taken away from the tranquility of his studies to engage in worldly polemic. We are left with a shadowy notion of the fine philosopher Augustine could have been, if only he had had the time to devote himself to undisrupted studies of a higher order.

To be sure, long before he became a bishop, Augustine was an ardent fighter with words. With at least some embarrassment, he recalled how he would win arguments with the orthodox in his Manichee days, and go from success to success with mounting self-assurance.[203] He spoke as if the habit had passed, but it's hard to see real transformation. Face-to-face, he did best when his opponent was weak and wavering, a potential convert. He could, and would, challenge his opponent to a public disputation, confident, usually justifiably so, in his debating skills, honed over the years. He was at his most vehement when the opponent was somewhere else, far away in miles but within the ambit of the textual world Augustine created. Mani, Pelagius, Julian—these men not only took the full brunt of Augustine's attacks, but took it repeatedly, almost endlessly, in obsessive detail. The affection of Augustine's friends for him tells us one thing about the man; his flair for hostility tells us another.

A man who could go forty-three years from conversion to his grave without ever a moment when one or another polemical work was *not* on his plate, and who can be shown, moreover, to have picked every fight he got into, must surely be thought to be part of the problem, not part of the solution. The Manichees were a moment's fashion in Africa, easily outlawed. By the time Augustine assails them with his lengthy *Against Faustus*, few were paying attention to the cult. The Donatists were the majority church of Africa. To attack them was to attack African Christianity, and to invoke imperial assistance was to change the history of Africa forever, and not necessarily for the better. Whether there ever was such a thing as Pelagianism may reasonably be doubted, but even if we conclude that Pelagius and a few others held doctrines that were at variance with Augustine's, the choice to hound those doctrines and those teachers with obloquy was just that—a choice. Augustine's opponents on the same issues in the next generation, the "semi-Pelagians" (that term is a sixteenth-century moniker for them) of Gaul were far more discreet and managed to rewrite Augustine's teaching without the billingsgate.

Augustine was not alone in defining himself by what he wasn't, by what he could defame. In his time, ecclesiastical controversy raged with furiously pursued claims of villainy against the most unlikely suspects. Priscillian of Avila, for example, offers to the modern eye little doctrinal irregularity and only mild idiosyncrasy of ascetic extremes of practice, at a time when the nature of asceticism was open to the widest variations of sometimes ludicrous practice in the Latin west. But Priscillian was taken out by the imperial government at sober ecclesiastical urging and put to death in 386 for his irregularities, which were trumped up to include alleged magic practices and illicit associations with women.[204] On both larger and smaller scales, similar obloquy was poured out in all directions. Histories of doctrine find a narrative line in the great theological arguments over Trinity and Christology and build a record of councils and conciliar aftermaths (building, indeed, on the choices of mainstream medieval clergy from east and west), but in so doing they are forced to overlook some of the gaudiest stories of the age.

The spirit of the time is well captured by Epiphanius of Salamis, whose *Panarion* tells the story of *all* the heresies of his world and ends as a catalogue of interest to the religious ethnographer, full of local variations, comical misunderstandings, and petty quarrels enshrined forever in an authoritative text. Epiphanius's book was much to the taste of the time, and Augustine himself would revise and digest it in Latin in his own *Heresies* (*De haeresibus*), and one of Augustine's own enemies would write a particularly witty and stinging attack on Augustine that included a revision of Augustine's catalogue.[205] Everyone (including many historians since) tried to picture a world with one normative model of religion and many forms of deviation.

These people were building what our contemporaries would call a "totalizing discourse" of Christianity. Christianity, to Augustine and many of his contemporaries, was not truly Christianity unless it was universal and all-powerful, like Christianity's god. But turning a welter of local doctrines, practices, and texts into a universal, all-powerful church was at best a nascent enterprise in Augustine's time. That this enterprise would spend another thousand years at least proving the impossibility of what it undertook has blinded many to the bravado of ambitious clergy like Augustine. In the meantime, diversity flourished.

Men of self-assurance prevailed and are remembered as having prevailed. Histories of the church and histories of doctrine recall and emphasize the stories of those who built structures, propagated doctrines, and exercised control at a distance. Pelagius or Paulinus of Nola or Priscillian, disinclined to thinking on a grand scale and preoccupied with cultivating their ecclesiastical gardens, are footnotes in the histories we receive. Ambrose, Augustine, Jerome—each in his own way a less attractive personality than the others just named, each far more successful in imposing his views of Christianity on contemporaries and successors—are central figures of western history. Augustine was a less important person in his world than in the intellectual history we have constructed since. To know him is to know his limits. Then we can understand how he transcended them.

V

AUGUSTINE
IN HIS BOOKS

There have always been people who know the life of Augustine lived in and of his books. We pay attention to the man *because* of books: those he read, those he wrote, and because he has influenced the way we write our own books. One must see him in his words, or try to *hear* him, in order to know him at all, but this part of his story needs to be told in layers. Start with the words he gave voice to every day, in private and in public.

AUGUSTINE'S TONGUE

The rule of history is that the larger your town or city, the more likely it is that you live among people who speak languages you do not. Modernity, industrialization, and political nationalism worked hard to make us forget this rule, and contemporary politicians often try to make us regret its resilience. But for most anyone who has lived in the metropolis or traveled beyond his home valley, understanding and making oneself understood to one's fellows is an achievement, not an automatic expectation.

So Augustine spoke and wrote Latin. If you think of him as a Roman citizen (which he was) and think of the Roman empire as a culturally and linguistically homogeneous place (which it wasn't), then to observe that Augustine spoke Latin might seem both obvious and sufficient to describe his experience.

But it is not. Bear in mind first that Latin arose in a small region in central Italy, coexisting with many other Italic dialects that more or less resembled each other. As Roman hegemony in the peninsula grew, Latin followed and flourished. But when the poet Vergil was a boy in Mantua, four hundred years before Augustine was born, he heard other natives of that region whose speech did not much sound like the vernacular of the city of Rome. To learn Latin well enough to become the leading poet of Rome required an effort and a concentration that went well beyond the abilities even of most well-born and well-connected sons of Mantua.

In and after Vergil's time, Latin spread well beyond its origins. Rome planted settlements of officers and bureaucrats to manage the conquests it made. These men generally found themselves in or adjacent to local communities, and so the opportunistic local population would find ways to learn enough of the conqueror's language to make it possible to do a little business.

With the passage of very little time, Rome followed conquest with colonization, both imitating and reinventing Greek practices. Roman colonies consisted of bands of retired soldiers, who were given land as a reward on retirement for their long service. It was shrewd management to reward soldiers this way, after a long itinerant career during which they were not supposed to own *any* property, and it was shrewd imperialist politics to locate those settlements strategically in conquered lands. Confiscated or unsettled land, chosen for location, became home for small settlements of Latin speakers who were by definition loyal and grateful to the Roman regime for which they had fought and were otherwise unrooted in the place they settled. The colonists acquired wives and children, time passed, and soon what had been an isolated encampment of aliens became a part of the local cultural fabric. The colonists went native but in the process the natives were Romanized, and on balance, over time, Romanization prevailed. These communities added their weight to the Latinization of the provinces, a process that progressed from the second century B.C.E. until the first stages of Roman devolution, the "barbarian" kingdoms of late antiquity, set it back temporarily.[206] That the setback was only momentary was evidenced by the spread of Latin, after Roman government and arms had vanished, to lands that had never had it, such as Ireland, Germany, and Scandinavia, and by the persistence of Latin in most of the former Roman territories (notably Iberia, Gaul, and Italy).

But Latinization had its limits and surprises. Though Roman Britain, for example, was a secure part of the Roman world for four hundred years, the abandonment of Britain by Roman generals at the end of the fourth century and the subsequent arrival of war bands from the east left the center of Great Britain speaking the newly arrived Germanic tongues, and the rest of the island speaking the Celtic (Welsh and Scottish Gaelic) tongues that had antedated Roman arrival. By contrast, Gaul and Iberia speak the conqueror's language to this day and are intensely proud to have made it their own. North Africa retained and spoke Latin through Vandal and Byzantine conquests, but lost it finally after the Islamic conquest of the seventh century.

Latin never established itself as a dominant language in the Greek-speaking eastern Mediterranean. There an earlier linguistic imperialism had taken Greek from the Aegean all around the eastern Mediterranean and planted it as the language of urbanity and politics, giving it a dominant role, which it maintained until subsequent Islamic, Slavic, and Turkish conquests. Latin was the language of empire in Constantinople until the sixth century, and as late as the fourth century the fashionable Greek rhetorician Libanius could still complain about young men going to Beirut to study law in Latin rather than coming to Antioch to study finer subjects with him in Greek. But Latin remained alien there, and though a wealth of Greek literature was translated into Latin or at least read by native Latin speakers, Latin literature never achieved comparable penetration in the east. Plenty of Greek, on the other hand, was spoken in the cities of the western Mediterranean by sailors, merchants, and others in pursuit of opportunity. Christianity at Rome was a Greek-language community until the late fourth century, when the liturgy was finally converted to Latin, and ample evidence indicates that maritime cities of the west had Greek communities till very late.[207]

But Latin did not paint the map even of the western empire a solid color. Down from the upper classes and away from the cities, local languages persisted everywhere. Ample testimony from Greek and Latin speakers reveals the persistence of other spoken languages, and from all around the Mediterranean fragments of evidence show us how even the most marginalized parts of society could find ways from time to time to commit their words to writing in local tongues. Nabatean Aramaic inscriptions from the Near East are matched with Celtic inscriptions found in Gaul and, more to our purpose, Libyc (Berber) inscriptions found in North Africa.[208]

Augustine's Tagaste, at the upper end of the Medjerda valley and as far from Carthage as one could get and still regard Carthage as the regional metropolis and path to the sea, provides a significant concentration of Libyc/Berber inscriptions, suggesting that the city had been at some point on a linguistic frontier. The names of Monnica and Adeodatus, for example, reflect local, pre-Roman religious practice,[209] but in the names (quite unusual, as it happens) Patricius and Augustinus, on the other hand, each derived from the title of a high Roman dignitary, a sharply willed Roman-ness sticks out, as it does with the evocative name of their wealthy friend and neighbor, Romanianus.[210] Yet the other socially ambitious Tagastan we know best, Alypius, had a name with Greek roots. To be Roman in name and style was something that marked you in the community as a person of standing, or at least of pretensions. (Augustine himself would change his name subtly when he became bishop. No longer known as Aurelius Augustinus, now he always would be Augustinus Hipponensis, Augustine of Hippo. In such a way did bishops claim a special social standing for themselves.[211]) When the bishop of Sitifis (modern Sétif), 175 miles west of Hippo, wrote to ask Augustine to send him a deacon skilled in Latin, he elicited an acknowledgment from Augustine that Latin was not the default language once you got away from the population centers.

We can't tell for sure what they did speak at Sitifis, for Libyc/Berber was not the principal non-Latin language of Augustine's world. He speaks repeatedly of the survival of Punic, the Semitic language that had come to Carthage with the Phoenician traders who founded that city—Dido's language. Punic had been in its own time an imperial language, spread through North Africa and into Spain by the Carthaginians, but was then in full retreat from the time of the Roman sack of Carthage in 146 B.C.E. A great deal of modern scholarly energy has gone into answering the question whether Punic is just Augustine's name for Berber, but the most natural interpretation is that the two are different languages. Berber was likely[212] a language of the lower classes and Punic the remnant of an upper-class literary language, a sign of the way social differentiation was maintained in even the most remote parts of the Roman world. In his exchange of letters with Maximus of Madauros, the traditionalist professor, Augustine is the one who speaks up for the prestige that still inhered in Punic books (though Augustine himself could not read them).[213] What was actually spoken in the country districts around Hippo was doubtless a patois Punic, mixed with Latin and Berber, even when the speakers were unaware of the mixture.[214] Berber persists in the Kabylie Mountains west of Hippo and elsewhere in Algeria to this day.

The household Augustine grew up in was likely not entirely monolingual, then, with linguistic and social fault lines running in many directions. In the course of his life, Augustine would find himself in many different moments of linguistic differentiation and confrontation. His Latin was the Latin of Africa, not Italy; it was Latin and not Greek; it was upper-class Latin and not vernacular (though he himself probably code-switched between "higher" and "lower" flavors of Latin in everyday conversation); it was Latin and not Punic; it was Latin and not Berber; it was Latin, marking him out as a Roman against whatever barbarian languages may have come his way; and for some discerning observers his Latin had a specifically Christian and modern flavor in a world where traditionalism was the accepted marker of prestige.

So, to speak of "Latin" in Augustine's time is to speak of a complicated thing.

The differentiation of Latin into regional variants sufficiently distinct to enable us to identify them as forerunners of the Romance languages that now occupy the same spaces was essentially complete in the age of Caesar Augustus. Though no African-Romance tongue (like the Gallo-Romance we call French) survived for us to examine, we should realize that even Cicero did not *speak* in exactly the way he appears in the chiseled purity of his texts. The local spoken Latin of Augustine's childhood stood thus at a significant distance from the Latin we now think of as classical. We have two or three ways to measure this distance.

First: Augustine's African accent. Even after years of schooling and professional success, when he went to Italy to pursue a career as rhetor, the Italians made fun of his African accent.[215] He shows in later years that he knows some of the distinct problems, talking carefully about problems in distinguishing two words that are spelled alike but pronounced *slightly* differently in correct Latin; but in Africa, he says, that slight distinction has long since been blurred.[216]

Then we have the example of Augustine's only effort as a writer of popular song. In the late 390s, making the case against his religious opponents, he wrote a "Psalm Against the Donatists," running almost three hundred lines and telling, in jingly and memorable form, the story of Donatists versus Caecilianists in a way that could be easily remembered and help understand Augustine's own position. Here's how it begins:

Everyone who loves true peace, judge the truth right now!
Sins are everywhere, the brethren are upset,

This is why our master wanted us forewarned.
The kingdom of the skies, he said, is like a fisher's net:
It snares all kinds of fish, every kind from here and there:
First they drag them to the shore, then they sort them out:
They put the good ones on one side, they throw the others back.
Anyone who knows his gospel, this story makes him scared.
The net's the church, he sees, the sea's the wicked world,
And the way the fish are mixed, that's how sinners and the just go on.
The shore's the end of time: that's when the sorting starts.[217]

And the refrain returns repeatedly: "Everyone who loves true peace, judge the truth right now!" Though Augustine knew and must have been able to write classical poetry in the classical meters, this poem is written in a more colloquial mode. Instead of measuring long and short syllables in the traditional way, he counts accented and unaccented syllables, does not shrink from rhyme the way a classic poet would, and even shows one or two pieces of distinctive pronunciation (revealed by the way he counts syllables) that were indigenous to Africa. He wrote this way to be understood and remembered as widely as possible.

But Augustine's Latin in his books is serenely regular and classical. How to explain the discrepancy?

There's concealment first of all. If you think about how we and our contemporaries speak and write in languages like French and English, the written word is anything but a faithful representation of the spoken. We notice the disparity most as a set of anomalies of spelling. But all the odd ways we spell words once matched their pronunciation. Writing systems are very conservative in this way, though the practice of spoken language changes constantly. Furthermore, the prestige of a written form of discourse exercises its own influence on all practitioners. Continuing to spell and write your language correctly (that is to say, following a norm of correctness laid down decades or centuries ago by people who *spoke* very differently from you) is a common and understandable practice. Particularly in far-flung empires, provincial mastery of the imperial tongue in its archaic forms is a vital cultural achievement and a sign of belonging to the larger world, as much as bearing a name derived from Roman titulature might be.

So the people around Augustine who wrote down and copied his books—the stenographers who wrote down his words, the copyists who transcribed them—were well trained to render whatever he and others of

his class said in ways that assimilated them to the official language of empire. For a comparison, see what happens when a modern politician falls
afoul of the journalists and they begin to quote his spoken words *exactly*
as he said them. He can easily be made to look like a fool, as indeed we
all could were someone to be so unkind to us.

But finally, Augustine had to learn his Latin the hard way. While still
a small boy, he was sent away from home in Tagaste to the upland city of
Madauros, twenty-five miles south, there to make or at least complete his
studies with a "grammarian." The function of a grammarian in this period
was to train the boys who came to him in upper-class speech and the writing that went with it. In a society that paid only lip service to mathematical training of any kind, or even to the serious study of history, mastery
of the imperial languages was the preeminent concern of upper-class education from earliest age to final teaching for those who went on to the
most advanced studies.

Just as the child Augustine was exposed to Latin in a new way in
school, so also was he trained in Greek. In the first book of the *Confessions*,
he talks about how he loved the one and hated the other. Modern readers
usually sympathize too easily at this point, thinking they understand what
it's like to have to study both one's own language and a difficult foreign
tongue in artificial literary form. There was ordinary common Greek in
Africa, notably in the person of old bishop Valerius at Hippo, a native
Greek-speaker trying to make do as bishop of a Latin community, and
you could also hear Greek-speakers swearing casually in the street.[218] But
Latin was undoubtedly more challenging for Augustine, and more like
school Greek, than English ever is to an upper-class British or American
student today. Bilingual immigrants to the United States, faced with class-
rooms in which the imperial language is the medium and the object of
instruction and does not always resemble very closely what they hear spoken outside the classroom, sense some of what Augustine encountered.

The mastery Augustine achieved of Latin was thus extraordinary.
Whatever else Augustine was and did, he always put on a show, and the
object of the show was not only whatever preachment or polemic he had
in hand, but the simple fact of his mastery of the spoken word. He never
found anyone to rival him in north Africa. His prestige in matters of doctrine undoubtedly owed not a little to his facility with words, and when
he transferred that facility to the written word as well and began sending
his writings around the Mediterranean, he must have felt again the benefits of the childhood education he later grew to mistrust. Augustine the

Latinist was, of all the Augustines we can talk about, the one most necessary as a precondition for all the others.

AUGUSTINE IN THE LIBRARY

Augustine lived much of his life sunk in an ocean of books, books he made and books that made him and books that made the world for him. He is like us in that way, creatures of media that we are, and unlike most of his contemporaries.

His life to age thirty was taken up among three cities: Tagaste, Madauros, and Carthage. In Carthage Augustine saw things that any small-town boy would see in a big city, things to shock and amaze: a fish *so* big, an old religious ceremony *so* decadent. . . . For four years, then, in his early thirties, he left his familiar world and went on to Rome and Milan, the two greatest and most powerful cities of the Latin empire in his day. Yet when Rome is sacked by hostile armies in 410, leaving other sometime residents (like Jerome) shaken to their core, Augustine is remarkably phlegmatic. When he writes hundreds of pages of *City of God* in response to the laments of others over that crisis, it's striking that the city he visited, the city he remembered, the city that so affected others seems to have had little impact on him. Milan likewise did not much claim his attention, apart from ecclesiastical events surrounding the church of Ambrose, which he recounts in the *Confessions* and a few other places.

After that, he went home to Africa, to his father's house, and for all we know might have stayed there a lifetime, except that he ended up in Hippo. But Hippo would have added little to Augustine's world that he had not seen already. From Hippo he would travel to Carthage again regularly, and on occasion his business would take him farther into the African hinterland—once on an inspection tour of some ecclesiastically controverted cities, once on a churchly errand hundreds of miles west to Caesarea, and once, late in his life, to remote uplands to find and speak with the most powerful man in Africa to talk him out of abandoning his military post to become a monk.

Still, Augustine does not speak of his travels or what he learned on them, and he hated the travel itself. He dismissed the inquisitive observation that tourists practice as culpable curiosity, which he regarded as a great sin. But he was not himself, in this way, very curious at all. Alas, that he had no sharp-eyed secretary in his retinue to bring his world to life for us more visually, more sensually!

Even in books he had his limits. The central classical texts of Latin culture were ones he made his own in the schools of Madauros and Carthage, with rare facility. Vergil and Cicero above all are the authors to whom he returns and returns, at a time when they were already as old as Shakespeare is today. He had read them with passion, imagination, and ingenuity, but while his reading was wider than the merely classical, it was not much deeper. We get surprises now and then, as when he turns up paying close attention to the polymath of the late Roman republic, Varro; but for the most part, when we think of the twenty years he gave to classical texts, their impact was narrow.

A second set of books is nearly invisible in Augustine's makeup: the ones he would have read during his twenties, when he was in the company of the Manichees. Occasionally we can see him reacting to these, as when he refutes the teachings of Mani's disciple, Adimantus, from books Augustine probably knew when he was in the sect himself. He barely more than began a reply to Mani's own *Fundamental Letter*, which would have been both a comprehensive refutation of central Manichean teachings and perhaps a revelation of Augustine's encounter with his own past. These books seem to have come and gone in Augustine's life, leaving questions and issues, but they are otherwise invisible. That they could so disappear is a reminder of how deeply rooted *and* socially acceptable the Latin classics were by contrast, and that Augustine could and would keep them in play all his life.

When he first fell among the Manichees, he had been reading the Christian scriptures and he would continue to read pieces of those scriptures all the time he was among them. He had been exposed to Christian writings at some distance in the churches of his childhood, but that reading at age eighteen seems to have been his first serious encounter, and the new medicine didn't take: stylistically and doctrinally, he found the texts wanting. The Manichees read Christian scripture selectively and with a distinctive set of interpretations. Augustine criticizes their approach but shows us little of what he himself made of those books in those days.

In his thirties, he was driven back to the Christian texts, but by a curious detour.

To follow the narrative of the *Confessions*, when first Augustine came to Milan, he was impressed by the sermons of Bishop Ambrose. Though Augustine went to those sermons as a connoisseur of fine speaking, he was quickly taken, he says, by the content of what Ambrose had to say. The sermons on the texts of the Hebrew scriptures particularly inspired him to think that, thanks to Ambrose's sophisticated way of reading philosophical lessons back into the adventures of the old Jewish patriarchs, who evoked for Augustine's world an "archaic, precivic world of the Old Testament,"[219] the texts could be rescued and made part of a gentleman's religion. The flavor of these sermons survives well in the pamphlets Ambrose made of some of them, such as the *De Isaac, sive de anima* (*On the Story of Isaac: That Is to Say, on the Nature of the Soul*).

But the intellectual shortcomings of Christianity (or, as he would think later, of what he thought Christianity was) still weighed heavy on him. One other set of books would intervene, and ultimately drive him to the books to which he would give the rest of his life.

Someone in Milan—he won't tell us who, because he later came to disapprove of the man[220]—put in Augustine's hands what he calls those "books of the Platonists" (*Platonicorum libri*), Latin translations of what were probably selected treatises of the third-century (neo-)Platonist philosopher Plotinus, and perhaps some materials by Plotinus's editor and biographer, Porphyry, as well. Those books, with their refined spirituality and high intellectualism (made, doubtless, more mysterious and perhaps more enticing by being translated badly into Latin from dense and difficult Greek), had a paradoxical effect on Augustine. They set fire to his imagination, but that fire then kindled into a true blaze only when he took the ideas he found there with him to read the Christian scriptures.

We should pause over this curious turn and feel its oddness. The narrative Augustine gives in the seventh book of his *Confessions* captures the puzzle well:

> You got for me (by way of a certain man all swollen with monstrous arrogance) books of the Platonists translated out of the Greek into Latin, and there I read, not to be sure in these exact words but in this sense all the same, with many and various arguments, that in the beginning was the word and the word was with god and god was the word.

He seems to think that what he found in Plotinus was nothing more and nothing less than the doctrine found on the first page of the Gospel of John, stopping short of the "word made flesh." But a greater strangeness lies here. A young man, reader of many books, searcher after truths, dabbler in arcana, falls upon books that change his life, and he lets them change his life—and then he resists them and finally leaves them behind, in favor of books that had been there whenever he wanted them all his life. Even then, what the Platonists drove him to was, he claims a decade

later, the study of Paul's letters. What he was thrilled by in the neo-
Platonists was their account of mystical rapture, and Paul was the preeminent Christian authority on that subject, having been taken up to the
third heaven (see 2 Corinthians 5 and 12) to see things that no one else
had seen.²²¹

Over the next several years, after Milan, he read more of the Platonist
books, probably including more by Porphyry, and some of his writings of
that period (such as a short and scrappy half-written treatise on *The Im-
mortality of the Soul*) are digests of what the Platonists had to say. But these
books faded nonetheless. When he was conscripted into the clergy at
Hippo, he left them behind entirely. In this way he is quite unlike Ambrose, who seems to have been reading Platonic and other non-Christian
philosophical works while serving as bishop and using them to fuel what
he wrote. In the first book Augustine wrote as a cleric he says that if Plato
were alive today, he would modify one or two of his opinions and become
a Christian.²²² It's hardly likely Plato would be willing to make such a
modification, but the real surprise is that Augustine thinks that the doctrines of the Athenian and those of the church were close enough to allow such an easy sidestep.

Ten years later, Augustine would discover (what he should have known
all along, but a world of scarce books could leave funny gaps in one's information) that Porphyry had been the outspoken author of the stinging
book *Against the Christians*, and his opinion of Porphyry decisively soured.
When in the 410s and 420s, Augustine came to write *City of God*, the neo-
Platonists, who had once meant so much to him that he could claim they
changed his life forever, were now the stooges for a philosophical dumb-
show. They almost get it right, Augustine argued, but missing by an inch
is missing by a mile, and so they will languish in hell for want of drawing
the right conclusions (the ones Augustine drew) from what they had
learned. They had right doctrine in most regards, but they did not learn
to worship the one true god.

Instead of the Platonists, the books Augustine read by preference were
unexpected ones: mediocre Latin translations of Greek and Hebrew texts
written hundreds of years earlier, mainly in Palestine.²²³ We are accus-
tomed to the stunning success of those texts in achieving wide readership,
but it is still somewhat surprising to see a sophisticated and worldly connoisseur of books like Augustine settling for what these texts had to offer.
When he was eighteen, he thought they were beneath him. When he was
thirty-five and fifty-five and seventy-five, they contained for him the sum

of all wisdom. Be that as it may, they brought with them a new imaginative world for Augustine, a world filled with the stories of old covenants and new. For a man with as little experience of the world as Augustine had, this was a powerful force.

Imagine a skilled and versatile actor, constrained to perform improvisationally on a stage filled with props and flats from a particular long-practiced tradition and set of stories—say, Shakespeare. Then imagine that even while the performer remains the same, all those sets and props vanish and are replaced by something quite alien to the cultural tradition in which the performer grew up: Japanese Nōh drama, perhaps. The performer is and isn't changed. He still remembers his training and his gestures, and when pressed can still perform in the old ways, but at the same time he throws himself into the new, offering heartfelt and enthusiastic performances, ones that would astonish and scandalize the direct heirs of the adopted tradition if they could observe what he was doing.

That is where Augustine ended up, impresario to a new culture made up out of old Jewish texts and traditions, half-understood and badly translated. What did he read, then, and when did he read it?

I'll talk about Augustine's Bible and how he read it in a couple of pages, but first a word on the sequence of his reading. To begin with, there was immersion in scripture in 391 and following, particularly the Psalms and Paul. (Before ordination, he had gone repeatedly to Genesis, seeking illumination among, and later against, the Manichees.) Over the next decades, his focus shifted and glided. In the 410s, he was driven back to Paul by his preoccupation with the "Pelagians" and continued to expound, explain, and embroider Paul for the rest of his career, but without changing the fundamental interpretation he had come to in the 390s.

What Augustine did *not* much read in his years at Hippo were the books of his youth. Not for him the histrionics of a Jerome, disingenuously telling us, almost boasting, about his nightmare in which his god remonstrates with him on the golden floor of heaven for being more Ciceronian than Christian. When Augustine entered the church, he left the classical authors behind. He left them behind so utterly that he could go back to them easily and with a clear conscience when he needed to, and in the 410s he decided that he needed to. In writing *City of God*, he first refreshed his arsenal of classical historians and poets to underpin the virtuoso first three books, in which the aging rhetorician proved once more that he could still write in the high classical style of his youth, drawing on the full range of reference to ancient texts that was the hallmark of a gentlemanly style. But he went on to read some of those books more closely (Cicero in particular, but also Apuleius), to find in them philosophical argument and straw men with which to buttress his own position. He even read Plotinus and Porphyry again at this time, and he was as cold and unmoved by them as by the Latin classics. You would never know what they had meant to him thirty years earlier. The new books had taken over to an astonishing degree.

Augustine's life in books moved in this way, by a deliberate transfer of allegiance from one set of closely meditated master texts to another. Beyond the master texts, he had little advice. In his *Christian Doctrine*, for example, first drafted in 396 and then revised and completed in 427, he has much to say about how to read scripture and what the scriptural exegete needs to know—but he has no bibliography for his readers. The library of Christian classics on which he could draw was modest in size, but it had some important things in it, writers like Tertullian, Cyprian, and Arnobius of Africa, or Lactantius, Hilary of Poitiers, and Ambrose from across the Mediterranean, and we know that at various times he paid attention to all these authors. Yet he never studied them with the single-mindedness he had the classic texts of ancient Rome and which he then applied to scripture, and he does not go out of his way to recommend reading such authors. As work on his complex and difficult *The Trinity* progressed in the 400s and 410s, he did some selective reading in the Greek theologians of his age, but he did not feel the need to quote what he read or to give footnotes. Rather, he imbibed what he could and used it to interpret his biblical texts, then discarded (as it were) the theologians, the better to have his own say. Even his reading in Jerome, whom he knew he had to respect, was always limited and sporadic, even though he could have learned a lot from the Bethlehem obsessive.

In this regard, Augustine was the last of his kind and no one after him could have the same insouciance toward intellectual and theological predecessors. For them, the colossal presence on the library shelves of Ambrose, Jerome, and Augustine meant they had no choice but to find a way to deal with non-scriptural authority. The fifth-century Gaulish Christian writers who resented Augustine's extreme doctrines of grace and predestination were paradoxically instrumental in shaping the idea of a textual tradition of "Fathers of the Church" and building something of its practice,[224] but similar lines of development can be observed in Spain, in Italy, and in Ireland in the fifth centuries and afterwards. Augustine was lucky that he never had to read anything like Augustine.

A word on Augustine's Greek: pathetic. This is not to say that he was completely ignorant of the language, but he had resisted it in school and never mastered it.[225] All his life he seems to have been able to look at a Greek text of scripture and make some sense of it if he had a Latin translation at hand (as many moderns can decipher some Greek or Latin with the help of a bilingual Loeb edition), but inevitably this left him at a disadvantage. To come at the end of the fertile years that were marked by the literary careers of Athanasius, Basil, Gregory of Nyssa, Gregory of Nazianzus, and Evagrius Ponticus, to name only a few, and to be heir to a Christian tradition that numbered Origen among its most learned and original figures, and to be unable to read any of them except in very limited and partial ways reflected through translation was bad. But to be cut off from direct reading of the gospels and Paul as well was ultimately very damaging to what he could say and do. Yet he never seems to have been truly distressed by his lack, though there had to be people around him who sniffed at him for it.

A last observation: when we hear of his library at Hippo, from him and others late in his lifetime, we're hearing of his *own* works kept there. A cheeky young correspondent wrote to him around 410 to ask some questions that drew on Cicero and others,[226] and Augustine has the nerve to write back that no texts of Cicero can be found in Hippo. That is a slander on the culture of his adopted city, but perhaps also a marker of what was not available in Augustine's own household and community.[227] Scriptural texts themselves were available for sale in Hippo,[228] for the Christian texts as *objects* were not treated with quite the reverence that Judaism and Islam would bring to their holy books.

AUGUSTINE'S BIBLE

Augustine's first psalm book was in his hands at Cassiciacum the winter after he quit his job to pursue a different life, before he and his friends came back to Milan for baptism in the spring. A decade later, in the *Confessions*, he remembered the enthusiasm of that time. He wanted to recite them to the whole world! He wished the Manichees could see and hear him now! (They wouldn't have approved of the Jewish Psalms.) It was probably the same book that came to hand a few months later in Ostia, when Monnica lay dying and Augustine's friend, the future bishop Evodius, picked it up to intone the Hundredth Psalm, about divine mercy and justice.[229] These psalms were "scripture" (texts of authority), but Augustine did not find them in what he would call a Bible, for he never laid eyes on a Bible.

The Christian scriptures impose an unusual burden on their readers. On the one hand, the collection is far too large for any one person to master all of it, to know all of it, to keep every part potentially in mind. The Qur'an can be, and is, memorized by individuals; the Torah can be known equally well. But on the other hand, they are small enough and have been credited with such authority that they do not simply offer a library of edifying literature, to be taken *quant. suff.* and *ad lib.* the way Christians do. Every page of Christian scripture is authoritative—so Augustine would say, quite unambiguously—but the canon is too large and too habitually filtered through the prism of summarizing doctrine to allow or require strenuous control.

In practice, readers always select. Some individual passages and some pages and some books of these scriptures are better known to a given reader and more often quoted than others. Some family affiliations connect these selections, but a wide range of choice is left for taste, habit, and chance. A given denomination or community, for example, may well choose to emphasize a given section or set of texts, especially when they are brought together to support a particular festival or ceremony. Any such selection is unlikely to be free of contradiction and most individual selections will contain things that speak against passages important to at least some other readers. Such contradiction often fuels rather than dismays devotion.

Augustine's Bible was like that. He never saw it in our familiar form of a complete set of Christian scriptures bound together. Such books, far bulkier and more expensive than books ordinarily bought and sold and read in antiquity, didn't come into use for Latin readers for another century or more after his death, though some Greek examples date from his time. What Augustine's age had were lists of books, authorized books, books inside the canon. For Augustine, the books that were inside the line, that were canonical, were what he thought to be inerrant. He would gladly read other things, parascriptural in various ways, but without the same expectations.[230] Augustine's list resembles closely that which Latin Christianity would maintain through the middle ages and which would be ratified at the Council of Trent.[231]

So he knew his scripture by physical subsets: a volume of Paul, a Psalter, a book of Gospels, and so forth. (At one point he encourages his listeners in a sermon delivered in one of Africa's larger cities to go out and buy a copy of the Gospels for themselves—they are readily available for sale—and spend time reading it rather than their usual trifles.[232]) If we look at his history as a reader, the Psalms come first in his affections, Genesis second, Paul's letters third, and the Gospel of John fourth. Nothing else quite competes. The synoptic gospels he knows well, but they don't move or impress him with their theological depth the way John does. While he was at Cassiciacum, he wrote to Bishop Ambrose to report his newfound devotion and ask advice on scripture reading. Ambrose replied by suggesting Isaiah, but Augustine made no headway with it. He found it too difficult and put it aside for later. But at no point in his career did the prophets seize his attention. Jerome wrote endless commentaries on the prophets, but Augustine never felt their magic (or dared to compete with the older master). And so we hear less than we might from Augustine about apocalypses and the millennium. He was more literal-minded earlier in his career, more agnostic later, but preaching the last judgment and second coming and reporting the details of that future history are less a concern for him than for many of his contemporaries. The Donatists, on the other hand, were great readers of the prophets and great students of the end times to come.

The Psalter was a book he loved and returned to all his life. He carried it with him in Italy, and from the time he became priest at Hippo he immediately started writing short exegetical treatises on individual psalms. Even before he was allowed to preach in his bishop's church, he wrote sketchy outlines of interpretation of the first thirty-two. Over the next two decades, from his pulpit he would preach and take care to have recorded sermons on all 150 psalms. In the 410s he realized he had come close to a full set and so made sure to dictate a discussion of the 118th Psalm (119 in the modern numbering), for the sake of completeness— that psalm was far too long to make the object of a single sermon. We don't know how many times Augustine may have performed a given psalm before getting it right, before instructing the scribes to retain a copy (and a few psalms are treated twice in the collection of written sermons). We have just under two dozen other sermons of Augustine on psalm themes, but these are ones where he concentrates on a very few verses of a given psalm. Devoting a whole sermon to part of a psalm was a distinct choice he made, particularly with the longer psalms, arranging to have the scribes at hand to take down what he said.

If a modern reader would like to get the flavor of Augustine's religion as his followers did, seeing and hearing him preaching in church week in and week out, those sermons on the Psalms are the best place to go to listen. His Psalms aren't quite ours, though. He exceeds modern readers both in his literality and in his flights of fancy. Here's how one of them, on Psalm 51 (52), begins:

> To the end: the understanding of David.[233] When Doec the Idumite came and reported to Saul and said, David has come into the house of Abimelech.

The words quoted are the *titulus*, the heading that Augustine found in his Latin manuscript. Since every word of scripture was inspired and informative, even these almost marginal words were no exception. When Augustine gave a sermon on this psalm, one day in perhaps 413, he made a point of having the relevant passage from Kings read first, and then he spent a third of his sermon on the rivalry between Saul and David. His point was not historical but allegorical and ethical. The audience was to get the point, a favorite one of Augustine, that David stood for Christ. (Those first words quoted above did not delay him every time they appeared, for similar words appear, hashed translations of the Hebrew, on many psalms. But Augustine took them as his warrant for seeing Christ wherever he saw David.) On this reading, Saul's persecution of David is the persecution that led to Jesus's death and David's eventual ascent to his kingdom is Jesus's resurrection. By implication, the same story is the hearer's story, trial leading to redemption. Before Augustine begins reading the psalm proper, he knows what it means.

Augustine knew he was taking his elaborate time, but he had his reasons: "This is a short psalm we're going to talk about, but the header has some business in it. Bear with us while we untangle that, as best we can, with the master's help. We shouldn't pass over these things easily, for my brothers have been kind enough to arrange for what we say to be taken in not only by ears and hearts, but by pens as well, so we have to think not only about the audience here, but the readers as well."[234] Not to be missed here is the way the late-antique schoolmaster gets excited about difficulty as a signal of concealed meaning. Bad translation was an opportunity for interpretation, for there was no phrase so gnomic or inapt that it could not be made the subject of close study and ingenious exegesis.

What followed was a patient and elaborate performance. Hebrew etymologies of proper names (Saul, Abimelech), more or less accurately known from reference works, and passages of scripture made parallel either by their verbal resonance or by their doctrinal content are brought to bear, as the tools that were at hand, and interpretation happens. An eerie clumsiness hangs about much of it, and a strange beauty, like the beauty of found art, in the results.

His treatment at the beginning is typical: "Doec means 'movement'; Idumite means 'earthly.' Just see what people this 'movement' of Doec stands for: he is not going to abide forever, but rather pass away. 'Earthly': why should you expect any profit from an *earthly* man? It's the heavenly man that lasts for eternity."[235]

Now, Augustine's text of the psalm, the one he had the lector read to his congregation, gave the name here as Achimelech, but he knows from elsewhere in his scriptures that it can be spelled Abimelech. He likes that because he knows that Abimelech[236] means "my father's kingdom" (*patris mei regnum*), and "the changing of the name [from one spelling to another] draws our attention to the mystery, so we won't just study the history and ignore the sacred things that are veiled here."[237] Augustine suggests that the name is appropriate, since David was betrayed when he came to the kingdom of his father.

So the verse "you loved malice more than kindness" (*dilexisti malitiam super benignitatem*) provokes a natural demurral, but two scriptural texts come to mind: Psalm 35 (4–5), "he plotted wickedness in his chamber" (*iniquitatem meditatus in cubili suo*), where the "malice" of Psalm 51 has called the "wickedness" to mind; but then a few moments later, Augustine thought of the gospel, and began a fresh line of thought, "but if he should do what is written, namely 'love your neighbor as yourself'" (Matthew 22.39): here the connection is substantive and verbal: *diligere* is the Latin verb in both passages. Time after time, a verbal echo will call up parallel passages for Augustine (this says something about how his very powerful verbal memory worked), of greater and lesser relevance to the passage under discussion.

All these interpretations make the audience dependent on the interpreter. To know etymologies, to know parallel passages of scripture: these are matters for experts, not for inspired novices. To hear Augustine preach in this vein is to understand that you, in the congregation, are watching a master perform.

The master's performances were crowd pleasers. The problem with reading Augustine's sermons on the page as we do is that we pay too much attention to these details of practice and cannot feel the emotive power:

the magic of place, of voice, of the intentionally dazzling effect that flashes of erudition will have, of the effectiveness, finally, of this style of making the psalm texts present and apposite.

What begins as a history lesson becomes a mystery and then becomes again a reassuring construction of the main messages of Augustine's church. Fall and redemption, the mixing of the good people and the bad people in this world, and hope of better things to come: the real magic of sermons like this came in three movements. The lector performed the biblical text itself, intoned with power in a solemn and sacred place, rendering homage to its mysteriousness, remoteness, and opacity. Then, by the virtuoso performance of the preacher the text was brought down to earth, given a meaning for the here and now. The sermon ended as reassuringly as an old-fashioned murder mystery, with the good news the audience already knew confirmed once again. Augustine knew how to find his endings with just the right tone, and so he did that day with this one. Here are the last paragraphs of the sermon, typical of Augustine in his church:

> "And I shall look out for your name, because you are delightful" [Psalms 51.11]. The world is bitter, but your name is delightful. And if there are some sweet things in the world, they are mixed up with the bitter. Your name is preferred not only for its greatness, but for its delightfulness. Unjust men have told me of their delights, but they are not like your law, Master.[238] If there weren't such sweetness, the martyrs wouldn't have endured such bitter tribulations so calmly. Their bitterness was felt by everybody, but not everyone can easily taste the sweetness. So the name of god is delightful to those who love god above all other delights.

Then Augustine echoes the psalm verse again, for effect:

> "I shall look out for your name, because it is delightful." And to whom will you show its delights? Give me the palate to sense its delicacy. Praise honey as much as you like, overstate its sweetness with what words you can: a man who doesn't know what honey is doesn't know what you're saying unless he tastes it. So what does the psalm say when it invites you to try it? "Taste and see how sweet is the master."[239] You don't want to taste it and you say: "It's delightful? How is it delightful?" If you tasted it, you would find it in your own pleasure, not just in words, no more than you would find it in sprouting leaves—you could deserve to be

shriveled up by the master's curse like that fig tree.[240] "Taste," he says, "and see how sweet is the master." Taste and see: you'll see, if you taste. But how will you prove it to a man who doesn't taste it? By praising the delightfulness of the name of god. Whatever you say, it's just words: taste is something else. The impious hear the words of his praise, but they don't taste how sweet he is—only the blessed do that.

So this author senses the sweetness of the name of god and wants to explain it and wants to demonstrate it, and he can't find who to do it for. For the blessed don't need to be shown, for they taste for themselves and they know. But the impious can't sense what they won't taste. So what does he do about the delightfulness of the name of god? He took himself away from the crowds of the impious: I will look out for, he says, your name, because it is delightful in the sight of your holy ones. Delightful is your name, but not in the sight of the impious: I know how sweet it is, but only to those who taste it.[241]

Augustine's performances often resemble an old-fashioned striptease, the kind with the blackout just at the moment of revelation. Has this audience, here and now, tasted the sweetness? Only by a great stretch of imagination and generosity would we dare to say that. Everything we know of Augustine in his church tells us of congregations extremely various in their predispositions and interests. Their minds wander, they mishear things, they don't get the point. If Augustine had a good day the day he gave this sermon, if he kept the crowd with him, they still went along on a performance that consisted of ostension rather than action: of Augustine showing and pointing to what revelation and direct experience were like. This one ends with both Augustine the performer and the Psalmist he interprets snatching themselves away from the crowds at the crucial moment. Everything important is left to the imagination overheated by the performance. The ideal congregant in Augustine's eyes would be the one who went away thinking indeed that she or he had seen something, had tasted something, had glimpsed the real thing. The eucharistic liturgy that followed the sermon (at least for the baptized faithful; it, too, was concealed even from baptismal candidates and left undescribed and undiscussed until the very night of baptism[242]) orchestrated a physical representation with exactly the same structure of anticipation, participation, and a lingering longing.

Augustine would be back the next day or the next week, every sermon a fresh start, beginning with another piece of scripture and essentially the same agenda. The best count suggests that he did this eight thousand times in his career.

And he did it as performer, not scholar. The pulpit and its extemporaneity offered the focus for his biblical interpretation. While his contemporary Jerome was dictating volume after volume of careful biblical commentary in his study, sometimes following Greek authorities and sometimes simply translating them, Augustine the exegete shied away from that practice as time went by. He only turned his hand to writing formal scriptural commentary a half-dozen times, and only once as a bishop, and never used an authoritative source or sources.

Already at Tagaste, he had tried to write on Genesis against the Manichees, to not much effect. While a priest at Hippo, he made several abortive attempts: at a detailed commentary on Genesis, at commentaries on Galatians and Romans, and an exposition of the Sermon on the Mount. He would return to gospel problems and issues many times, notably in his book on *The Agreement of the Evangelists*, that is, on the question of how the four gospel narratives can be taken as telling identical and complementary stories. He would also give a long series of sermons on the Gospel of John that stretched on and off for years. The only biblical commentary he wrote was his twelve-book opus on Genesis (*Genesis Taken Literally*), a work of many years and much effort. Instead of writing scholarly commentary, Augustine was always much more comfortable taking up individual issues and hammering at them exegetically, and so many of his treatises on doctrinal or moral issues turn out to be extended meditations on scriptural passages. But this style means that he habitually takes his scriptural text out of the context of the original creation (whatever book of scripture that happens to be) and reads it instead against the whole of scripture and against the doctrinal and polemical needs of his time. Much of what he says in that mode is brilliant, even memorable, but little of it stands up as a serious engagement with the text in any way that patristic, medieval, or modern readers would call scholarly.

MODES OF INTERPRETING THE SCRIPTURE

Augustine's struggle to enunciate principles of interpretation in the first book of his bishopric, *Christian Doctrine*, mixes the familiar and the unfamiliar in ways that elude all but the most resolute reading. What sets him apart clearly from moderns is his preference for the nonliteral sense of scripture as the truest sense. Most moderns are disconcerted at first by this preference and either discount or, seldom enough nowadays, disapprove with deceptive ease. But if every page of scripture is scriptural and Christian, then the Jewish scriptures get largely rewritten in ways that would have surprised the patriarchs of old. Augustine learned this technique of inscribing the new doctrine in the old scriptures from Ambrose and Jerome and passed it on to the Latin west, where it had a long run, until it was challenged by the Reformation. It came to the Latins from Alexandria, where Origen in particular had developed the technique with ingenious mastery.[243]

All this can be found in any standard history of biblical interpretation. What evades attention too easily, however, is the implicit authority of the literal meaning of scripture. It seems natural that the literal sense would come first. Literal interpretation belongs readily to the contrary worlds of either scholarship or fundamentalism, or so it would seem. But the oddity of Augustine's literal sense should be a warning that something else is going on.

For only when you create the idea of a second sense of scripture—call it allegorical or figurative or prophetic—can you give shape and meaning to the supposedly first sense, and the choice of making that the literal sense is far from obvious. Few ancient readers of a text like Genesis, for example, ever stopped to think what they were making of something like the six days of creation. Some readers would take it naïvely, others would see it metaphorically, and few would notice the difference or make much of it. But to ask the question of two senses is to divide meaning and segregate it in categories, categories that did not exist without the doctrine of the "higher sense." The lower sense was never so low until the higher sense made it so. Modern literal and fundamentalist interpretation of scripture is conceptually impossible without the creation of the allegorical modes of reading of the early church and the theory that writers like Augustine built on those practices.

In *Christian Doctrine*, Augustine repeatedly makes another point: that when matters of strict doctrine of the faith are not involved, multiple interpretations of scripture can and should flourish side by side. (Book 13 of the *Confessions*, a discussion of Genesis, is perhaps his best attempt at living up to this principle.) His view of what constitutes doctrine of the faith is (by modern standards) remarkably narrow, confining itself to the principles that can be laid down in a conciliar creed: Trinitarian and Christological doctrine, as moderns would understand them. On the express principle of *Christian Doctrine*,[244] if two or three expositors of scripture give differing interpretations of a text but are fundamentally in accord on the few things that are essential, then the diversity of opinion is not a bad thing but a good thing: a sign of the polymorphousness and polysemy of the infinitely rich Christian text. Many disciples of Augustine will point to this principle as an edifying and open-minded one, without recognizing that in practice Augustine often found reason not to be moved by it.[245]

Augustine's Bible is doubly hard for us to see. There was no book, no single physical thing to concentrate the attention, and so the separate scriptural books came to him behind a shimmering veil of meaning, something that both separated him from them and pointed the way, if the reader was graced and wise by his lights, beyond words to meanings hinted with delicate indirection. No modern book, emphatically including the things called Bibles and used abundantly for many purposes, has much in common with what Augustine knew and read.

AUGUSTINE THE WRITER

Isidore of Seville, almost two hundred years after Augustine, famously said of him that whoever claims to have read all of Augustine must be a liar, for too much survives for one man to read. Possidius had already anticipated the point:

> There's so much that he dictated and published, so much that he argued in church and had taken down and corrected, so much that he wrote against the heretics, so much he expounded concerning the canonical books for the edification of the holy sons of the church, that scarcely anybody would be able to read through and know all of it.[246]

What neither Possidius nor Augustine ever explains is why he had to write so much.

In the early winter of 419, for example, Augustine was counting up the lines he had written since the preceding fall. The total came to six thousand lines—not a bad sum, and if he was paying his secretaries by the line, it's probably an accurate figure.[247] Augustine was always busy with words. The five million or so we have from him were all written in the last forty-three of his nearly seventy-six years of life, and by far the majority during his thirty-four years as bishop of Hippo. The average is approximately that of a three hundred–page printed book every year for almost forty years. The sheer *cost* of this undertaking must not be ignored: the labor of preparation and transcription, the cost of materials, the further cost of preparing copies for others to read, and all managed in a relatively minor provincial city. In all the Latin world outside government bureaucracy, only Jerome in that age mounted a literary enterprise anywhere near so ambitious and successful. Even if you were an illiterate member of Augustine's congregation, you had to know that this bishop was a man of his books. He constantly reminded you that he would prefer to be in his study reading and writing. The stream of visitors, the busy staff, and the economic impact of the enterprise had to have impressed visitors as much as the content of the books themselves.

Augustine himself rarely had to be bothered with the burdensome material aspects of writing, and he benefited from this greatly. Writing was a messy, fussy manual technique in antiquity, ever concerned with the writing materials (papyrus or parchment, pens, inks), and working at handicraft pace. But the cumbersome technology had given rise to its own forms of mechanization: stenographic scribes. The later Roman empire lived on the paperwork produced by the imperial and ecclesiastical scribes (*notarii*) who could take down a speaker's words at speed and give them back as properly formatted manuscripts. The poet and government minister Ausonius praised a boy who served him in this capacity for his ability to get things right in a "hailstorm" of dictated words. To be supported by such a team was a sign of wealth and influence, and it was the necessary condition for production of text on any ambitious scale.

Whether in his study or in church, Augustine was attended by such scribes. The intimacy and intensity of the *Confessions* almost certainly came about as a performance before an audience of one or two of them. Writing that way does not encourage an author to revise as he writes in the modern way. Rather, he will most likely perform a large body of text, then review it by eye later. (Edward Gibbon tells of writing his *Decline and Fall* paragraph by paragraph. He would compose a paragraph mentally, while walking up and down in his garden perhaps, then, when he had it right, go in and set it down on paper. Augustine may be imagined doing something like that, composing abstractedly while the scribe sat patiently waiting.) At any rate, Augustine's scribes, a reminder of his wealth, explain his hugely productive writing.

His works took widely varying lengths of time to compose, and some hung on for many years. His books *The Trinity, Genesis Taken Literally*, and *City of God* in particular were all composed in fits and starts over as much as twenty years, and show it in the assurance of the material. This practice of Augustine's suggests that for his staff, managing the bishop's library and its works-in-progress was an exacting task. We know none of Augustine's employees by name or character. Like the servants in Jane Austen's novels, they remain invisible, anonymous, and indispensable.

Even in church, Augustine's bravura improvisational riffs on scripture and the issues of the day were captured and recorded for posterity. Every now and then we see the marks of scribal intrusion: a short note, for example, that the bishop asked the lector to read a particular passage aloud. In the case of his sermons revealing and teaching the words of the Apostles' Creed to baptismal candidates, the inserted note reminds us that it was not permitted to write down the text of the creed itself, though we can reconstruct the text from the individual sections Augustine then quotes as he explains the whole. The sermons may or may not have been seriously revised by Augustine himself. We don't know, for example, whether he could look over shorthand and correct it, or whether he took the time to take a first draft, revise it, and then demand a second copy from his staff. Nor do we know whether scribes were always on duty or if (more likely) they were summoned only when Augustine had an inkling that he wanted to retain a particular performance's record. What we have in the sermons is the largest body of oratory surviving from any ancient speaker, representing a record of text much closer to the spoken word than any other. The style of the sermons is more straightforward, more designed for oral impact in its rhythms, than is Augustine's other prose. This is surely a mark of the vivacity and fidelity of the transcripts.

Augustine had been a writer long before he became a cleric. He wrote his first book at Carthage during his Manichee days: *The Beautiful and the Fitting*, philosophy and esthetics in a traditional mode under Manichean influence. It would be a valuable document of cultural history even if, or rather especially if, it had been the only thing to survive from this eccentric African intellectual. (*That* Augustine would always have been spoken of in the same breath as Apuleius.) Augustine tells us he wrote it to impress, dedicating it to a famous rhetorician at Rome. The writing of it is presented to us in the *Confessions* narrative with no reference to Augustine's choice shortly afterward to move to Rome to pursue his career, but the idea of making himself known beyond Carthage was surely part of his ambition for the fame that Augustine would later achieve, using similar tactics, beyond all that he could have dreamed of as a young man. When writing about his first book in the *Confessions*, he reproached himself for his worldly ambition, even as, with the *Confessions*, he was carrying out an ecclesiastical version of the same social climbing.

The other literary products of his rhetorical career in Africa and Italy were speeches, very likely written down and distributed to discerning readers. When we know that he delivered grand public orations in honor of the consul or the emperor at Milan, for example, we should expect that the politesse of the profession and the time assumed that these would be written down, commented on favorably, and handed about as cultural tokens. We have a dozen or so such speeches from the fourth century and they give the best idea what these might have been like: polished, elaborate, exaggerated, allusive to the point of obscurity (for those not in the know), and highly professional.[248]

So when the autumn harvest came in 386 and Augustine gathered up his retinue of family, friends, and students to decamp for a country villa near Milan, it seemed quite natural that there was also a retinue of *notarii* to attend Augustine's professional needs. When Augustine conceived his literary project of that winter—to recreate life at Cicero's villa at Tusculum by staging dialogues with neo-Platonic content in the drawing rooms and on the lawns of the villa—the *notarii* were ready to hand, taking down every word just as it was spoken. Modern readers have wondered at the polish and structure of the dialogues that were produced in those months and have been skeptical about the story of the busy *notarii*, but they misestimate two things: first, the ability of these cultured men to perform the dialogue roles their master set out for them, more or less as actors playing a conscious part in a literary game; and, second, the skill of the *notarii* in preparing whatever rough drafts Augustine eventually worked into the works we now have. The making of the books themselves and their ambitious dedications to well-placed and learned gentlemen of Milan reveal something of the ambitions Augustine still felt in that winter of his conversion.

Somewhere along the line Augustine let his first book, the philosophical one written back at Carthage, slip away from him, preferring to edit it out of his resumé. The books of that Cassiciacum winter, on the other hand, followed Augustine for the rest of his life. In building up his own canon and choosing to begin it with Milan, he makes a statement about his past. Whatever his written works were meant to achieve, they always told as well a story about Augustine. (What is most regrettable, perhaps, about the loss of *The Beautiful and the Fitting* is precisely the self-presentation and the implicit or explicit narrative about Augustine that it would have contained, one that likely wouldn't much match the *Confessions*.)

Back in Tagaste in 388, the retired literary gentleman continued to read and write. His devout Tagaste home surely looked to his contemporaries like a proper gentleman's establishment, through with a rather larger than usual staff of scribes (where others might have employed musicians or huntsmen—or perhaps Augustine had some of those as well). The books he wrote in those years were a mix of neo-Platonic philosophy and anti-Manichean diatribe. The audience for such things must have included old and new acquaintances in Africa, especially in Carthage, where Augustine had been generously lodged and entertained by friends on his return to Africa.

The turning point in Augustine's career as writer was the turning point in his career in other ways: his ordination to the clergy at Hippo. In this unliterary community, a most unusual and literary cleric suddenly appeared. He tells us how his bishop authorized him to establish a monastery in the church grounds, but says nothing of the other investments that must have gone along with this. If the Greek-speaking bishop Valerius had a scribe or two for business purposes, Augustine needed a larger, more professional staff, and this was undoubtedly forthcoming. No one in the African clergy was like him.

From the moment of Augustine's establishment in Hippo, his literary ambitions expanded and intensified. In his time as priest, he undertook new literary projects with a will. The last book of his lay career, the abstract and unsatisfying *The Usefulness of Believing* (*De utilitate credendi*), was succeeded by a vivacious and persuasive tract called *True Religion* (*De vera religione*), one that reads like C. S. Lewis for its *bonhomie*, its polish, and its blithe assumption that all truly cultured men will understand that Christianity is the only religion for them. The sheer snob appeal of such works is often overlooked by their enthusiasts, but it is an important part of their power. That is where Augustine ventilates the opinion that if Plato were alive today, he would easily be persuaded to join the Christians. Surely this was the mark of a true religion, one that *gentlemen* could espouse. . . . Given that Augustine had chosen to associate himself in Africa with a church that appealed to gentlemen, or at least bureaucrats (who liked to think of themselves as gentlemen), the approach was deft.

The Manichees were still on his mind, an idiosyncrasy his new colleagues could tolerate easily, but those were the years of writer's block for him, for the man who would eventually write millions of words. As priest he tried to maintain his old posture as Christian litterateur and in that spirit completed, for example, his dialogue on *Free Choice of the Will*, the theologically unsophisticated piece that would come back to haunt him in later years, or worked on his treatises on the seven liberal arts, part of his Platonic enthusiasms from Milan days, while at the same time trying to undertake new genres of scriptural commentary and homiletics, writing on Genesis (taken quite literally) and the Psalms and Paul and the Sermon on the Mount.

Nothing came quite right in those years. Every literary project ran into trouble. What remained were scrappy and incomplete works, often quite unfinishable. His ecclesiastical role was neither fish nor fowl—no longer quite a free gentleman, but not yet able to claim real authority in the church for what he said. His bishop let him preach in his own presence, but that wasn't quite kosher and there was trouble for it afterwards. Augustine claimed they hadn't known the rules, but that is slightly disingenuous. The sermon as literary product was not yet something he had mastered.[249]

Even after Valerius finally ordained Augustine as his successor and then shortly after passed away, the writer's block persisted. His venture in Ambrosian Ciceronianism, his *Christian Doctrine*, dried up in his hands halfway through the third section and remained unfinished for thirty years. He found it difficult to sustain his voice through such an extended production, especially when thorny issues pricked at every turn. The mechanisms of exegesis he counseled were ones in which he was still nearly a neophyte. Whether there was a cultured clerical audience for Augustine's ideas at all in the mid-390s is also questionable. In more ways than one, Augustine seems to have overestimated the cultural attainments of the church he joined. (Other famous intellectual converts, from John Henry Newman to Ronald Knox and Graham Greene and C. S. Lewis, have had the same experience.)

One writer on his mind in these trying years was his near contemporary, compatriot, and rival Tyconius. He was the most impressive theologian the African church produced before Augustine. If he was indeed a member in good standing of the African church of his time, the late 300s, that would have made him in Augustine's eyes a schismatic. But his theology also put him at variance with his contemporaries in his own sect. Augustine seems to have thought that Tyconius's natural alternative should have been to join the catholic community. In thinking so, Augustine reacted with the self-centeredness with which a Trotskyite of the 1930s would believe that every disaffected Stalinist naturally should join his marginalized group. Augustine's nervousness in the face of this powerful but problematic mind is seen in the letter he wrote to Aurelius of Carthage in 396 or 397, asking insistently, and not for the first time, what Aurelius thought of Tyconius and his "rules of interpretation." We do not know how Tyconius came to his end, but he had faded from the scene by the time Augustine was made bishop. His rules, however, show up quoted more or less verbatim in the section of *Christian Doctrine* added in the late 420s. Was Augustine's dependency on Tyconius the reason he couldn't make the book come together any sooner?

Whatever were the explanations for the writer's block, it finally passed, for after *Christian Doctrine* comes the miracle of the *Confessions*—and it led to an explosion in his literary production that scarcely let up for the rest of his life.[250] The readers (of whom there had been few) of the Cassiciacum dialogues would have found the self-indulgence of this new book familiar, but nothing could have prepared any reader for the white-hot prose, the ingenious adaptation of scriptural texts to a new story made almost scriptural by their resonance, the bold philosophical ambitions, the self-revelation mixed with self-concealment, and the sheer scale of performance to be found in these pages. Even modern readers, indeed especially those who find the exercise the most questionable and its underpinnings the most specious, are compelled to admit the seductive power of the text and its ability to shape a consciousness that would resonate with its concerns. Not again until the Florentine *trecento* or the Romantic moment of Goethe and Wordsworth would there be writers who could unleash a book that so changed the sensibilities and expectations of its readers.

But even that book had its failures. Most of the contemporary readers we know of by name—Secundinus the Manichee, Vincentius Victor the Rogatist, Pelagius, Julian of Eclanum—found the book unpersuasive, even infuriating. They knew the man and didn't buy his story at all, so the intensity and the doctrine all seemed false. Others—Augustine's friend Possidius is the only one we can name, but in his *Reconsiderations* Augustine tells us there were many others—were immediately charmed and moved and changed. Augustine himself was changed.

Interpretation on this point depends somewhat on the conclusions we draw about the writing of the book. Was it, as most scholars assume, a work of long travail, spread out over several years? The conventional chronology assumes four years of composition, or perhaps six years. But Augustine's account of its making does not contain any suggestion of delay or extended composition, and the spirit of the work speaks against it. The book's making, certainly its inception, dates from 397, the year of Augustine's debut in Carthage. When in the tenth book of the *Confessions* he reflected on the temptations to which he was still prey and found that vainglory, arising from the admiration bishops are heir to, to be his greatest pitfall, he was probably thinking of the applause of Carthage as much as of any (surely more modest) praise from his own community at Hippo.

Most importantly, the *Confessions* broke Augustine's writer's block. In the months and years after he began the *Confessions*, a flood of books flowed from his pen, now on a larger scale, and most of them completed ambitiously: *Baptism* against the Donatists, and the huge anti-Manichee work *Against Faustus* (his old teacher) were undertaken and finished in short order. The bigger projects of *The Trinity* and *Genesis Taken Literally* both have roots in the closing books of the *Confessions*, and though both took many years, they were begun in the early 400s and eventually brought to successful conclusions. A flood of other texts followed, large and small.

Yet the 400s were not Augustine's most successful literary period. He wrote many works, few if any of which would be recognized by more than a handful of modern readers. Augustine's concerns in that decade were centered on his fight with the Donatists, the rival faction of African Christians he had chosen to demonize, and the books of that venture are of little interest today. In these years Augustine passed his fiftieth birthday in provincial obscurity, known to a few Christian intellectuals abroad, but with a variable reputation at home.

The years following 410 transformed Augustine into an international figure, and we will watch closely how the *annus mirabilis* of 411 brought him success (and notoriety) in his fight against the Donatists, and at the same time risky new battles with Pelagians. The next decade saw the completion of *The Trinity* and *Genesis Taken Literally*, the undertaking and half-completion of *City of God*, the completion of the long series of sermons on the Psalms that we know as *Enarrationes Psalmos*, and a torrent of pamphlets and polemical works against both Donatists (in the wake of the Conference of Carthage) and Pelagians. The latter campaign succeeded (or seemed to) when the African church obtained decisive condemnations of Pelagianism from two popes and an emperor, but Augustine engaged ferociously in rearguard battles for the rest of his life. The *Reconsiderations* in the 420s that gave his reputation weight and staying power came from a period of retrospection in Augustine's life rather than of fresh achievement.

Who read him? The people we know who read him were people like his younger and older selves, the Christian intellectual upper class, both clerical and lay. The hundreds of bishops who flocked to conferences probably included few who had the money to acquire or the time to meditate on the bishop's lengthy productions. Some of his books, such as the short *Christian Combat*, attempted to speak down to a broader audience, but we can wonder whether his *Genesis: Against the Manichees* really answered the pleas reported in its opening paragraph from those who thought that Augustine's earlier writings against the Manichees had been too difficult for their readership.[251] Short of actual reading, there was listening, and we have odd fragments to suggest that a fair amount of listening went on. On one occasion, for example, the painfully tedious book 18 of *City of God* was read aloud (at Carthage?) on three consecutive afternoons.[252] We see cases where books are copied and sent around to Augustine's highly placed literary friends, but we are much less well informed about the readership closer to home. In numbers, though, they will be (to a modern eye) surprisingly few: few because of the difficulty and cost of getting books, few because of the level of education they demanded, few because of the infrequency with which wealth, leisure, and religious inclinations found themselves looking for so much reading material. His real audience found him after he was dead.

NOT EVERY READER IS A GREAT READER

The gentleman Consentius, living in intellectual isolation (as he tells it) on his native island of Minorca, was an early reader of Augustine's *Confessions*. His reactions are instructive:

> About a dozen years ago, I went out and bought your *Confessions* and a number of your other works, not out of a good and praiseworthy zeal for your teaching, but just out of my damned lust for having them. Weighed down by my incredible sloth, I've kept them sealed up to this day. Just now I tried to read a few things there. I was struggling to understand some things and found them very finely discussed there. When I saw that the things I was thinking were laid out just like in a picture, I began

to realize that when it came to the rest of the things I want to know, it's
not the teacher that's lacking for me, it's the student that's lacking in me.
To tell the truth in the sight of the master at last, it was four years ago—
that is to say, before I started trying to get to know your holiness—that
I read no more than two or three pages of the first book of the *Confessions*. In your paternal way you like to compare the minds of the empty-
headed to eyes that are bleary and unseeing: that fit me perfectly.
Repelled by the painful splendor of what you had to say, because I encountered nothing there of the soft and gentle kind that would soothe
my damaged eyes, I gave up and went rushing right back to my usual ignorance and darkness and I avoided your books—not just the *Confessions*
but all of them, more carefully than I avoid a viper's poison.[253]

He goes on at length to talk of himself as a student of the commentators on scripture, and he has already learned to look beyond the substance
of what they say to their future fame.

Let us go over in succession all the commentators, the great ones, the
catholic ones! But it's hard not to note some spots of error even in the
fairest of them. For even if we say that bishop Augustine writes impeccable things, we still don't know what posterity will say about his books.
Not every perverse heretic writer—think especially of Origen!—was
condemned while he was still alive, but now, two hundred years and
more later, it's clear that he *is* to be condemned.

Consentius, postmodern before his time, reveals to us what he himself is
unaware of, that the cult of authority invariably carries with it suspicion
of the same authority.

Consentius is in other ways a good example of what Augustine was up
against in promulgating his ideas. The two fell into correspondence because Consentius wanted advice about lying—that is, wanted to be told
that it was all right to lie for a good cause. Augustine tried six ways from
Sunday to tell Consentius that it is never all right to lie (Augustine's position was firm on this point[254]), but we are indebted to Consentius for
what is in many ways the funniest story (Evelyn Waugh before his time)
of late-antique Christian heresy-hunting. In a letter to Augustine, Consentius tells of sending an orthodox spy from Minorca to the mainland of
Spain to infiltrate the "Priscillianists" there.[255] The spy is about as successful as one would expect a half-trained FBI agent to be on attempting

to infiltrate a communist cell in Ogallala, Nebraska, in the 1950s, when the "cell" turned out to be three local schoolteachers and a librarian who enjoyed sharing copies of the *New Republic* and talking about them at coffee hour after church on Sunday. Every appearance of success is reported back to headquarters, but we have to doubt whether the object of the infiltration is what the secret agent thinks it is. When the matter finally comes into the open, Consentius is dismayed that the Spanish bishops who take up the matter are far less seriously moved than he thinks they ought to be, and his indignation is marked throughout his long letter to Augustine. The story is funny and maddening and relevant here only as a marker of the pastoral difficulty Augustine faced as author and letter writer. None of Augustine's several interventions and none of his books made the slightest positive impression on his great fan Consentius.

VI

AUGUSTINE
IN PUBLIC

Augustine's background and upbringing had prepared him for the public life of a late Roman gentleman. He lived up to the type in most respects. Without a sustained day-to-day portrait of his life, we make do with the glimpses we get from scattered moments in his career.

AUGUSTINE IN CHURCH

Augustine's public life took many forms. We know best the part that he played out in the written word, but what he was and did in church was the real Augustine to the people who knew him face-to-face. And even as we grasp for a sense of what that Augustine was like, we are cut off from a vital part of his experience. What we know of his time inside the walls of the church with his congregation is mainly limited to the texts of the sermons he gave. These are marvelous documents, rich in vignettes of the confrontations, tensions, and opportunities that filled the air between him and the people for whom he was responsible. But precept and practice of the time enjoined reticence. Sermons were delivered to a broad audience, the faithful as well as the hangers-on and the curious, and "pagans" and

Jews for that matter, any of whom might, though more likely not, eventually be baptized. But there came a point at which all except the baptized faithful were expelled from the building, the doors were closed, and the eucharistic liturgy was performed.[256] That may be part, but probably isn't all, of the explanation for Augustine's seeming inattention to the details of liturgy. He has little else to say about the material church: he does not speak of church ornament, he did little building or renovation or ornamentation that we know of, he is not a connoisseur of church music, and he inculcates little such taste. His Donatist rivals, by contrast, preferred a livelier, more musical service.[257]

The hinge of the church year was Easter (Christmas was only gradually emerging as a feast in Augustine's time), and the hinge of the week was Sunday. While Augustine would often be away for many Sundays, as his business and ambitions took him to Carthage and elsewhere, he always tried to be in Hippo for Easter.

He had a high opinion of the ritual, without giving an absolutely unambiguous statement on the side of either real or symbolic presence of Jesus in the bread and wine. Later centuries of debate would try to invoke him as authority for one position or another, but the issue had not been raised and forced in those terms in his time, and so he used language that can be taken sometimes either way.[258] But whatever the language, the bishop in his church performed Christian doctrine in word (sermon) and deed (bread) for the assembled congregation.

To get into church and stay there could be an anxious business. Twenty-five years after his baptism, Augustine would ask rhetorically, "Are we so out of touch with our feelings as not to remember how conscientiously and with what anxiety we heard those who taught us the catechism laid down for us, when we begged the sacraments of that fount of life?"[259] Different people came to that moment in different ways, from children as young as seven (the age of truth-telling[260]), or visitors of varying motives and different degrees of seriousness.[261] It could be hard to make the final step of public profession of faith. Augustine told the story in the *Confessions* of Marius Victorinus's reluctance and how it was overcome,[262] with every implication that he had felt the same diffidence. A more dramatic story from Hippo tells of a man who promised to be baptized if his daughter recovered from illness. She did, but still he procrastinated. Suddenly he was struck blind and promised to be baptized if he recovered his sight. His vision recovered, but still he procrastinated. Then he was struck down by paralysis and could not speak or walk. Admonished in a dream, he awoke and wrote down his acknowledgment that he had been punished for not making his profession of faith. With that he recovered movement but not speech, and so finally he made the profession itself in writing. We do not know if he recovered his power of speech.[263]

Sometimes—we don't know how often and surmise it was infrequent—a member of the community would be banned from communion for grave and open sin. For them there was prescribed special dress and a curious form of exile. They were expected to be at church, outside the door, but their exclusion was calculated to solidify the identity and commitment of those still inside. The banishing bishop, who would embrace the penitent again weeks or months later, had the power to exclude not only from church, but from paradise.

BRINGING IN THE SHEAVES

The text read one Sunday in Augustine's church was Psalm 126 (5–6), "They that sow in tears shall reap rejoicing. Going out they went and wept, scattering their seed. But when they return they shall come in exultation, bringing in the sheaves." Augustine took up the theme:

> They go as they go and they weep as they sow. Why are they weeping? Because they are in the midst of unhappy people and they are themselves unhappy. It is better, my brothers, that no one be unhappy than for us to have to show pity. If somebody wished for others to be unhappy so that he could show pity on them, it would be a cruel pity—like a doctor wanting there to be a lot of sick people so he could practice his skill—that would be a cruel medicine. Better everyone should be healthy than that the doctor's art have to prove itself. So it is better that all men, blessed, should reign in that homeland of ours than that there should be people in need of pity. But for as long as there are those to whom to give it, then we should not fail to sow the seeds of happiness in this troubled world. Even if we weep ourselves while we sow, we will in the end reap the harvest with joy. Each man at the resurrection of the dead will receive his sheaves of grain, that is, the fruit of this sowing, the crown of joy and exultation. Then there will be a triumph in rejoicing and an exulting over death.
>
> But why say rejoice? Because they are bringing in the sheaves. Because they went as they wept and they wept as they sowed. And why say wept as they sowed? Because those who sow in tears will reap rejoicing.[264]

The urban audience thinks of its future happiness in the contingent and unsure image of a successful harvest, where some seeds, some fields, and some seasons will be lost.

NO PARTIES, PLEASE, WE'RE CHRISTIAN!

Not long after becoming bishop, in his *Confessions*, Augustine made a point of telling a story about his mother's religious practices. When she had lived in Africa, good Christian that she was, she would from time to time go out to the Christian burying grounds and participate in the rituals of eating and drinking that went on there in honor of the blessed dead.[265] But when she came to Italy, she found that the austere Bishop Ambrose forbade such things, and people showing up at the graveyards with their picnic hampers were turned away. Augustine praised his mother's willingness to take Ambrose's direction in this matter and pitched the matter as a difference of custom between Africa and Italy. The custom was known in Italy as well, and it was the authority of the high-minded bishop that marked a difference. When Augustine returned to Africa, he found the practice widespread and sniffed at it again as "pagan,"[266] though he had to notice that it was widespread among Christians of the Donatist community.

When Augustine found himself some years later in Hippo as priest of the Caecilianist church, his first most visible public engagement came when he set out, in tandem with his friend Aurelius, the newly ordained bishop of Carthage, to emulate his spiritual father Ambrose in uprooting at Hippo pious practices like those of his mother. It was a daring assertion of authority, but he carried it off (more or less), and it was the making of him in Hippo.

The story of Augustine's victory is told in a letter from Augustine to Alypius in 395, when Alypius was already bishop of Tagaste.[267] It began with an uproar in church.

Augustine had banned the *laetitiae*, the "festivities," that were to be held on the occasion of the annual feast of Bishop Leontius, Hippo's martyr bishop of many years earlier (about whom we know nothing reliable). Augustine thought the celebrants were trying to hide their lust for wine under a pious premise. But as the service began that Thursday—we have to imagine a world where a clergyman going into church could find himself face-to-face with a restive crowd far from ready for pious abstraction—Augustine saw his opportunity in the gospel passage for the day:

"Do not give what is holy to the dogs and cast not your pearls before swine" (Matthew 7.6). Augustine made a meal of the text, so to speak, looking to shame his audience into docility and modesty.

Then as now, Thursday services were always underattended. Nonetheless, the sermon was reported abroad, feelings were heightened, and a few days later, on the first day of the Lenten season, a large crowd was present for the sermon on the cleansing of the temple scene in the gospels. The master, Augustine said, would be all the *more* offended by scenes of revelry than he was by Jerusalem commerce. The Jews never had even sober banqueting in their temple, much less wine. Augustine told a story of an episode in Exodus where drunkenness led to idolatry. Gesturing for the codex, he read out the whole passage. He went on to rail a bit longer against drunkenness, taking up this time the text of Paul to make his point, first from one chapter, then from another. By then he had juggled three different books in front of his congregation, reading aloud to make his points.

Now, people who enjoy large, convivial celebrations lightened by alcohol may very often abuse the substance, but rarely are they willing to admit it. One man's drunken orgy is another man's happy hour. Augustine recounts his sermon-making with careful zest, but we can't see or hear the audience yet. The readings went on.

Then a curiously personal turn: he commanded them to think of their god, to think of Christ's suffering, and to think of him, drawn to preach to them. He tells how Bishop Valerius (somewhere discreetly offstage) had often said to them that his prayers had been answered with the coming of Augustine to Hippo. He asseverates his certainty that divine punishment will be visited on them if they do not reform, and so he concludes, *in tears*, though the congregation remained dry-eyed.

The next day the murmuring went on, even among those who had heard the sermon and seen (if not shared in) the tears: "Why now? The people before who didn't prohibit these things, they were Christians."

Augustine imagined his next moves: he could tear off and throw down his clerical garb and stomp out. But before the hour of the church service at which he meditated this dramatic move, a delegation came to see him. Peace was quickly made, and at the appropriate time the sermon was kept short: "Why not now?" he asked. He went on to say a little in explanation of how the history had come about. He gives birth here to a version of a self-serving story that was familiar in church histories even to our own time: how the wave of non-Christians who came into the church after the age of persecutions missed their feast days, and so it seemed wise to the elders of those days to spare their weakness yet a little while and to turn the feast days into days in honor of the martyrs, retaining the celebration but sanctifying the goal. Now it's time, he went on, to begin to live the true Christian life. He added the example of the churches across the water, some of which had never gone this way, some of which had changed their ways. When he was reminded that in the basilica of Peter in Rome, daily drunkenness was only too familiar, Augustine had excuses: the basilica was outside the city walls of Rome, far from the bishop's residence, and thronged with tourists hard to control, and he added a few pious words read from the first letter of Peter to rebuke drunkenness and other sins of the flesh.

The next day again, a still larger crowd gathered, with readings and psalms in the morning until the hour when he and Bishop Valerius left the church. Valerius made Augustine say a few more words, which he did rather relucantly, as one who would rather leave sleeping dogs lie. Up the street, the "basilica of the heretics" (that is, the Donatist church) was resounding with the customary celebrations—they were already in their cups—and Augustine made hay of the comparison. (He shows no ear or sense for those in his crowd who may have been thinking of drifting away to that livelier community.) The day passed quietly and there came time to say vespers, Augustine and Valerius together, with a crowd abiding and singing psalms till it was dark.

And so the story is told as a success, and Augustine had made his authority stick.[268] A year or so after the crisis, he was ordained bishop. The *dignity* of the Christian religion, always important to him, had been restored. Augustine regularly marked as "pagan" religious practices that he deplored, and did so of the conviviality of Christians.[269] "Pagan," then, is sometimes a label Augustine applies to Christian religious practices he deplores as insufficiently spiritual and transformed.

Augustine shows no sense of irony in ending the letter with a story of Donatist thugs he called "circumcellions" invading a church and destroying the altar in the town of Hasna. Those shock troops of the majority church (we'll see them again) had their own sense of the purity of religious observances, one that ran quite counter to Augustine's.

SURROUNDED BY DEMONS

Everywhere Augustine went, demons and angels hovered almost within reach.

One day in the holy days of the week after Easter, when many lay Christian brothers came to see me and we had sat down in the usual place, the conversation turned to the position Christian religion takes against the presumptuous and supposedly great and wonderful learning of the pagans. I decided to write down and expand in letters what we said. . . . Since we were talking about demons and their powers of divination, it was said that someone had predicted the overthrow of the temple of Serapis at Alexandria. I said it was no wonder if demons both knew and predicted that ruin was awaiting this temple and its image, since there are lots of things they were allowed to know and foretell.

The demons, for Augustine, were really the fallen angels of scripture, creatures who retained much of their innate power, despite their having turned to evil. In pre-Christian times, they had used their strength to amaze the gullible and so had passed themselves off as gods, the very gods of the "pagans." Now, revealed for what they were, banished from their temples, deprived of the worship of their victims, they lingered in the world, seething and seditious, looking for opportunities for petty victories and petty amazement.

Augustine is mainly consistent about the powers of demons throughout his career. The magicians of Pharaoh with whom Moses competed (Exodus 7) were a scandal to some of his flock, and he needed to explain that they derived their power from their illicit commerce with the demons. Passages like these still loomed large in the first great anthology of Augustine's writings, the *Excerpts from Augustine*, compiled by the Italian monk Eugippius, working from a good library outside Naples in the mid-sixth century. The number and arrangement of extracts on these topics in his collection suggests that the question was still a lively one for his readers, and if we read the *Dialogues* attributed to Pope Gregory I and likely written later in the sixth century, we see a world in which demons are at large and powerful. Perhaps most telling, though, is a tiny prescription in an early sixth-century monastic text called the *Rule of the Master*, from which the author of the *Rule of Benedict* took much of what he said. The "Master" includes among his prescriptions this one: "Someone who is praying and wishes to spit or blow his nose should point himself not forwards but back, on account of the angels standing before him."[270] Such vivid perception of the presence of spirit beings makes more sense of the old passage in the Roman liturgy, immediately after the consecration of the elements, where the priest prays that the angel of god will take the sacrificial elements to the holy throne above—no hard thing if the angels were standing right there. Augustine himself wasn't sure but that the sun and moon were visible angels, but he took little interest in the question: not relevant to human life and so better left uninvestigated.[271]

Though he later changed his mind, at one time Augustine believed that demons could insert their ethereal bodies into the body of a human being and thereby present lively pictures to the imagination.[272] That belief came about as part of a larger puzzlement he felt all his life about dreams and their workings. He could not resist the idea that some dreams were truth-telling, but he could not explain them to his satisfaction, and then he bogged down in worrying about moral responsibility in dreams. Did sexual dreams signify that "consent" had been given to acts that the waking mind would not agree to? Did that consent carry guilt? He answers in the negative, but just needing to ask the question is significant.[273] The mystic powers of the world were more numerous and more alarming than we might expect a monotheistic universe to contain, and that was true for all early monotheisms. That a hell and a heaven would lie beyond and above the world of the visible was quite unsurprising to such early believers, for whom the everyday city street held hidden perils quite unfamiliar to us.

But Augustine was a moderate in his time and place. A gentleman named Publicola (whom some scholars think to be a very wealthy gentleman indeed, the father of the Melanie the younger we will meet later) wrote to him, probably in the late 390s, a letter full of fears.[274] Barbarians on the frontier well south of Carthage came and negotiated with Roman officers there and swore by their own gods—demons, in Publicola's and Augustine's eyes—to make and keep the peace. But Publicola fretted— could a Christian benefit from such a defiled oath? Publicola went round and round that issue, asking related questions in half a dozen ways, enough to make us think that it was just that frontier-life confrontation with demons that had distressed him. He went on, once worked up, to ask another set of increasingly improbable, scruple-driven questions. *What if I'm traveling*, he wonders, *and will perish of thirst unless I drink from a fountain in a temple of demons? What if someone, barbarian or Roman, is going to kill me—may I kill in self-defense?* On the last point, Augustine was cautious, offering his consent most readily if the defender is a soldier, killing not on his own behalf but for others, and in this we see the muddled moderation that led to his acceptance of the notion of "just war." But on the superstitious points, Augustine was sturdy and unanxious. The Christian is not defiled by what others do, but by what he does himself. This position is *strictly* inconsistent with belief in the power of demons, for then their words and food and drink and shrines really would be polluted and dangerous. Without coming explicitly to the point, Augustine seemed to be saying that the power of the Christian god so far outran that of the demons that a blithe disdain could accompany the truly faithful and confident Christian in an ambiguous world.

THE BISHOP UTTERS A HARD SAYING

Here is a fragment in Augustine's voice newly heard just in the 1990s, a short sermon he gave as visiting preacher in another bishop's pulpit somewhere in Africa. A wealthy and well-regarded man had died, a Christian who had not been baptized, a candidate member of the community. This fourth-century practice of postponing baptism often gave rise to whispers, as we have seen, that it was for people who would wait until the last minute after a lifetime of sin and peccadillo in order to get washed in the blood of the lamb just in time for it to do some good.

This man miscalculated and died suddenly, but his family wanted him buried in the church. Augustine took it on himself to say, hard and straight, that it couldn't happen. He was adamant that the man's wealth shouldn't get him favors. He defended a tough doctrine, and he was uncompromising: die unbaptized and you are *really* dead. Take that, he says to the unbaptized in the church, as a warning. Get right with the master now, or run the risk of eternal damnation. The sermon is short, and not sweet.[275]

> Our master, your father and brother [the bishop where Augustine was visiting], asks that I say a few words in your holy presence about the burying of catechumens. It's really his concern, but in the divine love through which we speak we share all things with you so we can be sharers of Christ. Grief happens and anger is forgivable sometimes. Who doesn't forgive somebody who is grieving and upset if he says something angry? But you all have to know, dearest, what many of you—almost all of you—know, that according to the rules and practice of the church, the bodies of deceased catechumens shouldn't be and can't be permitted by anyone to be buried among the bodies of the faithful, where the sacraments of the faithful are celebrated. To do otherwise would be a reprehensible "accepting of persons."[276] For why should we grant this to the

rich and not the poor, if there's solace for the dead there? But the merits of the dead are looked for not in the places you find their bodies but in the disposition of their souls. My brothers, learn to think about these things as faithful Christians. For the sake of the sacraments, bodies cannot be placed where they don't belong.

We lament and grieve that this particular man, this catechumen, has passed away. And so we encourage you, brothers, to think that no one of us is certain that he will be alive tomorrow. Run to grace, change your ways: let this be a caution for you. Who was healthier than he was? Who was sturdier of body? Suddenly he's dead. He was healthy, now he's gone, and would that he were only gone and not truly dead. What am I going to say, brothers? Shall I be soft-hearted and say that catechumens go where the faithful go? Should we go so far in deferring to the griefs of men that we argue against the gospel? We can't, my brothers. We must run while we are alive, so we won't be mourned for when we are really and truly dead. If we took vigorous action for the sacraments for the living, as much as we worry about the graves of the dead, no one in his right mind would weep: because if he did, it would be a carnal feeling that was coming out. We shouldn't weep for the one who has won better things, left behind the temptations of the world, slipped free of anxiety, secure in Christ, not fearing the devil as adversary, not shying from a man who might curse him.

Maybe that Lazarus in the gospel wasn't really buried, when the dogs licked his wounds: for god didn't talk about his burial. It was only said of him that when he died, he was taken to the bosom of Abraham. It wasn't said that he was buried. The man who was condemned for his hunger when he was alive, perhaps when he died he was cast out unburied. And nevertheless he was taken up by angels to the bosom of Abraham. "He died," it says, "but the rich man was also buried." [Luke 16.22] What did it profit his soul in the underworld to have a marbled sepulchre, thirsting for a drop from a fingertip and not getting it? I don't want to say more, my brothers: it's enough to frighten you this much, to keep from adding to the grief of some of our brothers who are shaken by this event. For we shouldn't have to say these things, but we are forced to encourage and admonish you.

Think about human fragility, my brothers: run while you are alive, so you can live. Run while you are alive so you won't really die. Don't fear the discipline of Christ. He cries out, "My yoke is easy and my burden is light," in the very chapter we were talking about a little while ago: "Learn from me that I am gentle and humble at heart, for my yoke is gentle and my burden is light." [Matthew 11.30] And you come back and say, "I don't want to be faithful yet"?[277] "I can't"? What's this "I can't," unless Christ's yoke is rough and his burden heavy? So your flesh is telling you the truth and Christ is lying? He says, "It's gentle," and your vanity says, "It's rough." He says, "It's light," and your vanity says, "It's heavy." Trust Christ instead, because it's his yoke that's gentle and his burden that's light. Don't tremble, give it your unfearing neck. The yoke will be gentle to your neck the more faithful your neck can be. So, brothers, know that we've said and admonished these things to your charity for two reasons: so no one will ask for this and be sad if they don't get it, and so each of you, O catechumens, while you are alive, shall watch out so you don't perish in real death and leave you and mother church unable to provide you this help, however much it is.

THE BISHOP TRIES TO OFFER COMFORT

On other days, the bishop meant to be far more forthcoming and comforting. Here is one of those days, probably in 406 or 407, delivering one of the ten sermons he gave on the brief and uplifting first epistle of John.[278] The "love" of which he speaks here comes to his hearers in the Latin word *caritas*, a word particularly common among Christian writers, particularly common in translating scripture, with somewhat less erotic overtone than the customary Latin *amor*. One could equally well, and equally misleadingly, translate *caritas* as "charity" or "affection."

> "There is no such thing as fear in love, but perfect love casts out fear."
> [1 John 4.17] But there's another text, one that seems to contradict this
> one if you don't understand it carefully. It's in a Psalm: "The fear of the
> master is pure, abiding forever and ever." [Psalms 18.10]

The problem Augustine sets for himself is a false one. That the apostle and the psalmist should say things that are at variance with one another is scarcely surprising, but once Christianity insisted on pulling many diverse texts together into one body of scripture and then on arguing that every text of scripture is in agreement with every other text, an endless supply of such contradictions presented themselves.

> He's showing us a fear that lasts forever, but it's pure. But if there's a fear
> that lasts forever, isn't that contradicted by this epistle that says, "There

is no such thing as fear in love, but perfect love casts out fear"? Let's put the question to these two oracles of god. There is one spirit, even if there are two books, two voices, two tongues. The one was said by John, the other by David: but don't think that the spirit is different in either case. If one breath fills two flutes, can't one spirit fill two hearts or arouse two tongues? And if two flutes that share one spirit, one breath, are still in harmony, do you think that two tongues moved by the spirit of god can be out of tune with each other? There's a harmony there, there's agreement there, but it needs a canny listener.

So the spirit of god inspired and filled two hearts and two mouths and moved two tongues to speak. And we heard from one of them, "There is no such thing as fear in love, but perfect love casts out fear," and from the other, "The fear of the master is pure, abiding forever and ever." So what's this? Are they clashing with each other? No: clean your ears out and pay attention to the melody. It's no accident the one adds "pure"[279] and the other doesn't, because there's one fear we call "pure" and another we don't. If we can distinguish those two kinds of fear, we'll understand the harmony of the flutes here. How can we do that? Please listen to me in all your *caritas*.

There are people who fear god so they won't be sent to hell, so they won't burn with the devil in eternal fire. That's the fear that brings us love: and love comes so that fear goes. For if you still love god because of the penalties he threatens, you aren't really loving the one you're really still afraid of. You're not longing for what's good, you're trying to avoid what's bad. But when you fear what's bad, you change your ways and you begin to long for what's good. When you do that, you will have pure fear within you. What is that pure fear? Fear of losing the good itself. Listen: it's one thing to fear god so he won't send you to hell with the devil, and another thing to be afraid that god will go away from you. The fear of being sent to hell—that's not a pure fear. It doesn't come from the love of god but from the fear of punishment. But when you are afraid that god may abandon you, you're really embracing him, you're longing to enjoy him fully.

The best way I can explain how these fears are different, the one that love casts out and the other that abides in its purity forever and ever, is to think of two married women. One of them is thinking about having an adulterous affair and she takes pleasure in that wickedness, but she's afraid she'll be condemned by her husband. She's afraid of her husband, but she fears him because she still loves her wickedness. For her, the presence of her husband isn't pleasing but bothersome; and if she lives wickedly, she's afraid her husband will come along and catch her. That's what people are like who fear the day of judgment. Now think of another woman who loves her husband, pays him the pure embraces she owes, and stains herself with no adulterous filth: she hopes for the presence of her husband. And how are these two fears different? The first one is afraid, and so is the second. So ask them, go ahead: ask the first one if she's afraid of her husband, and she'll say she is. Ask the other if she's afraid of her husband, and she'll say she is. One expression, different ideas. Ask them why they're afraid, and the one says, I'm afraid he'll come home, and the other says, I'm afraid he'll go away. The one says, I'm afraid I'll get in trouble, and the other says, I'm afraid I'll be left alone.

So transfer this to the way Christians think and you'll find the fear that love banishes, and the other fear that abides in its purity forever and ever.

Finely done, so far, and an illuminating point. The underlying sexism is native to Augustine's time, for the good wife's fear that her husband will abandon her is implicitly the fear that *she* will be found unworthy. God might indeed abandon the Christian soul, not out of divine irresponsibility or infidelity, but in response to the error of the wifelike soul. Augustine does not know how to transcend that limit, but he can end this section of the homily in a way that still charms and reassures, perhaps more by form than by substance:

So that's it: we're heard the two flutes singing as one. The one speaks of fear, the other speaks of fear, but the one speaks of the fear of a soul that wants to avoid damnation, and the other of a soul that fears to be abandoned. The first fear is driven away by love, but the other abides forever and ever.

The undercurrent of anxiety, the anxiety that shadows every hope, cannot be missed.

KEEPING THE FLOCK IN LINE

A letter to a grieving girl gives us a snapshot of Augustine at work. She has lost a brother to death and is inconsolable, but she has sent Bishop

Augustine the cloak that she had woven for her brother with her own hands and that he used to wear. "I'm putting it on to wear as I sit down to write to you," replies Augustine,[280] "for whatever solace it may bring." The lived experience of a bishop in an African city in late antiquity brought him in contact with the diversity of human fates and wishes and left him many choices how to play his role. Augustine is such a virtuoso performer that the focus always zooms in on him, but we should pull it back to see him among his flock if we are to see him clearly. His touch was characteristic in the small things as well as the large. A sermon on swearing reveals him to have hesitated long whether to take up the theme at all, for fear of making people feel worse without being able to amend their bad habit, but Augustine is sure that they can break the habit in just three days and he has the method for them.[281]

He was quite sure he knew what his job was:

—to chastise troublemakers, to comfort the faint of heart, to welcome the ailing, to refute those who argue, to watch out for the treacherous, to teach the ignorant, to arouse the passive ones, to calm down the boisterous ones, to rein in the arrogant, to pacify the quarrelsome, to set free the downtrodden, to support the good, to endure the evil, and to love everybody.[282]

That pastoral Augustine is hard to see unless we read his sermons with great patience. The role deserves some attention, for in its mix of the educational and the authoritative and in its vocabulary, it represents a reinvention of fatherhood. A similar transformation of role was making the teachers of late antiquity similar figures of prominence.[283] But fathers in the natural state very often don't teach very well. More successful, in late antiquity and after, are figures of Augustine's sort, carrying displaced fatherly authority. Christianity had the effect in this world of creating social roles that went beyond the ordinary familial and local ones, not only liberating bearers of those roles from the tyranny of the home town but in other ways liberating church members from some at least of the tyranny and isolation of the family. Protestantism, it has been argued, reconnected fatherly and religious authority in early modern times and makes this late-antique relocation of paternity seem anomalous to us.[284]

The congregation grew dependent on Augustine in more ways than one. When he had been away at Carthage for a long time, he had apologies to make, and sometimes the people seemed more fractious and less malleable on his return.[285] On one occasion, he wrote home to the congregation in some embarrassment.[286] Some time before, a man named Fascius had taken refuge in church to evade the bill collector. When the bill collector complained, Augustine offered to take up a collection, but Fascius refused the charity. So Augustine borrowed seventeen *solidi* from a layman named Macedonius and gave it to Fascius with the understanding that if Fascius defaulted, Augustine would tell the story publicly. Fascius had now, no surprise, moved and left no forwarding address, so Augustine had to write home to the congregation to take up that collection. We don't know how that idea went over.[287]

On at least some days, Augustine had few illusions about what the congregation, or at least some of them, thought of their clergy. "Sometimes you see people coming out of the theater or the amphitheater in a disgraceful mob, their heads still full of the images they've seen there, remembering all the things there that weren't just useless but downright pernicious but rejoicing in it all as if it was pure and sweet. They will come across servants of god and recognize them by their dress or their haircut, or will just see ones they know, and they'll say to themselves and each other, 'Oh, those poor guys—think what they're missing!' "[288]

But there was plenty of devotion on the streets and in the churches. The people Augustine knew and lived with prayed often with sighs and tears. Some would develop calluses on their knees from their kneeling. They banged their foreheads on the ground in prayer and went about disheveled. A poor man went to a martyr shrine to pray for the money to buy a cloak, making a sufficient spectacle of himself that boys in the street came laughing after him, but they stopped when the man found a huge fish beached on the shore and took it to a market and sold it for enough to buy some wool. (The story goes on to say that the cook found a gold ring in the fish.)[289]

Sometimes Augustine's sermons went over well, sometimes they didn't. On one occasion, when he had preached rather longer about a psalm than he had expected to, he was astonished by the enthusiasm the crowd still showed as he moved the end. "Oh, I know I've gone on a long time," he exclaims (I think we must imagine him shouting over the din), "but I can't satisfy you! You're just too much! I wish you were as enthusiastic about going to heaven!"[290]

On other occasions, the crowd was harder to win over. He took up the challenge one day of bearding his congregation about the current local scandal. An abusive government official had been summarily taken out and lynched. Augustine pleaded with his flock, giving signs of his strength and weakness at the same time. After all, he said, many houses in Hippo can be found where there are no "pagans" any longer, but none where there are no Christians, and none where the Christians don't outnumber the "pagans." He was trying to send his congregation home to play the good Roman part, reining in children, friends, servants, and clients, to give over violent behavior. Right there we see the boundary of his power, for he needed to make this appeal even to the core of his Christian congregation, and what he had to ask of them was that they impose traditional paternal authority in their households.[291]

He found one other boundary to his authority, which was always shifting, when he ran up against competing ideas of how to organize a Christian community. At every period, the will of the pulpit to impose a standard model has crossed the enthusiasm of those who know better, somehow or other. One letter shows him responding to a priest who had the latest fashionable book from Rome, written by someone named Urbicus, who insisted on strict fasting on the sabbath (as a way of distinguishing Christians from Jews more clearly). Coming early in Augustine's career, his reply demonstrates moderation by opposing such austerities at about the same time when he was himself attempting to get the congregation to give up what he sees as their "pagan" excesses in the *laetitiae*.[292] But other excesses of devotion abounded. To another bishop he responded with advice on how to handle parents who have had their infants baptized *and* put through purification rituals of other kinds, the better to keep away *all* the evil spirits. One such child came back from the alien ritual and was given Christian communion . . . and spat it out.[293] And then there were snobs, like Hilarus, the high-ranking layman at Carthage who could not get used to the new custom of singing songs at certain points in the liturgy.[294] Augustine wrote a pamphlet explaining the new custom and trying to calm him down. His congregants were neither unbelievers nor half-Christians. They had plenty of belief, but also a strong desire to make sure that no reasonable prospect of spiritual protection slipped past them.

The extreme, perhaps, of such aberration (from Augustine's point of view) was found in the congregation of the Abeloites, who lived in a farming community not far from Hippo.[295] In Augustine's time, they were down to a tiny group in one place. The name is Punic in form but comes (some say) from the name of Abel, son of Adam. Their distinctive contribution, anticipating the Shakers, was that they did not engage in sexual intercourse at all. Men and women lived together as couples in perfect continence, each adopting one boy and one girl in order to have a succession. The poor of neighboring communities knew they could give up unwanted children to the Abeloites and assure them a prosperous future by doing so.

The excesses of late-antique life were with him in other ways as well. The rich had their elegant funerals, whatever their mortal lives were like: fine tomb, expensive funeral garments, the most expensive perfumes, a mighty marble monument above their bones.[296] Augustine speaks of such things in order to chasten, but his congregation was skeptical when, on one occasion, he introduced to them an elderly banker of shady reputation who suddenly wished to become a Christian. The congregation suspected ulterior motives, beyond merely a yen for heaven: "It's not public office I want," he had to exclaim, to general disbelief.[297] But Augustine was glad to have him. A younger bishop, Auxilius, was tougher with the wealthy, and excommunicated a wealthy man and his whole household. Augustine reproved him and encouraged him to find a more moderate path.[298]

KEEPING THE SHEPHERDS IN LINE

Christianity began without a formal clergy but ended by having a group of dedicated male individuals sharply distinguished from ordinary society. Gradually those distinctions were supported and then enforced by church and civil law. The boundary was not always an easy one to cross, precisely because of the changes in status. A young man (named Laetus, or "Happy") thought about making the transition, but his mother protested.[299] Modern readers naturally wonder about the mix of motives of son and mother, but Augustine keeps it simple. Respect, he said, the mother's anxieties over her own economic and social position. Laetus should make sure to settle on her the worldly goods that he would leave behind: then would he find her more accommodating.

Perhaps it was sometimes that simple. Augustine had been skeptical as a young man, and even for years after baptism. The mystic in him did not think it would be possible to cling to the best way of life and keep the soul at peace when torn by the duties of ministry.[300] Living at home in Tagaste, he was suspicious of the clergy and reluctant to become one of them.[301] When he did join, his bishop allowed him to live like a "monk" and to gather a community around him. That practice was relatively new and not uncontroversial. Eusebius of Vercelli in Italy, who had been to Egypt and

seen the monks there around 340, is thought to have been the first west-
erner to be monk and bishop at the same time. The practice of ordaining
monks to the clergy (when there was a shortage of other candidates) was
approved by the emperor Honorius as late as 398.[302] In the Latin west, the
practice did not prevail or even become common until much later, but has
always been more common in the east. The case of Pope Gregory I
("Gregory the Great" [590–604]) shows the hostility that the so-called
secular clergy could and would easily display toward a high-minded
monastic leader. Although he was praised as a great spiritual thinker by
later generations, the people of Rome were delighted to see the end of
him and his austere ways.[303] Some lay Christians thought that monks were
idle parasites and needed to be persuaded to be otherwise. And though
notionally monks would be free and equal, in practice, ex-slaves in monasteries were expected to work harder than the freeborn, because they were
used to it.[304]

We know something of the details of Augustine's establishment in
Hippo only for the last decade of his life, a decade after the absorption of
the Donatist community. In 421 or 422, he had three priests and at least
six deacons. Five years later, in 427, he had seven priests (two of whom
had been deacons in the earlier count) and still two deacons.[305] But however closely they lived in that monastic community in Hippo, Augustine
paid little or no attention to the financial management of the community
and was thus remarkably blind to the behavior of his staff.[306]

And clerical behavior was a plague to Augustine, at Hippo and everywhere else. Some clergy were marginal characters on the make, sometimes needing charity, sometimes looking out for themselves. Donatianus
of Suppa[307] was one such, a priest who left his home to seek his fortune
but fell to taking the role of doorkeeper at a shrine in return for a pit-
tance. He still dreamed of returning home as a priest.

But much more often in the sources (which we can suspect of underre-
porting the evidence), bad behavior, real or alleged, has to be dealt with,
often where it might least be suspected. One of Augustine's longtime colleagues, Urbanus, superior of the monastery at Hippo for years, became
bishop of Sicca Veneria, where he found himself the target of complaints
by his own cleric Apiarius, a controversy that went on for years until it
reached the judgment of the very bishop of Rome.[308] The church of Vige-
silitana, south of Carthage, came to Augustine's attention because the
bishop had been ousted for bad behavior, the priest was in trouble, and
even their reader had run away.[309] Congregations were often scandalized.[310]

The catalogue could go on. Augustine's priest Abundantius, from a tiny farm community near Hippo, went bad. He had misused money and been seen dining on a fast day with a woman of ill repute, and even staying in the same house with her. Augustine wrote to the primate of Numidia to alert him that he, Augustine, had given the man leave to go and live elsewhere, on condition that he not function as a cleric.[311] Another embarrassing monk in Augustine's care, with the ironic name of Spes ("Hope"), fell into mutual recriminations with the priest Boniface; Augustine's response was to send them both to Nola, in Italy, for a de facto trial by ordeal, to see which one the saint there would miraculously approve.[312]

Equally common were clergy working the boundaries between the two large and mutually hostile Christian communities. When one grew too hot to hold them, for whatever reason, they could make a new life on the other side, where they would be touted as glorious converts. Three letters tell the story of a subdeacon of Augustine's who had gone bad and was on his way to join the Donatists in Hippo. Another of Augustine's shepherds, the subdeacon Primus, also from the country near Hippo, had been defrocked for associating with religious women. He went over to the Donatists, took two of his female colleagues with him, and they were all welcomed and rebaptized. Augustine was shocked that he now associated with circumcellions and "flocks of vagrant women." We only hear Augustine's side of the story.[313]

Not only the Donatists ensnared Augustine's men. A subdeacon, an old man by Augustine's standards, was found to have been a secret Manichean hearer and to have been teaching the sect's doctrines. Augustine banished him, and we know the story from his letter warning another bishop not to be taken in by the man if he came his way. Another cleric, in the early years of Augustine at Hippo, needed to be warned not to allow Manichean texts to be read in public.[314] Augustine addressed that behavior as an oversight (and some seemingly devout texts might well find readers who did not appreciate the doctrinal fine points), but others might not be so tolerant. (And those who would think that Augustine had never really left the Manichees behind would treat these cases as shocking revelations.)

The most exceptional group of people devoting themselves to the religious life under Augustine's care turn out to be no easier to handle than the priests and deacons. Augustine's sister was ensconced at Hippo as the leader of a religious community for women. A letter Augustine wrote to her[315] has long been taken as a "rule for women" and forms part of the disciplinary basis of numerous modern religious orders. Read attentively, it reveals not only the glories but also the challenges of such a community.

It begins with a foul breath of discontent in the air. The women want him to come and visit them to straighten things out, but he thinks that this will only make things worse, and that they know that. Their community is riven with quarrels, rivalries, hostilities, disagreements, backbiting, insolence, and muttering. He has several particular requirements to impose on them (including the assignment of a male supervisor). There was to be no singing of impermissible songs (old Donatist hymns?). They were to avoid all forms of unchastity, and he realizes that the absence of men from the community does not make such misbehavior impossible: "The things that people do when they take no thought of modesty, even women with women, when they are laughing and playing shamefully, shouldn't be done—I don't say just by widows and virgins devoted to Christ with holy purpose but not even by married ladies or by girls who will be married."[316]

Class distinction persists in the women's house. Those who have been somebody in the world outside should not turn their noses up at those who came to religion from poverty,[317] but neither should anyone take it amiss that some of the more delicate sisters got special treatment in the way of clothing, bedding, and food.[318]

There was embarrassment also in what Augustine found in his own house. A series of variously disastrous and mediocre clerical appointments left Augustine surrounded with friends and disciples he could better have done without. In two embarrassed sermons when he was a little over seventy, he was compelled to outline in personal detail the financial affairs of each priest and deacon who worked with him in Hippo, and almost every one had some bit of awkwardness to get over, some financial transaction or personal relationship that required just a little more explanation than was seemly. To follow that account opens a picture into his world that can't be gotten any other way.[319]

First, there was the priest Januarius. He had entered the clergy in mature years, with a daughter and son who had each entered the sworn religious life. The daughter was not of age, but he wanted her to have some money of his. But as he grew older and she was still not of age, he made a will and named heirs. Augustine was shocked by this, shocked that one of his own should make a will and name an heir to his estate. After all, the clergy of Hippo lived in ostensible communism: no one owned anything; all was held in common, in the way of the apostles (Acts 4.32). And what heir did he name? The church! Augustine would have none of it and declared that the church wouldn't accept the money—let his children do with it what they would! But they fell in turn to quarreling over the matter, and Augustine was disgusted.

Augustine knew that some criticized his fastidiousness, claiming he just didn't know how to accept a gift for the church, but he insisted that he took all the good gifts that came his way, like that of Julianus, who died childless. On the other hand, he had turned away the gift that came from the estate of Boniface, who died in a shipwreck, because he didn't want to get into the nasty legal practice of the time of asking that the survivors be tortured to find out what had happened to the ship.

Telling the story of Januarius was enough for one sermon. The second, the next day, began with a reading from the Acts of the Apostles, with the passage about communal property in context. The passage was read twice. The deacon Lazarus read it aloud in the usual way (junior clergy did the scriptural readings at the bishop's direction) and then Augustine himself read through the crucial handful of verses again.

Then he went on making explanations for his clergy. There were Valens the deacon and Patricius the subdeacon (the latter Augustine's own nephew, probably the son of his brother Navigius). Valens still owned some property with his own brother, because his mother was still alive (though she had just died). Valens meant to give it to the church, but it hadn't quite happened yet. And he still owned, well, this is awkward—some slaves, on the same terms. He really does mean to set them free, Augustine said, he really does. (The brother he shared it with? Well, he, too, was a subdeacon, in the church of Milevis, where Augustine's dear friend Severus was bishop.) Patricius had a similar awkwardness, regarding a mother who had just died, but he also had some sisters, and he had to clear things up with them before he could do anything. (Was Augustine making excuses for a family member that he wouldn't make for another?)

Then there was the deacon Faustinus, who came to the church from government service. Now baptized and ordained a deacon. It turns out that he still owned property that he had left behind with his brothers, but now he was going to straighten things out right away, splitting the proceeds, fifty-fifty, between his brothers and the church.

Then there was a deacon, another Severus, who was blind. He had bought a house for his mother and sister when he wanted to bring them to Hippo from their home city. He bought it with money he got by taking up a collection among other religious men (Augustine had, not surprisingly, asked him just who these other affluent clergy might be). He now fell to quarreling with his mother, but asked Augustine to judge and settle the quarrel. Then, whatever was left of the property, he would give it to Augustine to do as he pleased with. Augustine wanted him to turn the property into largesse for the poor in his home town.

Another deacon, unnamed, gave away his money and property but before he was a cleric he had bought some slaves, which he still owned. So *today*, the day on which Augustine gave this embarrassed sermon, he would set them free in the presence of the congregation in church. (One can hear echoes of the congressional committee asking the witness why he waited until *now* to sell that questionable stock.)

The deacon Eraclius was a special case, and he came next. He had provided the funds to build the shrine of Saint Stephen (whose coming to Hippo we will witness with suitable astonishment shortly). He had also bought a house and donated it to the church, just a few days ago, by an extraordinary coincidence, and he, too, would set free a few slaves later that day. "Don't let anybody say, 'He's a rich man,' " Augustine entreated the congregation. "Don't let anybody think it, don't let anybody speak ill of him, don't let anybody go gnawing at him and his fine spirit."

Happily for Augustine, his subdeacons seemed to be ethically clean, but not so the priests. They were poor men, and, well, a couple of explanations were in order.

First, there was Leporius. He was wellborn but came to Augustine and the clerical life in poverty, the poverty that came from selling what he had and giving the proceeds to the poor, not here in Hippo, but Augustine knew where he'd done it. Leporius also looked after the expenses of Augustine's monastery, and of course he had built a pilgrim's hostel for the church: Augustine told him to. Oh, and a basilica in honor of the eight martyrs, he built that as well. And bought a house so he could use its stone for his hostel, but then the stone wasn't necessary, and so the house had been rented, the income going to the church. People call it "the priest's house," but it's not—really, it's not.

And then one last piece of good news. Remember the son and daughter of Januarius, quarreling over their inheritance? Augustine had been planning to resolve it, but sometime since the first sermon they had spontaneously kissed and made up and there was no quarrel left. Augustine was delighted.

After a warning to the congregation to beware of giving gifts to clergy (give to the monastery and all the clergy will benefit equally), there was the case of the priest Barnabas. Had he really bought a house from the fine gentleman Eleusinus? No, Eleusinus had *given* it to him.

The sermon breaks off about there. These sermons tell us all we know of this band of brothers, this holy and pious tribe of self-sacrificing ascetics. Whatever the truth of Augustine's protestations, we are left with an unmistakable flavor of a community less drastically cut off from the secular world than Augustine wanted, one of ordinary people with ordinary wants and quarrels, too ordinary for Augustine's comfort. That's what he had to live with. And it wasn't the worst. We'll reserve the story of Antoninus of Fussala, the worst of Augustine's bad boys, for its place in a larger story.

"Who will guard the guardians?" was Juvenal's famous question.[320] Augustine knew it was his responsibility to do so, but he was not what we would call today a "proactive manager." The embarrassments ended when he died, and we have no information about the state and fate of Augustine's clergy after his lifetime.

A GLIMPSE OF THE SAINTLY BISHOP

The oldest biographical novel about Augustine dates to his own time. Sometime in the fifth century, probably fifteen to twenty years after Augustine's death (to judge by mention of the Huns in one passage), an unknown writer composed a series of letters supposedly exchanged between Augustine and the Roman general Boniface.[321] They don't come anywhere close to being authentic, and the compiler could not have thought they were. He likely had seen Possidius's *Life* of Augustine and perhaps was the first to feel those pages lacking in appropriate drama. These letters come to us only by the chance survival of a single manuscript.

The story they tell represents a memory and image of Augustine that is not defined by books and doctrine, but by his engagement in the military politics of Africa in his last years. Boniface, the Roman general charged with protecting the African province, is known to have been a slightly difficult friend for Augustine, moving from initial appearance of intimacy and religious devotion to a more distanced position after a trip back to Italy from which he returned with a new heretic wife and concubines besides. The novelist knows something of this story and of the invasions that troubled Africa in Augustine's last years, and he attributes to both parties in the correspondence stereotypical roles. Augustine is high-minded enough to chastise and then to forgive, while Boniface is the military man who expects war to be hell.

So the collection begins with a devout Boniface and a reprimanding Augustine. A Gothic soldier in Roman service has sexually approached a consecrated virgin and Augustine demands discipline; Boniface promises that the man will rot in jail; oh, please, no, replies Augustine, I didn't mean quite that. Let him have a chance to repent himself, for after all, if we wanted to punish *all* the sins of barbarians, there wouldn't be many barbarians left, and they wouldn't be much good for fighting. But now Boniface goes wrong, arresting a man on the church steps—or was it just inside? Has he violated the sanctuary principles of the law? Called to account, he is apologetic and promises to make things right.

Then the most stirring scene. Augustine writes to report that he saw Boniface pass by at the head of his forces. "Your gentle yet awe-inspiring appearance as you passed was a delight to my eyes. But after you with your anointed brow had passed out the gate of the city with a few others, suddenly the buildings erupted with horsemen, the city poured out an army, weapons were clattering and clanging, trumpets were blasting, torches flickered in the breeze, the armor breastplates of brave men weighed them down, horses and men veiled in silk came by, and bows were at the ready. It was all beautiful to me, but I saw nothing better than Count Boniface."

The exchange of letters presents two more rounds of misbehavior and chastisement among the military and government officials for whom Boniface is responsible, then ends with the sounds of war approaching. Boniface survives a difficult battle; Augustine replies that he lies abed and sees his final day draw near. "I rejoice in your victory. Save the Roman city, I pray you, and govern your men the way a good count does. Don't be overweening in your power; remember to boast of the true author of your virtues [i.e., god] and you will never have to fear an enemy. Farewell."

To those last words of Augustine, Boniface replies with good wishes and his own hope for the bishop's prayers to see him through the crises ahead.

None of this, remember, happened this way. But someone old enough to have seen Augustine in the flesh could imagine him in this way, and that is itself a part of the way Augustine went through the world, creator and prisoner of familiar stereotypes.

VII

AUGUSTINE
AND THE INVENTION
OF CHRISTIANITY

AUGUSTINE THE GLUNCHIST

What would we think if the story we told of Augustine included this discussion of the rather oddly named religion he belonged to?

> We can discern precious little of the authentic origins of the Glunchist cult from the disparate and mutually contradictory collection of biographies and hortatory texts that come to us from its first age. It was a renegade Jewish sect with vaguely stated political aims, capitalizing on the political execution of its leader by making him the object of miracle stories. Some seemed to think he had risen from the dead, while others awaited his return (as others awaited that of the once and future king of Britain), and many apparently thought that he had already risen from the dead, then gone away only to return again. At all events, it was a cult focused on the fact of the leader's absence.
>
> Outcroppings of this cult can be found scattered around the Mediterranean for most of the ninth and tenth Roman centuries, and there was some limited communication among them. Naturally enough, great diversity of belief and practice existed, though the reliance on texts made it possible for one and another group of communities (usually aligned

around some larger social structure, be it linguistic, ethnic, or political) to make common cause and share a mutual sense of belonging over a range of places and times.

Occasionally suppressed by Roman governors or even emperors (usually as a sideshow to some larger political struggle), the cult came to brief and perilous notoriety when the emperor Constantine and his successors patronized it and sought to control it. They were broadly successful in creating a state church whose priests might almost have been functionaries of the Roman state, for indeed they broke out into quarrels and factions as often as civil servants and soldiers did. In Augustine's time, it was possible to invoke the imperial state church in local quarrels and use government support to quash rivals not so successful in winning state approval.

But such a religious structure was as dependent as other ancient cults on the political and military success of its sponsors, and as Roman government found more and more ways to weaken itself, lose battles, and miss opportunities, the Glunchist church was at a disadvantage precisely for having come to rely so heavily on the patronage of the state. The decisive blows that led to the extermination of all but a few curious local sectaries (who can still be found as living fossils on Mount Athos in Greece, in Iran, and in India) were struck when the Frankish king Clovis invoked his ancestral deities against the pretensions of the Italian and Gaulish Glunchists, who belonged entirely and mindlessly to the state church, and thus Clovis returned western Europe to its traditional religious diversity; when two centuries later the Islamic conquests took the Near East and Africa away from the Glunchists, and then in the third century B.C. ("before Columbus") when the assimilation of Greek and Turkish realms in eastern Europe and Anatolia . . .

Such counterfactual history eventually breaks down, or at least its fantasies become too far-fetched to sustain interest. A harder task than writing this narrative would be to imagine in some detail what modern societies would look like had Christianity been mainly eradicated or at least marginalized throughout the old Roman territories at some point before the age of exploration began to draw disparate continents into a single world.[322] The thought experiment can be sustained at least far enough, however, to let us begin to think how we could see Augustine and his age if the very things about it that seem most familiar to us and most connected to our own time lost that prestige of appearance. If we only read the term "Christian" for the first time somewhere in university courses and found it as jarring in form and unfamiliar in denotation as the reader will find "Glunchist" in the foregoing fantasy or "Donatist" on other pages here, our reading of him and his time would be quite different, even if all the surviving evidence were identical in form, content, and abundance.

Everything about Christianity is subject to controversy. How many people are Christian, how devoutly they believe and practice their faiths, and how these allegiances affect their behavior outside the sphere of religious ritual are all questions that will be answered very differently, depending on who answers. But the cognitive and social structures of Christianity have been deeply implanted in the whole of our planet's social consciousness. Educated people everywhere, first of all, know whether they are Christian or not; second, they share some broad conception of what that entails; and, third, they participate in cultural forms that would be meaningless without Christian history to explain them. The biggest practical stumbling block to writing the above revery lay in deciding how to name the times through which people have lived. Other reckonings of time are in use in the world today, but few educated practitioners of non-Christian systems fail to know how to convert their own reckoning into the European one; yet few Euramericans have the remotest idea how to make any reverse equivalence. The Year 2000 fears and fantasies we lived through all made sense at the time, for a global audience.

The story of Christianity that I have just told under a dissonant pseudonym is demonstrably true on all points, as far as historical fact and verifiability are concerned, at least down to Augustine's time, but unfamiliar for the range and character of interpretation it includes. The chief unfamiliarity is in the outcome, the failure of the cult to sustain itself. But in the fourth and fifth centuries, Christianity was far from certain to survive and thrive. Christians have commonly claimed that early Christianity was homogeneous, even miraculously so, and that division and disagreement are later degenerations. Though scholars have long since exploded historical claims to homogeneity, it remains a theme of conventional discourse, and the outcome of all the early stories seems to be the rise of a single Christianity. So we tell all the stories of early diversity to one another fully knowing that homogeneity of some kind awaits. Eastern and western branches of Christianity both aver that homogeneity was achieved, but do so only in the face of the evidence of their long mutual mistrust, misunderstanding, and near millennium of outright excommunication.

The religious movements of medieval, modern, and postmodern times that carry the name "Christian" have chosen to associate themselves with a body of ancient religious movements and, for the most part, with one or two lines of development within that body of movements. The notion that what one sees today on an evangelist's television program, in the cave monasteries of the Pechersk Lavra in Kiev, and in an African cathedral welcoming a papal visit, to say nothing of an upper Manhattan Episcopalian Sunday service regularly attended by house pets and their owners, are all of a piece with what happened in Augustine's lifetime in the Syrian desert, in farming villages in Africa, and among perfumed socialites in Rome is to make a quite extraordinary theological assertion in the guise of history. The doctrines and practices of Christian groups are at sharp variance with each other in almost any period of Christian histories, but the gap separating even the most past-reverent of contemporary Christians from Augustine's contemporaries simply boggles the imagination. If a time machine could juxtapose moderns with ancients, it would take a great deal of effort merely to keep them from killing one another, and much more to get them to comprehend each other's beliefs and practices. They would require the intervention of very high authority indeed to acknowledge mutual communion.

Augustine matters as much as he does because of the movement he aligned himself with *and* its self-proclaimed successors. If repeatedly we feel on reading stories of his life that we understand the issues, concerns, and attitudes he and his contemporaries shared, that's *not* because we have seen and understood them and made a serious historical attempt to compare them to our own, but because they (and their modern translators) use names and labels that elide the gaps that separate us and make their issues and their affiliations seem relevant. This elision is nowhere so powerfully effected as in the use of the word "catholic" in discussions of African religion in Augustine's time. We will see below what happens to our perspective when we deny ourselves the use of just that word.

FEASTS OF STEPHEN

The full story of Augustine in Africa is impossible to tell because so much of it has been erased. The first twenty years of his clerical life were defined by the conflict between his community and the other African Christian church, the majority church, the one that descended from the earliest days of Latin African Christianity two hundred years earlier. A fragment of narrative from the way the story ended can provide us a framework for understanding the whole story. An attentive student of the New Testament writings who knew nothing else of Christianity might be surprised to learn what a place relics of the saints held in Christian worship for a very long time. The doctrine of the resurrection and ascension, after all, taught that there were no remains of Jesus's physical presence on earth. But by the fourth century, Constantine's mother had found the true cross in Jerusalem, and Mark Twain, centuries later, would make a show of calculating the considerable total weight of all the fragments from it that he had found on his travels in Europe. Relics could be potent in themselves (Pope Gregory I in the late sixth century reported that attempts to meddle with Peter's remains under his basilica at the Vatican were fatal to those who came in contact with them) and the object of a bizarre and lively trade in stolen property. Augustine's own body turned up, so we are assured, in Pavia, where it can still be seen in the same church as the body of Boethius, after an intermediate stop for Augustine in Sardinia.[323] In 1845, when French Catholics in Annaba, Algeria (ancient Hippo), were planning construction of a new basilica in his honor, they prevailed on the authorities in Pavia to let them have Augustine's elbow, which duly made a ceremonial pilgrimage across the Mediterranean and is on display to this day, carefully fitted into the appropriate place on a life-size sculpture of a recumbent and anachronistically mitered bishop.

Augustine himself when younger tried not to speak or think of such things. The idea that such tokens of the dead could be powerful and worthy of special treatment grew on him slowly. In his early baptized days, he said outright that the age of miracles had passed, that these things were necessary in early days but now no longer. At about the same time, as we have seen, he was saying something similar to the convivial members of his flock: drinking in church was appropriate in earlier days, but now no longer. In many such ways, he sought to enhance the dignity and cultural level of his congregation. In later years, to be sure, he remembered that he had seen and then written in his *Confessions* about the wonderfully convenient "discovery" by Ambrose of the remains of the martyrs Protasius and Gervasius during Augustine's Milan days.[324]

But times change and people change. Augustine changed when Stephen—or what was left of him—came to Africa in the late 410s. Stephen the "protomartyr" was stoned to death and his story told in the Acts of the Apostles (7.59–60) with the unconverted future apostle Paul standing aptly by. After almost four hundred years, his relics appeared.

Good relics come with good stories: indeed, without stories, relics are just old trash. This saint has one of the best collections.[325] First we have the letter of Lucian, the priest of Caphamargala in Palestine, who tells of sleeping in a shrine (a common ancient practice for inducing visions) and seeing in a dream the saints Stephen, Nicodemus, and Gamaliel. With the usual reluctance to believe found in dreams, he is led to discover the remains—bones and dust—of Stephen and reports the event to Bishop John of Jerusalem, who was at that moment in Diospolis (modern Lod, Israel) for the famous synod that acquitted Pelagius of charges of heresy. At just that moment, the Latin church would find itself saying afterwards, god had providentially chosen to manifest the power of one of his great saints. The reported discovery was followed by the usual cures and the end of a drought.[326]

Orosius, a friend of Augustine's from Spain, whom we will meet again, was in Palestine to attend the synod at Diospolis and generally to create trouble. He was the vector who carried the relics and the passion for them and their miracles to Africa. There, shrines popped up and ecclesiastical travelers carried the infection hither and yon.[327] (And there is one other gaudier story of the transfer of Stephen's relics, this one taking him to Constantinople. A senator has himself buried next to Stephen. A few years later, his wife wants to take her husband's remains to Constantinople, but cannot tell the saint from the senator and so takes the wrong one. On the voyage, Stephen appears to the travelers in a storm, then calms the waters; later an earthquake, demons, and angels come into play, before the saint finds rest in another new land.)

From Africa, we have miracle stories, but Orosius voyaged beyond Africa and back to Spain, stopping off in the Balearic Islands. If in Africa the saint's dust generated fairly ordinary pious enthusiasm, in the islands he inspired terrorism and his enthusiasts mobbed to force the Jews of Minorca to convert to Christianity in one of the ugliest episodes of anti-Semitic hostility to come to us from this period.[328] But stories went on begetting stories. Back at Uzalis in Africa, where Augustine's old friend Evodius was bishop, the letter in which Severus of Minorca detailed the uproar in his homeland was received and read from the pulpit to great enthusiasm. We know this because we are told the story to introduce a collection of the signs and wonders Stephen worked there.

By this time it is Easter week, 425 or 426. Augustine is old, in his seventies now. He has probably already designated his successor and begun to pull back from daily involvement in the affairs of the church. But Easter is the great feast of the year, and the bishop himself must be present throughout. This year we have a series of his sermons from that week, all having to do with Stephen, who is flourishing at Hippo. One sermon we have was held on Sunday, one on Monday, two on Tuesday, and one on Wednesday.

Augustine will never say just why Stephen is so useful for him. In the 410s Augustine had acquired a new flock, the ex-Donatists, among whom reverence for martyrs ran hot and high, and they had their own martyrs—some of them done to death by other Christians. Stephen, in that environment, was a trump card, an undoubtedly ancient and authentic and powerful martyr, greater than the local ones. Years before, Augustine had mentioned in passing[329] that the Donatists "adore the dust" that had been brought from the Holy Land. Now he had dust of the highest value for them to venerate. (Similarly, in the same post-Donatist period, new shrines to martyrs would be found springing up around old circumcellion sites near Hippo, to satisfy the old tastes.[330])

When Stephen's relics arrived, Augustine had a shrine built for him,[331] within earshot of the main church—or was an older shrine in the old Donatist basilica Augustine now claimed remade for a new tenant? Whatever the facts, the shrine carefully told the story of the new tenant in pictures: "There's a wonderfully sweet picture there," Augustine observes in almost the only place where we can see him noticing church architecture or decoration, "where you see Stephen being stoned, where you see Saul watching over the garments of the ones doing the stoning."[332] Four verses of text, presumably of scripture, were provided to accompany the pictures, but for once, Augustine told his flock they needed no book.[333] "A little dust has brought together such a crowd," he said one year on the feast day. "The ash lies hidden, the benefits from it are well known. Think, dear ones, what things god holds for us in the land of the living, who has given us such great things from the dust of the dead."[334]

Stephen's influence is in the air on that Easter Sunday, but Augustine begs off reading the miracle stories until the morrow: he is too exhausted with age, fasting, and the demands of the Easter liturgy. On Monday, he is still unready, but the congregation is chafing for stories.

Finally, on Tuesday, we get the story, the full text of a "Pamphlet made by Paul for Bishop Augustine." (It was the custom in those days to turn miracle into text by writing such a *libellus*, a pamphlet, for public reading and circulation. Sometimes it was hard to make a congregation remember the difference between canonical scripture and locally produced and exhilarating pamphlet.)

Here is Paul's story: when they were living in Caesarea of Cappadocia, his elder brother assaulted their mother. She was going at dawn to the baptistry to curse him when a demon in the form of their uncle appeared to her and asked her where she was going. She told him, and he persuaded her to curse her whole family. She tore her hair, bared her breast, and prayed that all of them be made exiles. The elder brother came down with a persistent case of the shakes, and the others in the family fell victim to the same penalty within a year. The mother, full of remorse, hanged herself. "All of us went abroad, unable to bear our shame, and left our common homeland behind to scatter through the world." Some of the ten brothers followed the eldest to the shrine of Lawrence in Ravenna and were cured, or so Paul was told. Paul was the sixth and wandered the earth with his sister (next in age), going wherever he had heard of miracles. "I did not fail to visit Uzalis in Africa, where the blessed martyr Stephen was said to do great things quite often. But it's three months now, just on the first of January, that my sister and I—she's here with me, suffering the same illness—were instructed by a clear and vivid vision." They saw a venerable man, white-haired and striking in appearance, who promised them good health within three months.

> You yourself, Augustine, appeared to my sister in a vision and told us to come here. We arrived fifteen days ago and I have prayed daily in the shrine of Stephen. But on Easter Sunday, as the others who were here have seen, while I was praying with many tears and hanging on to the altar rail, I suddenly collapsed. I took leave of my senses and had no idea where I was. After a little while, I got up again and found that the trembling had left my body. Deeply grateful for this blessing from god, I offered this *libellus*, in which I report what you may not know about our calamities and my recovery. I hope you will pray for my sister and give thanks for what has happened to me.

Augustine now goes back to tell of their earlier adventures. They had been to Ancona in Italy, where there was a shrine to Stephen erected before the relics were found. "This man could have been cured at Ancona, but it did not come to pass for *our* sake, because it easily could have happened there. Many people know how many miracles were worked through blessed Stephen in that city, where his shrine had been of old." (It seems that one of the bystanders at Stephen's martyrdom had taken one of the stones that had been thrown at him and brought it to Ancona and made it the basis of the shrine. Misinformed people believed that

Stephen's arm was there, but it was only a stone that had bounced off Stephen's elbow. Or not, as the case may be.)

Then, just as Augustine starts to tell the story of one of the miracles of Stephen's power that had occurred at Uzalis, suddenly there is an exciting interruption:

> . . . and while Augustine was saying these things, the people began to shout "THANK GOD! CHRIST BE PRAISED!" from the shrine of Stephen. In the middle of that continuous uproar, the sister, who had been cured, was brought in to the apse [of the main church]. When they saw her, the people continued shouting—no words, just noise, a mixture of joy and tears—and went on for a long time. When Augustine had calmed them he said, "It is written in the psalm 'I have said it, I shall declare against myself what I have sinned against my master god, and you have forgiven the impiety of my heart.' 'I have said it, I shall declare': I had not yet said it, but you forgave the sin. I commended this pitiful one—no longer pitiful—to your prayers. We determined to pray, and we were heard. Let our joy be our thanksgiving. The mother church was heard more swiftly than her mother was heard when she cursed her to misery."[335]

And with that Augustine has the sense to bring his remarks to an end and let events take their course. He represented his god to these people, but the dead saint could commandeer the stage at will. No wonder Augustine preferred to make his name and solidify his influence in the world of texts.

HOW AUGUSTINE'S RELIGION WORKED

Augustine's god was off the charts. He was one of few ancient gods who could shed foible and whimsy and seek to stand ostentatiously beyond the reach of human outrage and indignation. (Those Christians who tried to sever the god of Christianity from the god of Israel were attempting to protect that majesty and impeccability from the vagaries of the often angry and unpredictable antecedent. It still cost Augustine some effort and special pleading to explain how god could "repent" of what he had done.[336]) Though some of Augustine's contemporaries would fret at the ways of a god who could condemn little babies to hell, Augustine himself would be unperturbed. "God" was for him a set term, absolute and inviolable, beyond question or doubt.

But the name alone would be the telltale sign of an idiosyncratic generalization. This god has no given name, nor even any namelessness. Instead his name is the generic term for any god (*deus* in Latin, *theos* in Greek), taken over into common parlance by a detour through the translationese that represented Hebrew scriptures in Greek and Latin. This god was timeless, unchanging, all-powerful, existing at the extreme limit of what language can say. He reached this exaltation through the intertwining of biblical texts with Platonic thought, and Augustine had acquired him already as a young man in Milan. Indeed, acquiring this god beyond reproaches was a condition of Augustine's willingness to settle for the religion of his mother, whose god had seemed very ordinary and impugnable. (The thrill of Manicheism was that it both admitted the problem that the existence of evil offered and gave back a resolutely impervious and sure-to-be-invincible deity.) As long as he thought about god in material, limited, attackable terms, Augustine was unable to find a deity that suited him. Once he found that bodiless god, he hung on for dear life.

We will come back to that god when we know Augustine a great deal better. But for now, if we found that god more unfamiliar, we would be more inclined than we are to realize that the theological extremes to which Augustine found himself driven late in life were reflections of the god he had chosen. That is to say, a god who is all-knowing and all-powerful and all-good so far transcends ordinary categories of behavior that any narrative into which he intrudes will be seriously disordered. Storytelling doesn't work if one character violates all the rules and transcends all the limitations that the other characters endure. A jealous, arbitrary, limited god who favored his chosen ones and ignored other humans would be deemed capricious, but he could not be blamed for the misfortunes of those he ignored. Augustine's absolutist god could not lift a finger in human affairs without becoming responsible for all human affairs, and so Augustine would spend the last two decades of his life evading this quite reasonable conclusion, the *reductio ad absurdum* to which his contemporaries repeatedly tried to press him.

The one category in which that god of Augustine's would be limited would be, ironically, in how human beings could perceive him. This utterly transcendent and supreme being lay hidden in the world to all but the most discerning eyes. Sin had so far separated people from this god (Augustine argued) that mortal sight had darkened and the "invisible things of god" (Romans 1.20) that should be intuited by all those who looked upon the things he had created were obscure to all but a few—most likely, Augustine thought, those to whom god had chosen to reveal himself. Humankind lived in a world dominated by a supreme and irresistible force that lay maddeningly just beyond its ken. When Christians assert that the divine is knowable, they have to accept that their god is at the same time obscure, difficult, and absent.

Human beings facing such a god felt, not unnaturally, fear and anxiety. Throughout his life, Augustine found Christianity for himself and preached it for others as a religion in principle founded on hope, but no one is hopeful who is not also fearful. Not until the last moment of life could one say with assurance whether salvation had been achieved, whether what Augustine came to call the "gift of perseverance" had been among the gifts god had given. He could describe an old man of great piety and chastity who took up with a dancing girl as lacking this ultimate gift.[337] The Augustine of the *Confessions* who can say that he does not know to which temptation he will next submit is the Augustine of that anxiety.[338] To be sure, some of Augustine's contemporary Christians seem to have lived with more settled expectations and a more secure hope in the future. Not surprisingly, most of them were ones to whom Augustine's ideas about his god, and his conclusions about the implications of that god's nature for human freedom, were at least unfamiliar and perhaps unwelcome. But the terrifying images of the last judgment from the Book of Revelation found already in Christian art of this period are reminders that some strains of Jesus's message came through more loudly and clearly than others.

If Augustine's Christianity were unfamiliar to us, one other aspect of his teaching would strike us with a jarring note of dissonance, a doctrine that descends from, and is reinforced by, his idea of god: his notion of a "catholic" church.

Augustine's catholicity was no invention of his, any more than his idea of god had been, but both are stamped with his absolutist interpretation and asseverated throughout his career in ways that many contemporaries found unsettling. The notion that Christian communities in all places make up a single community and that they should be in harmony in matters of doctrine and practice is a theological rather than historical doctrine. It has proven to be very powerful in welding together disparate Christian communities into socially potent forces, but its appeal has never been universal. In the early churches, some were persuaded to think in translocal terms, while others were content (in a world in which many people did not think much beyond the boundaries of their own communities, after all, except to ponder the wickedness of the tax-guzzling Roman empire) to find catholicity (wholeness) in the possession of the totality of Christian teaching and the enactment of the totality of Christian practice, without much regard for what others elsewhere would accomplish. When communities banded together, it tended to be by natural geographical unit, and the Christians of Africa, who had been the first Latin Christians and who were the most abundant and ferociously faithful of Latin Christians, did not by and large deeply care about the fate or habits of Christians elsewhere.

Augustine cared. He acquired a notion of geographic catholicity that arose not long before him among African Christians of the faction with which he aligned himself, and he proclaimed that idea heroically and consistently all his clerical career. Numerous passages in his correspondence and polemical writings show us other African Christians hearing these impassioned and, to us, quite reasonable and predictable arguments and simply disregarding and disavowing them. Those were the people he called Donatists.[339]

The catholicity of Christianity has multiple implications for society and politics. The most notable is that it reduces the number of categories by which the religious geography of the ancient world could be described. If there are not multiple Christianities but only one, or at least if all others than the approved one are marginal and irrelevant, then a bright sharp line is drawn between that one supereminent religion and the rest of the human world. If that line could be as sharp as one would like to make it, then Christians/un-Christians would be all the categories one would need. And for "un-Christian" a suitably offensive term was "pagan."

"Pagan," from the Latin *paganus*, originally "dweller in a country district," roughly "hick, rube," was an old Christian term revived in Augustine's times. He himself used it cannily. *Paganus* in the second century had been in use in Latin in idiomatic opposition to *miles* ("soldier"). Across the Roman countryside, soldiers fought and were fed on tax revenues, revenues often collected in kind from the peasants, the *pagani*, the commonest word for describing those who lived outside the cities. So a "pagan" in this metaphorical usage was a civilian in the cosmic struggle, not a "soldier of Christ." A modest stream of texts dating from about 200 and a little after recorded this Christian usage, but then it faded from use.

"Pagan" returns in the late fourth century as a word of abuse with a new explanation. Christians who had seen it in older texts did not understand the derivation and decided it must have meant that un-Christian religion was found surviving most abundantly in the countryside and was "pagan" in that sense. The revived use made it possible to divide the world between those outside and those inside, the new chosen people and the new gentiles (and indeed *gentiles* is sometimes attested as a word for "pagans").

What made the term "pagan" particularly attractive was that it could be launched against precisely the most polished and urbane of un-Christian citizens of the late fourth century with particular effect. The perfumed gentlemen of Rome, who had not deigned to add the slightly vulgar Christian god to the discriminating collections of cults they patronized, could now be insulted as bumpkins. The tables of disdain were thus turned on men especially sensitive to such mockery. Augustine uses the word about these men, but not to their faces. It is almost entirely missing from his great work against "paganism," *City of God*, where it might have given offense, but it is very familiar in the safer polemical space of the sermons preached to the already converted.

Augustine worked hard to turn his world into one with sharp lines separating "pagans" and Christians. But when we ask what was left of real "paganism," that is, of ancient religious practices that Augustine would characterize that way, we find some odd things. It might seem, for example, that his vast refutation of "pagan" principles and practices in *City of God*'s first books would be a place to look for reflections of the religious spirit of his age. But what might have been a precious ethnography is anything but. A few glimpses of what the rites of the goddess Caelestis were like in Carthage in Augustine's youth come through in a story of his we heard some while ago (pages 17–18), and we have a parallel story from Quodvultdeus, a follower of Augustine who seems to have been present in Carthage in 399 when the great temple-busting purges of that year brought Caelestis down, but Augustine isn't much of a witness for us.

So Augustine stays mainly among his own kind, contenting himself with telling the faithful how they can see the ancient prophecies of the fall of the gods coming true around them.[340] His world is Christian, and has been for a while. So in a sermon sometime after 411, he speaks of Donatists who are reluctant to come over out of respect for their elders who had been of the same party, then adds: "Your parents were Christians in the Donatist faction, and maybe their parents were Christians, but their grandparents and great-grandparents were certainly pagan."[341] To get back to those ancestors, we need to go back to the first quarter of the fourth century, almost a hundred years earlier than the time at which Augustine speaks.

Hence his disdainful interest in one of the media events of the time, a scene in the modest town of Sufes.[342] There, probably in 399 and also connected with the imperial steps taken against "paganism" in that year, a riot broke out in support of the old rites and buildings. Sixty Christians were killed, Augustine claims, and the city council seems to have demanded that it be given its statue of Hercules back. Augustine writes a letter to them for no good reason except to make a public statement of mockery of their ideas and aims. Elsewhere we see similar outbreaks reflected, as Christian mobs run amok on an estate to destroy hated old shrines.[343]

The "paganism" that Augustine attacks has less to do with old rituals and more to do with his fears about the Christians in front of him and their lingering attachment to ideas and practices that he finds unworthy of them in various ways. So we have Christians who turn their noses up at sermons on the resurrection[344] and plenty of Christians who go to enjoy the wild entertainment of the circus,[345] and even some who are to be found among the actors and prostitutes of the city of Bulla Regia.[346] He imagines another who says, "Okay, so I visit idols in their shrines and pay attention to lunatics and fortune-tellers—but I don't leave god's church. I'm a catholic!"[347] Augustine can see only "paganism" lingering on under false pretenses. But what are we to make of the boys who go reveling for the feast of John the Baptist, which falls at the summer solstice? The bonfires of that night were scarcely Christian in origin, and we can be sure that they persisted despite the bishop's disapproval.[348]

But failure to recognize the way Augustine uses the "pagan" label to attack Christian practices has misled many modern readers. His attack on the "pagan" practices of feasting in church and at graveside was really an attack on Donatism, and several distinguished figures we encounter in Augustine's later career who are commonly spoken of as "pagans" prove to be churchgoing Christians of whom Augustine has reason to disapprove. "Pagan" was, like "pinko," a privileged epithet, shorthand for a basket of disreputable practices, and a substitute for more nuanced argument.

Perhaps the closest we get to a true "pagan" is the engaging fellow of whom we hear in a sermon on John's gospel in the early 400s.[349] As best we can tell from Augustine's label for him, he was a priest of the old god Attis, and wore the "Phrygian cap" as a sign of office. He had the mother wit to claim that his god was really Christian, and Augustine suggests that others had added the name of Christ to their spells and chants, adding honey to their poison to seduce the unwary. Very likely.

Other contemporaries could see things ambiguously as well.

Calama was a modest city not far from Hippo, in fact the closest respectable town. The suspension of traditional rites after 391 and the forced overturning of traditional shrines and facilities after 399 were unprecedented acts of interference from outside in local habits. Around 408, Augustine began to hear from a local dignitary named Nectarius whose position is easy to mistake. He is generally taken as a "pagan," but on careful reading he emerges as a perfectly ordinary Christian whose main allegiances are not religious but social. He writes to Augustine in dismay,[350] appealing to him gentleman to gentleman and particularly as one educated man to another, implicitly encouraging Augustine to intervene on the side of the established order to protect the old ways and the old institutions. The bishop's social position was such that a request of that kind seemed worth bringing to him, even if we know with hindsight that Augustine would reject it.

Augustine was the one who dragged religion (which Nectarius left discreetly unmentioned) into the conversation.[351] As he would often do later, Augustine sought to carve out a space for Christianity that was both dignified and classical on the one hand and unyielding on the other. He addressed Nectarius as the son of a Christian and as a gentleman,[352] pointedly calling him brother (*frater*, usually reserved for Christian correspondents) and brought a full panoply of Ciceronian and Terentian references to bear. Like his master and model, Ambrose, Augustine insisted that Christian Romans do everything worthy and dignified that their classical forebears had done, and more and better besides.

But there was also the matter of the riot. An old non-Christian festival took place on the first of June in 408, some customary local rite not sufficiently disinfected for Augustine's taste, whatever mix of Christians and others might participate.[353] Things got out of control. A rambunctious crowd was passing by the city's church when the Christian clergy tried to stop the procession—they and the church were stoned for their trouble. The bishop remonstrated with the town council, to no avail. Eight days later, the church was stoned again. A third stoning ensued, and then a mob tried to set fire to the church. One ecclesiastic was killed, and Bishop Possidius hid in a secret place in the church. He could hear the mob rooting about and complaining that if they didn't find the bishop, their whole attack was pointless. The raid went on from afternoon into the night before fading away.

Augustine visited the city shortly afterward, hearing the story from his Christian friends, then engaging a group of "pagans" in a frank conversation. No good came of it.

Nectarius's reply to Augustine's indignant and accusing letter is a mas-

terpiece, evoking the spirit of late Roman civic patriotism and showing us
the oddity of Christianity in a bright light.

To my honored and respected brother Augustine, Nectarius sends his
wishes of salvation in the master:

When I had received the letter of your excellency, in which you attacked the cult of idols and the rites of the temples, I thought I was hearing the voice of a philosopher, not one from the Lyceum of the old
Academy—not the one sitting on the ground in a dark corner, pulling his
knees to his head deep plunged in thought, with no ideas of his own and
waiting to attack the distinguished ideas of others—but rather it was Cicero himself whom your voice called to my mind—I could almost see
him. He had saved the lives of countless citizens and brought the symbols of his victory before us, wearing the laurel crown as all the mobs of
Greeks stood amazed. He had put his great resonating voice and tongue,
a veritable trumpet against criminals and traitors, into service . . . and
had stripped himself of the toga in favor of the Greek pallium.

So when you make a powerful case for worshiping and following the
god who is over all, I listened with pleasure. When you persuaded us to
gaze upon the heavenly homeland, I was delighted to hear it. For you
were not speaking of a city that has a circle of walls around it, nor even
a city that the books of the philosophers argue we all belong to in this
world, but rather a city that a great god and the souls that have deserved
well of him occupy and make their own, the kind that all the laws are
seeking to establish by their different paths and ways, which we cannot
express in words but perhaps can imagine in thought.

So far, what Nectarius says differs very little from what Augustine will say
a few years later in *City of God*. He continues:

This city is to be sought and loved above all, but I still do not think we
should abandon the one in which we were begotten and born: the city
that first bestowed the gift of light upon us, that nurtured us, that educated us. To come to the point, if we have done well by it, done well by
the city of our birth, the most learned men will argue that a home will
be prepared for us in heaven after the death of the body as an elevation
to higher things. The people who will live with god are those who have
made their homeland thrive by their counsel or by their deeds. As for
your whimsical remark about how our city is troubled not by weapons

but by fire and flame, and produces thorns more than flowers—that's not the worst criticism to make, for we know that flowers often grow from thorns. It's true of roses and of heads of grain, that the sweet is often mixed in with the sharp.

The last thing you said in your letter was that the church demanded in punishment not heads or blood but the things that people most feared would be stripped from them. In my opinion, if I'm not mistaken, it's worse to be stripped of your property than to be killed. As you know very well from your reading, the death of bad men takes away their sense entirely, but an impoverished life leads to eternal ruin. For it is worse to live badly than to end with a bad death. You prove this by your own efforts to support the poor, to cure the sick, to take medicine to afflicted bodies: you do this in every way so that the afflicted will not feel the endlessness of their ruin. . . .

I've said my piece, as best I could if not as best I should, more or less. I ask and beseech—I wish I could do it face-to-face—that you consider my tears and think about who you are and what you profess and what you are doing. Think about the sight of that city from which people are being dragged to punishment—think of the lamenting of mothers, wives, children, relatives. Think how embarrassing it is to have to come home after being tortured, with the sight of wounds and scars refreshing the pain and the groaning. When you consider all these things, think of god first of all, and think of the good name of men and friendly good will and your close connection with us, and look for your praise in forgiving rather than in punishing. And all this has to do with things where people have confessed what they have done. Forgiving them out of regard for the law is something I praise without hesitation. But think how cruel it is to go after the innocent and summon into a serious criminal trial those whom it is clear had nothing to do with the crime. If they are cleared, think how much hostility will turn on the accusers. . . .

May the highest god protect you and conserve you to be the guardian and the ornament of his law.[354]

Augustine's reply[355] to this made much of the fact that Nectarius had waited eight months to reply to Augustine's original letter, but failed to see the dignity and measured calm that Nectarius was careful to display. (If Nectarius had traveled, as some think, to Ravenna in the interim to defend his townsmen against the complaints that Bishop Possidius was making there, the delay in replying to Augustine would have been perfectly understandable.) He mocks Nectarius for speaking of patriotism when the real issue is terrorism and Nectarius's condoning of it. The correspondence breaks off here, as far as we know, with Nectarius still trying to establish a community of interest between two gentlemen and Augustine still trying to turn the occasion into a debate between a "pagan" and a Christian.[356]

The one group to escape this "pagan"-Christian bifurcation of the world was Jewry. The Jews were unique in the Christian taxonomy Augustine inherited and propounded in that they worshiped the correct god, but worshiped him incorrectly, or rather incompletely. Their fault was entirely moral: they had the scriptures, they had seen Jesus, they worshiped the correct god, but they had not put two and two together correctly, and so they would be damned. Augustine's reading of the reasons for their survival in this anomalous state was anything but generous. They were kept around, he argued, as independent proof of the validity of the prophecies of the old dispensation and their fulfillment in the new.[357] Without them, Christians could have been accused of making up their Old Testament to make the New look good. Augustine's Jews live a shadowy half-life as a result, attesting ignorantly to the truth but not sharing in it. They, too, are familiar to us because of their name, yet very different from anything we know in today's world of Judaism.

The Manichee Secundinus, on the other hand, accused Augustine of having gone over to the Jews when he apostasized from Manicheism, because he acquired a more positive view of the Jewish scriptures and the link between its god and its teachings and those of Christianity. Augustine was left in an odd position, defending the historicity of Jewish scriptures, proffering a generous reading of the Jewish past (by comparison to such anti-Jewish preachers as Mani or Marcion, who would not allow that the gods of the Jewish scriptures and of Paul were really the same god), and treating real living Jews with cautious generosity, as when he defended the Jew Licenius against the seizure of his property by a bishop.[358] His manner of patronizing was not directly toxic, but in his own time, forced conversions, which he condemned in principle,[359] would be harbingers of future persecution.[360] To be as little positive as Augustine could be was its own contribution to the climate of hatred that would prevail too often in the future.

Every half-educated or educated modern who comes to the period in which Augustine lives still lives with the unthinking binary categories he nourished. The "pagan" category has triumphed over its sectarian origins and is now commonly used by interpreters and scholars of every stripe to accept the imposition on the late-antique world of the black/white divide that Christians sought to create. Eighteenth-century sympathizers with un-Christian cultists did not realize how much of the combat they were giving away in accepting the name and preferring the style of "pagan" for their heroes in the period. To be sure, few if any real "pagan" heroes stood out in Augustine's time. Most of the modern melodramas of the decline and fall of "paganism" suffer from the fundamental failing of taking Christian parody and polemic too seriously. The poignancy and loss of old ways in Augustine's time was rarely felt so deeply by votaries of the old religions as their modern sympathizers would have us believe.[361] Christianity succeeded by the way it outlasted the Roman empire and defined itself against its culture of origin. It persuaded those who came after to see some linear transformation, even progress, between old and new, with Christianity granted presumptive ownership of the new. We say glibly of Augustine that he is both Roman and Christian, ancient and medieval, and in so doing make claims that could only be true in retrospect, and only if we accept a set of theological categories that were very much controverted in Augustine's own time.

Once again, if we could imagine Augustine without the future we know he had, he would engage a broader but less intense debate about his merits. Without legatees and legacies, real and imagined, he undoubtedly would be one of the most fascinating and broadly studied of ancient men. But we would think of him as resembling in the first instance not so much Aquinas or Heidegger as Cicero or Pascal. Indeed, he and Cicero would be found to be brothers in many ways: failed family men and political upstart machinators whose prestige and creations succeeded beyond their lifetimes even while they themselves died amid the ruins of their earthly hopes; heirs of Platonism consciously rewriting their master for their own times, and living at a moment when new political orders they little imagined would invoke *them* as founding patrons.

Men like Cicero and Augustine earn grudging respect mixed with polite belittling from their descendants. Absent sainthood, Augustine might well have heard some later sage say of him what he himself said of Cicero: "In the ordinary run of the curriculum, I came upon the book of someone named Cicero, whose eloquence almost everyone admires, but not so his heart."[362] This phrase introduces Augustine's acknowledgment that one of Cicero's books changed his life as dramatically as any book of Christian scripture ever did and so only underlines the ambiguity of the inheritance.

If Augustine could be read without an enfolding notion of Christian supremacy, or at least of Christian legacy, he might have been as inspiring to many young men, and at the same time esteemed as weakly.

Christianity has changed in another way since Augustine's time, by changing its competitors. Christianity in our world competes with a variety of other systems of discourse. Some of them are religious, and some of those are either younger than Augustine's age (e.g., Islam) or unknown to his world (e.g., Asian cultures of great antiquity), while some of those are themselves complexly related to things that existed in Augustine's world and have similar problems of identity. Thus "Christianity" and "Judaism" were at loggerheads in his time and in ours, in various ways, but the lines of filiation between the ancient and modern avatars of each tradition are complicated and often broken.

More important, the modern world has seen the emergence within western societies of modes of thought that have consciously created and differentiated themselves with Christianity in mind, and in so doing they have compelled Christianity to define itself against them, and so have forced Christianity to change as well. The empirical scientist, the empirical economist, the medical researcher or practitioner, and the post-Enlightenment political theorist have created alternatives to all or part of what Christianity speaks of in ways that have made it impossible for *Augustine's* Christianity (embodying as it did the best of science, the best of philosophy, and the best of social science known to that time) to exist any longer. A Christianity that sought a similar embodiment of contemporary excellences today would be very unlike Augustine's.

CHRISTIANITY AS WE KNOW IT . . .

The version of Christianity that exulted in the discovery of Stephen's relics seems almost not to need comment. Medieval religion was like that. The only hesitation heard when people speak of Augustine is to compare his late support for the miraculous and for relic cult with his early skepticism, as though he were somehow an Enlightenment skeptic who had fallen, through long familiarity with ordinary church folk, into practices his better mind had once stayed away from. It wasn't that simple.

Augustine instead stands at the head of a line of Enlightenment thinkers who rationalized the position of Christianity in the world by a two-tier theory of interpretation.[363] On this theory, two domains of religious thought exist, one for the world of the body, one for the world of the spirit. Real religion is religion of the spirit, but fallen mankind lives in a corporeal world of rituals. In his short book *Taking Care of the Dead*, Augustine both confronted the division in practices and established the two-minded way of speaking. Caring for bodies of the dead does no harm, and making them a focus of liturgical activity is entirely acceptable, *because* the truth lies elsewhere, in the realm of the spirit. Augustine in this way re-creates the attitude of traditional Roman aristocrats who philosophized at home and participated in quite fantastic religious cults in public. But he had the advantage of a deeper rationale, one that held that it was indeed the same religion in both cases, the same god, seen in different ways.

Augustine internalized the ideas about two modes of religion so well that he probably forgot he had done so and began to live in the two worlds simultaneously. One motive for his amphibiousness was still his desire to rescue his mother's religious reputation for orthodoxy, and with it his own reputation. But that is only the beginning of an explanation. Deeply rooted in Augustine's version of Christianity (and in western ways of Christianity since) is a divide that appears in various ways: body and spirit, science and religion, therapy and punishment.[364] The bridging of that divide and the notion that it need not fundamentally exclude religion from the advance of civilized life is an extraordinary, and extraordinarily powerful, invention, still cherished in most of mainstream Christianity and rejected outright among Christians only by the most resistant of Evangelicals. The relative failure of a comparable notion to take root broadly in Islam and the strength in religious discourse of those for whom the claims of religion are unmitigated by other social forces is proving now to be an expensive failure for humankind, and especially for Islam itself.[365]

This division of practices matching division of social classes in matters of religion has a curious appeal to intellectuals when they see it as a way of separating permissible from impermissible forms of religious expression. The danger of such a separation needs also to be seen. For such spiritualization will eventually support complicated and, to most eyes, pathological disenfranchisement of the body, sexuality, and women in mainstream western cultures. Much of the labor expended on elaborating incarnational spirituality and other recent theological ventures could have been saved had the fundamental and unnecessary lines not been drawn long ago.

But Augustine's case can lead to a wider set of reflections. Thinking that we know something of Augustine because we know that he was a

Christian goes along with thinking that we know what Christianity was in his time. The "triumph of Christianity" in the Roman empire is a familiar enough story and underlies many of the narratives we inherit. A small community struggles, resists persecution, grows quietly and irresistibly, and eventually wins over the rich and powerful of the earth. It is a story literally too good to be true.

For the organizational idea of Christianity, the idea that Jesus left behind a community that has self-reproduced, grown, diversified, but remained in some fundamental aspects the same—that idea is a theological proposition, not a historical one, and can be reconciled with history only with the greatest difficulty. The historian has the obligation to ask why one would bother. My sketch of the history of "Glunchism" earlier in this chapter made that point in one way. We have reached a moment where we should look more closely at how the story of Christianity of Augustine's time can and should be revised.

The history of Christianity is not as a musical score prescribing a continuo accompanied by melodies and variations that come and go. Rather, it is a room full of musicians, quarrelsome and opinionated, many of whom come and go, tooting their instruments randomly at times, at other times seeking to make music together in smaller or larger groups that never quite fill the space. Even at its greatest geographical extent and social penetration, the orchestra of Christianity never played as one.

After the disappearance of Jesus, astonishing stories grew up around his passing, stories that took a long time to resolve into a common narrative of resurrection, forty days of visible presence thereafter, and then ascension into heaven. Telling these stories, groups of enthusiasts spread through the Jewish communities of the Near East. In very short time, communities of widely varying beliefs and practices sprang up. The earliest documents of Christianity, the letters attributed to Paul, came into being because it was both possible and difficult to impose similar notions of belief and practice on people living in different places. Paul (and the segment of the Jesus movement he stood for) had intense and fundamentally unresolved quarrels with Peter and the other apostles, whose views of Christianity in the long run yielded to those of the ex-persecutor, who told a story of his own miraculous conversion to justify his authority. Through the first three centuries of their existences, Christian churches showed an extraordinarily wide variety of ideas and practices. The texts they wrote confirmed this. Even the texts that were redacted eventually into the New Testament (and the final list of books accepted into that canon may date no earlier than the fourth century) reveal on close examination considerable diversity of understanding and interpretation, both about the historical events of Jesus's life and the theological interpretations that might be imposed on those stories. The other texts we have that were in circulation in those days, such as the so-called Gnostic Gospels,[366] show conclusively the breadth and depth of the variety and disagreement that separated the earliest Christians. In Augustine's own time, there was a new Latin translation of the *Recognitions*, a first-person narrative attributed to Clement, the early bishop of Rome, yet readable as the first Christian novel, in which many earlier practices (those associated with the followers of Peter rather than those of Paul) could still be seen and spoken of and a not-quite-authorized version of early events passed on.[367]

Christianity in those first three hundred years rarely came to the attention of government authorities, and then was looked on mainly with mild amusement. That Christians every now and then fell afoul of the law and were punished did not, and does not, add up to a history of "persecution." To imagine (as Christians of the fourth century already did) that Roman authority could have such a consistent and widely held view about these disparate and insignificant bands of zealots is to flatter early Christianity too much. But the Christian enthusiasm spread and flourished in its way. In some parts of the Mediterranean world (Asia Minor, the Syrian hinterland back of Antioch, the Egyptian delta, Africa around Carthage, the Greek-speaking communities of Rome and Gaul), churches flourished and fought. Elsewhere, the map remained largely empty of Christians.

Other books tell the story of Christian persistence and eventual Christian good fortune. The patronage of the emperor Constantine, starting around 312 C.E. was the making of Christianity as a force in history.[368] The shifting of financial resources to support one particular stream among Christians, the demonstrations of imperial social patronage, and the prestige given to groups of Christian bishops brought together to argue their doctrinal issues all sent an unmistakable message of support and created an environment in which this Christianity could flourish. Even so, Christianity was still most visible in the traditional locations; the emergence of a new capital at Constantinople added a further focus. The four apostle-founded bishoprics of Rome, Constantinople (whose claim to apostolic foundation was a bit of a stretch to sustain), Antioch, and Alexandria retained their prestige for centuries. (Jerusalem, by contrast, even while it remained an important Christian bishopric, had lost all pride of place in the formal hierarchy, for the city itself was economically, socially, and politically insignificant.)

Africa's Carthage ranked fifth, at best, with the the first evidence of

Christianity in Africa coming late in the second century. In very short order, the Christians ran afoul of the local authorities for their outspoken
contempt for public order and religion, and at various times in the third
century, government action sought to control them, gaining only a reputation for persecution and leaving behind martyrs. The story of the pious
women Perpetua and Felicity, mauled by wild beasts, then killed by exe-
cutioner gladiators, quickly became a bestseller.

Taken in one direction, the natural future of this Christianity was the
future that Donatism tried to have. That native African Christianity remained insular, idealistic, and highly suspicious of the Roman government. Its believers awaited the coming of their god patiently, venerated
their martyrs, and did not much care what the rest of the world thought
or did. For them, the important thing was to grasp and hold the true faith
that had been handed down to them. Augustine stands, on the other hand,
for the Christianity of the future in the fourth century. He and the other
visionary leaders of that time, many of whom have been long acclaimed
as "Fathers of the Church," more appositely than their admirers knew,
were indeed the people who invented the belief system we call Christianity. It is one of the lasting and monumental achievements of civilization,
on a par with the Roman empire, differing chiefly in the way it imagined
endless possibilities of growth for itself and saw all political systems as
candidates for its support. Like all great empires, this Christianity is to
some extent an independent social organization and to some extent a par-
asite on other systems. Large-scale organizations succeed when they can
leverage their influence by absorbing the energy and resources of other
social groupings they subsume.

What was that revolutionary fourth-century Christianity like, which
shaped Augustine and was in turn shaped by him, living on after him, in
and beyond the territories of the old Roman empire?

First, Christianity is wealthy, visible, and respectable, for all that it
preaches humility and poverty. There had been wealthy Christians here
and there in the third century, but the widespread building of large basilicas and other church buildings, the expectation of financial support from
public and private sources, and the presence in church of the wealthy and
well-connected were all novelties made possible by Constantine and his
heirs. Second, and equally important, the emergence of an educated, sophisticated, socially well-connected (but not *too* well-connected) clergy
was only possible when the church had come into the bright light of social
prominence. In the Latin world particularly, the emergence of figures like

Augustine, Ambrose, Jerome, Paulinus of Nola, and the poet Prudentius gave the churches they were associated with a very different character from what had gone before. All those figures encountered suspicions in their Christian communities, suspicions arising out of their close association with the institutions of traditional Roman culture and government. Ambrose was a governor and the son of a prime minister, Paulinus of Nola a wealthy landowner. Augustine, with his provincial roots, was by comparison a piker, but his wit and fortune had made him every bit the man of the establishment as he made his way to Carthage, Rome, and Milan.

The new model prevailed: an aristocracy of clergy emerged, with the educated and theologically sophisticated at a pinnacle, women marginalized, and the half-educated increasingly subservient to their social betters.

The Christianity of this world made for itself new enemies by its new way of defining itself. Jesus, his first disciples, and the first generations of Christians lived in a world full of overt competition. But in 391 C.E. the emperor Theodosius banned all public religious sacrifice and with it effectively shut down the religious competition to Christianity. No longer would it have to compete with a welter of diverse religious communities and practices. If you wanted religious assurance, if you wanted to believe that you would benefit from divine favor, Christian churches were the only place to go. The underground persistence of practice did not succeed in keeping a place for non-Christian allegiance in the public realm or common discourse.[369]

So two new classes of enemies were invented, and two old ones reconstructed. The old ones seemed familiar enough: the Jews and the heretics. Both were family members for Christianity, hated and feared as one hates those one knows too well. (Jews were now increasingly pushed outside the family and increasingly withdrew from any hint of association with Christianity, but that is another story.[370]) But now "the world" was also invented in a new sense: the world of temptations of the flesh and worldliness *without* religious overtones, a world that tempted by its seductions and its appeal to the senses.[371] Where Christians had earlier hated the shows and games of Roman civil life at least in part for their association with Roman religion, now they could hate them for their own sake. Augustine in *City of God* is the poet of this hostility to the secular, building on what he found in scripture and early Christianity to be sure, but taking the opposition to new intensity. In Augustine's world, even if every form of overtly religious opposition to Christianity were to be eliminated, "the world" would remain implacable and opposed. The narrative of triumph comes into its own accompanied by this notion of endless struggle against an enemy that will be surmounted only at the end of time.

But the *idea* of religious opposition needed to survive, and so Augustine's contemporaries created and increasingly relied on an artificial and convenient picture of non-Christian religion: hence the function of "paganism."

The greatest evolution occurred inside, in the way the church was organized and behaved. The establishment and maintenance of a church system that would achieve universality of doctrine and practice in a threatening world gave rise to a whole set of management techniques new to that period but profoundly influential in later centuries. The most fundamental is the reliance on standardized texts as vehicles of authority and discipline. Curiously enough, the Bible came last in this process of standardization.

First came doctrinal disputes. The successive battles of the fourth and fifth centuries took repetitive form. Idiosyncratic (in the eye of the beholder) expression of Christian ideas would attract negative attention, attempts would be made to repress the idiosyncratic, and then theological effort would be devoted to demonstrating the incorrectness of the views already opposed. In the normative cases, the figures marginalized at the outset of the controversy would be rendered permanently alien and branded as heretics, like Arius or Nestorius. In extreme cases, they might be killed for their beliefs and practices. In some cases, however, which side would ultimately prevail remained uncertain for a long time. Both evolved complicated and subtle theological arguments and called upon friends near and far (and in high places) to support their claim to having the one acceptable form of truth. The fourth century saw a series of comedies in which the bishop Athanasius of Alexandria went from hero to villain and back in his home city and at the imperial court. He was the greatest theological diva of the age and ended as the undoubtedly orthodox and saintly leader of the dominant party; but he could have turned out otherwise and very nearly did.[372]

The years after Constantine declared his patronage for Christianity saw a sequence of these quarrels. The puzzles that took root and lasted longest asked how Jesus was to be understood in relation to god—as god, as son of god, and/or as man at the same time? In a way, they never came to conclusion, as the trinitarian arguments that gave rise to the Arian controversy led, once forcibly settled by the Council of Constantinople of 381,[373] to Christological arguments that were again forcibly settled at the Council of Chalcedon in 451. But those arguments never really went away, and orthodox, monophysite, and Nestorian stripes of Christianity survived through the middle ages and to the present day.[374]

What was new was both the possibility of such deep disagreement over doctrine, carried out at a distance, and the *idea* that disagreement could and should be resolved in doctrinal harmony, with imperial backing. The difficulties of achieving such agreement were only multiplied by the sharp cultural and ideological differences that separated Greek-speaking and Latin-speaking Christians (to say nothing of their colleagues writing in Syriac, the language closest to the one Jesus spoke). Boethius in the sixth century would observe that the very fact of translation contributed to disagreement, and he gave examples of how the natural way to translate given theological terms inevitably led to misunderstanding.

To resolve the disputes of doctrine, councils of bishops were called with increasing frequency. This brought together the leaders of churches, ostensibly under the guidance of a divine spirit, to reason together and agree. Agreement sometimes followed, but, in the process, the role of the bishop was subtly and surely elevated.

Those gatherings could and very commonly also did deal with issues that fell far short of the heights of theological doctrine. The standardized management of the Christian church began to express itself in the disciplinary rules for laity and especially for clergy laid down by these councils. As bishops gradually took on the role and trappings of civil authority (even sitting in judgment on civil disputes in what looked very much like courts of law), they gradually acquired the staff to help them do their jobs, and over time those staffs took on more and more of the familiar trappings of civil government.[375] In the extreme case, at the end of the sixth century, we know in great detail the management structure of the papacy of Gregory I, and it can be shown that every official in his entourage had an exact equivalent in the civil government of the time, while he was very much engaged in the civil and military government of an Italy increasingly abandoned by the empire at Constantinople.

Doctrinal dispute gave rise to creeds, that is to say, negotiated formulas of words designed to exclude error and state a minimum truth necessary to salvation. The so-called Apostles' Creed, still current today, was already in wide use and had been for a long time; it took final form (with the addition of a phrase to say that Jesus had descended to hell after his crucifixion and before his resurrection) in the late fourth century. It was the form of words that new Christians had to memorize (along with the "Lord's Prayer") to be admitted to Augustine's community. But each council that dealt with matters of high doctrine had to find new formulas, and so the Council of Nicea had its own hotly disputed text. Its bishops had to employ a newish and unscriptural word, "homoousion" (literally "same in being," rendered in churchly English as "consubstantial") to make their point, and others would accuse them of departing from the true biblical doctrine to do so. Later councils would need to issue their own statements, and today a new scholarly edition of all the creeds of Christendom fills four volumes.[376]

This textualization of Christian authority made people pay attention in new ways to the Christian scriptures. Here the eastern and western churches were in very different positions. The New Testament was all written originally in Greek and could be read thus in the original, while books making up the Old Testament (on Augustine's reckoning) had been written some in Greek but mainly in Hebrew. Centuries earlier, Hellenized Jews had prepared a Greek translation of the Hebrew books, accompanied with an authorizing legend of how it had been commissioned by the Egyptian king Ptolemy and prepared by seventy bilingual Jewish sages. Each, the story went,[377] was sent into a tent by himself to translate the whole of scripture, and when all seventy emerged many weeks later, each had miraculously produced a translation identical to all the others. With that combination of Jewish authority and divine patronage, it was easy for Greek Christians to accept the translations they had in hand, even though at least several distinct versions were in use; but that of the "seventy" (nicknamed from the Latin number as the Septuagint) had the greatest prestige.[378]

The early Latin translations came from the Greek and none had wide authority. Many of the translations in circulation were manifestly inept. It would appear that it was the high-living Bishop Damasus of Rome who sought to promote the use of Latin. He switched the liturgy of the city of Rome from Greek to Latin and also asked Jerome (then a priest in the church at Rome) to prepare a revised and improved translation of the whole of scripture. From his place of retirement at Bethlehem in the years between the 380s to the 410s, Jerome carried out this task, studying Hebrew and returning to the original texts of the Hebrew scriptures. The texts he produced, combined with some earlier versions that he did not succeed in replacing, came to be known as the Latin Vulgate, so named from its broad acceptance in general use. Of greatest importance was the common agreement that translation would suffice and that it would not be necessary for believers—or even, in practice, most theologians—to have recourse to the original texts of the biblical books. Judaism and Islam are not so lenient with their sacred books.

So by the time Christianity was firmly implanted in the highest circles of Roman society, had acquired the allegiance of the best-educated and most ambitious men, and had regularized its doctrinal and textual affairs, the identification of religion with secular society was essentially complete—and, for some, troubling. What became of the original spirit of the religion with its aloof and dismissive air toward ordinary society, with its strict moral demands, with the thrill of the forbidden enshrined in stories of martyrs done to a hideous death for their faith?

That spirit found its own characteristically modern expression in the fourth century in multiple ways. If no more martyrs were being made— with no good persecutors to make more of them[379]—then at least two direct compensations could be counted. The old martyrs themselves could continue to be present in their shrines and in their bones. Martyr sites became chapels or cathedrals, and eventually bits of martyr bones and clothing moved into circulation. The great martyrs, like Cyprian of Carthage, great for his position before his martyrdom as bishop of Carthage, would have large shrines, and the contest for control of their spaces between factions of the church would be intense. The annual festivals memorializing dates of martyrdom would be high points of the Christian year. When Augustine would go to Carthage for the summer, he did not leave his own flock until Easter, but he would characteristically stay in Carthage until late summer, for the festival of Cyprian on September 14. Stephen's relics, as we saw, brought special prestige, but moved into a very familiar role. If the martyr's shrines were not sufficient, martyr stories abounded. The fifth and sixth centuries, particularly, would be the great age of flourishing reading and writing of martyr stories in the world of Latin Christianity. Some of these stories even had basis in fact, but many of them either took rise from mere names on lists maintained by faithful churches, or were simple fictions told for a purpose. If we cannot suffer, then to remember that others have suffered provides a satisfactory emotional release from guilt or anxiety.

This was the age in which a male, celibate elite emerged, competing for power with traditional authorities. The fourth century saw its emergence in the Greek east, in the desert away from the city clergy who tended the ritual needs of the faithful. The history of eastern Christianity for many years after was the history of the increasing influence and domination of the monk over the ordinary cleric.

In the Latin west, things were rather different. For decades, westerners played an envious game of catch-up with eastern holy men. Augustine's age was highly unstable, even volatile, for the debates among Latins about how best to emulate the Greek successes, and a stable western pattern of "monasticism" settled into place only gradually over the next several centuries. But it was settled that *ordinary* Christianity would never suffice, and so there emerged a willed and established system of fundamental spiritual hierarchy, in which the ascetic few would stand before the carnal many. This was not just a hierarchy of responsibility for management but a hierarchy of value. The *theological* implications of such a social system were tangled and probably finally impossible to work out, so egalitarian were the gospel and other biblical texts on which the theologians had to work. But the social emergence of the clerical aristocracy was assured. This was also the age in which stories of heroic contemporary Christian ascetics began to circulate widely. Once again, if you could not suffer, reading about the suffering of others made you feel almost as good.

In one last area, in many respects the most obvious, the Christianity invented in the fourth century had a long life ahead of it. When Augustine entered the church, he knew of the practice of infant baptism but could not quite make sense of it.[380] He would spend the last twenty years of his life trying to explain publicly how it was that he had now decided infant baptism was a right and good and necessary thing. Meanwhile, he had to learn to cope with success.

For as long as Christianity was a minority religion and its adherents came to it from outside, adult baptism was easily accepted as the norm. That assumption had begun to change in the fourth century as whole households and communities found themselves inside the Christian world. The liturgical practice of infant baptism grew up in such circles,[381] and much of the theological development of Christianity from that point forward had to derive from and defend that practice. That practice in turn seems to have reified superstition and fear. If baptism works, and if many tiny babies die, and die in agony, then surely baptism cannot be denied to children. No professed theologian could say that, but every pastor had to cope with parents demanding baptism on those terms, and pastors increasingly conceded the point. Augustine would proceed, in his literal-minded way, to interpret the fact of infant mortality as a sign of infant sinfulness. We will see how this puzzlement and his accommodation to it led him to his most distinctive and regrettable doctrinal innovation.

The prevalence of infant baptism revealed the new ubiquity and universality of Christianity. Nothing in Christian scriptures prepared believers for this eventuality, and it can be argued that Christianity has never really theorized a way to live in such domination. For it could gradually come to seem that Christianity was everywhere (within the sway of Roman dominion) and was believed by everyone (heretics and Jews excepted, while surviving adherents of other old religions were simply declared nonexistent). The fear of persecution would vanish, and no one worried about the tyranny one's own party might employ. Augustine never theorized a world in which Christians would dominate the secular realm indefinitely and with confidence. Even in *City of God*, though he praises Christian emperors, he still fails to see what is happening before his eyes. Instead he perilously accepts that imperial military and civil power can be brought to bear in what he still sees as the desperate struggle to bring humankind to its senses. The triumph of Christianity, spoken of transparently in the history textbooks, depended in fact on the brute force of empire and law to bring it about, a force to which Christians were slow in breaking their addiction many, many centuries later, an addiction that still flourishes in some surprising places.

Others were slow in seeing that future as well. The bishop of Rome in Augustine's lifetime was still only a prestigious and sometimes influential figure, but he was not yet "pope" to Christians at a distance from Rome in any meaningful sense; that would take another hundred years. But in that respect and others, the fifth and sixth centuries saw the working out and institutionalization of the religious and social creations of the fourth century. Such institutionalization was probably far from inevitable at the time, but in retrospect, the fundamental choices and alignments were in place by the time Augustine died, and those were, in the main, choices that had been made in his, or even in his parents', lifetime.[382]

The homogenization of Christianity into a more or less successfully single international movement and the branding of that movement as "catholic" (in the west) or "orthodox" (in the east) is a further result of this process of invention. Augustine's part in shaping the catholic identity was the central achievement of his career, and we will pursue that story in the next chapter.

Several important conclusions should be drawn from reviewing this history. First, if "Christianity" has any specific historical meaning, it should be thought of as that fourth-century church and its descendants and branches. This observation runs sharply against the theological tradition, common in all denominations, of seeing a linear descent and filiation from Jesus to the present, always culminating in the community of the particular observer—but it does far more justice to the evidence.

Second, the thing "Christianity" denotes is only tertiarily a religious movement. It is always accompanied by religious claims and practices, but the fundamental impact of Christianity on the world has been in the organization of civil life and society. Christianity became not a religion but an umbrella surrogate for religion. If you had Christianity, you had, by definition, religion, whatever your own views or practices might be. Where Christianity takes root, to be sure, it links up with local religious practices and indeed becomes a religion, to the embarrassment of its theoreticians. The hierarchy of believers comes into play again, as the two levels (sophisticates and devout) each concoct a story to explain the other. Augustine would always believe that the ignorant and the intellectual were very different in many ways and that the ignorant had, if anything, the better chance at heaven.[383]

DON QUIXOTE OF HIPPO

What if we could laugh at Augustine? Hasn't anybody ever done that? Not to judge by the books he wrote, not to judge by the vast literature about him. In the tens of thousands of pages about him, in the thousands of pages he wrote, vast humorlessness stretches as far as the eye can see. When Augustine attempts a lame joke[384] or when a bitter enemy allows himself a snide remark, we are astonished, we remark the event, and move on solemnly.

Why?

Is it because Christianity is a religion that takes life so seriously that every moment of consciousness is notionally written down in a book somewhere? That an impertinent wisecrack is somehow a sin and, even if not a great sin, still something to be toted up in the minus column of that unironic accounting ledger? Christian liturgy is certainly jokeless and virtually humorless, for all that it remembers to speak of joy. In it, wine becomes blood, the most successful men and women are virgins and martyrs, the central action commemorates a brutal judicial murder, and song is an afterthought.

Given five million humorless words by Augustine, and heaven only knows how many more solemn words by his exegetes, opponents, historians, biographers, and adulators, we'll probably never find an easy and natural way to laugh in his presence, that's true. And that's sad.

What if you take the blinders off? What if you stop seeing "Augustine" or "Saint Augustine" and instead really ask yourself who this guy reminds you of? What comes to mind?

Look at him in his last years in Hippo. He has given up on his adventures and resides now at home, reading over again all the books he has written, and reading back before that the books that he read when younger. He has been shaped, decisively, by the books he has read, but he was less unusual when he was still trapped in the books of the educational system he grew up in. As long as a whole community is trapped in certain books, the common hallucination they share is easily pardoned. Fish don't know they're wet.

But Augustine had abandoned the common culture in favor of books that had not yet made a culture. They told heroic tales of olden days, set among the exotic Jews of Palestine, and he believed them all, lock, stock, and barrel. He believed them so much and read them so obsessively that he began to act as if those books defined the world, as if they could be used as an operator's manual for real human life.

When he took these books seriously and applied their lessons to his own life, he managed a functional adaptation. Almost any book or set of books can be useful in that way.[385] Some aspects of that life of his were asocial at best: abandoning to plunge into rustic retirement, then abandoning family and property to let himself be remade into the high-priest figure of a new-age cult. But it worked for him, and when he told the story in his memoirs, he made a persuasive and beautiful work of art from it.

And there's a lesson there. The diversity of fates and lives that men and women choose for themselves is extraordinarily broad, and it is beyond belief difficult to predict what will seem a functional adaptation and what will seem derangement. Think, if you seek comparisons for Augustine, perhaps of Nietzsche: brilliant, successful, and rescued from responsibility for the consequences of his more idiosyncratic ideas by the fortunate fall of his illness. Or think of Wittgenstein: fleeing from wealth and family into a social disaster during his years as schoolteacher in rural Austria, but then falling—rather like Augustine falling into Hippo—into a fellowship at Cambridge, where his eccentricities were the mark of a more nearly satisfactory socialization. Or think of Emily Dickinson: by most reasonable standards a gross failure at establishing and maintaining normal human relationships, but in the eyes of her contemporaries able to maintain a sufficient façade of normalcy to escape all but the most ordinary censoriousness and interference.

Is Augustine so different? Is Augustine so odd? Nietzsche, Wittgenstein, and Dickinson all took their books as seriously as he did.

But another figure, this one fictional and standing at the head of the chronological line of modernity, long antedating the three prisoners of nineteenth-century textuality to whom I have compared Augustine, comes to mind as a better model.

An old man, living too much by himself in the country, too much absorbed with his books and the adventures of former times that he has fallen among, takes those stories seriously, as true histories, and goes out to shape his life as if those stories were reasonable models. He has one set of misfortunes, the ones more familiar to modern cartoon iconography, when he is alone in his fantasies: a golden helmet that is really a barber's piece of crockery, looming giants that are really innocent windmills. But Cervantes' hero has a far more interesting set of adventures in the second half of his history, when the world has begun to read about him, the demented hero, in books, and when it begins both to take him as seriously as he takes the heroes of old. The second half of *Don Quixote de la Mancha* is the story of the world that takes him seriously and sends out its champions to fight him.

So who is Augustine, on those terms? He is Don Quixote in a world that *really* takes him and his obsessions seriously. That world, it must be emphasized, is Roman Africa, or at most the Latin western Mediterranean. Recall that the space Augustine inhabited is the eastern Maghreb, from Hippo to Carthage, and the world that could be reached easily from there: across in one direction to Rome and Italy, across in another to the Balearics and Spain, and, because of the fellow zealots who were blazing the trail, east to Palestine. The Greek world may as well not have existed, and Augustine's particular backwater certainly did not exist for the Greek cosmopolites of the eastern Mediterranean.

Christianity was still new and fresh in his world, particularly in Augustine's class and community. The upper-class Christian, the one for whom the religion really was a matter of something you found in a book, was a clumsy newcomer in Augustine's Africa, as in Paulinus's Italy. For many, the scripture books were too badly written to merit serious attention and were introduced into serious conversations only with some awkwardness.[386] Their clumsiness betrays itself as well in their fumbling with the practices and ideology of ascesis, but it ran much deeper. Augustine and his contemporaries, busy inventing Christianity as we know it, had all the deftness of garage-hobbyists, and some of their constructions had the daffiness and improbability of garage-creations that don't quite make it.

Will the whole elaborate notion of the seven days of creation, charmingly fantastic when the writer of Genesis ventures the riff, sustain Augustine's killingly literal-minded attempt to make it a serious piece of cosmology? Could the Rube Goldberg notion of *seminales rationes*[387] (implanted by the divine creator in the first creations and left to sprout and blossom into apparently new beings later) ever persuade an objective observer? Do his explanations of the historical and logical inconsequences of scripture ever come across as more than special pleading?

Dig one level deeper and start there. Jesus spoke of salvation for people who were distressed, alienated, dissatisfied. On a given day in Palestine, it could all make great sense.

But once Jesus was gone, somebody had to work out, if the Jesus idea was to persist, how to rationalize and mechanize the hope of salvation into a set of behaviors and expectations. The failure of Jesus to return for a third coming (counting the post-resurrection appearances of Jesus as the second) posed one set of difficulties, difficulties that were heroically overcome by Paul and the other followers. (And bear in mind that without Paul, who never met Jesus, the Jesus idea might well have faded very quickly or become something very different.) The power and attraction of the message that those followers retained from Jesus is best measured by the stretches to which they could go in order to reconcile their disappointments with what they remembered him saying in a pattern that could keep hope alive.

But more time passed. As long as Christianity was like a bowling league or condominium association—and to envision the quality of governance in early Christian churches, one would probably do well to recall such other earnest and well-meaning and amateurish efforts at human self-organization—it was reasonable to expect adults to come to join the club, pay their dues, and acquire the benefits. Once Paul was read as saying that the Jewish requirement of circumcision no longer applied, the club could be quite attractive and reassuring.

Then more time passed. Success happened. An emperor (no less!) bought in to a Christian club. Pretty soon imperially sponsored bowling leagues were springing up everywhere, and huge new 199-lane Bowl-O-Ramas, with marble foyers and gold ceilings, were being built all around the Roman world. Joining was no longer a rare, discretionary choice. There was a stampede to get in.

People began taking the rules of the league more seriously, insisting that membership was necessary to happiness and salvation. Necessary for whom? For all? What about babies? Many of them would die before ever they achieved the age of league-joining. What would become of them?

The logic of the arguments created long ago in Palestine would begin to weigh on all sides: of *course* one had to baptize these infants, it made sense.

And so the practice, scattered at first and then widespread, becomes increasingly popular. The young Augustine is baffled by it, the bishop Augustine capitulates to it, and the middle-aged Augustine begins to explain it: but he could only explain it by constructing a theological notion, original sin, that defies logic on various points. It has the qualities of a mathematical equation that requires you to fail to notice that it divides by zero on two or three occasions in order to get to its results.

If it were only Don Quixote, alone in his study, worrying about these things, no one would take them seriously. The world's history is full of comparably obsessive ideas, worked out in elaborate detail, that make no sense when seen from outside. What is different about Augustine's original sin is that it was a doctrine elaborated in a community of obsessives, people who had willingly bought in to the same history, the same odd-lot jumble of pretexts (their "scriptures"), and reinforced one another's anxieties. It was their reality, even if others around them could not see it.

And when Don Quixote of Hippo came to elaborate his notions, plenty of people resisted. Those resisters came in three camps: the aristocratic, old-fashioned, Christianity-lite folks, for whom the new religion was a charmingly fresh way of enacting old pieties; the extreme zealots of the monasteries, for whom mere infants and women were of no interest in comparison to the heroics of the true Don Quixotes, whose stories were told in all the bizarre legends of the desert fathers; and the well-intentioned middle, who could not accept the ideas but could not bring themselves to resist Augustine, and so tamed him, gradually and carefully, to the point where, by the time a century had elapsed after his death, the council held at Orange in southern Gaul in 529 could adopt a series of dogmatic statements that abandoned all of Augustine's extreme positions at the cost of incoherence: yes to infant baptism, and yes to salvation by a series of sacramental and ethical good works.[388] And yes to Augustine.

Let me interrupt myself there. The last few paragraphs present a partial and inadequate view of Augustine. They betray a contemporary set of judgments about modern Christianities, projected back on an ancient religious movement of great subtlety and complexity.

Does that make them either true or untrue? Try this thought experiment: suppose we discovered a society exactly like ours, except that in that alternate society, a group of stories with no reasonable likelihood of truth-to-history were widely and enthusiastically accepted as history, and the moral and political lessons drawn from those stories were taught in schools and homes and public places as the fundamental moral and political lessons of the society. How would living in that society differ from living in our own?

Leave aside the last two thousand years. We admire the Greeks and Romans because they are the ancestors of our rationality. But they did live in exactly those kinds of worlds. If we look abroad, beyond our ancestors, we find that the ancient Chinese or Native Americans, or whomever we looked for, lived in just that way. We know how to read those pasts selectively, admiring intellectual achievement and moral insight, but feeling no obligation to believe, or even to consider believing, the stories.

Looking in that way, we see suddenly one of the defining features of the Christian tradition: the claim to supervening truth for its stories. I say "supervening" to mean that Christian cultures don't just treat their stories as though they were true. Lots of cultures do that. They do not even simply disregard other people's stories politely when confronted with them. Lots of cultures do that. Christianity, the brand of Christianity, that is, that won wide adherence, actively propagated the notion of its own truths as demonstrably and exclusively superior to those of other cultures and devoted itself to maintaining that truth in a historically and naturally multicultural environment.[389] If the ancient Jew said, "We have a better god than you," it was the Christian that perfected the addendum, ". . . and we can prove it to you." It doesn't matter whether that proof was carried out by documentary history, philosophical argument, or the persecutor's ax: the principle was the same. The Inquisition would add, ". . . and if we fail to prove it to you, the fault is entirely yours." Dostoevsky's Grand Inquisitor is a reminder that such attitudes are not demonstrably tied to a close attention to Jesus or his own words.

Now, today many people might find it problematic to accept that the particular stories of life in Palestine in olden days on which Christianity was erected are superveningly true. Remarkably enough, most *believers* have a pretty good idea what the problems are with validating those old stories. And it makes little or no difference. The principle that survives is the principle of self-assertion of stories. We are who our stories tell us we are, we live the way our stories tell us to, and we feel deeply that we are right to do so. And if someone comes along later with another set of supervening stories, be he Muslim or Mormon, we are under no obligation to take his stories seriously but we may insist that he acknowledge ours.

But then it turns out that the most rigorous historians of human history, the most objective and dispassionate scientists, the most versatile wizards of the truth of what has actually happened in history (granting all the difficulties that we are able to see nowadays with ideas of rigor, objectivity, and truth) are heirs of the western Christian traditions. If we do not claim, in western cultures, the truth of the resurrection of Jesus with the near unanimity that we once could have brought to that proposition, we know what it is to talk with near unanimity, founded in extraordinary patience and rigor of argument, of the truths of history going back tens of millions of years, or only tens of years. We have created a world of textualized, external, objective truth. Augustine's fantasy world, the fantasy world of earliest Christianity has come eerily to be real. If many of the *specific* propositions he entertained have been discarded, the cultural practice whose power he attests remains with us. Anti-Darwinist literalizers of Genesis take such practices to extremes Augustine himself would never dare to venture.

Don Quixote gets the last laugh.

VIII

THE AUGUSTINIAN PUTSCH
IN AFRICA

AUGUSTINE THE CAECILIANIST[390]

Augustine encourages us, quite successfully, to take it for granted that his affiliation with the Christian church makes him naturally part of the "Catholic Church" (which he already called *catholica*— not even *catholica ecclesia*, just *catholica*), and when he does this, we immediately know how to fit him in a master narrative of Christian history. As we recognize the polyphony of early Christian voices, even the best late-antique scholarship remarkably often accepts the notion of a single unitary "catholicism" in late antiquity, surrounded by heresies. But that catholicism is something that was invented and propagated, and Augustine's own history is a part of that process. To understand how he came to be a catholic (and the senses in which he was never one entirely), we need to trace his religious history objectively and carefully.

Augustine was born in Tagaste, a town few would ever otherwise have noticed. Christians had been there before there were Christian emperors, and at least one story was told of a doughty bishop pursued by the emperor's men but keeping faith even when hauled before the emperor himself.[391] In the mid-fourth century, this town's Christians belonged to the majority, traditionalist faction of African Christians. The status of that majority church was not, however, unchallenged.

The persecutions carried out in the reign of Galerius and Diocletian, fifty years before Augustine's birth, had left behind a residue of bad blood among Christians, and a fraction of well-connected Christians at Carthage found themselves at odds with the majority. Soon two bishops faced each other in Carthage, Maiorinus from the larger faction (he died soon after and was replaced by Donatus, who would preside for thirty-five years) and Caecilian for the minority. Each faction accused the other of collaborating with the authorities in time of persecution. The majority faction denounced the minority claimant, Caecilian, for having been consecrated bishop by clergy who themselves had lapsed under pressure. Their alleged crime lay in handing over copies of the holy books to be burnt by the persecutors, and for this they were called *traditores* (traitors). Such charges of collaborationism would be vetted and reargued for decades. Though the majority Donatist claims against Caecilian's consecrators did not sustain themselves (and though the behavior under persecution of the consecrators of the majority's own bishops was suspect), both parties numbered collaborators in their midsts, some of whom it was convenient to disown, and some of whom it was convenient to forgive and forget in silence.

If the quarrel were only over behavior in time of persecution, the passage of years and the passing of the principals would have assuaged it. But within a few years the sides had found a liturgical issue to use as touchstone: the question of how to handle those who returned to Christianity after lapsing in time of persecution. The Donatists, in line with African tradition, took the sin so seriously that they insisted the seriously lapsed be baptized again: only thus could they be purified. The Caecilianists, on the other hand, took the sacrament so seriously that they insisted baptism could be administered only once.

A remarkable series of appeals to the emperor Constantine was inconclusive. (He had barely declared himself inclined to favor Christianity when the idea of seeking his support arose, and his theological understanding was never more than an inch deep.) Though the faction of Maiorinus and Donatus initiated the appeals (more about that below), the faction of Caecilian was successful in winning recognition from imperial and ecclesiastical leaders on the other side of the Mediterranean, a legal fact that Augustine long after would harp on incessantly.

But the fact of imperial approval meant little on the ground in Africa and the Caecilianists did not turn that approval into popular support and remained isolated, mainly among the urban upper classes and the Romanized sections of the population. The majority church thrived throughout Africa and benefited from the inspired leadership of Donatus, whose oratorical ability and ecclesiastical charisma carried him through an extraordinary reign at Carthage. W.H.C. Frend scandalized readers fifty years ago by arguing that Donatism was the religious expression of the less Romanized parts of Africa, catholicism that of the Romanized cities and their populations.[392] He still thought of catholicism as the norm and Donatism as the divergence. The facts now seem to indicate the reverse of that situation.

A long generation passed after the outbreak of controversy before the next disruption in the African church. In advancing age, Donatus and his colleagues took a gamble in the late 340s that seriously backfired. Thinking to consolidate their position at last, they sought recognition and assistance from over the water again, now from the emperor Constantius. The empire responded by sending a legate named Macarius to Africa. On arrival, Macarius and his retinue demonstrated in force their support for the Caecilianist faction. The majority church quickly found itself on the defensive in the face of a concerted campaign to put Caecilianist leadership in place, uproot followers of Donatus, and change the map of ecclesiastical Africa.

The Donatists recognized what was happening: once again, imperial officers were persecuting faithful Christians. The "Macarian persecution" remained a rallying cry for the rest of their history, the event that proved the bad faith and wickedness of their opponents. The Caecilianists accepted the support of the government as something they deserved for their righteousness and profited by seeing many towns either turned over entirely to their control or at least given into a joint custody, where two churches would confront each other, the one with government support (legal and financial), the other not.

We do not have good information to say how consistently this enforced Caecilianization was carried out or how firmly it was continued in every locality. In the countryside, Donatism generally prevailed, even on the property of wealthy landowners who were themselves members of the other party. Augustine's repeated pleas to some of them to intervene and save the souls of their farmhands do not seem to have been very persuasive. A man named Celer, for example, goes along with Augustine at one point,[393] but a few years later, even after official imperial repression, Donatists are reopening churches on his property.[394] One wealthy senator, Pammachius, will get credit for "converting" his dependents,[395] but other great gentlemen were unimpressed by the need to do so.[396] Donatism had some outright support in that class, as in the case of Crispinus of Calama, who bought Caecilianist land and began to have the people there (who spoke only Punic) rebaptized. Eighty souls were lost this way, Augustine feared. We hear of this because Augustine wrote to challenge him and threaten him with legal action.[397]

Tagaste was one of the towns that changed its stripes when Macarius came to Africa. Until approximately 348, that is to say during the years when Augustine's parents were growing up there, Tagaste had been a largely Christian town with a perfectly ordinary ecclesiastical regime recognizing the bishop of Carthage. We don't know how far in a town like Tagaste people of the 330s and 340s perceived themselves as taking sides in a controversy. The Caecilianists were probably so marginalized that for most of Africa they existed only as rumor. Conversion created problems in at least two ways: first, by disrupting communities in foisting new leadership on them (presumably from outside); and, second, by puzzling and disorienting the congregation that was trying to understand just what had changed. By now the factions taught identical doctrine and differed outwardly only in the practice of rebaptism. Not many opportunities for such rebaptism, however, had come up in the years before Macarius where there were so few Christians outside the fold of those following Donatus. Ironically, in the years after Macarius, Donatist rebaptisms would increase, as the factions fought for control and those who abjured the state-supported church sought refuge and accepted reinitiation in the other community. In the short run, most Christians saw little difference in practice, however much they resented the interference and whatever they thought of the new leadership. To be bishop of a newly converted community was no particularly pleasant task, and the more aggressively such a bishop presented the novelty of what he stood for, the more hostility he was likely to face. Newly installed clergy in many such places must have chosen to make few waves.

The details of Tagaste's turnaround are unknown to us, except that Augustine says that the town had once been entirely Donatist. Monnica's religious history, in particular, must then have included a Donatist upbringing, a baffling conversion, and a long life thereafter of compliance with the Caecilianist regime. (Years later, Augustine exchanged letters briefly with a blood relative named Severinus who was still a Donatist. Augustine expressed a longing to see and talk to his relative, but we sense this will never happen.[398]) Such alienation within families was a common side effect of the schism.) As we have seen, when Monnica went to Italy, however, she took with her and surrendered only reluctantly the traditional African Christian practice of (mostly decorous) feasting in graveyards. When Augustine sought to ban conviviality in churches broadly in Africa, we saw him describe the practices as "pagan." Non-Christian antecedents could be found for them, but the traditional African, that is to say Donatist, church had known the same practices and propagated them widely. The history of the African church came to the child Augustine as muddled rumor at best. He spent a substantial portion of his awakening later childhood, moreover, in Madauros, where Christianity seems to have played little part in public life. As far as Augustine knew, his Christianity was Caecilianist. But after Madauros, with short interruption, came Carthage and Manicheism, then Rome and more Manicheism. His first mature encounter with traditional Christianity in Milan, where he claimed status as catechumen in Ambrose's "catholic" church, the Italian equivalent of the church Augustine had been brought up in, was crucial for his future development. The functional utility of finding a church in a distant land that was the same as your own church seized his imagination. For him ever after, the argument for geographic "catholicity" was a powerful one, although he failed to see how often it failed to impress less worldly and less well-traveled fellow Africans. That the catholic Christianity he found in Milan was a minority group led by an impassioned and articulate bishop fighting a dominant church he stigmatized as heretical is at least a striking coincidence. It was also surely an encouraging model for Augustine as he worked to think more clearly about the choices Christians faced in Africa.

When Augustine accepted baptism in Italy, he was sure he could make himself accepted in Africa as well, sure there would be a churchly home for him there. Late-antique Christianity created a truly portable cult, one with communities throughout the Mediterranean world. The non-Christian traveler could not expect to find his own style of worship in distant lands and instead floated as a religious tourist, graciously participating in rituals quite disparate from his own. Judaism, Mithraism, and Manicheism were also cults, each with its own models of dissemination in the Roman world, and each, like Christianity, attracting its own kind of benevolent voyeur.

Though Augustine says the Christianity of Milan meant everything to him, he remained remarkably aloof from churchmen and churchgoing when he returned to Africa. His letters from the period 388–91, when he lived in semiretirement in Tagaste, include not only no sign of contact with the church of his town or province, but also some glancing remarks of disdain. Clergy were objects of some suspicion to him, the laity included "crowds of the ignorant" sunk in backward ways, and if any religious role other than that of curious gentleman appealed to him, it was increasingly that of the monk.[399] At the same time, he spoke most naturally in a Platonic vocabulary and said some things that are hard to square at first glance with traditional Christian orthodoxy.[400]

But his loyalties were still Caecilianist. He was inside their walls in Hippo when he was seized and ordained in 391, having gone there on a visit to pursue a possible convert to the higher life, a government official, notably, and therefore someone likely to be found accepting the call of state-approved religion. Childhood loyalty and official convenience had combined to lead Augustine to the walls that he would defend ever after. We can only really see him enter those walls to stay if we remember how easily it might have been otherwise.

The Caecilianist church in Hippo in the 390s was to all appearances a poor place. The community was substantially smaller than the Donatist community in the same city, and its bishop, the aging Valerius, was a Greek-speaker from across the water. (The choice of Valerius suggests that local talent must have been unable to carry the day at the time of his election.) We have already discussed the landscape and architecture and the likelihood that the grand basilica whose traces we see did not at the outset belong to Augustine's community. The Donatist church in Hippo was not only larger but more enthusiastic. In the years since the Macarian persecution, the majority church had flourished throughout Africa. The time of direct repression after Macarius ended in 361 with the accession of the emperor Julian, who refused to go along with the Christianizing tendencies of his predecessors. Whatever his own religious practices and ideas, Julian was bent on leveling the playing field among religions and then tipping it against the Christian state church he resented.[401] Accordingly he took various steps that infuriated the Caecilianists of Africa and the orthodox everywhere. The majority church in Africa accordingly rebounded and entered its last phase of growth and prosperity, a phase that lasted through the 390s, until Augustine and his colleagues could begin to undermine their opponents' tranquility. Many cities in this period looked like Hippo: a small Caecilianist community holding on by its thumbs in the face of majority hostility and even ostracism. Donatist history thus consisted of two long periods of preeminence (312–47 and 361–98) interrupted by this one wave of persecution. If we try to estimate the state of affairs in Africa when Augustine comes on the ecclesiastical scene, we must realize how normal Donatist predominance seemed to all sides, even if it was not everywhere welcome.

The world looked very different for the members of the different communities. At Hippo, the revival of Donatist hopes under Julian was something Augustine recalled with horror and stories of violence and abuse. The Donatist bishop Faustinus had ordered the local bakers not to bake bread for the Caecilianists.[402] By the 390s, relations between the communities were at least somewhat more mannerly, no doubt because the Donatists had little to fear. But angry encounters erupted, such as this one Augustine reports:

> There was a sharecropper on church property whose daughter was a catechumen with us but she was enticed by the Donatists against her parents' will to take baptism and become a *sanctimonialis*[403] with them. The father wanted to bring her back to the church, but I insisted that it had to be done of her own free will, and so when he began to beat her, I flatly prohibited him from doing so. In spite of that, one day when we were passing through the Spanianus estate, the Donatist presbyter there, standing in the middle of the property of a catholic and worthy lady, cried after us with a shameless voice that we were *traditores* and persecutors; and he even made the same insulting remark about the lady of our communion on whose property he was standing. When I heard what he said, I didn't just refrain from arguing with him myself but even shushed the large group who were with me.[404]

The 390s was the decade when the Donatists would practice on one of their own factions, the Maximianists, the same exclusive and coercive tactics they would later bemoan when they found them directed against themselves. Augustine thought they were hypocrites and overconfident, but at the time their confidence in their own powers was entirely justified. The pre-Augustinian years are hard to know, but even the Caecilianist bishop of Carthage before Augustine's friend Aurelius, a man named Genethlius, had read the signs cautiously. Some unspecified legal mandate against the Donatists he prudently chose not to enforce, a tolerance that the Donatists would remind Augustine of later.[405] The majority church had gone repeatedly and confidently to law through the fourth century. They had appealed to the emperor Constantine, to a church council at Arles, to the emperor Constantius, to the emperor Julian, and to the local imperial government in the case of Maximian. It was not until 399–400 that the Caecilianists felt strong enough, in the wake of Gildo's rebellion and Donatist complicity with him, to make the same move.

Augustine, to hear him tell it,[406] had originally resisted the notion of coercion but had then been persuaded by the example of his own hometown's experience. Such wholehearted conversion to the truth, he thought, was an argument in favor of the means that had brought it about, whatever they were. But many, including his eventual ally Count Boniface, needed to hear again and again just how it all made sense.[407]

The rival bishop of Hippo when Augustine arrived was Proculeianus. Early on, Augustine tried to engage him in public disputation, and Proculeianus professed through intermediaries to be willing, but the promised engagement never came to pass.[408] Macrobius succeeded Proculeianus, then fell afoul of an anti-Donatist purge of 405 and lived on the lam for four years, returning around 409 in a swarm of circumcellions bellowing their customary chant, *"Deo laudes!"* ("God be praised!"). But in a day or so, Macrobius turned on them and rebuked their excesses (through an interpreter who spoke their native Punic), and they left town as quickly as they had come. Augustine wants to appear brave about it all, but at the same time he lets us sense that such bands of rabble were a threat to his own faction and to the public order.[409] It was surely an unsettling moment, and Augustine makes the most of it: slaves threatening their masters and running away, Donatist congregations retaking the basilicas that had been seized from them in 405, with the Donatist clergy washing down the floors with salt water to purify them of Caecilianist taint.[410] But these reverses led to the approach to imperial power that, in turn, led to the final conflict of 411 and Augustine's eventual success.

If you lived inside the Donatist community, on the other hand, you were quite without what Augustine would think of as the fear of god. From a sermon of his: "You can say to one of them, 'You are going to perish in that heresy, that schism of yours. God will inevitably punish such evil and you will come to damnation. Don't flatter yourself, don't follow a sightless leader; for when the blind lead the blind [Matthew 15.14], both will fall into the pit.' 'What's it to me?' he replies. 'I lived this way yesterday, I live this way today. What my parents were, that's what I am.' "[411]

And many were just uninterested in the differences. "So, god's here, god's there—what's the difference? That's the result of men quarreling, but god can be worshiped anywhere."[412] When Arian Goths began appearing in Africa in the 410s and after, the Donatists were resourceful enough to suggest a common cause against the government-sponsored church and tried to persuade the Goths that the two communities really believed the same thing.[413] They may have had a point, for years earlier Donatists, in a debate, had cited the Council of Sardica (modern Sofia, Bulgaria) of 343 for writing to African bishops of the Donatist communion. That was when the keen-eyed Alypius pointed out to Augustine that the document quoted attacked Athanasius and the bishop of Rome by name, and so realized that it was an Arian text. On the day of that debate, Augustine won his point, but it's worth bearing in mind that the Donatists will have had sincere reason to think they had evidence of being in communion with churches across the water from Africa, whatever Augustine may have thought of those churches.[414]

And rumors flew. Some Donatists, Augustine says, were deterred from taking the Caecilianists seriously because they had been told that the minority sect engaged in strange and secret eucharistic rituals: "They go around claiming that we put something or other very strange on our altars!"[415] More mundane suspicion suggested that the Caecilianists were really out to gain control of Donatist property, and that claim wasn't entirely false.[416] Complacency, suspicion, and indifference were not so much barriers to movement as reinforcements to a natural human tendency to stay in one place.

Augustine could see how the land lay, and in his first years as bishop he was forthright but diplomatic in his dealings with members of the other community. We can watch him as he flatters, seeks dialogue, expresses regret for misunderstanding, and shows all the signs of hoping that good will and brotherhood can bring people together, but no sign of willingness to compromise his own position.[417] He never engaged the Donatists as people with a perspective that might have merit or explanation. Labeling them as "schismatic" made it unnecessary for him to deal with them as people. His other favorite labels—"pagan" "Jew," "heretic," "Manichee"—all worked the same way, to defer discussion and leave the bishop alone with the divine.

Augustine's first surviving letter to a Donatist clergyman,[418] from sometime in the 390s, is courteous and at the same time public. He expects what he writes to be read in public, and invites his correspondent to respond on the same terms.[419] If they cannot have a public debate, they can at least discuss their differences publicly by letter. His friend Evodius met the Donatist bishop of Hippo socially one evening, and they conversed about how a public disputation might go, the Donatist resisting the idea of writing down the results and publishing them.[420] Augustine at this point already had firmly in mind his view of catholicity, one that swings on two hinges: sacramental integrity (no rebaptism) and global universality (interpreting as sharing communion with churches across the Greco-Roman world). The first position was unacceptable to his opponents, the second largely irrelevant. For the Donatist, to be catholic meant having the totality of faith—that is, possession of the whole of Christian doctrine in a given local community.[421] If that betrays a provincial perspective, we should not be surprised. For most citizens of the ancient world, the world beyond their personal ken had an abstract, even (literally) mythical quality. (There was a Donatist bishop at Rome, because, as Augustine would have it, the faction guiltily needed some such representation; we have no independent way of confirming how or why that bishop came to be. Rome had old prestige but the desire for connection did not necessarily entail a notion of catholicity.)

The Donatists resisted debating Augustine. He would have us imagine that in part this reflected fear of his rhetorical skills, but the reluctance may have run deeper. At one point, in a sermon on Psalm 21 directed against them, Augustine characterizes their attitude thus: "And sometimes we come to them and say, 'Let us search for the truth, let us find the truth [in dialogue/debate].' And they say, 'You have what you have. You have your sheep, I have mine; don't trouble my sheep, because I don't go troubling yours.' "[422] One cannot miss the note of disdain in the unconcern of the representatives of the larger community, brushing off the buzzing fly that is the smaller. The net effect, then, of Augustine's wooing and challenging the Donatists did not change the ecclesiastical landscape. For that, *force majeure* was required, and it was forthcoming.

Meanwhile, one day in 396 or 397, Augustine came together in the up-country town of Thubursicu with the Donatist bishop there, Fortunius.[423] It may have been the best forum Augustine could find for a confrontation at that moment. The appeal was less than completely dignified. The crowd was there, Augustine tells us, "more to gawk at our quarreling, more or less as if they were going to the theater." The crowd wouldn't keep still or listen properly, but Augustine and Fortunius persisted in their efforts for several hours. They tried and failed to get a transcript made by *notarii*; the letter we have summarizing the events is all they could manage. The event ended inconclusively with talk of a rematch at a neutral site, a villa in the country where neither side had a church.

But the tissue of encounters between members of the two communities was infinitely complicated. By chance we hear from Augustine of a Caecilianist churchgoer who has met a Donatist priest.[424] It seems the priest had written a pamphlet and given his acquaintance a copy; it was a pamphlet written at the instruction of an angel no less, an angel who described how the religious life of the city should be arranged. Augustine responded indignantly, mocking the idea that it might have been an angel and insisting that Christianity must be a religion for the whole world, not just a particular community. As always, his argument has greater impact for cosmopolitans like ourselves; but it would be less persuasive for somebody who lived in a world bounded by material horizons and defined by a single city or town, for whom an angel might very well trump a smooth-talking bishop.

A COLD WAR HEATS UP

Opportunity played into the hands of Augustine and his colleagues soon enough. A local chieftain in Africa in 398, Gildo, was in revolt against the government of the adolescent emperor Honorius across the sea in Italy. The majority church in Africa saw prudent advantage in collaborating with him, and the powerful Donatist bishop Optatus of Timgad threw in with Gildo. (Timgad was a wealthy farming city whose ruins are impressive evidence of the ambitiousness and scale of the city, which was situated far from the coast and was a hotbed of Donatism.) When that rebellion was crushed, the Roman government was unhappy with the part played by the church and engaged in some fairly heavy-handed retaliation, closing churches and exiling clerics.

For the Caecilianists, this was a godsend, and they happily interpreted events as foretelling a hoped-for patronage from Rome for their own position. Diplomatic negotiation between the smaller church and the empire quickly found common cause, and the government remained willing to accept the allegiance of the minority and to support its claims against the majority. The years that followed were years of governmental action against nonstandard religion anyway (the anti-"pagan" laws and reprisals of 399 and after were notorious) and the Donatists could expect their share of oppression as well. Laws in 399 and again in 405 were passed and some steps at least were taken to give those laws effect; in the latter case the Donatist church was formally disbanded, leaving its members at large

and "unchurched."[425] The Donatists found themselves in a defensive position for the first time in over a generation, and the climate soured badly.
In the town of Bagai, for example, which lay high in the Numidian plains,
well south of Hippo, a Caecilianist bishop managed to claim the basilica
there by law in these years. But he was not well received, as Augustine
recounted:[426]

> The bishop of Bagai had gone to law and won a judgment by which he
> gained control of the basilica there. Because he was catholic, the Do-
> natists swarmed into church, horrible in their onrush and cruel in their
> rage, and assaulted him as he stood at the altar. They had clubs and sticks
> and weapons of any old sort, destroying the altar as they cut him down.
> He was knifed in the belly and would have collapsed lifeless except that
> their own greater savagery saved his life. For when they were dragging
> him along the ground, gravely wounded, the wound from which his life
> was flowing was stanched by the dirt. When they finally let him be, our
> own people began singing psalms and tried to carry him away. But the
> Donatists were so enraged that they snatched him away from the hands
> of those who were carrying him, beating and chasing the catholics
> (whom they far outnumbered) and terrifying them with their savagery.
> They took him up onto a tower nearby. Then, thinking he was dead
> (though he wasn't), they threw him off the tower. He landed on a certain
> soft heap.[427] Passers-by later that night caught sight of him by lantern
> light, recognized him, and took him to a devout household nearby,
> where they showed him great care. Over many days he gradually recov-
> ered from his desperate condition, but widespread rumor—even reach-
> ing overseas—had it that he had been killed by the Donatists. When he
> traveled overseas and showed off his scars—fresh, ghastly, and many—
> everyone saw that it was no irrational rumor that had marked him down
> as dead.

While he was in Italy, showing his scars to the emperor, his enemies
burned down his basilica anyway.

That simmering violence of the countryside—and sometimes the
cities—pervaded Augustine's times. We have no way to measure quantity,
but the edginess that rumors of terrorism create need not be closely
matched to the number of incidents or even their magnitude.

The most tantalizing stories of life in the African countryside in this
period all come down to the same people, the violent gangs of circumcel-

lions found outside the cities and sometimes swarming into them, bearers of Donatist violence against Caecilianism. East German Marxist scholars of the last generation were sure they could see in them the disempowered rural proletariat, unemployed agricultural workers. More traditional scholars imagine them as monks or religious zealots, clustering at religious shrines in the country. It is tempting to try to equate them to modern terrorists, but in fact their behavior is not unlike that of the stereotypical British football fan of our own day, and they may well have been as socially diverse (despite some common tendencies) as contemporary hooligans. No one in antiquity speaks up for them, and we see them only through the eyes of their enemies, chiefly Augustine, who credits them with organizational loyalty that may overstate the case.

So Augustine regularly bemoans those cases where individuals who left Donatism were attacked, beaten, and their houses burned.[478] He felt himself a marked man, particularly at the moment of Donatist revival in 409–10,[429] but the most notorious incident may have happened earlier. Going from one town to another, Augustine happened by accident to take a long way around, the less logical route, and so allegedly escaped an assassins' ambush.[430]

But there was plenty of violence to go around, and not all of it from Donatists against Caecilianists. Florentius, the fire-breathing bishop of Hippo Diarrhytus (modern Bizerte, east of Augustine's Hippo) kept his opponent, the Donatist bishop, imprisoned for many years and tried to have him executed.[431] Augustine came to preach at the dedication of the new basilica there.[432]

The Donatist community, for its part, had an intensity that reads now as zealotry, and it led even to suicide. The Donatist priest of Mutugenna, himself named Donatus, was arrested by the secular authorities and carried off on a donkey. En route to prison, he went limp and let himself fall from the beast and was injured, while a more cooperative colleague continued along unscathed. Then Donatus threw himself into a well, presumably to do himself in, but was shortly after dragged out by his captors.[433] We have other stories of Donatists throwing themselves down to death from high rocks[434] and doing themselves in by fire and flame as well. "This was their everyday game," Augustine coldly remarks.[435] They assuredly still thought themselves persecuted as in the old days, and had in the old days thrown themselves in the way of violence hoping to be killed: "especially in the days when idols were still worshiped. They would go to pagan festivals in great crowds, not to destroy the idols there, but so they might be struck down and killed by the idol-worshipers."[436] The formal banning of "pagan" religion in 391 and the official Christianity of the emperors seems to have had no effect on their ethos. After 411 and the defeat of their hopes, the suicides only got worse.

The most dramatic near miss was probably that of Bishop Gaudentius, successor of Optatus in the Donatist stronghold of Timgad. He retreated to his huge basilica and threatened to burn it down with him and his congregation inside. Augustine's *Against Gaudentius* responds to the media event in an entirely heartless way. He also writes directly to the imperial agent at Timgad, Dulcitius, urging and justifying repression in unambiguous terms.[437] In making his case, Augustine gives us our most lucid account of the Donatist perspective.[438] The Donatists take the case of Razias in the books of Maccabees as a justification for holy suicide. When the general Nicanor sent to have Razias arrested, Razias first stabbed himself, but the onrush of the enemy kept him from inflicting a serious wound, so he went up and threw himself down into the crowd on his neck; still alive, he then went up to a high place, pulled out his entrails and threw them at the crowd, and so finally died! Augustine wrestles with this because the scriptural text says that Razias died "nobly and like a man"—and Augustine has to add, "but surely not wisely."[439] That story also suggests that the Donatists were ready to see themselves as the new Maccabees, cherishing the true religion against imperial persecution.

The anti-Donatist legislation of the early 400s faded in effect as quickly and surely as had the "persecutions" of Christians before the days of Constantine. With the overthrow of the powerful general Stilico at Ravenna in 408, the empire became less dependable an ally for Augustine and his colleagues; still, they continued to press forward. That year was marked by a stream of clerical visitors sent from Augustine's church in Africa to the imperial court in Ravenna, all in various ways anxiously canvassing support that had suddenly become less reliable and rehearsing the tactics that would bear fruit over the next decade.[440] Augustine and his allies had been eager and active in using imperial protection to spread their community through more of the towns and cities of Africa than ever before, seeking to make a numerical claim of at least parity with the more well-established native church.

The upshot came in 410 with the appointment by the emperor of an imperial commissioner to visit Africa to resolve the dispute between the two churches once and for all. Winning that appointment was a vital success in the Caecilianist campaign, but we do not know how they managed it. The arrival of Marcellinus in Africa was epochal for many and a particularly sobering moment for the Donatist leadership. Marcellinus was one of those few Roman military and governmental leaders who not only went to church but took his churchgoing seriously. His choice as commissioner could mean only that the imperial government had decided to decide in favor of the Caecilianists. This expectation was soon borne out in Marcellinus's decision at the conference at Carthage in 411, the story of which we will hear shortly.

This time the imperial decision stuck. Donatist churches were directed to accept Caecilianist leaders, but with the unusual provision that Donatist clergy who accepted the new regime could retain their clerical rank and share their bishopric with a rival, the survivor inheriting the post. That was a remarkably lenient move, one that recognized the immensity of the task the Caecilianist church was taking on. Augustine naturally went on the polemical offensive, summarizing and digesting the proceedings of the conference quickly, but as late as 420, his years were not without a variety of embarrassments and he was still writing refutations of new Donatist pamphlets by Gaudentius of Carthage. Once more in the years after 411, up and down the countryside, traditionalist churches were accepting new leaders with a variety of outcomes. Augustine's catastrophic history with the church at Fussala in his own diocese will occupy us soon: it was one of hundreds of such stories of hostility and constraint that was played out in those years.

Augustine does not much talk about the impact on his own congregation at Hippo of absorbing the larger church of Donatists down the street. We do not even know how the buildings were managed: Did Augustine move churches to take the new property? Most likely he did, for symbolic reasons, and to gain the larger space. In any event, the congregation Augustine addressed after 411 in Hippo was no longer the loyal remnant of Caecilianists he had started with but now numbered as many of the old Donatists as could stand to face him inside the walls of a church. If Augustine in his later years takes on more and more of the coloring of the African traditional church he had scorned when he was a child, one reason at least for the assimilation was the gravitational pull of all those new faces in the crowd. Nothing suggests there was any violence in Hippo at this point, but nothing we know rules out the possibility. In the far west of Roman Africa, a funeral inscription seems to record a Donatist perspective as late as 434; it memorializes an elderly virgin, the sister of a bishop, who was murdered by *traditores* in that year and earned the rank of martyr in the process.[441]

The later history of Christianity in Africa is still strongly marked by the Donatist-Caecilianist controversy. When the Vandals took political control of Africa, they quickly imposed their own brand of Christianity, which others rejected as Arian.[442] For a hundred years, until the forces of Justinian destroyed the Vandal kingdom, that brand of Christianity owned the public space in Africa. Victor of Vita, a catholic writer from that period, gives us a lurid history of strife and persecution as the new-comers fought with the old residents. What is unknowable in that history is the extent to which the disruption of traditional loyalties and hierar-chies by the putsch against the Donatists, led by Augustine and his friends, weakened the cohesiveness and powers of resistance of African Christianity. When, a century and a half after Justinian, Islam swept across Africa, the last native Christian dominance was washed quickly away. With the oldest and strongest-rooted Christianity in the Latin world eradicated, Italy and Gaul were left the beleaguered heartlands of western Christendom for another hundred years, until the kudzu-like church in Ireland sent its missionaries back to the continent to convert the Germans and to shape up the Frankish church. Did Augustine strike the initial blows that weakened that oldest church in critical ways?

Through these years and controversies, to some at least, he was the bishop of a small church in a city of little charm, but he was undeniably ambitious and ruthless. By dint of invoking Roman governmental inter-ference, he succeeded in an extraordinary act of suppression and takeover. If many Africans resented the "times of Macarius" as an unsurprising ex-ercise of governmental persecution power, the events of 411 and after would only have confirmed their suspicion and hostility. Augustine, as the most outspoken local leader of the Caecilianists, would have absorbed the full brunt of that hostility.

And what of the church he thus led to prosperity and state protection? We follow the story through his and his friends' writings and so give it an ecclesiastical rather than political cast. The African story as seen from im-perial Ravenna was another matter, and in that story, ecclesiastical debates took second place to political control. African prosperity was vital to Ro-man strength. If it began to look as if a series of African generals might seek to make the province too independent for comfort and fall in league with the local churches, it was in Ravenna's interest to ensure that the churches understood who was boss. The bargain struck after Gildo's revolt in 398 served both Caecilianist and imperial purposes. But who was boss?

In 413 another revolt broke out. Heraclian now was the military leader in Africa who led troops against imperial forces until he, too, was broken and killed. In the months that followed, another purge ran through the province, and it finally carried off among its victims Marcellinus, Augustine's friend and partner. The devout layman who had come to Africa to do the government's bidding and in so doing rescued and enthroned Augustine's church was suddenly and brutally taken out and executed, just when Augustine thought that diplomatic efforts had succeeded in sparing him.[443] Augustine took that killing as a direct hit. It told him indeed just who was boss, told him that churchmen served at the pleasure of the most powerful military force and were well advised to align themselves with it. Augustine went back to Hippo to recover his bearings and stayed away from Carthage longer than he had in quite some time, perhaps three years in all. Ambrose had challenged the emperor Theodosius and succeeded after the emperor ordered a massacre in the circus at Thessalonica;[444] Augustine never challenged any imperial authority. After his return to Carthage in 416, he showed that he knew where authority lay, and in his last years chose to curry favor not with the wealthy aristocrats he had sought out in the 390s and 400s, but now with the hard men, the military and political enforcers Rome sent to Africa: men like Boniface, Darius, Macedonius.[445] In his last years, Augustine resembles nothing so much as one of those pious churchmen of Francoist times, leader of a state-promoted church, followed prudently by many, despised quietly by some, and opposed fiercely by a remnant quite sure of its own fidelity to a truer church.

Boniface was the strongest figure the Roman government had seen in Africa, and for a long time, he and Augustine were as close as either could have hoped. At one point, the devout general went so far as to indicate that he was thinking of entering a monastery, and Augustine and Alypius made an arduous and uncharacteristic journey up into the Numidian country to meet with him at Tubunae and talk him out of his particular form of devotion. He was more urgently needed to stay in command and defend the province from unspecified depredations from the desert south.

But not long after, Boniface had been widowed, gone away to Italy on a visit, and returned with a new bride, herself a Christian but of the wrong sort (Arian)—in other words, probably a "barbarian." The man had even taken concubines; few besides Augustine would be surprised. Getting it right ecclesiastically was vital to Augustine, and he could not control himself. In a lengthy letter, he berated his erstwhile friend for his personal failures and bemoaned the military misfortunes now being experienced at the hands of African barbarians (*Afri barbari*).[446]

Like other Roman generals operating at a distance from court, Boniface seems to have found himself isolated and at the same time empowered, and to have used his position for self-advancement. He was not the first to assume that if he did not keep climbing the ladder, he would be thrown from it. Whatever his actions, they attracted the attention of the imperial court. The ungluing of Roman Africa came as one generalissimo faced another. Boniface invited the Vandals from Spain to support him, while Darius was sent from Italy with mostly Gothic support to negotiate at least, fight if necessary. Augustine, having cooled on Boniface, was also in touch with Darius. The epistolary conversation with Darius is elaborate and flowery. Darius asked, shrewdly, for a copy of the *Confessions*, and professed himself lately depaganized. He'd been reading the letter that the king of Edessa in Mesopotamia was supposed to have written to Jesus.[447] Augustine was delighted by the thought of a soulmate general and replied, quoting Persius and Horace. Such quotations were always a sign of Augustine's preening in the virtual presence of his Roman social betters. He sent along the *Confessions*, but cautioned his reader: "Look at me there, but don't praise me for more than I am. Don't believe what others say about me, believe me. Watch me there and see what I was in and of myself. If there's something in me that pleases you, praise along with me the one that I think deserves praise for me"—in other words, god.[448] He sent along a few more of his books, notably ones that were a little shorter and directed to more elementary students of Christianity: pamphlets on faith, patience, continence, and providence, and the slightly longer *Handbook on Faith, Hope, and Love* (*Enchiridion*), in case the *Confessions* turned out to be a bit much for the general.[449]

Augustine was no bit player in the Roman Africa of the 420s and his turning away from Boniface may indeed have been part of the story of the ultimate downfall of Latin and Christian Africa.[450] A Boniface ruling Africa in league with Augustine and Augustine's church, therefore a Boniface who didn't need his Vandals, a Christianity that had not needed to quash its Donatists: together they might have strengthened Africa enough to resist eventual subversion and conquest.

Augustine, however, had come to inherit the worst of two worlds: imperial masters who kept him on a short leash and surly ex-Donatist congregants who declared their resentment with their eyes or with their absence. Dependent as we are on Augustine and his circle for our stories of him, we must know this by inference rather than report. Augustine would rather we did not know it at all.

AUGUSTINE'S YEAR OF CRISIS

The transformation of Augustine, his church, and Africa can best be seen through the lens of the year 411, a turning point for all of them, if we follow Augustine through its events. Every important thread in his life is knitted into this fabric, and only after 411 did the patterns of motivation and action that we now see in retrospect come fully into the open.

In the spring of 411, Augustine was fifty-six years old. Twenty years had passed since his ordination as priest at Hippo, fifteen since his consecration as bishop. He was a popular preacher and a well-connected churchman in league with the higher civil and church authorities, at the apparent peak of his power and influence. But the year opened with him in retirement from Hippo, spending time in a villa somewhere outside the city, recovering from an unspecified illness. For all anyone knew, this was the onset of old age or worse, the beginning of an old man's fading away.

The traditional reading of what happened this year is to see it as the fortuitous coincidence, driven to some extent by a single acquaintance, of several important streams of Augustine's concerns. Coincidences happen, but some coincidences are deeply rooted in the character of the person they happen to. So it is with Augustine in 411.

In the preceding August of 410, the overseas news, already thunderous for some years, took an unsettling turn. After several years of threats, bribes, and negotiations, the general Alaric, after falling out with the empire he had once served, chose to make an example of the city of Rome by entering it with his troops and giving them a few days' opportunity for plunder. Sung from that day to this as the "sack of Rome by the Visigoths," the event was both more modest and more threatening than the label implies. As long as the emperor Honorius's prime minister Stilico, himself of Germanic origin, was in power, he could negotiate with Alaric and at least hold him off. Alaric led a migratory people seeking permanent settlement but content in the short term to move from place to place, winning limited advantage by a show of force and implicit threats of more. With Stilico's overthrow and death in 408, the new regime had chosen to emphasize Alaric's barbarian connections in order to manage him, and that had the effect of self-fulfilling prophecy.

To this day we cannot say just how much Rome suffered at the hands of Alaric's mainly Christian troops. The wealthy and well connected had endured more in the years preceding, when they were repeatedly called on to fund the bribes paid to Alaric, but they also inevitably incurred some losses in the siege. The aftereffects of the siege were, on the other hand, insignificant, and order was quickly restored. Death and destruction on a scale unparallelled in the city since the sack of the city by the Gauls exactly 800 years earlier were shocking, but the episode lasted only three days and the city and its inhabitants then went on very much as before. The emotional impact of such an event, as we know today, can run well beyond a cool assessment of the actual damage, aggravated by fears of repetition. "I was so distressed," wrote Jerome, "that it was like the old proverb: I didn't even know my own name."[451] Augustine revealed none of the same visceral sense of shock. Indeed, he is so immune at this moment one might think he had never laid eyes on the great city a quarter-century before, on his way to and from his prospects of a great career. On the way north, at least, he must have looked upon the glories of the city with the eyes of a devotee of empire brought up reading Vergil.

But even before 410, the horizon could look threatening to Augustine in many directions. In one letter, to Victorianus in 409, he evokes already a "whole world" with no place to hide from violence and barbarism.[452] Egypt, Italy, Gaul, Spain—no relief anywhere. To be sure, this picture is designed to help dramatize the Donatist-Caecilianist hostility in Hippo, where the circumcellions make the barbarians look peace-loving in comparison. The circumcellions come across as terrorists, throwing lime and vinegar in the eyes of opposing clerics, burning houses, ploughing up fields, forcing people to accept rebaptism (forty-eight at a time in one place). But such tales of irreligious woe reminded him of others, and he drifted off into the story of a consecrated virgin at Sitifis a few years before who had been taken by the barbarians and then the slave-trader had given her back to her parents. What strikes the reader most in such a catalogue is the inability to see a big picture, the inability to find perspective.

But in 410 he would have been ready to respond to the news from Rome with an Eeyorish "I thought as much." Only with the writing of *City of God* in the years that followed did he begin to find perspective, and even then it's not clear that he could really hear what he had to say—and some of his most devoted disciples couldn't hear him at all, as we shall see.

Those who could flee in comfort from the Rome of 410 did so. A stream of "refugees," we are regularly told, arrived in Africa. One must not imagine tramp steamers and squalid steerage passengers. Think rather of the fortunate Lebanese of the 1970s, who could keep their places in Beirut, fly to Europe when they had to, and set up fortified luxury resorts in the suburbs as an intermediate refuge. Goody's gourmet grocery

store in Beirut did a fine trade in luxury foodstuffs before, during, and after the bad years; its equivalent undoubtedly flourished at Rome in 410,
and another such would have greeted the refugees in Carthage or Hippo
when they landed.

Many Roman dignitaries had property in Africa already, and so when
the attractions of a winter spent away from Rome grew powerful in 410,
the fortunate few had places to go, along with their hangers-on. Ammianus Marcellinus, a generation earlier, wanting to slur the first families of
Rome, told how in time of famine the rich revealed their priorities. Foreigners and people of any literary pretensions were expelled from the city,
but hordes of actresses and dancing girls were kept on.[453] Their priorities
were equally clear when they fled, and Augustine found them in Africa
preoccupied with the games and shows of Carthage.[454] But Ammianus
would also have observed, acerbically, that the best people were now also
accompanied by their chaplains.

Augustine missed most of the excitement in the winter of 410–11 by
being out of town. He therefore missed the passage of a charismatic
younger man, a monk said to be from Britain, who had won a great following among the devout upper-class Romans of the moment. No lean
and meager zealot he, nor was he one of those preachers who insisted on
the most extreme standards of behavior for a self-selected elite. Rather, he
had found his market by preaching firmly a religion of moral rearmament
and self-satisfaction. The demands of Christianity were moderate and def-
inite, and their accomplishment was something that reasonable men and
women could find within their powers. He had found a way to be both demanding and understanding and to present his version of Christianity as
very much the thing the best sort would pursue. His name was Pelagius.

Jerome and Augustine both saw in him, though they never admitted it,
a more accomplished and probably more successful version of what they
themselves might have been. Had Jerome not been politely ridden out of
Rome on a rail in the 380s, he might very well have been chaplain-in-
ordinary to the wealthy, or maybe even bishop of Rome. He may, indeed,
have known and crossed swords with Pelagius when they were both on
the make in the big city.[455] Augustine never took concrete steps (so far as
we know) to pursue the role Pelagius mastered, not least because he was
unready, when still in the company of the rich, to abandon his own wealth
and property back home. But the religion Pelagius preached—serene, optimistic, cultivated—was much like the one Augustine thought he was giving himself to, back in Milan.

By 410, Augustine and his world had changed. He had every reason to think, incorrectly, that what he had succeeded in imposing on his community in Hippo, and was about to make the norm for all of Africa, was the very same religion he had given himself to in the 380s. But the disenchantment[456] he had experienced in the 390s had changed his doctrine, and long years of association with the church in Africa, rich and poor, had remade Augustine. He never acknowledged or dealt expressly with this fundamental reorientation of his view, more of a conversion in many ways than his original adhesion to catholic Christianity. Pelagius, an avatar of his old views and old self, was an unwelcome reminder of Augustine's compromises. When, moreover, he found that Pelagius had been quoting the young Augustine in support of his teaching, in ways that did not quite square with what the older Augustine was teaching, Augustine was incensed.

But suppose Augustine and Pelagius had met in Hippo in the fall of 410? Would the two have hit it off, or at least come to the self-absorbed mutual understanding that would have made it impossible for Augustine to demonize the other man later?[457]

Augustine came back to Hippo in the spring of 411 for Easter preparations and the great annual celebration, knowing that the summer would see a decisive turning in his long quarrel with African Christianity. The literary remains let us stalk him through the summer. We have one sermon from that spring in Hippo, and then by the first half of May he was away to Carthage. A handful of sermons and a couple of letters are dated to that spring. June was absorbed by the labors of the conference with the Donatists, but several more surviving sermons almost certainly date from that year, and perhaps another dozen can plausibly be assigned to it, all at Carthage. Sometime that year as well, his sermon "on the destruction of the city of Rome" (*De excidio urbis Romae*) was performed. We see him last in Carthage that summer on the great feast of Cyprian in September at the Basilica Restituta, delivering sermons on Psalms 88 and 72. He made his way home along the coast road this time, stopping off at Hippo Diarrhytus for the dedication of the new basilica built by the ruthless Florentius.

Among the stately refugees from Italy to arrive in Africa in 410–11 could be found a young couple named Melanie and Pinian.[458] The offspring of near-preposterous wealth, they were now about twenty-eight and thirty-two respectively, completing fifteen years of marriage whose ostentatious piety was marked by their much-remarked abstinence from all sexual relations. Melanie's grandmother, whom we know as the elder Melanie, herself famous already for piety and renunciation, had made a special visit to Rome to help them set themselves up in religion (against family prudence) when they married, and over the next decade they had come into their own shares of vast inheritance, with estates stretching from Britain to Spain to Africa. Given the implications of divestiture from such wealth,[459] the wife of the all-powerful general Stilico, Princess Serena (niece of the emperor Theodosius), had to use her authority to intervene in 408 to assure that they would be allowed to sell what they had and follow the gospel's command to poverty. Such intentions were generally imperfectly carried out. (The elder Melanie held on to property in Sicily for thirty years after her own retirement to the east.)

When they arrived in Africa, Pinian and Melanie made their way to their estates at Tagaste, ostensibly to sit at the feet of Alypius, whom they had heard to be most skilled in scriptural matters, though they observed of the town in passing that it looked extremely poor to their eyes.[460] Such an arrival created a huge stir among the notables of the town. Augustine probably never saw any such thing in his years growing up there, when his family's friend and patron Romanianus was the richest man they had to do with. The estates that Melanie and her husband had inherited were, in the absence of such visitors, large economic facts of life but detached from the practicalities of local society and politics.

Alypius, as bishop of Tagaste, naturally welcomed the visitors. A delicate process of "relationship management" followed, as the bishop let his guests know just how welcome their intention to divest themselves of their wealth could be, for reasons both spiritual and temporal. The local church could hope to benefit in both ways.

Not long after coming to Tagaste, Pinian and Melanie made a visit to Hippo and found themselves in Augustine's church. Things went badly that day, and Augustine found himself writing a long self-exculpatory letter to Melanie's mother, Albina.[461] The very first thing he needed to tell her was that Pinian had never had any reason to fear for his life, a reassurance that had to be sobering in its own way! It had been, he went on to admit, an unruly situation and some outbreak of violence might have been possible, but happily the moment had passed.

What had happened was simple and, in its way, predictable. Just as this same crowd twenty years earlier had pounced on the visiting Tagastan Augustine and forced him to accept ordination as priest, so too this day they wanted to claim Pinian for their clergy and their community, and with him his wealth. As the storm of acclaim erupted in church, Augustine intervened and told the congregation that he had promised Pinian that no such thing would occur and that if they forced Pinian to become a priest, he would no longer be their bishop. With that, he turned his back on the congregation and went back to his episcopal seat at the end of the apse. The crowd paused, and then roared back with their demands. A small group of the more distinguished members of the community came up to talk privately with Augustine in the apse, but he held firm, while the larger crowd roiled in the nave a few feet away. The situation grew ugly. Augustine insists in his account that he had stood firm, while admitting that he thought of walking out of the church, either alone or together with Alypius, but he feared violent outcomes no matter which course of action he followed.

At this juncture Pinian sent a messenger through the crowd to Augustine to say that he wanted to proclaim publicly that if he were ordained against his will, he would leave Africa altogether. Augustine approached Pinian and heard him say the same thing, adding that if he were not ordained, he would remain in the area. Augustine said nothing but, seeing a glimmer of hope, went back to his colleague and friend Alypius. Alypius disavowed all responsibility for what was going on and left his friend exposed. Augustine quieted the crowd—they must have been ready to explode by now—and told them what Pinian had said. The crowd responded by demanding one further promise: that Pinian agree that if he were *ever* to accept ordination, he would do so in the church of Hippo. Pinian agreed.

When it came to making the actual oath, the promise proved a hard one to swear to. Pinian wanted a loophole, allowing him to leave the vicinity if military invasion threatened. Melanie unhelpfully chimed in that an outbreak of malaria might equally be cause for flight, but Pinian dismissed her suggestion. Augustine told Pinian that he quite understood the position, but feared that any proviso added to the promise would be rejected as subterfuge. When one of Augustine's deacons read out proposed language, including the proviso, to the crowd, that is just how they reacted, and so Pinian agreed to remove it. Finally, Pinian read out what he would swear to, and the crowd was delighted and insisted it all be put in writing. When he had signed, a few of the leaders of the congregation came up to suggest that the bishops sign the same document, but as they began to comply, Melanie objected. Augustine was puzzled, but held his signature back, half-written on the page, and no one else intervened to encourage him to finish signing.

And so the service could continue and the day came to a quiet close.

But the storytelling was not quite so simple. Albina, to whom Augustine was writing, had heard some other things. She had heard, for example, that Augustine had *told* Pinian to swear to what he swore; Augustine denies this. She also had the notion that the crowd wanted Pinian for his money; but Augustine vehemently denies this as well. Here he tells Albina that he had left his own father's property to the church at Tagaste when he came to Hippo, alleging that the Hippo congregation had taken this in stride. (Quite apart from the fact that the event had occurred twenty years earlier in a very different ecclesial setting, Augustine admits he had not been anywhere near so rich a catch as Pinian.) He even has to admit that the suspicion of greed might affect not so much the congregation as the clergy and even the bishop—himself! He is forced in his letter to swear his innocence.

The oath Pinian took remained a problem. Just how firmly was he bound by it? What elasticity might it contain? In the end, Pinian and Melanie moved on from Africa, never to return, and Pinian was never ordained, leaving Augustine with a lost opportunity and a broken connection. The richest and most powerful patrons and associates he could have had in the church in Africa had slipped away, like many others, to the holy lands to the east, and he was left explaining himself, deferentially and awkwardly, to his colleague Alypius and to Melanie's mother. Contact was maintained, and years later Augustine wrote a pamphlet (*Grace and Free Choice, De gratia et libero arbitrio,* in 418), explaining his views on some of the issues raised around Pelagius's ideas and addressed it to Pinian and Melanie. The sense of what might have been is a shadow on his life.

Augustine left for the summer in Carthage not long after this episode. There he met the new imperial representatives in Africa. The new proconsul was Apringius, a traditional man and firm executor of imperial will, but we have no sign that he was of particularly high birth; he and his brother traveled in the same circles as the eminently well-connected Volusianus, proconsul either just before or just after Apringius. It was Apringius's brother, Marcellinus, who caught Augustine's eye. This younger brother, himself on the imperial career track but still in the subordinate rank of "tribune and notary," fitted a type then fresh and novel in the Roman upper ranks: the devout bureaucrat, ethical and modest, seeking out the company and counsel of churchmen. About thirty at the time, he had been a child in 391 when the last legal public sacrifices of the old religious world were seen, and so he was in a way the first man of the new "post-pagan" age.[462] He had been assigned to investigate the split between the two factions of the African church. Given his devotion and his later friendship with Augustine, the fix surely seemed to be in place for the debates to follow. Devout Christians from over the sea would be welcomed and embraced by the Caecilianist party, and viewed with suspicion (particularly those thought to be in league with the persecutorial Roman government) by the Donatists. Many already believed there was only one possible direction events could take.

IN THE BATHS OF GARGILIUS, JUNE 411

In mid-January 411, the official decree had gone out requiring the two parties to appear in Carthage within four months. On the first of June, the sessions began in a private hall in the Baths of Gargilius in Carthage, a public space, ecclesiastically neutral.[463] The events that followed gave shape to Augustine's greatest victory. He did not have much to say those days, but his will dominated.

As volatile as public opinion was, why did the imperial side decide to risk a public confrontation and invite all the bishops of the African party to gather in Carthage? Part of it was a show of force, at last. Finally, after the years in which Aurelius, Augustine, and their colleagues had struggled to establish the Caecilianist position, there were enough Caecilianist bishops throughout the country to stand face-to-face with their Donatist counterparts.[464] Second, there was a propaganda war to be waged, and a media event would help. And, third, there was imperial authority to bring to bear with the full show of justice and impartiality, a show that fooled no one.

The Donatists meanwhile took cover in public opinion and the tangles of the law, both redoubtable places of refuge. They made their appearance in Carthage in mid-May in grand style, and they continued to meet and rally support, culminating in their show of presence on the first day of the conference itself.

Marcellinus followed the imperial edict with one of his own setting forth the conditions of the debate. Each side would have seven bishops to speak for them, seven more to advise the seven speakers, and four to supervise the official transcription. They would debate in comparative privacy, away from the public eye, but every word would be transcribed and published immediately. Marcellinus's edict also made some further concessions: (1) any Donatist bishop who had been evicted from his church would be allowed to return pending the outcome of the debate; (2) the

Donatists would be allowed to pick a judge of their own to join Marcellinus on the bench; and (3) the Donatists would be assured protection during their stay in Carthage. In the event, the Donatists decided not to avail themselves of the second judge. They seem to have suspected that taking up that option would disadvantage them in objecting to the inevitable decision of the imperial commissioner, who could accept a colleague, but still had the ultimate authority and responsibility.[465]

The Donatists balked in their document at the requirement of limited representation and held out for having all their bishops present. The Caecilianists, meanwhile, telegraphed in their letter what the outcome of the meeting would be, and from their position of strength it was a remarkable move. If the Donatists were found to be in the right (which was not going to happen), the Caecilianists would agree to give up their episcopal authority and submit themselves to their colleagues (and in so saying they were laying out the terms for the certain-to-be vanquished Donatists). But if the Caecilianists prevailed, they would welcome their Donatist colleagues into their churches and share their episcopal rank and title with them. A city with two bishops and two flocks would now have two bishops over one flock. When one passed away, the remaining bishop would succeed; and if the dual bishopric was unacceptable, both would step down and await election.

We infer that this offer, which was in fact put into effect, could only have been made on several conditions:

1. Marcellinus had to be sure that there were enough Caecilianist bishops to go around and that this arrangement would not leave powerful Donatist bishops in control of towns where there was no Caecilianist colleague. This was very different from the situation sixty-plus years earlier, when Macarius came to Africa and imposed Caecilianist bishops on many local communities against their will because there was no other way to unseat the Donatist bishops.
2. There had to be assurance that the Caecilianist bishop in such a position would not simply be done in to leave the Donatist in control.
3. The Caecilianists must have been confident that the merger of the two flocks would produce communities that would soon cohere and subside into peaceful coexistence.
4. Everyone was aware that to defrock the Donatist clergy would leave them in a volatile position—deprived of their social status and thus virtually of their social identity, impoverished, and on the loose.

Such dereliction would be personally disastrous, but would also leave those clergy more likely to seek extralegal remedies—to continue to function illegally as clerics, to become outlaws and a force for disruption.

The political strength and the social weakness of the Caecilianist position are both on view here: confidence of victory accompanied by the expectation that victory would make little difference, except in the names of the people who would lead the resulting communities.

The sessions took place in the "private hall" (*secretarium*) of the baths. It could hold all 600 bishops in a pinch, but was meant for ceremonies on a smaller scale. Each session began with a crier asking the presiding judge whether to allow the parties to enter, and him then indicating his formal approval. Next, the participants streamed in. When the first session opened on the morning of June 1, time was spent reading the constituting edicts of emperor and commissioner and the responses of the two churches, and then a Caecilianist reply to the Donatist *notoria*. With that, the wrangling was under way.

Marcellinus asked the Donatists if they accepted the conditions of the contest. During the opening formalities, the Donatist voice on procedural matters had been Petilian of Cirta (modern Constantine), from the heartland of Donatist strength, but now for the first time we hear the voice of Emeritus of Caesarea (modern Cherchell, a little west of Algiers and nearly five hundred miles west of Carthage). Emeritus emerges from this account as a vivid personality: terse and tedious at the same time (every sentence pithy, but many of them), carefully but not effusively polite, willing to state bald facts bluntly, and tenacious when it came to the rules of the game. Augustine had been wooing him, to no effect, with letters for years.[466] "The whole case is already in fact settled," he opens, "and we're still fussing with procedural questions."

The fussing continued: Did Marcellinus say that this was more an ecclesiastical matter than a legal one? Could we agree, Emeritus asks, that the rules of the day will be purely those of the scriptures? Marcellinus passes that one by and turns to the Caecilianists, who ask to have a manifesto (*mandatum*) of theirs read. The Donatists demur, not wanting the debate to begin with a lengthy Caecilianist screed, but the Caecilianists insist that they can only answer the question about procedure by introducing their document.

Another Caecilianist, Fortunatianus of Sicca, intervenes to push for the Donatists to name their delegates. A distinguished crew will represent the Caecilianists (names given in order of seniority in office): Aurelius of Carthage, Alypius of Tagaste, Augustine of Hippo, Vincent of Culusi, Fortunatus of Constantine, Fortunatianus of Sicca, and Possidius of Calama. Marcellinus approves the documents submitted by the Caecilianists and asks that the names of the principal signers be read out, then asks how many signatures in all their declaration bears: 266 is the answer.

Petilian leaps to the challenge. Where are these 266 bishops? Ah, Aurelius says, the judge asked for only seven to appear here. But who knows how authentic all these signatures are? asks Petilian. Lesser clergy could have signed and not real bishops. He insists on a formal count. Marcellinus lets himself be drawn into a discussion of how you would do this: Are there two bishops in every town, where one from each side could recognize the other? This gives Petilian room to complain of Caecilianist practice. I have an opponent in my own town of Constantine, he says, but then they have set up another bishop still in part of my territory, so it seems they have two to my one. The purpose of a count would be to reveal the real nature of the Caecilianist numbers game.

The Caecilianists oppose, but realize they are defending a difficult position. Aurelius insists that if all came in the resulting crowd would produce tumult. Augustine chimes in for the first time, supporting the suggestion that only disputed names be invited to enter. But Emeritus craftily observes that the Donatist bishops have been present all day, sitting quietly in prayer, making no disruption. Ah, says Aurelius, but when there's another crowd to blame for the uproar, it will be different. So, says Emeritus, you're saying that it will be bringing in the Caecilianists that causes trouble! With that zinger, the quarrel is effectively over, and after a few more exchanges, Marcellinus yields. The idea is that each bishop will be summoned against his name, identified, and then dismissed.

And so begins a long, tiring shuffle. Each Caecilianist bishop is called by name, acknowledges his presence, and is in turn acknowledged by his Donatist rival. Most of the confrontations pass quietly, but outbursts happened. One Caecilianist is called and a Donatist named Januarius recognizes him. "It's *my* diocese," he says. "But he's got nobody there," the Caecilianist retorts. "It's *my* diocese." "But you've got nobody there, no church, no communicants." "How many did *you* have before you forced your way in?" Petilian intervenes to complain. Four Caecilianist bishops lurk in various parts of Januarius's diocese, planted to bulk up the numbers.[467] Some went unchallenged as the other party acknowledged it was unrepresented in a given community; death and ill health were blamed for some absences; sometimes a Caecilianist was recognized as ex-Donatist. "That one was ours," said Primian of one. "You should do as he did," retorted Alypius. Other barbs punctuated the tedious routine: "I got to know him by the wrong he did me," one Donatist says for the record of his Caecilianist townsman. Another Caecilianist adds, when his name is called, "If anybody called himself a Donatist in my town, he'd be stoned."

Or consider this snapshot:

The clerk recited: "Severian, bishop of Ceramussa, I approved the *mandatum* and signed it at Carthage before the distinguished tribune and notary Marcellinus." When that had been read, Severian said, "The diocese is all catholic." Habetdeum, the deacon of [the Donatist] bishop Primian [of Carthage] said, "We have the elderly Adeodatus there." Severian, bishop of the catholic church, said: "Show him." Adeodatus, bishop, said, "Ceramussa near Milev[468] is part of my people." Severian, bishop of the catholic church, said, "The whole church there is catholic from the beginning. There were never Donatists there." Adeodatus, bishop, said, "It's part of my people. It was his violence that drove my clergy and priests away." Severian, bishop of the catholic church, said: "He's lying, as god is my witness." Marcellinus, distinguished tribune and notary, said, "Let your holiness just say this clearly, whether there's a bishop there now." Adeodatus, bishop, said, "It's part of my people, everything around it is mine. All of my people there have succumbed to the terror." Severian, bishop of the catholic church, said: "He's lying."[469]

The Donatist Victor of Hippo Diarrhytus makes his point: "I'm here. Write it down whether Florentius recognizes me in person: he's the one who had me thrown in jail awaiting execution for three years, in all my innocence."

This is a family quarrel. An overarching decorum and commonality of language and even grudging mutual respect mark the space in which they argue passionately. People have moved back and forth between the two communities, but these people on this day know no outside world, no third place to go.

Memories are short and convenient. When Augustine's friend Alypius is called to endorse his own signature, he adds the wish that other towns could rejoice in the same "ancient unity" (*antiqua unitate*) that Tagaste enjoys, by which he means, since the Macarian intervention in the 340s, some sixty years earlier—not quite "ancient" by most standards. Petilian knows this and responds obliquely: "The unity that comes from mixing innocence and villainy is a bad thing: you can't have it both ways."

When it comes Augustine's turn, he and Macrobius of Hippo acknowledge one another politely.

When all the Caecilianists have taken their turn in the hall, Marcellinus tries to smooth the wearied tempers of the room by encouraging the bishops, who have stood for all this back-and-forth, to be seated, saying how awkward he feels, sitting while so many venerable gentlemen remain standing. Petilian receives the offer graciously, but then declines: Christ stood to face his persecutors; so, too, shall the Donatist bishops.

Just when some might heave sighs of relief, Aurelius of Carthage rises to insist that the Donatists be made to do as the Caecilianists had done, and the weary routine of identification and recrimination starts again. One of the first names to attract attention is that of Felix, the Donatist bishop of Rome. Petilian suggests that he is in Africa along with the rest of the nobility of the city, refugees from the sack of Rome the year before. The Caecilianists don't want to count a non-African bishop and Marcellinus grants their point but allows he will indulge this one rather special case. Marcellinus repeatedly tries to shorten the process, but objection and counterobjection thwart him at every turn. The roll call starts again.

The Caecilianists regularly challenge the list. At one point Alypius observes that a string of names belong to people who are bishops "of villas and farms, not cities."[470] A Donatist priest has signed for his blind, absent bishop: Are the Donatists trying to pack the list with the names of the absent? Another bishop seems not to have known what town he was from, to judge by his signature—an error or forgery? If a bishop died on his way to Carthage, how is it he seems to have signed the *mandatum* there?

When, at the end, Marcellinus declares that he wishes the staff to total up the number of bishops on both sides, Alypius intervenes to make sure that a few bishops who are present but did not sign the *mandatum* for his party get counted. That is controversial: 273 Donatists plus six more names on a challenged page, but 266 Caecilianists, not counting the ones who were present but had not signed. Marcellinus has those bishops brought in to identify themselves. When twenty of them have appeared, the count stands at 286 to 279. Then Alypius claims that 120 Caecilianists are absent. Petilian counters, asserting the existence of an unknown but large number of absences plus vacant sees, so Fortunatianus interjects that there are sixty-three vacant Caecilianist sees, and Marcellinus has it all entered in the official record.

About an hour of daylight is left now and the parties have been at it since early morning, standing face-to-face in the hall of the baths. Marcellinus wins easy approval of both sides to put off the proceedings for another day.

The second session is a fizzle. The secretaries had been working as hard as they could, but with the requirement particularly that every speaker sign next to every intervention, they had not been able to complete the transcripts. Eventually they agree to reconvene when the texts are in hand, and the third meeting occurs on the sixth.

Once the formalities of the third session had been completed, the Donatists had a new tack to take: they sought to put the opposition on the offensive. They took the position that they were the victims of treason and persecution, but they would make no such claims. They waited for the other party to declare the nature of its complaints, which they could then defend. The Caecilianists resisted this approach by taking on a generous and open persona: we're just here to talk through our differences and see if we can make peace. The redoubtable Emeritus firmly and insistently kept the focus on the Donatist request for an agenda.

The Donatist leaders begin repeatedly insisting that they have the true and proper right to use the word *catholica* of themselves. "It's our pure observation of ritual and your vices and sins that prove that the *ecclesia catholica* is to be found with me and not with you," says Petilian.[471] Or another time, when Marcellinus has said that it was the catholics who sought the conference, Petilian exclaims: "Let the acts contain the fact that *we* are catholics!" Marcellinus: "I am required to call them by the name the emperor uses for them." But later, in the long Donatist letter to Marcellinus read aloud in the conference,[472] we still hear from the "bishops of the catholic truth, the church that suffers persecution and does not inflict it."

The Donatist Emeritus takes up the argument of catholicity and maintains that the rest of the church beyond Africa does not care who wins in this debate.[473] "Whoever is proved to be Christian according to law and justice, he is a catholic to me"—so he represents the words of the church at large. The question of universality, he thinks, comes after the question of authenticity. Since by definition the universal church is authentic, then you must be an authentic Christian in order to be the local representative of the universal church. Augustine replies with his unvaried argument from catholicity. Gaudentius of Timgad rejoins: "They think the catholic name has to do with provinces and nations, when it really means the fullness of sacraments, perfection, spotlessness—nothing to do with nations."

The wrangling grows mind-numbing, and Marcellinus shows himself incapable of moving the proceedings forward. In this, if nothing else, the Donatists feel the power of their position.

As the argument seemed to be subsiding into an examination of the guilt or innocence of Caecilian of Carthage a hundred years earlier, the Donatists managed to get permission to read into the record the fundamental statement of their own position.[474] It begins with the point that has always differentiated them. Against the Caecilianist insistence on a universal church in which both sinners and saints are found mixed, the Donatist position begins with a chain of biblical texts taken as insisting on the purity and integrity of the church. The sequence includes the famous text from Ephesians 5.25–27 about the church not having spot or wrinkle, but also includes texts taken allegorically in the same vein, such as Canticles (Song of Songs) 4.7 ("You are entirely beautiful, my sister, and there is nothing to criticize in you"). They reread one of Augustine's favorite parables to insist that the place where good and evil coexist is not the church but the world (*mundus*), within which the purity of the church is all important. "Latent" sinners may also, they admit, lie within in the church, unknown and invisible now, to be sorted out at the last judgment. This last position is not so very far from the Augustinian position, but the flavor is palpably different. To the Donatist, Augustine sounds as if he is justifying an indifference to known evil in the church. Their references keep coming back again and again to the prophetic books of the Jewish scriptures, the ones with which Augustine generally seems least comfortable. Their not unimpressive tract ends with the reminder of the persecutorial zeal shown by assorted anti-Donatist representatives of the Roman state, from as far back as 320 and as late as the 370s. All of them shed the blood of saints in Donatist eyes, and the Caecilianist church was fatally compromised by its association with them. Augustine, in his summary and criticism in a pamphlet he wrote shortly after the conference, was quite deaf to this outrage. He fails to report it, not because he was suppressing it deliberately, but because he simply couldn't *hear* it.

Augustine sets out to respond, but at this point the stenographers ask for attention. "We've been at it since early light," one says, "and we've filled two notebooks [*codices*]. Can we have some replacement stenographers so we can go out with our monitors and begin putting our notes together?" Marcellinus agrees.[475]

We now get a paragraph of Augustine's rebuttal and at that point our transcript breaks off. We can reconstruct what is left of the debate from later sources, but from this point, though we have a good idea of the content, we lose the *voice* of the Donatists. And so when the argument comes back, after Augustine's lengthy showpiece refutation on points of church doctrine and factual questions of history, we are at the mercy of a very partisan report. The Donatists apparently let themselves be led into an argument about the sources and the initial weakness of the Caecilianist party, localized in the person of Mensurius, bishop of Carthage at the time of the persecutions, and about his successor, Caecilian. The Caecilianists were ready for this and had refutation available with documentary proof quite satisfactory to modern scholars and to most of their early fifth-century contemporaries.

Here we come to a fundamental challenge in reading Donatism. Based on the surviving historical evidence, it would appear that they were in the wrong about Caecilian.[476] The documentation, moreover, survived and was known in Augustine's time. On those terms, Augustine had the best of the argument, and this has given him the pride of place in all arguments and assessments since. In that sense, the Donatists were obsolete and doomed.

But they were the victims of a style of argument at which they were less adept than their contemporaries. Traitors (*traditores*) could certainly be found on both sides; the schism surely arose over claims by the Donatists that the other side was guilty and lax in dealing with the guilty; and in that moment of controversy in the early 300s, the majority position carried the day, whether true or false or somewhere in between. The Caecilianists were always in the minority, always localized, protesting their innocence, always good at invoking imperial contacts to help them when they needed it. That the Caecilianists were apparently right on the history and the Donatists wrong is as near irrelevant as can be. Charges of collaboration were, as they always are, toxic and volatile. In the politics of the moment—and truth rarely has much impact on politics—the Donatists emerged as the natural majority party, pure and holy, scoffing at the minority and in a position to accuse them of treason without having to prove it. The minority Caecilianists, moreover, tried and failed repeatedly to make their case, and when they finally made it successfully in Augustine's day, it was not because they spoke truth that they prevailed, but because they had imperial force on their side. Might sometimes sides with truth, but it should not be ignored even when that quite uncharacteristic stroke of good luck happens.

If our sources are to be believed, the Donatists finally went off the rails when the argument over documents went against them. Petilian finally begged off speaking: he was losing his voice to hoarseness. One last document was called for, and it turned out badly for the Donatists as well: very badly, inasmuch as it proved that the people they had been attacking from the early days of Caecilianism as guilty of treason to the church were found to be quite innocent. It was evening when the Donatists threw in the towel and Marcellinus issued his decision: he found for the Caecilianists.

Afterward, the Donatists complained of everything. They had been held prisoner in the meeting room and the decision passed off in the dead of night. Augustine made light of it:

> The matter was settled by night, but it was so that the night of error might end. Sentence was passed at night, but shining with the light of truth. They claimed they were shut in like prisoners, but we were there too. Either both suffered, or both were respected. How can we say we suffered, when we recall being in such a spacious and light and airy place? And how was it a jail, when the judge was there with us? We were there with them, and we didn't feel imprisoned. How would they think that, unless it was because they wanted to run away?[477]

We do not have the text of what Marcellinus said that night, but we have the fuller edict he issued two weeks later. It ordered the Donatists to yield their churches and rejoin the Caecilianists. If they did not do so, they were barred from meeting, their property was confiscated, and the property of anyone who continued to harbor circumcellions was similarly at risk. But if they submitted, they would be treated generously.

IX

LOOMINGS

ictory can be hard to handle. The infrastructure Augustine had created for absorbing the Donatist population into the one church that now prevailed was shaky at best. Throughout Africa in the following years, catholic clergy would find themselves facing congregations grown suddenly larger by addition of multitudes of hostile or, at best, indifferent people. Donatist clergy were allowed to come into the catholic church with their clerical status and rank intact. In some places, this meant that there was change in name only: Donatist clergy still preaching to Donatist faithful, with a few catholics swallowed up in the crowd. The difficulties, however, were real and persistent and are underreported by the surviving sources.[478] Augustine's official line was that the results of the Carthage conference of 411 were a great success.

But he himself faced one crisis in the wake of the conference that his misjudgment turned into disaster. The story comes straight out of Willa Cather.[479]

One way to gain control at such a time, slightly circumventing the terms of the official policy, would be to divide and conquer. If a former Donatist bishop had several communities under his supervision, taking one or more away from him and giving them to more assuredly catholic supervisors would extend the tentacles of influence. So it was that late in

411, a newly converted church in the farm country about forty miles southeast of Hippo needed a bishop of its own, or so Augustine judged. There hadn't been a single Caecilianist there before 411. The first clergy who went in to reclaim the town for the state-approved church were seized, stripped, beaten, maimed—some were even killed.[480] But on the day of ordination, the chosen candidate failed to present himself satisfactorily. It's easy to suspect that he found himself unable to face the challenges and likely threats of the position. The moment was full of embarrassment and inconvenience for Augustine, and so he reacted quickly. A young man who knew enough of the local Punic to be able to function and whom Augustine had known for years as a child and student in the church at Hippo was present. The impoverished son of a family fallen on hard times, he had been brought up around the church from earliest childhood. On what he later represents as essentially the spur of the moment, Augustine had him ordained, and so he found at last what it was like to have a prodigal son, one who was never to be reconciled to him.[481]

His name was Antoninus and his see, a *castellum* or walled hamlet in the country, was called Fussala. Augustine's hasty choice that day let him in for a decade of embarrassment. Antoninus swiftly became a petty tyrant in his domain, high-handed and grasping. Augustine was reluctant to believe the first wave of accusations against him, and his tolerance then put him at a disadvantage when he did decide to crack down later. Worse, Antoninus proved a tenacious opponent to Augustine as the years passed. A master of delaying tactics, he seemed to yield to discipline, only to claim a right of appeal. Augustine had to call in an outside bishop to arbitrate the case. When it came to the time for local investigation, Augustine himself could not accompany the investigators, so unwelcome would he be in that neighborhood for having foisted Antoninus on the congregation.[482] We last hear of him when we see signs that Antoninus had bested Augustine at his own game: social climbing. Augustine was reduced to writing painful and embarrassing letters to Italy, one to the bishop of Rome himself, telling the story and exclaiming that if things go badly for Fussala, he, Augustine, would even think of abdicating his see in disgrace.

Then Augustine had to write to a great and wealthy lady in Italy to whom Antoninus had gone and found hospitality as he pursued his appeal for reinstatement to his bishopric at Rome: "Please forgive this letter, for it has a lot that will pain you. I hope you can share with me in our mutual love of Christ the pain I feel and join your prayers with ours. . . . I don't want you to hate him, but give him true and spiritual advice to keep him from continuing to hurt himself. For whom else is he harming when he tries to upset and overthrow a church that he ought to be winning for Christ, not for himself?"[483] Modern readers are inclined to take Augustine's side in the quarrel, such as it is, but they should bear in mind that we take his side largely because of a letter that must have seemed quite alien and unwelcome in the chaste and serene drawing room to which it came in Italy, where the persuasive Antoninus was ready to defuse its every allegation and insinuation.

If we know this one case in such detail, and if it reached such extremes of abuse and frustration, we must realize that dozens of lesser cases surely played themselves out throughout Africa in these years: unwelcome new clergy, restive congregations, and machinations galore. In that same summer of 411, while Augustine was still at Carthage or on the way home, he had news of the murder of two catholic priests from Hippo by Donatists.[484] One had been tortured first—a finger chopped off and an eye gouged out.

MARCELLINUS'S FRIENDS

But other stories were unfolding simultaneously in a moment full of possibilities and futures for Augustine. Marcellinus's friendship in the wake of the conference of 411 brought Augustine valuable entrée into the world of distinguished refugees and other Christian dignitaries in Africa. The introductions Marcellinus furnished led to one of Augustine's greatest books and to his most bitter and unnecessary controversy. Without Marcellinus's patronage, Augustine's fame might well never have materialized.

Marcellinus is generally said to have come to Augustine with reports of conversations being held among "pagan" aristocrats dismayed at the "fall of Rome" and inclined to blame the Christian god. Closer study of the letters that tell us this story reveals that the leading figure, Rufius Antonius Agrypnius Volusianus, was the son of a Christian mother, while his sister was the mother of Melanie the younger, and all of the aristocrats involved were members of one of the two or three very best families of Rome.[485] He had served as proconsul of Africa, so he counts as a "refugee" only with some difficulty. In after years, he would serve as prefect of the city of Rome, carrying out imperial strictures against the Pelagians,[486] and still later as praetorian prefect (prime minister, more or less). In 436, he went on a diplomatic mission to Constantinople, helping to arrange the marriage of the western emperor Valentinian III with an imperial cousin at the eastern court. When Volusianus fell ill there, his pious niece Melanie came to visit, inducing him to accept baptism as he died—appropriately, on the Christian feast of the Epiphany in 437.

Read in that light, Volusianus's "paganism" was anything but natural or obvious, and it was Volusianus's Christian mother who encouraged him to write to Augustine.[487] Moreover, it had been twenty years, at the time Marcellinus reports his conversations to Augustine, since anyone could possibly have participated in traditional "pagan" public religious ritual. What we see in him is a style and a posture of class and culture, taking a learned pleasure in verbal toying with the ideas of Christianity. The unsexed and arrogant Christian clergy, it seems, were beneath his dignity.

In short, he was exactly the sort of "pagan" Augustine needed: well connected, well read, urbane, and (thanks to Marcellinus) socially accessible, at least through the written word. A sequence of letters, introduced by Marcellinus but later engaging Augustine and Volusianus directly, sketched a series of quite conventional issues that learned critics of Christianity had posed for generations. Jesus, in this patronizing view, was no god but a divinely blessed human, with considerable powers of wonderworking to be sure, though hardly any different from many other such figures. This view was not uncommon and probably underlay sympathy for the rather more nuanced philosophical position that had very nearly prevailed inside Christianity in the fourth century but was eventually rejected as "Arian." The notion of Jesus-the-wonder-worker was in many respects commonsensical and benevolent. One need not imagine any allegiance on Volusianus's part to any *other* form of religion than Christianity in order to see him take these positions. (The Latin world never found an anti-Christian writer with the intellect or ambition of Celsus, Porphyry, or the emperor Julian, all of whom wrote against the Christians in Greek with energy and effect.[488])

Augustine was delighted to confront Volusianus; he'd held similar ideas about Jesus himself while at Milan, not long before his conversion, and so he was able to situate such a "pagan" just outside the Christian boundaries, but close enough to be the welcome object of persuasion and dialogue. Augustine leapt to respond in two ways: first, by his series of letters to Volusianus and Marcellinus. Here Augustine tried to play the part Ambrose played in his own life—encouraging Volusianus to go away and read Paul and the prophets, while professing himself too busy for more conversation.[489] Such aloofness suited Augustine, not least because a figure as elevated as Volusianus might have been difficult to approach, especially in the aftermath of the Melanie/Pinian debacle.

But Augustine had grander ideas. The book that Augustine soon began (*City of God*—*De civitate dei*) was addressed to the lesser of his correspondents, Marcellinus, but it was a book of great ambition. It would unfold over the next decade and a half in twenty-two books. Augustine's best reader was the vicar of Africa (second to the proconsul in rank), Macedonius, who read some of the first books in 414 and exclaimed in a letter:

> I read your books. . . . They grabbed me, snatched me away from my other business and shackled me to them—for god was kind to me. I didn't know what to admire in them first: the priest, the philosopher, the historian, or the orator. They draw in even the general reader to keep reading until he's finished, and leave him wanting more. . . . You used the example of the recent calamity [at Rome] to strengthen your case, though I could wish you hadn't had the chance. But since that's where the foolish complaints came from, truth had to take its arguments from there.[490]

In the long ancient conversation about the good life and the good society, Augustine's work is his considered and artful reply to Plato's and Cicero's books on the "republic."[491] The subtle shift that Augustine makes turns the good society into something that is no longer a matter of a people and its property (*res publica*) but a community and its privileges. The word from its title, *civitas*, is originally the Latin for citizenship and thus by extension "body of citizens" and *thus* eventually becomes the Italian *città* and the English "city," deriving its meaning from the concept of people and community, not fortifications and buildings. Christians are members of their god's community and thus live in the world of Rome and Africa as *peregrini*, noncitizen aliens sojourning for a time (Augustine's interpretation of *peregrinus* helps it eventually to become the English "pilgrim"). The relocation of true community to heaven was already implicit in his models (both Plato and Cicero ended their dialogues with visions of an afterlife, as Augustine did in *City of God*), but Augustine devoted the full measure of his rhetorical skill to demonstrating that the misfortunes of life here below are insignificant by comparison with the rewards beyond, and the injustices suffered here irrelevant to the final accounting in heaven.

Augustine's view, elevated and devout, was deeply corrosive when it came to real secular societies, and his alternative to them was more potent than those dreamt by Plato and Cicero, because Augustine could claim that he was not dreaming but describing a spiritual reality. And so he could be punishingly dismissive: "What are kingdoms without justice?"

he asks sneeringly (meaning any kingdom not animated by and devoted to the spirit of Augustine's god). "They're just gangs of bandits."[492]

Thus his reply to those who would say that the Christian god had failed Rome was twofold: (1) no, he hadn't; and (2) so what if Rome suffered, a city that had no natural claim to lasting grandeur? Such nonchalance came as a shock to those who had been brought up—as every reasonable man had been brought up—on Vergil's notion of a Roman "empire without end" (*Aeneid* 1.279) or thought of Rome as the "eternal city" (first spoken of that way by Vergil's near-contemporary Tibullus). But for Augustine, what success Rome knew was success divinely ordained to achieve a purpose, the spread of Christianity. And if Rome suffered, no lasting harm was done. Here again, Augustine's position was not unique to Christianity. Serene philosophers had been saying similar things for centuries, but the mass of both classical and Christian learning and the retelling of the story in a fully fleshed Christian account were meant to have the effect of taking over the Rome story once and for all to serve Christian purposes. Constantine's panegyrist Eusebius had done a similar thing for the church in his own Greek histories almost a century earlier.

Macedonius's remarks, quoted above, give us a good idea of the effect of the rhetorical performance. Augustine had rehabilitated his classical learning (for the first time since he returned to Africa he put some serious attention, at this time, into reading some classical books) and came back, like the old fighter, with one more championship in him, for a virtuoso performance of the kind that he had mastered in his youth. The first three books, in particular, are a masterpiece of rhetoric, learning, and style. Augustine had spent many years in his youth seeking acceptance and status via his rhetorical abilities. In his sixties, in a very different world and a very different setting from any he could have imagined, he achieved that goal.

But every success of Augustine's advancing years was matched by paradox. While he was working on the first books of *City of God*, the young Spanish priest Orosius passed through Hippo on his way to the Holy Land.[493] Orosius made mischief wherever he went, and we have seen his name before in connection with Augustine's crises of these years. One way in which he disappointed Augustine was in his misreading of Augustine's ideas in *City of God*. In book 3 Augustine had dismissed the idea of becoming a mere writer of history, only to return to the task and become de facto a historian in the eighteenth book, which was written over a decade later. In the meantime, he had apparently suggested to Orosius that it would be a good thing to have a text of world history, written from the Christian point of view, available in Latin. The "chronicle" of Eusebius, as Latinized by Jerome, was probably available, but it was dry and sketchy, so perhaps Augustine had something with more narrative and interpretation in mind. At any rate, narrative and interpretation are what he got, but instead of a lofty philosophical disdain for worldly empires, Orosius gave him arrant Christian imperialism. Orosius tells the story of human history as a sequence of empires created by god to propagate his people, starting with the Babylonians and culminating in the Roman Christian realm.

Augustine never had the gumption to disown Orosius, though a close reading of his work, especially the history in book 18 of *City of God*, reveals traces of disappointment. But Orosius was on to something. The story he told was very much in line with Christian teaching after Constantine, however unacceptable Augustine now found it. Augustine himself had not, in *City of God*, been able to avoid the conventional rhetoric of flattery directed to Christian emperors.[494] Orosius took such politesse to its logical next step. He saw the interaction of catholic church and Roman state all around him, saw the way each supported the other, saw in particular the way the emperors of the fourth and fifth centuries had made the making and shaping of Christianity their own business, and told the story that resulted. Augustine could not deny it, and in his failure to deny it he gave tacit approval to the later generations of Christian imperialism that would invoke his name. The emperor Charlemagne, it was said, kept a copy of *City of God* at his bedside four hundred years later, implicitly as model for what he was about.

The Augustine-Orosius tension leaves its traces.[495] On the one hand, western societies that have learned from them find ways to underpin the state with religious ideology (the Orosian contribution), without ever identifying the two and while maintaining an idealized notion of the just society (the Platonic-Augustinian contribution). The two elements are probably unimaginable without each other, and each has exacted its costs in after times.

Augustine had one other piece of business in *City of God*, one often overlooked: dealing with Donatism. Just as the *Confessions* are often seen as eerily devoid of discussion of Donatism (the chief issue on Augustine's official mind at the time of writing), so, too, Augustine is believed to have compartmentalized his targets and dismissed all thought of Donatism from his mind while attacking the "pagans" in *City of God*. This assumption would make more sense if the "pagans" were a genuine threat to him, but the "paganism" of *City of God* is a straw man, built to create an imaginary other against which to define his version of Christianity. The Christian of *City of God* is the one who has all the virtues of the classical world and none of its vices.

That Christian lives in a world divided sharply in two, between citizens of the earthly city and citizens of the heavenly city. In principle, this divides the world between members of the catholic church and all those who stand outside, but the actual dividing line is invisible. The visible church includes some, very likely many, who will not be saved in the end. Insistence on this point made Augustine's Christianity focus on the imperfection of the church as it exists in the world, over against Donatist insistence on seeing the church as "without spot or wrinkle."[496] It was a matter of emphasis, with the Donatist more than mildly baffled at Augustine making a difference where the Donatist (happy to concede that some of the moment's Christians would fall away before they died) could see none. The Christian of *City of God* is on the inside of the anxious and uncertain church of Augustine, there because it is the right place to be, but radically unsure of both himself and his colleagues—that is, utterly dependent still on god for future salvation. The old classical wheeze attributed to the early Greek law-giver Solon, "Count no man happy until he has died,"[497] was literally true again for Augustine and his followers. The story told in *City of God* is the same one told in the *Confessions*, only now generalized to the whole church.

In the creation of "paganism"—creation in the sense of elaborating and theorizing a hodge-podge of received opinions about "pagans"[498]— Augustine did his cause lasting damage. We may find inside his version of Christianity indications of an expansive and embracing modern notion of Christian community, one in which the "visible church" of later theology has a leadership position in a world that is genuinely all on the move toward divine reconciliation. But in practice the drawing of hard and sharp lines between the two cities left Christianity with no alternative but to imagine itself as forced to convert or condemn all those it encountered. At a moment of Christian universalism such as the fifth century, the costs seemed bearable, but in the ages of European colonialism, for example, a great price would be paid, and in a world of twentieth-century pluralism, Christianity would never quite be able to portray itself as the welcoming and embracing community that its best instincts and judgment told it to be.

The understanding of history and promised redemption that Augustine evolves here is one already seen by at least a few of his contemporaries in the Donatist Tyconius, the renegade Donatist. (Augustine must have realized the irony.) Only in the 420s could Augustine acknowledge his influence openly, in the completion of *Christian Doctrine*. Even then, the credit that Tyconius will get from Augustine is hardly generous. But if we can see Augustine's stamp on the doctrine of the two cities, he had seen something very like it in Tyconius and had been impressed.

City of God took Augustine at least a decade to write, and it can be argued that it was still on his mind and plaguing his shorthand secretaries as late as 429. The circumstances of composition faded: the wealthy "refugees" went back to Rome, Marcellinus was dead, and the pungency of the constructed version of "paganism" that Augustine attacked had faded. The last books show Augustine in a new ecclesiastical world. The one persistent relevance was the model of interpretation that set it as a book that rejected any lingering attachment to Donatism.

MARCELLINUS'S FRIENDS—AGAIN

But we should return to 411 one more time. Marcellinus's influence on Augustine's agenda was not limited to his role as government enforcer against the Donatists and as social go-between with the aristocrats Augustine chose to construct as "pagans." He also claims credit for bringing to Augustine's attention the ideas circulating among his class that owed their currency to the persuasive influence of Pelagius and the zealotry of Caelestius.

The first trace of this future storm in Augustine's writings is a pair of books begun probably in 411–12: *What Sin Deserves; or, Infant Baptism* (*De peccatorum meritis sive de baptismo parvulorum*), and *The Spirit and the Letter* (*De spiritu et littera*). In both of these books, Augustine represents Marcellinus as having presented him with the seemingly novel idea, in circulation in Africa and attributed to Pelagius, that Christians believe that a perfectly virtuous life is possible. Augustine responds in these earliest works gingerly and moderately. Yes, he says, it is *possible* that individual humans can live without sin, but it has never really happened, so pernicious are the effects of "original sin." He presents his view as the obvious, traditional Christian doctrine, though many then and since have failed to see the obviousness, which depends on a particular reading of Paul.

Given his druthers, Augustine would have left things at that. Pelagius was pious and well connected, after all. Slowly Augustine turned sour on the rival who resembled his younger self. A year or two after the initial discussions, Augustine read Pelagius's older book *On Nature* (*De natura*), and it was then that he found himself quoted (from his book *Free Choice of the Will—De libero arbitrio voluntatis*) to support doctrines that Augustine himself would now reject. By the time Augustine made "Pelagianism" a hot issue in Africa, Pelagius himself had left for the Holy Land, where he would weather the toughest years of the controversy. Back in Africa, a local priest named Caelestius, who was probably more Pelagian than Pelagius himself, was the most direct object of attack for some time, until he, too, left for the east. After Augustine left Carthage for Hippo in the fall of 411, other churchmen sat in judgment on Caelestius and found his resistance to infant baptism disturbing. That condemnation undoubtedly encouraged Augustine further, but he seems not to have been involved in it.

Augustine's rejection of Pelagius is doubly complex. First, there was the rivalry for the affections and attention of the well-connected Romans whose support Augustine craved so strongly throughout his career. At the same time, Augustine and his world had changed, and what was needed now was to bring official teaching into line with views that had evolved over time. The teachings of the younger Augustine that had shaped his vision of Christianity as a religion that gentlemen could share had evolved as he read scripture and as he found himself embroiled in the struggles of the African churches. The evolution of the Pelagian controversy over the last twenty years of Augustine's life depended on the choices he made in 411–12, choices he could have made quite differently.

The anti-Pelagian venture was an endless struggle for high principles with no prospect of success. Augustine failed to see that his doctrinal positions were unsustainable as a matter of pastoral practice and thus would be subject to attacks in his own lifetime and for centuries after, from the best-intentioned of his coreligionists.

Jerome had shown the way here. Augustine rarely shows us how deeply conscious he was of the anti-Origenist theological wars of the early 400s, but he seems to have missed their main lesson, perhaps because Jerome was the persecuted, rather than the persecutor, in that case. But the "Origenist controversy," like the "Pelagian controversy" was marked by the same willful creation of a polemical target by those with good intentions and high principles but insufficient detachment and objectivity. It ended with the same mainly counterproductive results.[499]

So Pelagius sailed away from Africa in 411; the aristocratic refugees from Rome sailed away as well; and the Donatists stayed behind. Augustine always wrote as if it were the other way around. The battles with Pelagianism that sapped Augustine's energies for years are ones we will return to.

THE SILENCE OF EMERITUS

Caesarea in Mauretania (modern Cherchell) is as far from Hippo as any place to which Augustine ever traveled as bishop. He and a few other bishops went that far west in 418 on a difficult piece of business involving the choice of a new bishop.[500] Officialdom had disapproved of the local choice, but the populace rioted in favor of their candidate, not least because he was a man who had been abroad to the imperial court himself and could reasonably be expected to be an effective patron. When he arrived there, Augustine found standing in the square the old Donatist bishop Emeritus, one of the spokesmen of the losing side in 411. Emeritus had never made his peace with the new order, but Augustine invited him into church, hoping for a pleasant scene. After the death of the local catholic bishop Deuterius, there must have been voices in the town that spoke of bringing Emeritus back to his throne, whether on terms Augustine would have found acceptable or not. If Emeritus played his cards right, Augustine must have thought, a great coup was possible: restoration of Emeritus to the catholic fold and the happy acceptance of him by the congregation that had long respected him.

Emeritus came along. When they were inside, Augustine addressed him:

"Brother Emeritus, you're here. You were at the great conference. If you were defeated there, why have you come here? If you think you weren't defeated, tell us how you think you were the victor. You were defeated if you were defeated by the truth. But if you think you were defeated by force and that you were yourself the victor in truth—well, there's no force here. Let your townspeople hear you say how you think you are the victor. [Presumably there was a pause here.] But if you know that truth defeated you, why do you reject the unity of the churches?"

Emeritus, the Donatist bishop, said: "The acts of the conference show whether I was loser or winner, whether I was defeated by the truth or oppressed by force."

Augustine, the Catholic bishop, said: "So why have you come here?"

Emeritus, the Donatist bishop, said: "To answer your question."

Augustine, the Catholic bishop, said: "I'm asking why you've come here; I wouldn't ask if you hadn't come."

Emeritus, the Donatist bishop, said to the secretary who was taking all this down: "Do it."

The Latin for Emeritus's last remark is one word: "*Fac.*" No one knows exactly what he meant, but he was probably saying something like "go on," "just do your job," thus dismissing the whole conversation.[501] Emeritus said no more that day in church.

So it came Augustine's turn to deliver his sermon. This is how it went that day:

SERMON DELIVERED BY SAINT AUGUSTINE, BISHOP OF HIPPO, TO THE PEOPLE OF THE CHURCH OF CHERCHELL WHEN EMERITUS WAS PRESENT

Augustine: You know how joyful we are to see the throng of your graces here. For we exult in our master god, of whom the apostle says, "For he is our peace, who brought both together as one." [Ephesians 2.14] So we give thanks to the same one, our master and savior Jesus Christ. He is the one who let us understand how much our brother Emeritus loves unity even though we do not yet have him willing to share that unity. Let me tell you the principles that god wanted us to hear from Emeritus's own mouth. As soon as he entered the church, standing in that place where we started our conversation with him, as the master inspired him, the master who informs the heart and controls the tongue, Emeritus said, "I cannot disagree with what you want, but I can want what I want." See what he promised, when he said that he could not disagree with what we want. For if he could not disagree with what we want, he knows what we want. We want what you want: we all want what the master wants. But there's no mystery about what the master wants. We can read his testament, the one that makes us his co-heirs. In it we hear "my peace I give to you, my peace I leave to you." [John 14.27] Whether early or late, then, Emeritus cannot disagree with what we want. But his second sentence leaves room for some delay—"I can want what I want." He can want what he wants, but he can't disagree with what we want. We see what he says he can do. For now he wants what he wants—but what he wants, god does not want. For what does he want now? He wants to be in dissent from the catholic church, to be still part of the Donatist communion, to be still a schismatic, to be still among those who say, "I belong to Paul, or I belong to Apollo, or I belong to Cephas." But god does not want this—he rebukes this notion thus: "Christ is the one who is divided." [1 Corinthians 1.12–13] So he can want what he wants, but just for now, just for the moment—but wanting what he wants will be reckoned to his shame, not his wisdom. For now this is what he wants, and he can want what he wants. But because he cannot disagree with what we want, then may god disagree with what *he* wants and may he do what we want. Don't let this little delay bother you, my brothers, while he wants what he wants. But pray that he will do what he promised, that is, that he won't disagree with what we want.

And one and all [that is, the congregation that stood in the church in support of Augustine] cried out: "Either here or nowhere!"

Augustine: All of you who proclaimed with your words what is in your hearts, help us with your prayers. Powerful is the master who teaches us unity, teaches us to change our wills for the better. When your graces cry out "Either here or nowhere!" we recognize the love you show him, and we love it. This isn't the first time we've thought this: we always think it, we always hope it. Your bishop and our brother and fellow bishop Deuterius feels exactly the same way, just as he should.[40] We've known how he feels for a long time: he prayed to the master for this with us, along with the council that promised and offered reconciliation to those who were outside. Now our signatures bind us to this. We have never been so self-seeking that we should begrudge reconciliation to anyone. . . . We know just how to invite weakness upon ourselves in order to achieve unity.

After a discussion of the importance of conversion and the risk to the souls of those among the Donatists who resisted it, Augustine turns again to address Emeritus:

Listen, then, brother, listen, I beseech you. You say to me, "Why do you come after me?" Here's my answer: Because you are my brother.

If a dramatic reconciliation scene were the goal, Augustine was to be denied. He goes on with a long defense of the Caecilianist/catholic history and repeated assertions that Emeritus is not the object of any persecution. The sermon ends, in the face of Emeritus's continued intransigence, with Augustine's address to those in the church who were on his side, Augustine encouraging them to abide patiently for the master's will.

From a text like that, we get some idea of what Augustine was like in the pulpit, but we probably underimagine his power and presence. It was on the same visit, to hear him tell it a few years later, that Augustine made one of his most dramatic personal interventions in a city's affairs. In the completed version of his *Christian Doctrine* of the late 420s, he tells the story as an example of what oratory can accomplish:

> The grand style very much burdens the voice with its weight, but it wrings the tears out of us. So it was not long ago when I was in Cherchell and trying to put down the form of "civil war"—or rather worse than "civil"—that they call the Mob Scene.[503] They are divided into two factions by the brickbats they throw, not just citizens against citizens, but relatives, brethren, parents and children—for days on end, at a fixed time of the year, they are ceremonially at war, everybody killing everybody, however they can. I spoke as grandly as I could, to try to uproot and banish this cruel and habitual wickedness from their hearts and their habits by my speaking. I didn't think I had gotten anywhere when I heard their applause, but only then when I saw them weeping. When people applaud, they show that they are informed and delighted, but tears are the sign of persuasion.[504] When I saw those tears, I really believed that this monstrous tradition that had been passed down to them from their fathers, their grandfathers, all their ancestors, and which had conquered their hearts like an invading enemy—that it had finally been vanquished, and I believed this even before they could prove it in fact. As soon as the sermon was over, we turned our hearts and lips to giving thanks to god— and, look, it's now eight years and more under a benevolent Christ in which nothing like that has been tried there.[505]

The Augustine whose voice quells riots is one the printed word doesn't quite prepare us for.

PEACE AND WAR

Augustine is often cited as the patron of "just war" theories, a role that fits him awkwardly. Good men bewail every war, even the just ones, he thinks.[506] And the bloodthirstiness of the Hebrew patriarchs was often carried out at divine behest, so there must be *some* good wars.[507] Such texts offer a grudging form of patronage, and he is far more eloquent on the theme of peace, even if he lived in hard times and accepted the support of a brutal imperial regime.[508] Here he is, writing in the 420s, a time of war fears.

> If you consider with me human affairs and our common nature, you have to admit that just as there is no one who does not want to be happy, there is no one who doesn't want to have peace.[509] Even people who want war want nothing except victory: and so by their war making they want to reach a glorious peace. (What else is victory but the subjection of opponents? And when that's done, there is peace.) So even wars are fought with peace as their goal, even for those people who work to display military virtue by command and by blows. So it's clear that peace is the desirable goal of war. For every man, even when he makes war, longs for peace, but nobody makes peace in order to achieve war. People who seek to upset the peace they dwell in do so not because they hate peace but because they want it changed to suit them. It's not that they don't want peace, but they want the kind that suits them.
>
> So, peace for the body is the orderly accommodation of the parts to one another. Peace for the irrational spirit is the orderly quieting of the appetites. The peace of the rational soul is orderly agreement between knowing and doing. Peace of body and soul is the orderly life and health of the person. Peace of mortal man and god is orderly obedience under eternal law through faith. Peace among men is an orderly harmony of hearts. Peace in a household is the orderly harmony of those who dwell together in commanding and obeying. Peace of a city is the orderly harmony of its citizens in commanding and obeying. Peace of the city of the skies is the most completely orderly and harmonious coming together in the enjoyment of the presence of god and of one another in god. Peace for all things is the calm that comes from order.[510]
>
> Order is the arrangement of like and unlike things that assigns each its own place. So, unhappy people, because their unhappiness denies

them peace, are lacking the calm that comes from order, where there is no such upset. But because it is right and just that they are unhappy, they could not be in their own unhappiness except in a way that is fundamentally orderly—not joined together with the truly happy, but separated from them by the law of order.[511]

Augustine had little knack for finding or living that kind of peace. Desire and deferral were as often his lot instead.

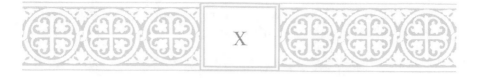

X

AUGUSTINE'S
GREAT FAILURE

F ew students of church history or theology are unfamiliar with at least
a stereotype of Pelagianism: generous support for human free will
against an Augustinian/Pauline acceptance of divine predestination.
Pelagius, the British monk, is cast as the optimist, Augustine the
gloomy pessimist. Augustine fought the great battle for his view of divine
power against the upstart, and he prevailed.

Or so the story usually goes.

"I AM AUGUSTINE"

Orosius, the "muscle" in Augustine's spiritual family, was there at a
Jerusalem meeting of clergy in July of 415 when Pelagius was interrogated about his beliefs.[512] Orosius had been invited to attend by the local
bishops and came up from Bethlehem, where he had been "sitting at the
feet of Jerome." The bishops asked Orosius what had transpired in Africa
to make Pelagius the object of controversy, and he told how a church
council had convicted Caelestius of heresy and how Augustine had written to refute Pelagius's *De natura*. Orosius had one of Augustine's latest
pamphlets in his hands and he read it to them. Then John, the bishop of
Jerusalem, called Pelagius to enter. Here is how Orosius tells it:

When Pelagius came in, you all asked him whether he acknowledged saying the things Augustine had refuted. "And who is Augustine to me?" responded Pelagius. And the bishops all exclaimed, "He's blaspheming against the bishop by whose preaching the master granted healing unity to all of Africa. He should be thrown out, not just of this meeting but of the whole church!" The bishop John told him that he was just a layman, defendant on a charge of heresy in a meeting of priests, and that he should sit down in the midst of the catholics. And then John said: "I am Augustine." His words meant to assume the persona so he could more easily offer forgiveness (on the authority of the one who had been offended) and calm the angry minds around him. So we said, "If you take on the role of Augustine, then follow Augustine's teaching!"

When Orosius came back to Africa, Augustine gave a sermon (recently discovered)[513] explaining how he came to be such an opponent of Pelagius and in which he used lurid tales brought by Orosius as his chief justification, though those who lived in Palestine (even Jerome) seemed to find Pelagius's presence less upsetting than Augustine thought he understood it to be.

But Pelagius had already met the virtual Augustine. Years before in Italy, perhaps at an affair arranged by Paulinus of Nola, Pelagius had been in the audience for a reading from Augustine's *Confessions*, a pious social evening. Augustine heard about it and told the story very late in life:

> But which of my books has been read with more delight and more often than the books of my *Confessions*? I had published them before the Pelagian heresy came to be, but in them I most assuredly said to our god, and I said it often: "Give me what you command, and command what you like."[514] One time there was a brother and fellow bishop of mine who quoted these words in Pelagius's hearing at Rome, and Pelagius just couldn't stand it. He argued back excitedly and almost came to blows with the man who had quoted them.[515]

Just as we regularly see Pelagius receding over a horizon away from Augustine, never quite in reach, always chased by artillery shells of rhetoric, so we need to imagine Pelagius, hearing Augustine's words before he ever crossed him and hearing him again years later, hounded by the name and rhetoric of a man he admired, a man who exasperated him. The exasperation of Pelagius is one mark Augustine made in the world.

Augustine's engagement with Pelagius grew out of three provocations.[516] We've seen how, just as with the "pagan" ideas of Volusianus, Marcellinus came to Augustine with news of provocative ideas in circulation among the upper-class visitors to Carthage, and Augustine responded didactically.[517] The response Augustine makes is puzzled and unsure (by comparison to the reaction that takes shape in *City of God*) and mainly polite. The second provocation was Augustine's reading of the *De natura*.

But Augustine also sought to control that controversy by his writings. Pelagius, meanwhile, was in the Holy Land, where controversy caught up with him. The local bishops called him to a synod at Diospolis in 415 (we have seen Bishop John of Jerusalem getting the news of the discovery of the relics of Stephen while attending this synod). This had the effect of taking control out of Augustine's hands and enraging him by giving Pelagius a clean bill of health. The next several years would be devoted to regaining control.

The fairest way to describe what happened at Diospolis is that an inquiring body that did not fully understand the issues interrogated a man who was confident of his own innocence and who answered circumspectly. Augustine was able to find in the replies enough traces of what he thought were unacceptable ideas to justify his campaign, but the bishops who passed Pelagius were equally able to find what they were looking for in his answers.

Augustine's natural move at this point was to write more books, for Augustine always tried to keep the matter in that natural domain of his. He was thoroughly scientific and analytical and literal and systematic in what he made out of the welter of conflicting texts in the scriptures. His opponents—even friends who were baffled by what he had to say—preferred to remain commonsensibly at the level of the biblical narrative.

Pelagius aimed at vindication as a person and a teacher, whether at Diospolis or later at Rome. His approach, moreover, was to conceal and minimize difference, to state his *distinctive* case subtly enough to attract a broad, perhaps unsophisticated audience.[518] He had worked out this approach before Augustine ever attacked him, for he had been controverted before.[519] So Pelagius went nowhere near attacking Augustine directly and indeed tried to deal with him as an epistolary friend and colleague. He condemned Manichees and the controversially easygoing monk Jovinian as the extremes between which he was proud to hold the middle ground, letting his audience decide whether Augustine was a man of the middle or rather an extremist. The device is effective, and it would have prevailed in the end had Augustine and his colleagues not succeeded in bringing down on him the power of the government they had in other ways colluded with for the last decade.

Through the mid-410s, Augustine went on winning over the hearts and minds of African Christians to his view of Pelagianism. In some cases, as when he got the former disciples of Pelagius, Timasius and Protasius, who had brought Augustine one of their teacher's books, to recant and offer him their full support, his sense of victory must have been strong.[520] On other days, it was an uphill struggle, as when he wrote a letter of almost seven thousand words to Paulinus of Nola to persuade him (and through him, Paulinus's influential friends in Italy) of his case, with little effect.[521] At about the same time, a layman at Carthage named Vitalis had been speaking against Augustine's teachings, and so Augustine wrote to him carefully and politely and gave him an anti-Pelagian catechism to subscribe to.[522]

We surmise that Augustine heard on some grapevine in about 417 that Pelagius was making ready to appeal to Rome. This was bad news for Augustine, who had insisted on Rome as the center of orthodoxy and discipline in his war against the Donatists. In a preemptive strike, he went directly to Innocentius, bishop of Rome, and won from him, with what must have been a limited body of documentation, an outright condemnation of Pelagius. But Innocentius died in 417 and his successor, Bishop Zosimus, saw no need to sustain the ban.[523] Augustine, panicking again, sought intervention from his highly placed contacts at the court in Ravenna, and Alypius's visits to the court were timely, strategic, and effective. At Ravenna's direction, Zosimus eventually caved in and added his own voice to the condemnation of Pelagius and Caelestius.

That was a costly victory for Augustine, for it won him a potent new enemy, one we will meet shortly.

ASCESIS AND AGONY

Mediterranean late antiquity was a special hothouse for the growth of group ideologies of bodily control along a particular axis of denial. "Flee from the body," commanded Porphyry,[524] and many agreed. The story has been elaborately retold, and recently, by a master, as far as the history of Christianity goes, and he was consciously following in the traces of another more tendentious master, whose thoughts on the subject may be surmised and may yet someday be known.[525] What we still want and may never get is a more comprehensive treatment of the late-antique war with the body, which is also its fawning, obsessive love affair with the soul.

Such histories are condemned to be written. We know what people said about the body and its practices in the books they wrote, and from those books we form conclusions about how they behaved.[526] They are seldom, however, as indiscreet as we would like.

It would be, for example, a great thing to know more than we do about the habits and practices of late-antique men of all social classes regarding sexual relations with women not their wives. Men of the higher social classes slept with the slave women on their property, and this was widely tolerated. Even the bishop expected them to distinguish between a concubine and a mere prostitute and thought the concubine's role a defensible one.[527] We do not know who else slept with those women. Did they have monogamous spouses within their own class? Or was slave sexual commerce more indiscriminate and less possessive? Generalization would probably be error here. And we do not know what happened when men slept with their own wives. I do not see that we even know who slept in whose bed, and how often. Nor do we know what happened there.[528] Were late-antique husbands considerate and companionable, or did they regularly approach their wives in ways that now would be marked as abusive?[529] When we write and speak about the much more abundantly documented and theorized practices of ascetics, who would leave all such behavior aside, fretting about their wet dreams, we should remember that their neighbors were going about more conventional and perhaps more interesting lives in much greater numbers all around them, without bothering to write it all down.

When Christianity began it was Jewish, Greek, and eastern and it flourished in those worlds. Every important step in Christian history was taken first in the east and only later in the Latin west, and the outbreak of ascetic passions and practices of late antiquity conforms to that rule. That said, we needn't believe very much of the literal sense of the first narratives of the heroic Christian desert-tamers. The tale-telling began with the *Life of Anthony* written by Athanasius in the fourth century to support his own very urban political agenda, and it sets out a perfectly satisfactory history of increasing heroism, increasing popularity, and doctrinal regularity. Some of that history is probably true.[530]

More to the point for Augustine, though, is that dazzling desert stories were in circulation already in his time. Athanasius was not the only one spreading stories of the ascetic heroes of the east, for many others told such tales. There were even asceticism tourists, like the high-born lady Egeria from Gaul, who toured the Holy Lands to see sites and saints and wrote home to her sisters to tell the tale;[531] but we should not forget Jerome and his sometime friend Rufinus, who came from their homeland in the northern Balkans together to find ascetic release in the east, then fell famously to quarreling and forcing their great lady patrons to choose between them. Augustine's later account of his conversion includes explicit reference to the Anthony story, which he encountered in the high court and church circles he frequented in Milan.[532] Those heroes fled the wicked world and all its ways, but made sure that the world heard their stories.

Augustine was not the only one affected by these stories. A great frustration can be felt in Latin Christians of the late fourth century as they hear the wonders of the eastern heroes and struggle to emulate them. A modern legend, told to me when I was young, and very likely no truer than any other legend, comes to mind.

It seems that in 1896, when the first modern Olympics were being planned, a virtuous team of scholar-athletes from the playing fields of Princeton was recruited to attend. Since there had been no such games in living memory, rumor and speculation were part of the planning. Just what to expect of the various field events in particular was somewhat mysterious. Those planning to participate in the discus throw discussed among themselves just what sort of thing a discus might be, and ended by constructing their own implement. Taking two dustbin lids and tying them together with a filling of heavy sand, they began flinging these ungainly objects about the New Jersey countryside, with increasing if improbable dexterity.

When they reached Athens, they found themselves handed something quite a bit smaller and lighter with which to compete, and as they were overprepared, they won the event hands down.

A lot of such dustbin lids were being flung about by Latin ascetics in the late fourth century. Everybody—that is, everybody of a certain class of mostly newly arrived Christians—knew about the eastern heroes and wanted to emulate them. For most people, the wanting was sufficient, and was pleasantly stimulated by hearing more good stories. But others really did try emulation, often with comical clumsiness and outsized ambitions.

Ambrose of Milan had not married during his worldly career as a young provincial governor, and as bishop he was the first Latin to write praising sexual ascesis in abundant detail. Virginity was his preoccupation, and he was delighted to see it in his sisters as in himself. His praises were mild and abstract, but they came from a man of a family recently rooted in government service, and that origin pinpoints the controversy that would arise in the generation that followed. Ambrose embodies the two models of fourth-century *arriviste* culture, both the newly made governing class passing itself off as a continuation of traditional aristocracy (and thus adopting traditional models of male authority and transmission of authority through children) and the new class of celibate clerics frankly rehearsing different models.[533] Ambrose abandons the old model in favor of the new.

Priscillian, the charismatic teacher in Gaul, was not so restrained. His enthusiasm for chastity brought him in close contact with religious women, and he fell afoul of suspicions that his religious practices were irregular and his beliefs worse. "Crypto-Manichee" was the charge. Ambrose took an interest in the case and sought to intercede on his behalf, but to no avail. Priscillian was put to death, the victim of a crusade against a heresy that didn't exist.[534] After his death, heresy-hunters in Spain would be on the prowl, looking for signs of Priscillianism and seeking to suborn witnesses to prove their case, while the official church wearily tried to get past the last generation's obsession.[535]

Meanwhile, the prestige of ascetic renunciation flourished in Gaul. Augustine's future friend Paulinus (not yet of Nola) was just a wealthy gentleman who kept getting himself into scrapes.[536] In the 380s, he fled Italy one step ahead of a usurping general's invasion, only to find himself the object of calumny in Gaul (perhaps *he* was suspected of Priscillianism);[537] he subsequently made his way to Spain and was almost hooked into the local clergy, but finally succeeded in fleeing back to Italy, to Nola and the shrine of a safely martyred saint of an earlier age. There he organized the sale of his vast estates (but seems to have controlled the dispensation of the proceeds, much as a modern billionaire might turn his wealth over to a foundation of his own shaping), swore a life of chaste cohabitation with his wife, and settled down to be the gracious impresario of Italian Christianity, entertaining visitors, engaging in a wide correspondence, never traveling, always *au courant*. He was friends with everyone, both Jerome and Rufinus, Augustine and Pelagius and Julian of Eclanum, while Melanie the younger and her husband, Pinian, were special friends. Paulinus promoted some lightweight books (including apparently the translation into Latin of the *Recognitions*, that supposed autobiography of one of the earliest popes but really a novel about clerical life at Rome in the olden days) and was the master of a new Christian style in poetry and prose—we've seen some of it rubbed off on Augustine—and succeeded in making himself his own greatest creation. The life he led was ascetic, if one accepts that a spartan but well-prepared diet counts as asceticism in a world where people are starving to death. Paulinus was always happier to display a nonthreatening form of Christian excellence than to preach it or even to decry its absence in others too indiscreetly.[538] He is still remembered in Nola and in Brooklyn.[539]

Among Paulinus's correspondents was Sulpicius Severus, rusticated in a remote part of southern Gaul, there engaged in his own literary panegyric directed toward ascetic practices he did not quite emulate himself. Sulpicius wrote the life of Martin of Tours, a monk turned bishop. That book would have a great afterlife centuries later when Merovingian kings took up Martin as their patron, after which his cult spread also to Christian Ireland. Sulpicius wrote as well *Dialogues* that recount the stories of local Gallic worthies in competitive terms. If you think the Egyptians know about miracles and self-denial, the text repeatedly says, look at what we have in Gaul!

But the center of the buzz was Jerome. At Rome, he had made his way as an ascetic and patron of fashionable ascetics, especially fashionable female ones. Like Paulinus, he took a long time finding a town he wouldn't be asked to leave, and eventually that meant settling at Bethlehem, though his fights even there with the local bishops and his old friends more than once brought him risk of dislocation. For Jerome, the great screaming extremist of his generation, virginity was absolutely superior to sexual experience. (He proclaimed this with the considerable authority of an ex-virgin.[540]) He was embarrassed when one of his protégés, the young Christian woman Blesilla, of a very good family at Rome, died suddenly and rumor had it that excesses of fasting and self-denial had done her in. He was embarrassed again by the rumors that his relations with his wealthy patroness Paula were not quite as chaste as they should have been. The great patron of asceticism was run out of Rome, on one argument, for hypocrisy and extremism.[541] Jerome, in his book *Against Jovinian*, made himself particularly offensive as the shameless excoriator of Jovinian, a monk who had a good word or two to say for marriage. None could admit that the very ideal of chastity made temptation and suspicion necessary and inevitable, with peccadilloes and worse highly likely to follow.[542]

All sides could agree on at least some things. That is why when the rich young woman Demetrias chose the religious life a few decades later, she was the object of the pastoral attentions of all the best writers, from Augustine to Jerome to Pelagius, all vying to be seen as the patron at a distance of so distinguished a convert to the higher life. Modern readers may have trouble seeing what there was to disagree about.

This was the world in which Augustine found himself fumbling toward his own idealized version of monasticism, or something. Augustine flung his own share of dustbin lids, only gradually becoming aware of what other people were doing and saying. Augustine has a considerable reputation for shaping later Christian ideas about sexuality and takes the blame for what are seen as extreme positions. But his positions emerged slowly and clumsily. To be sure, from the time he encountered Ambrose in Milan he thought chaste continence the highest form of life, though he must have thought similar things during his Manichee days, when he was impotent to enact his belief. In his later years, Augustine quoted Ambrose on these issues repeatedly, as a way of signaling that his views were orthodox and moderate, and that whatever hostility had sought him out, he was the true mainstream figure.[543] He could not stand that Pelagius seemed to have staked out the moderate position for himself and made Augustine look like the extremist, though Pelagius was himself a monk and presumably as personally ascetic as Augustine.

Then Augustine attacked Pelagius. In doing so he was led to extremes of statement that begat rejoinders, and those rejoinders in turn begat greater extremes. For the author of the *Confessions*, as for many of us, it was perilously easy to generalize from personal experience a set of rules that would be prescribed for all.

Augustine still held out that sexuality had its own order of excellence and potential, and on his best days he seems to hold out for the place in Christianity of the normal, concupiscent, imperfect Christian:

> Suppose there's a man who does good works and has the right faith that expresses itself through love, but he's not perfect. He takes care of his urges in the honorable married way, giving his spouse what he owes and seeking what is owed him in bed, and so he has sex, not just for the sake of having children but even just for pleasure—but only with his wife, as the apostle allows [1 Corinthians 7.6]. He doesn't take injury kindly, but gets angry and thinks about revenge—but, thinking of where it says, "as we forgive those who trespass against us" [Matthew 6.12], he forgives when people ask him to. He has his property and gives alms, but not all that abundantly. He doesn't take other people's property, but he certainly

demands his own back—going to an ecclesiastical court, not the public law courts.[544]

This ordinary man, Augustine is sure, will go to heaven, because he goes to the right church and has the right faith. For the moment, we sympathize, brushing aside the suspicion that other men just like this one but who happen to find themselves in church buildings of which Augustine disapproves will not be treated so kindly.

But one need only read his unintentionally comical description[545] of what sex would have been like in the garden of Eden, if only Adam and Eve had had time to get around to it before the fall,[546] to see how wildly idiosyncratic his ideas really could be. Sexual arousal is summoned calmly and rationally at will and pursued to its goal in a thoughtful and tranquil fashion, with no perspiration or heavy breathing, entirely for procreative purposes. The "normal" Christian seems far removed from such pages. Julian of Eclanum, a married bishop, whose chastity-in-marriage Paulinus of Nola had praised,[547] repeatedly attacked Augustine on this issue. Did Augustine really mean to denigrate marriage? Wasn't Augustine still in his heart of hearts a Manichee?

In the end Augustine proved to be nearly irrelevant to the history of ascetic practice, and with him Ambrose and Jerome and the others. Their writings would be gratefully and selectively quoted for centuries, but the practice of asceticism in the Latin west was defined and stabilized in unexpected quarters. In about 415, the Scythian monk John Cassian, who had spent time in all the best deserts of the east, came and settled in Marseilles, there to practice what he had learnt and to write, in his *Institutes* and *Conferences*, maxims and dialogues for the practice of monasticism that would finally instruct the Latins sensibly and soundly.[548] Among such monastic circles, serious men pursued a serious asceticism (without the posturing that intervened whenever the wealthy and well-connected took up the habit) and knew its rules and discourse. Augustine's own theology of grace and predestination was too much for them, and so they made their objections known and then quietly and discreetly, over a couple of generations, dispensed with the objectionable parts, retaining what pleased and served them. The first voices of resistance were heard from Hadrumetum in Africa.

Some monks at Hadrumetum, south of Carthage, had fallen to reading Augustine's work enthusiastically, so enthusiastically that they came to what even he recognized as an extreme position about grace. They'd read his letters to the Roman clergyman (and future bishop of Rome) Sixtus and, without telling their abbot what they'd been doing, derived from that a view that would later be called "quietist"—that effort and activity are unnecessary for the Christian and that divine power is irresistible and all-controlling.[549] It's easy to sympathize with the monks, who wondered what the point of all the self-denial and hard work might be if divine choice determined all. Augustine objected to this reading: taking me out of context does me a disservice, he complained, he who had taken many others out of context over the years. Their abbot, Valentinus, was angry with them and sent some of them to Hippo to be set straight. When they got there, Augustine kept them there longer than expected to make sure they got what he was trying to teach them, and sent them back with more books to read with their brother monks. We have no way of knowing what became of these fans, not the last ones who would embarrass the object of their enthusiasm.

The Gallic monks who took up the debate were serious men and passed their line of monasticism in its essential features to Italy, where it was picked up in the *Rule of the Master*, the *Rule of Benedict*, and the *Dialogues* of Pope Gregory I. Gregory gave the author of the *Rule of Benedict*, whose name may even have been Benedict, a biography, replete with angels and devils and wonders, and so finally canonized him as the archetypal western ascetic. The ninth century would make that canonization normative and in so doing confirm the irrelevance of Augustine and of the quarrels of his generation.[550]

But Hadrumetum and Gaul belong to the traditional histories of doctrine about Augustine. We need at this point to address seriously the doctrines that were evolved to explain and justify ascetic practices.

WHAT WAS AT STAKE
WITH PELAGIUS

So here is the puzzle. Pelagius resembles no one so much as the young Augustine: ascetic, outgoing, with an eye for an audience among the well-educated and well-connected. In the first decade of Augustine's baptized religious opinions, much that he thought, said, and did was far more continuous with who and what he had been before than with what he became later. He still held on to the optimism and idealism of ancient high culture and he was still emphatically Augustine the gentleman, or the would-be gentleman, seeking a role for himself based on what he knew of the traditional culture of his world. In that world, philosophical inclinations were highly acceptable, so long as they did not undermine fundamental social alignments.

With those inclinations came an ethical expectation. A gentleman was self-contained, self-sufficient, and autonomous. A gentleman comported himself well and made it look easy to do so. Augustine knew his goal, and the struggle we see in his youth was the struggle to make this personal goal align with the religious phenomena and demands of Christianity. That he made the match should not surprise us. Plenty of polished young men around the Roman Mediterranean were finding such compromises in those days, men like Paulinus of Nola or the African from remote Cyrene, Synesius, whom some scholars can't quite believe really believed in his Christianity, but who accepted a bishopric nonetheless. What is remarkable about Augustine is what Hippo does to him and what, eventually, Donatism does to him. The Augustine we know is emphatically the Augustine who has been transformed by Africa.

But what if he had avoided that Hippo ordination? What if he had never come back to Africa? Freed of the gravitational pull of African Christianity, he would have had the time and inclination to develop the persona he had sought all his life. We can combine what we know of Pelagius, of the younger Jerome, and of Paulinus of Nola to help us imagine an Augustine who ended his career as he began it, elegant and knowing it,[551] finding expression and social success for himself in adapting that elegance to a religious posture. For this, Augustine would have needed the wealthy patrons that Jerome and Pelagius found.

That is where Augustine the Pelagian would have been: not marked (in all likelihood) as heretic or heresiarch, for doctrine was not the chief attraction in Pelagius's case, and few besides Augustine could ever really see what was so odd or divergent about what Pelagius taught. Rather, Augustine would have been known as a discreet chaplain and guide to the Christian elite. He might very well have run afoul of the cantankerous Jerome in this role (most people did). Instead of Augustine and Jerome trying hard to be friends for political reasons despite their keen differences, we might have been able to see them genuinely at one another's throats. If we grow weary at the thought of Augustine's polemical books thrown back and forth to Julian of Eclanum, we should shudder and be amazed at the same time at the thought of the war that Augustine and Jerome could have had, fighting it out for the attentions of the same few wealthy Christian ladies, if only both had found it in good conscience necessary to do so.

Here we come to imagining how *Christianity* would have been different if one of these other Augustines had prevailed over the one we know.
To take away the pessimist and the pragmatist and leave behind an active,
articulate optimist could well have thrown the balance a different way in
western Christianity. Whether a Christianity less ardently monastic and
world-weary would and could have survived, thrived, and shown such a
flair for power as did the western Christianity we know well is a question
that probably cannot be resolved, but it remains an intriguing possibility,
forever lost.

And so Pelagius came to Africa, crossed Augustine's path, and the
drama gradually began. No one doubted Pelagius's zeal for Christianity
or the orthodoxy of his intentions. Whenever pressed, Pelagius would
find a way to say the things that pleased the most rigorous of questioners.
Pelagius himself recognized Augustine as a like mind, even quoting Augustine's early works in his own writing. When he came to Africa in 410,
he attempted to pay a courtesy call on Augustine and, failing that, the two
exchanged polite letters.

To be sure, Pelagius was perhaps not *quite* the right sort: Orosius objects to some of the language of Pelagius's letter to Demetrias as indecent,
but blames it on the misfortune of Pelagius's upbringing: "for saying this
thing neither well nor seemly, we ought not to blame you, since you were
not born in such station as to be trained in the finer studies, nor does it
come to you naturally to display wisdom."[552] The snobbishness is overt,
and in the circles in which Augustine now traveled, a chaplain monk who
offended would surely be seen as having transgressed above his station.
Pelagius and his followers could afford, because of their prosperity and
the security of their class position, to preach against wealth and its evils.
Augustine and his flock were not wealthy or well connected enough to
follow suit.

But what could have made these two men so opposed to one another
in doctrinal matters?

A traditionalist approach would consider the contextualized history of
Pauline interpretation in the Latin world in the late fourth and early fifth
century. In a single generation, Paul came to preoccupy the attention of a
diverse collection of the best minds of the time, and then to divide them.
Augustine himself famously progressed from one view to another, best seen
in the way his opinion changed regarding the seventh chapter of Romans—
"I delight in the law of god as far as the inner man goes, but I see another
law in my bodily limbs, fighting back against the law of my mind and holding me captive under the law of sin that is still in my bodily limbs."[553]

Who is speaking? Optimistic and careful readers have always tried to put these words in the voice of a generic seeker after divine help, thinking they describe the plight of the unredeemed. But a more somber reading of the passage, one that began to come on Augustine more and more as he grew older—though few other readers of Paul have found it[554]—thinks that Paul himself is probably talking, the converted Paul, the redeemed Paul, a Paul still not quite in control of himself. Augustine began to resonate strongly with that view and to see in it the perplexity, the temptation, the loneliness, and the threat of Christian life.

Pelagius never took the text that way.[555] The same can be said of a few other key passages.[556] For Augustine was an outlier in Pauline interpretation. Latin Christendom (including European Protestantism) has been marked since his time by his focus on the knotty issues that perplexed him, but the Greek church has always been less preoccupied by those concerns while still holding Paul in high esteem and reading him more optimistically and finding inspiration in him.[557] Augustine preferred to parse the texts as literally as he could and to insist that everything Paul said add up to one systematic and true body of doctrine.

So that is one way to read the history: reasonable men disagreed about an interpretation of Paul, and Augustine was often in the right, by standards of later western Christianity. But Pelagius had a trump card of his own. When he was challenged by the synod of eastern bishops at Diospolis in 415 to defend himself for claiming that baptized Christians might indeed end by burning in hell for their sins (a position on which Augustine would have agreed with him), he had a retort: he could quote Matthew 25.46 ("and these shall go away into everlasting punishment, but the righteous into life eternal") and tell his opponents that to disagree with him was to be an Origenist, one who believed in the eventual resurrection and happiness of *all* and thus, finally, in the irrelevance of Christian belief and practice. (If all will end in heaven, eventually, then the discipline demanded by Christianity needs to be evaluated on a cost-benefit basis. How much more quickly do I get to heaven as measured against how much pleasure of this life might I give up?) The power of Pelagius's argument lies in the fears of his interrogators. Origen and Origenism, as we saw, were the *bêtes noires* of Palestinian and Roman Christianity in the early 400s, and to tell his questioners that they risked becoming Origenists was to strike a keenly effective blow.[558]

A more skeptical reading would put exegesis aside and look at personalities. One would observe the possibilities for rivalry between older and younger men, the way older men resent young men who succeed in their own footsteps, and a particular resentment in Augustine for someone who succeeded and at the same time quoted the now-abandoned younger Augustine contradicting the hard-won ideas of the older one.

To do so is still to fail to grasp the sources of the intensity of the controversy. One may reasonably appreciate, for example, the charms of overweight middle-aged hippies playing bluegrass music without quite understanding what it is about the Grateful Dead that made them for decades an object of a cult familiar to historians from pilgrimage sites for late-antique holy men. Can we, without attempting to explain the Dead, get closer to the source of the baffling intensity here?

Consider what was at stake for Christianity in this conflict. Christianity begins, as far as the historical record goes, in the teachings of Paul, derived from what he heard about the teachings of Jesus. Even Paul insisted on making Jesus, the itinerant preacher of Palestine, the center of the religion. Teachings that come from Jesus are privileged beyond all others. And those are the teachings of a marginal figure in a marginal province of a world that had grown larger and less controllable with the years. Jesus's Judaism was a religion finally beginning to realize how irrelevant and impotent it was. The world outside would so control and master the world of Judaism that Judaism would be allowed to continue. It was not even worth destroying. (A generation later, that might have seemed an optimistic view.)

In that setting, Jesus, as taken by Christians like Augustine, said that if Rome and its world didn't care about any particular local community, there was a divine power that cared deeply. He evoked for them an alternate stage setting, all but invisible, that allowed the believer still to have a leading role. This was both reassuring and at the same time risky. Success would depend upon the individual. Temple, cult, and priests mattered less than they used to. Both Jewish and Roman traditions emphasized religious actions taken by leaders of the community on behalf of the community as a whole. Though such a view would grow more prevalent in Christianity as ritual became less participatory and more performance, the individual at the judgment seat of god was still going to be very much alone.[559]

Christian language about grace and freedom evolved to explain life enacted on that new scale. The god thus imagined is a mighty figure, on the model of the great men of this world, powerful, knowing, arbitrary, yet ultimately just and fair. But he has his favorites and bestows his favors as he wishes. And he pays attention to everybody. The god who converted Paul was certainly that kind of god.

The mature Pelagius and the young Augustine have not yet internalized the implications of that personality in the divine. Augustine's account of the events of his own conversion is remarkably free from the personality of the deity, though the *Confessions* themselves are an intimate address to him. For Pelagius, the Christian religion is a superior religion measured against all earlier models, but still fundamentally similar to them in type. It describes a divine power that acts rationally and fairly, aloof from the world, benevolently disposed toward it, certainly malleable now and then in response to prayers, but fundamentally distant. This divinity rules not by personal relationship but by the rule of law.

On this view, the human condition has its undesirable aspects but is fundamentally sound. A benevolent maker reveals rules, wise men follow them, and an orderly world ensues. Those who are imprudent enough to disobey are punished, and that, too, is orderly.

This view of Christianity might seem to hold within it the core of something more irenic, rationalist, and open than the Christianities that eventually emerged. Throughout late antiquity, some voices spoke up for such readings of Christianity, voices usually controverted by others. The reading of Jesus's relationship to his father promulgated by the Arians of the fourth century, for example, had this in common with Pelagius, that each interpretation imagined a fundamental ordinariness about Christianity and about the world it described, while both Nicene Christology and Augustinian grace imagine a world that has been deeply disrupted by the intrusion of the divine rescue mission.

Those are the views facing each other in the 410s. Pelagius and his like will always be puzzled and hurt by accusations of unorthodoxy and eager to deprecate them and make peace. Augustine will always be shocked by the failure of worldly men to see the urgency of man's plight and appreciate the drama of the divine intervention. Neither side can find a vocabulary that lets them discuss what is really at stake.

Left to face one another, these views could seem to be at loggerheads, and a modern reader is probably inclined to root for Pelagius. Certainly very, very few readers except the most devout Calvinist will find themselves agreeing with the Augustinian view, even in a notional sense. (By a notional sense, I mean in the way that uninvolved moderns often find themselves agreeing with Augustine or some other ancient figure as against their opponents, without sharing their fundamental views. So I take it that many modern readers find Augustine's view of catholicism more coherent and persuasive than the Donatist ecclesiology, even moderns who belong to no church themselves. In this case, if moderns agree with anyone, they probably prefer Pelagius.)

Why, then, does Augustine trump Pelagius in the short run and pre-vail as an authority figure, even if controverted, so easily in the long run? The answer to that lies in the evolving consensus among Christians, one that Augustine and Pelagius share, about the location of authority in the church. Before translocal hierarchies of bishops and eventual popes and patriarchs ever evolved to have any doctrinal authority, Christians had come to agree, without noticing it, without debate, and without anybody planning it, that scriptural texts, gathered in collections of apostolic authority, would prevail.

The emergence of a canon of scripture and the underlying idea of scripture is extraordinary. We have no history for it, no real discussion, just fragments of lists of debatable date. Sporadic debates erupted about whether the Jewish scriptures (already a more or less settled body of texts) were to be taken as scriptural in authority. From the first century onward, Marcion and others who had a high estimate of the reasonableness and power of Christ rejected the old scriptures, and the Manichees picked up their hostility in that tradition. Many gospels and epistles attributed to apostles were in circulation, some even gaudier in content than the ones that survive in the Christian scriptures. Insofar as there seems to have been a first principle of evaluation, it was apostolicity. Was the book writ-ten either by an apostle or by the friend of an apostle (e.g., Mark the dis-ciple of Peter, or Luke the disciple of Paul)? This required that everyone agree to accept Paul's own remarkable self-definition as an apostle, even though he never met Jesus and had no authority except his own story of his conversion.

What emerges is a remarkable agreement to accept the Septuagint col-lection of Hebrew and Jewish-originating Greek texts as authoritative, and to add to them roughly the list familiar to modern Bible readers of gospels and epistles, bringing in tow the explosive "Revelation of John" behind them and adducing as well the "Acts of the Apostles" to help the story stick together. The fundamental agreement that all these books would be scriptural in authority is something that Augustine can call upon in every argument with the mainstream Christians of his time—Donatist, Arian, and all others save Manichees—and use to his advantage. (The agreement is more remarkable given all the other noncanonical apostolic texts that were available and in circulation. By the fourth century the choices had largely been made and they remained very stable.)

But collecting those books and reading them with each other turned them into very different books from what they had been when they were being written. Paul, who wrote as a Jew explaining to Jews and gentiles how the two might both benefit from the enlightened views of the Jew Jesus, is a different thinker from Paul, the undoubtedly Christian writer of the fourth century, writing to attack Jews and liberate Christians from their legalistic clutches. That second Paul never lived and walked in first-century Palestine, but he is the Paul who has thrived in Christian imagination since at least Augustine's time.

That Paul was a problem for Pelagius. It was on Paul that Pelagius had to write his one detailed scripture commentary, because Paul as read among Latins of the late fourth century tested and pushed Pelagius's optimism to the limit. For that Paul, the divine power is ever-present and quite personal and directive, and the story of salvation is played out in myriad individual encounters of that sort.

As the drama and debates of the 410s played out, Augustine was on the offensive against Pelagius and Caelestius, and as long as he was on the offensive, he had the advantage and could count on all ecclesiastical authority accepting the terms of the debate that Augustine proposed, that is, the debate over the interpretation of these Christian scriptures. Once that victory was achieved, Pelagius was doomed to be marginalized. Gentlemanly Christianities would survive in the city of Rome longer than anywhere, but monastic-ascetic Christianities, still of a gentlemanly sort, would prevail in the west.

The last and decisive victory of the battle that Augustine fought was not a doctrinal one but a cultural one. Its symbol is Pope Gregory I, at the end of the sixth century, the sometime prefect of Rome and offspring of an exceedingly gentlemanly and prosperous clerical family there. He fled that life to enter a monastery, becoming bishop of Rome in 590. Though he was anything but popular with the local clergy, who seem to have been delighted when he passed away, his ascension and his widespread later reputation as "Gregory the Great" assured that the monastic-ascetic model of Christianity, which depended on the personal engagement of the individual with god and was every bit as anxious, depressive, lonely, and distraught in its hope for eternal joy as anything Augustine ever imagined.[560]

LAST ENEMIES

The Roman upper crust of the fourth century was as self-consciously self-creating and self-created as any gang of Proustian arrivistes. One line of their enthusiasm led them to putting on all the costumes and playing all the parts of traditional Roman dignity. They patronized the arts and took on the literary tastes and pastimes that they understood to be the tradition and prerogative of their class.[561]

But the upper crust of the fourth century had been transformed by the infusion of new faces under the emperor Constantine and his successors. His patronage of Christianity and the shift of public money away from traditional religious monuments and practices made it possible for Christian leaders in the churches of Rome and Italy to make significant inroads with those families. With the transfer of wealth into the hands of Christian churches, moreover, it became possible to reimagine the role of a bishop. Churches and episcopal households on a grander scale created the opportunity for a new cleric, himself a near-peer to the best families. We know far too little about the way these families chose their religions affiliations as individuals, but more and more of the best families found that they contained members who practiced the fashionable new religion patronized by the emperors. An appreciable number of such folks had made the shrewd transition by 391, when the zealot emperor Theodosius ended the period instituted by Constantine when old religions had been merely disadvantaged vis-à-vis Christianity and imposed an outright ban on their public practice. In the generation that followed, the aristocracy found its place inside the new church, or rather found a place for the new church in its midst.

Augustine moved among several Christian worlds, looking like one thing to the snobbish aristocrats of Rome and another to the olive farmers and farm laborers of upland Numidia. His position was bound to be a difficult one. The great plague of his middle years in Hippo was the conflict with the African social world where Augustine was a member of the thinnest upper crust himself. Augustine established his allegiance unmistakably on the side of Roman government and a vision of pan-Mediterranean Christian society. His last two decades, on the other hand, saw him in a reversal of roles—now stereotyped in his last public battle as the African, the provincial, the uncouth outsider.

His earlier success in making a name for himself in the world beyond Africa had been pleasant and bracing, but that reputation came back to haunt him. In his middle years, he could imagine himself among the circle of his correspondents in Italy, friends-by-letter like Paulinus of Nola, to be sure, but also Memor, bishop of Beneventum, not so very far from Nola in southern Italy. We have a letter Augustine wrote to Memor, responding to a request for a book. Memor asked Augustine for a copy of one of his more tasteful productions, the *De musica*, from his projected cycle on the liberal arts. Just the thing (Memor might imagine) for the cultural education of a gentlemanly cleric, his own son, a youthful deacon. Augustine is somewhat reserved in reply:

> After the weight of ecclesiastical cares was placed on my shoulders, all those old pleasures abandoned me, so much so that I can scarcely lay hands on a copy of the book now. But I can't think of resisting your wish, which is not a request to me but a command! If I sent you the whole book, though, it's not that I'd be sorry I sent it, but you'd be sorry you asked for it so vehemently. . . . [Augustine expatiates on the technical difficulty of the first five books. Then . . .] To be sure, I have not hesitated to send the sixth book, which I found in a clean copy and which has the meat of the whole work in it. . . . The first five books are scarcely worth reading and knowing for your—for *our*—son and fellow deacon, Julian (for he is already in service with us!). I wouldn't dare to say I love him more than I love you, for it wouldn't be quite true, but I do dare to say that I long to see him more than I long for you. It can seem puzzling that I love the two of you equally but long to see him the more, but after all there's more hope of my seeing him. I think if he came to see me at your suggestion he would do as a young man should and can (for he has fewer serious distractions than we do) and he would thus be really bringing you to me![562]

Augustine has to close by admitting that his ignorance of Hebrew makes him unable to answer a question about the meters of the Psalms. The gracious and discreet invitation went in vain and Augustine would never lay eyes on the promising young man. Paulinus of Nola, on the other hand, knew the family and provided the wedding poem in honor of the young cleric's marriage:

> *Join hearts and souls in chaste love,*
> *virginal lad of Christ, virginal maid of Christ,*
>
> . . . .
>
> *Let all the bawdiness of the silly world stay away,*
> *Juno and Cupid and Venus—those names for debauchery!*
> *Let the holy offspring of the clergy be joined in a sacred bond:*
> *Let peace and decency and piety come together here!*

And so on for 240 tasteful lines reflecting the ceremony and dignity of a high-society wedding with fine clerical sensibilities. The mixture is as much a part of the old Roman aristocratic spirit as of anything specifically Christian.[563]

The young man prospered and was a credit to his family. Still at an early age, he became bishop of Eclanum and settled into what should have been a comfortable and well-esteemed life as grandee of a sort in his community. But we know Julian best not for his gentlemanly upbringing and demeanor, nor for the respect and admiration of his neighbors. His writings propelled his name beyond the boundaries of his home community, just as writing had done for Augustine, and left him known to history as a blistering polemicist. He is generally characterized as a hot-headed young man, but he may very well have been one of those people who come across very differently in their writings than in their everyday dealings with people.[564]

He comes to our attention because he, not surprisingly, took umbrage at some of what Augustine had said in his anti-Pelagian writings. Wherever we imagine Pelagius in the social hierarchy of his time, Julian stood higher and more securely and acquired his Christianity as an adjunct to his social role, without the admixture of zealotry and Platonism that marked Augustine's religion. Augustine's posture on matters where Christian ascetic enthusiasm found itself confronting the traditions of marriage and family particularly affronted Julian. Paulinus's praise captures the austerity of Christian marriage for a cleric like Julian, but that austerity was more on the order of decorous restraint than any outright hostility to marriage. Julian's notion of the clergy, moreover, recognized that whatever the restraint of clergy, the clerical role was designedly and understandably different from that of the ordinary Christian. The dignity and seemliness of Christian marriage in the families around a dignified Christian bishop was something Julian could not question. Augustine, launching increasingly angry blasts against Pelagius, had given his hostages to fortune in things he said about marriage. Augustine had picked the fight.[565]

Augustine makes it very easy for us to see Julian from his point of view. He is young, hot-headed, disrespectful of the older scholar, determined to make a case for a version of Christian teaching that is (in Augustine's view) insufficiently open to a deeper understanding of scripture or (in the view of modern scholars looking over Augustine's shoulder to see Julian) insufficiently aware of the subtleties of Christian theology.

So what did Julian make of Augustine? Julian was indeed younger than

Augustine, but nothing would incline him to think of the African with respect. "Patron of donkeys," he called him, and that was upper-class disdain speaking.[566] To be African, from a town no one had heard of, with no money, no family, no past—none of this boded well in Julian's eyes. The Augustine he saw was an upstart who had succeeded in imposing himself on the Christian world by force of personality and literary ability, carrying obsession to fame without regard for the truth. Julian had visited Africa and probably took from that a sense of what the Manichean tinge in Augustine's thought amounted to.[567] He recognized the pattern: a "tenured radical," that's what Augustine was, an aging ex-Manichee, never really converted, an obsolete relic of a discredited generation. Julian was a close and hostile reader of the *Confessions* and would use what he found there for his own polemical purposes.[568]

And Augustine's obsession with Pelagius was just unintelligible and bizarre. Julian was galvanized into action by his quite transparent and natural shock at the success Augustine had in gaining imperial and Roman episcopal support for that obsession. It seemed a small matter—so far did Julian misread the strength of Augustine's political connections—to overturn the decision.[569] It was certain that the more he read of Augustine, the more outraged he became.

The decisive turn came in the spring of 418 with the decree at Rome of Zosimus banning Pelagius and Caelestius from Rome and putting their supporters on notice of legal jeopardy.[570] That was what drove Julian to react.[571] Augustine's influence at the imperial court, won through Alypius's astute lobbying, stood him in good stead. Julian was baffled at every turn. He wrote a public letter attacking the decision, only to see imperial support building against him. By the summer of 419, he had no choice but to be deposed from his bishopric and go into exile. He passed the rest of his life, perhaps thirty years, living in the eastern part of the Roman empire, for a time as a guest of another theologian who would come under suspicion, Theodore of Mopsuestia in southern Asia Minor. From that exile came most of his writings against Augustine, rocketing back westward.

One letter of Julian's addressed to a Roman audience and another letter he wrote jointly with other Italian bishops to the bishop of Thessalonica, seeking support, came to Augustine's attention. Augustine responded with a stinging polemic, *Against Two Letters from the Pelagians*. Another letter of Julian's went to the influential Count Valerius at the Ravenna court, a strong ally of Augustine's in getting imperial condemnation of Pelagius. To that Augustine responded with a pamphlet *Marriage and Libido (De nuptiis et con-*

cupiscentia). With each attack, Augustine's position sharpened and offered more points of attack. Imprudently, he wrote the first book of that pamphlet on the basis of hearsay, before he'd seen a copy of the letter, then corrected and sharpened his remarks with a second book when the actual text of Julian's remarks came to him. Julian naturally took this all badly and responded in kind (still in the heated year 418–19) to the first book of *De nuptiis* with a work in four books, *To Turbantius*. Augustine's response came partly in the second book of the *De nuptiis* and then at great length in six books *Against Julian* in the early 420s. Julian in his eastern exile received a copy of the second book of *De nuptiis* from a colleague at Constantinople named Florus, and so the last directly anti-Augustinian book from Julian is the *To Florus*. That in turn reached Augustine and he spent his last year or so of life writing obsessively in reply, in what we now have as the six books of *The Incomplete Work Against Julian*.[572] Julian may not have ever seen that book, but Augustine died knowing that his battle was unfinished and that the ideas of his enemies survived.

Julian went on to write other works of theology and exegesis and remains a great might-have-been of Latin theology. He was learned and eloquent and stood more nearly in the mainstream of the Christianities of his time than Augustine did, but he is forever marginalized as much by the condemnation of Pelagianism as by the misfortune of seeming for so long to be Augustine's punching bag.[573]

The last hundreds of pages of Augustine's writings against Julian have probably been read less often than any of his other works. To read much of Augustine requires or facilitates a respectful bond between reader and author. Call it codependency or Stockholm syndrome at its mildest, call it religious partisanship at its most extreme, but even Augustine's severest modern critics find something attractive or fascinating about the man and his work. The anti-Julian works, however, resolutely deter affection, fascination, or even respect, and they make wearying and dispiriting reading, even for his most kindly disposed students. Augustine has the worst of the argument in modern eyes because of the unrealistic extremes to which he took his suspicion of marriage, sexuality, and the fundamental processes of the human body. Julian is scarcely more attractive on these points and has no coherent alternative to offer. Julian is naïve and unrealistic in his own expectations of the working of Christian morality, and Augustine has at least the merit of recognizing that the most strenuous and traditional precepts of Christian sexual morality are simply difficult to observe—are, indeed, rarely observed by any individual consistently for a lifetime. Julian seems to have imagined that virtuous restraint was, for the dignified gentleman, a matter of merit, to be sure, but merit relatively easily achieved, whatever excesses of irresponsibility the mass of Christians beyond the highest social circles might display. Neither man comes across well.

Julian must be granted his victories. When Augustine, for example, argues for the power of baptism, Julian is on him in a flash.[574] If on the one hand baptism is so powerful, he argues, but if on the other hand people who have been baptized and liberated from original sin still pass on that original sin to their children—well, how powerful can baptism really be then? Augustine's unwillingness to sort through the issues of the origin of soul and take a coherent position leaves him weakened rhetorically. His failure is a sign of the inner incoherence of the position he occupies.[575]

To avoid settling for partisanship when gazing on the spectacle of Augustine and his enemies in his lifetime, it may help to cast the gaze forward a dozen centuries. Then we can find another figure, just as obsessed with the ins and outs of Augustine's later ideas as was Julian. He, too, is linked to a generation and more of aristocratic Christians determined to demonstrate the excellence and purity of their vocation.

Cornelius Jansen, bishop of Ypres in Belgium (died 1638) and author of a powerfully influential book that few people have ever actually read, did not oppose Augustine. Quite to the contrary, his obsessive study (he is said to have read all of Augustine's works ten times, and his writings against the Pelagians thirty times) led him to write a determinedly Augustinian book—indeed, *Augustinus* was the title—summarizing and recasting Augustinian ideas in the language of sixteenth-century scholastic theology. The book was published posthumously, but his ideas were taken up by the elegant Parisian school of Port-Royal, who numbered among their company the brilliant and lucid Blaise Pascal and the bulldog-like Antoine Arnauld. (Pascal and Arnauld as a pair are not altogether unlike, for their complementary strengths and weaknesses, Augustine and Alypius.) The positions of Jansen and his followers were fiercely Augustinian in the sense that they emphasized divine power and grace and consequent predestination. The great bugbears of Jansenism were the Jesuits, who vied with them for control of the hearts and minds of the French upper classes. Jesuitry won the battle in the seventeenth century and lost the war in the eighteenth, and French aristocratic catholicism remained marked (and remains marked, to the extent that it still exists) by the high-minded disdain and sense of distinction that the original Jansenists enacted.

Jansen and his followers were as much enemies of Augustine as was Julian. Both did him the unkindness of taking his last arguments as seriously as he wished them to be taken and left him forever marked by them. If the modern generosity toward Augustine arises out of enthusiastic readership of the *Confessions* and *City of God*, the broader theological and historical impact of his work has been perceptibly lamed by the quarrels of his last years. To take this late Augustine seriously is to expose him to criticism that he is finally unable to sustain, and his partisans and opponents are of one party in this.

AUGUSTINE IN PARODY

Best to keep things in perspective by ending this account with the story of a parody.

In 1643 a hitherto unknown text of late antiquity was published, untitled and attributed to an anonymous author whom modern scholars call "Praedestinatus" ("Predestined").[276] The work falls in three books and is a challenge for interpreters.

The first book outlines the heresies of Christendom down to the time of writing, ninety in all. In so doing, the author closely follows, but does not quite copy, Augustine's own book of *Heresies* (*De haeresibus*) and shares his view of the world in which the single path of truth is planted thick around with byways and detours and errors of every sort. But the ninetieth heresy listed is one that Augustine didn't mention: "predestinationism." Summarized in the first book, it becomes the theme of the second book, which espouses and *defends* predestinationism and is presented as a work wrongly ascribed to Augustine. Then the third book attacks the heresy of the second.

Readers have naturally been confused by this apparent mish-mash. Some have gone so far as to hold that the second book is the authentic work of a real "predestinationist" defending an extreme form of Augustinian doctrine. The truth seems to be subtler.

The most recent serious study assigns the whole work to a figure otherwise known only slightly, "Arnobius the younger," writing in Rome in the mid-fifth century. The core of the work is the second book, now revealed as parody and pastiche. The line of argument goes roughly like this: here are all the Christian heresies, and most readers would recognize many of them and be familiar with the idea. To be sure, the earlier Christian father Origen is more kindly handled (and indeed nearly rehabilitated) than was the case in Augustine's own treatment and in most church discussion of the fifth century, and the view of Pelagius presented here gives him as a heretic, to be sure, but softens the Augustinian view (apparently under the influence of Julian of Eclanum) and leaves him better off than in any other anti-Pelagian treatment we know.

So the author presents the second book as if it were a real book handed around in Augustine's name, as a representation of his own ideas on issues of grace and free will. But then there are two twists: first, the author knows perfectly well that Augustine didn't write it, because he wrote it himself, as a caricature of extreme doctrine; second, the allegation of false attribution has the effect of defending Augustine's memory while warning extreme defenders of Augustine to go carefully. (In Africa this would mean the writer Quodvultdeus; in Gaul, Prosper of Aquitaine; in Italy, Marius Mercator.) The author pretends that predestinationism is an *old* heresy, long known to be an error and thus of little relevance to Augustine and to Africa. In writing parody, the author goes further than Augustine or any Augustinian would actually go in apparent defense of predestination, and in so doing would hope to have the effect of ruling out much that *was* current among Augustinian disciples.

So we see a contest over Augustine's inheritance, carried out with an unusual sense of humor and ingenuity. On the best interpretation, the work is meant to defend what the author regards as mainstream Christians in Gaul and Italy against accusations of Pelagian sympathies by seeking to seize the middle ground from what he sees as zealots. If hard Augustinian views could be excluded as un-Augustinian heresy, then it would be harder for Augustine's moderate opponents in Gaul to be tarred with the Pelagian brush. We have no idea how persuasive the book turned out to be, but the performance is clever and witty. Most important, perhaps, is the realization that the name and fame of *Augustine* are secure in its pages, even if Augustinian disciples and ideas are under attack.

XI

AUGUSTINE THE THEOLOGIANS

The most common visual representation of Augustine in the middle ages, in manuscript illuminations or later in paintings in churches, reflected a familiar story. I can take the story from an obliging website:

The story is told in Christian lore of how the brilliant theologian and Doctor of the Church, St. Augustine of Hippo, used to ponder long and hard on the greatest mystery of the Christian faith, the Holy Trinity, as he tried to understand it. Strolling along the seashore one day while pondering how there could be three Persons in one God, he noticed a small child seemingly at play on the beach. He watched how the child repeatedly scooped up water from the sea in a shell and carried it to a hole in the sand into which he emptied the water. Then returning to the water's edge, the child refilled the shell and repeated the process over and over. Curious, Augustine walked over and asked the child what he was doing. Smiling up at him, the child said, "I am emptying the sea into this hole." Amused at the child's naïvete, Augustine replied, "Why, even if you spent your whole life at this task, child, you could never complete it. The sea is far too vast and deep to be contained in so small a hole!" The child looked up solemnly at Augustine and said: "Yet I will complete

this task before you can ever understand the Mystery on which you ponder"—and with that, the child vanished. Augustine then realized that he
was a messenger sent to him by God to point out the futility of his efforts to understand this Mystery.[577]

The late and pious story, alas, isn't within a country mile of being true,
and even gets Augustine's view of the Trinity wrong.[578]

But that is the Augustine whose memory has persisted most durably, Augustine the deep thinker, Augustine the master of theology. In Proust's
telling of the story of Charles Swann, smug and self-satisfied people who
only saw Swann at Madame Verdurin's house, where he pursued a rather
improbable love affair, thought little of him. When they heard or surmised
that he otherwise moved in the highest social circles of Paris, they scoffed at
the possibility. A reader who knows Augustine *only* from my treatment of
him to this point might risk a comparably embarrassing belittlement.

The title of this chapter is not a misprint, but is meant to emphasize
something important about Augustine—his moods and voices, and even
his counterfeits. We have seen him already on the rampage against the
Donatists, where mother (and father) church must be defended with fe-
rocity and skill. We have seen what was at stake when he took out after
Pelagianism with hammer and tongs, at that point defending a particular
ecclesiastical role. Those personae are the two that had in his own time
and after the deepest and most lasting theological influence on the existing churches of his communion, but the favor those personae have found
has faded sharply over the past century.

A third Augustine is the one still most deeply admired by many and always the most sympathetic: if not a purveyor of mystic crystal revelations
and the mind's true liberation (though on some days that language would
not have been foreign to him), at least a theologian of a deeply intellectual and spiritual religion, one so exalted as to be in touch with the ordinary religious Christians of his time only by the fact of mutual presence
in the same church building. *That* Augustine is the one who is generally
given pride of place in organizing discussions of his thought in our time.

And there are the counterfeit Augustines. The pious story I just told is
one example, but many others can be told. Works attributed to Augustine
that he did not really write were abundant in the middle ages. Some were
attributed to him in all innocence, but even where deliberate counterfeits
were in circulation, those who received them did so blithely and inno-
cently. Bear in mind, for example, that the first work of "Augustine" ever
to be printed was not by Augustine himself. It was a little pamphlet titled

The Christian Life (*De vita christiana*), published in Mainz around 1465, and it enjoyed a broad circulation. After many generations in which hand-written copies of Augustine's books had circulated widely and his name was sometimes applied to things that merely *seemed* to be his, this book was readily taken to be Augustine's and it was doubtless meant to express his spirit and thought accurately, but it wasn't him, whatever the printer and his public thought.

Samuel Beckett tormented his interpreters with a story he told one time, supposedly to help them understand *Waiting for Godot*.[579] He used to read, he said, a lot of Augustine in the Bibliothèque Nationale in Paris and recalled one passage in particular: "Do not despair," he remembered Augustine saying, "one of the thieves was saved. Do not presume, one of the thieves was damned." Thinking of Vladimir and Estragon as the two thieves crucified with Jesus is intriguing, to say the least, and it is won-derfully Beckett-like that the particular passage cannot be found any-where in the surviving writings of Augustine or anywhere in the pages of *Patrologia Latina*, for all that the language and tenor are quite perfectly Augustinian. Did Beckett make up the quotation? Is he the most modern of pseudo-Augustines?

Augustine himself, moreover, cannot escape responsibility even for the counterfeits. By the acts of gigantic self-creation and self-perpetuation in which he was so successful, he created a cultural phenomenon that in its broadest sense includes all that people *think* they know about him, all that people attribute to him. The fake designer handbags sold on Canal Street in New York and seen in use on fashionable streets everywhere are a real part of the impact the imitated merchants and their marketing have on the domain of style.

The construction of a successful interpretation of Augustine, there-fore, typically depends on finding a line of argument that reduces the multitude of theological Augustines to one. My practice is to try to do jus-tice to the multitudes. The wisest reader will go away from these pages to read Augustine unmediated (except if necessary by translation), and will go not only to the *Confessions* but to some of the other places where Au-gustine built bridges between himself and his god.

AUGUSTINE'S GOD

Any number of good treatments of Augustine the philosopher have been written,[580] and there is at least one good treatment of Augustine the theologian,[581] but this is not the place to reproduce them. Both approaches normalize Augustine to the practices, outlook, and disciplines of a community of thinkers that has emerged in modern times, and, particularly for members of those communities, such treatment can be very valuable. If we are to start from Augustine, however, and try to explore the world with him, we need to think about the part of his life that looked beyond the visible and the social to the divine and the immaterial, to the part of him that was devoted to thinking intensely about the divine and speaking and writing those thoughts. That appetite for transcendence is the most consistent and characteristic feature of his thought.

The chronological outline of that thinking is easy to establish: preoccupation with evil and god from his late teens; revelation and restoration by a reimagination of god from his early thirties, and with it an allegiance to religious exaltation; then reacquaintance with a more sober view—call it his age of temptation, muting the sense of exaltation and introducing a cautionary pragmatism in his early forties; and then the sharp turn of 411, back toward anxiety, a sense of the power of sin and the arbitrariness of human experience, very short indeed on exaltation.

That trajectory matches in many ways the outward events of Augustine's life. Becoming a clergyman was hard on him, and growing to be an old clergyman very hard indeed. His god stayed with him all those years. Augustine never wavered, but he himself changed and changed again, without ever seeming to notice.

In the *Soliloquies* (*Soliloquia*—Augustine coined the word for use in this book) that he wrote at Cassiciacum, in which "Reason" and "Augustine" set out together on a quiet series of conversations, the conversation proper begins with this terse exchange:

AUGUSTINE: Okay, I've prayed to god.
    REASON: So what do you want to know?
AUGUSTINE: Everything I prayed for.
    REASON: Sum it up for me.
AUGUSTINE: God and the soul.
    REASON: Nothing else?
AUGUSTINE: Nothing at all.
    REASON: So go ahead, ask me about them.[582]

God and the soul remain the poles of Augustine's thought and experience throughout his writings, and his theology and his "anthropology" define what he is interested in, and his notion of god that drives, and even derails, the rest.

Best to begin by hearing Augustine call on his god. The wordplay, the assonance, the alliteration, all disappear in translation.

quid es ergo, deus meus?	What are you, then, my god?

summe, optime,	Highest, best,
potentissime, omnipotentissime,	most powerful, most all-
misericordissime et iustissime,	powerful;
secretissime et praesentissime,	most merciful and most just;
pulcherrime et fortissime,	most hidden and most present;
stabilis et incomprehensibilis,	most beautiful and most
immutabilis mutans omnia,	strong,
numquam novus numquam vetus,	standing firm and elusive,
	unchangeable and all-changing;
	never new, never old;

semper agens semper quietus,	ever working, ever at rest;
conligens et non egens,	gathering in, yet lacking
portans et implens et protegens,	nothing;
creans et nutriens et perficiens,	supporting, filling, and
quaerens cum nihil desit tibi.	sheltering;
	creating, nourishing, and
	ripening;
	seeking, yet having all things.

et quid diximus, deus meus,	And what have I now said,
vita mea, dulcedo mea sancta,	my god, my life, my holy joy?

aut quid dicit aliquis	Or what does anybody say
cum de te dicit?	when he speaks of you?
et vae tacentibus de te, quoniam	And woe to him who keeps
loquaces muti sunt.[583]	silent about you,
	since many babble on and say
	nothing.

The paradoxes of the divine nature reveal the limitations of human language and its unsuitability for the impossible task of theology. Not yet for Augustine the mannered style of an Eriugena in the ninth century, for whom god is good, but god is also not good (not good in the human way, at any rate), and good is finally "super-good" (*super-bonus* is the word he uses) in a way that lies beyond the human category of goodness, but some of the same impulse is there. Human words used by humans fail in the presence of the divine, he thinks, and whatever can be said is only approximation. Most human discourse fails to say anything of god at all, despite endless loquacious efforts. The limitations of language thus discovered have the effect of proving to Augustine yet again the rightness of his fundamental view of a high, unapproachable, ineffable god.[584]

For a rhetorician as polished as Augustine to admit failure in a matter of rhetoric is striking and not without significance, as most experienced readers of Augustine will have felt. For all the clarity and definition that Augustine can give to his writing elsewhere, it cannot be without significance that at the center of his concerns lies this finally unsayable Other, who eludes all his attempts to define and delimit. Augustine's elusive god needs to be taken seriously, in all his elusiveness, in order to do justice to the things that Augustine says about other things, particularly things that are perplexing or repellent. Whenever Augustine is saying something that moderns find troubling, the best first resort for an interpreter is to look closely to see what text or scripture he has in mind and how it more or less forces him to say what he says.

Augustine's narrative of his discovery of this god in the *Confessions* is artful in several ways, but probably in the main reliable, and even revealing. The sequence emerges if we look carefully at the way he reports the attraction Manicheism had for him and the way he sublimated it. The questions the Manichees pressed hardest and with best effect on the adolescent Augustine were these: Where does evil come from (in other words, is god good)? Does god have a body? How do we understand the seeming inconsistency between Jewish and Christian versions of divine justice (in other words, can god be just if he is so inconsistent)? The short answers to these questions were simple: god is good, god is spirit, god is just. Each of those answers raises problems.[585]

Finding those answers took Augustine to Milan. Ambrose's sermons, with their emphasis on the Pauline distinction of letter and spirit as a means of interpreting the chasm that was thought to fall between the Jewish scriptures and the Christian ones, rescued god's justice, but the issue resurfaced at the center of the Pelagian controversies.[586] The first encounter with the books of the Platonists revealed to him a god who was not like the all-penetrating sea soaking into the sponge of material creation, but instead a spirit, although neither Augustine nor anyone else could ever explain what that might mean. The final stage in that revelation came on his second look at the Platonists. He was staggered to hear them teaching that evil did not exist at all. Everything is good and what is apparently evil is only a deficiency in the fullness of good. The moment was revelatory and inspiring, but it must be admitted that to make such a proposition requires significant adjustment in the ordinary meaning of the word "good."

For Augustine, the justice of this god was an adequate answer to those who were appalled by the stories of the Jewish patriarchs and their fleshly ways; the spiritual nature of this god offered a refutation of the "pagans"; and the goodness of this god and this god's creation offered the decisive argument against the Manichees. We need to do Augustine the favor of allowing that the questions that long plagued him did indeed speak to the heart of his religious experience of the divine, and that when he had re moved those obstacles, he found a way to a god who was not a phantasm but real and true. That doesn't mean the original questions went away. His anti-Manichee answers to Manichee questions (such as their insistence on asking where evil came from) have the unintended effect of keeping them alive. When Augustine makes his most cherished assertions about his god, we need to hear that he is at the same time giving tacit voice to his deepest anxieties.

This way of imagining the divine nature made both possible and necessary the further struggle for encounter with the incarnate word of god that came to a completion in the famous garden scene in the eighth book of the *Confessions*. But a seeker who does not share Augustine's questions and anxieties is unlikely to come to the same conception of god.

For Augustine's god is a silent god. Though god is everywhere, though god watches over and cares for humankind, though god hears human prayers, the response is, to every mortal ear, silence. For a god whose mediator to humankind was the incarnate word, silence is remarkable. The incarnate word of the liturgy and the superabundance of divine words in scripture make up for that silence as best can be, but the silence is still deafening.

What does this god come to in the end? Imagine yourself a fourth-century "pagan," imprudently cast in Augustine's way some afternoon, and challenging him to defend his novel religious ideas. You will suggest to him, as Symmachus had proclaimed in his speech on the altar of Victory in

384, "One does not approach so great a mystery by a single path."[587] (Augustine himself might have been open to such argument in his youth, and said something similar himself that he later regretted.[588]) You—still a "pagan"—think yourself tolerant, broad-minded in your acceptance of many cults, though in practice you are probably quite snobbish about preferring your own, and curiously disdainful about the excesses of others, perhaps even downright hostile to some. Augustine speaks to you of the unity and spirituality of his god, his ubiquity, and his timelessness, and thus of a god who is not the exclusive property of anyone, who forms no closed community, no sect, no cult, but (and this would be jarring) who is accessible to one and all. "Pagan" monotheism always had something abstract about it. It was a notion about religion, but not a part of the religious experience itself. Augustine's Christianity took philosophical monotheism to church and insisted on linking it to prayer and worship. That particularization of the universal was hard for many to follow.

This god of Augustine's could not be so powerful, so remote, so perfect without inspiring (or, perhaps better, arising out of) fear. What fears are mapped in this theology's shadow? Mystic union and transcendence might be one ending to a line of god-thought of the kind Augustine practiced, and if his god had taken him away at about the point at which he wrote the *Confessions*, that is how we would remember him. But the aging Augustine remembered and lived the possibility of temptation, gained a sense of the arbitrariness of god, and came to resent and resist his own youthful optimism when Pelagius thrust it in his face.

Augustine believes in, hopes for, and loves his god. The most sympathetic treatises of Augustine's later years (*Spirit and Letter; Treatise on the Epistle of John;* the *Enchiridion*) bring that Trinitarian image to the fore. What are their opposites? Disbelief (that is to say, the failure of the project to know god and soul), despair arising from disbelief, and isolation and chill—the isolation and chill that some find, or fear to find, in old age, perhaps.

And Augustine the polemicist? He attacks ostensibly misdirected faith and hope and love with a vehemence that gives expression to his many fears. He cannot allow that others, others with easier views of the divine and of humankind, can be right, for then not only he but his god would be rendered useless. And that is what, to the end, Augustine hangs on to: the firm conviction that god is not useless.

HOMO AUGUSTINIANUS

The human person (*homo* is the gender-neutral word in Latin whose equivalent we lack in English) is the necessary complement to the divine in Augustine's picture of the universe. If this seems obvious, Augustine is in no small part responsible.

The fundamental fact about the human person for him is that it is created "in the image and likeness of god" (Genesis 1.26). Augustine insists on that point relentlessly. Early and late he pursues triadic patterns of behavior in god and man at the same time: being/knowing/loving perhaps the most common of them, as we saw in talking about how the *Confessions* were put together. The similarities reside fundamentally in the soul of humankind, not the body, and they sharply separate and distinguish human beings from the animal kingdom. (Making that distinction was an old project of ancient philosophy—for example, in Cicero—and not something specially Christian. Human beings are what come between the divine and the bestial. In other words, we know what we are by knowing what we are not.)

The desire to see these similarities changed both god and man. Each begins to be squeezed into a triangular frame, defined by the geometry and its tensions. The three persons of the trinity appear reduced in role to parts of a machine and lose some of their affective impact. The human being is shaped in the image and likeness of god so idealistically that human qualities are squeezed out. We've already seen how the *Confessions* undervalued the role of the human, fallible, experiential person, the person different from every other. In that person's place, the image and likeness of god becomes an Everyman character. The more nearly redeemed the individual becomes, the more he loses his identity and becomes like every other saved soul. There, the legacy of Platonism is strong in ways that never surfaced in Augustine's express doctrine. He certainly thought that individual identity persisted in eternity, but he spoke and wrote in ways that were nonetheless compatible with other thinkers, such as the philosopher Plotinus and the Christian Origen, who anticipated an ultimate submersion of the individual in a shimmering reunion with the divine One.

Seeing the redeemable part of humankind in the soul led to certain difficulties. Augustine speaks very little of the ultimate resurrection of the body, and his readers can be forgiven for thinking that he still imagines a bodiless and entirely spiritual heaven. But the soul plays two ways in Augustine. On the one hand, when he philosophizes about the soul and its nature, he is quite certain that he finds it to be immaterial, intellectual, and immortal. Many people that he would encounter, and many others in the ambit of Christianity in late antiquity, would be inclined to find a material basis for the soul. If it took its origin as a concept based in the physical breath that goes in, comes out, and vanishes at death, it could surely seem to have a material dimension, even if of the lightest and airiest kind. On this point Augustine is resolute. The soul is spirit, not body (though spirit is hard to define except by an absence of bodily qualities like measurability, weight, tangibility, and changeableness), and finds its truest expression in the conscious life. Animals have souls that are and are not like human souls—devoid of the essential features of intelligence and expression. (Modern discoveries in the field of animal intelligence might perplex Augustine.)

And the soul cannot be destroyed.

But at the same time, souls can go wrong, perilously wrong. They did indeed go wrong, back at the dawn of time, when Adam and Eve sinned. When he could get away with it, Augustine would gloss over the question of the *mechanism* of transmission of sin to emphasize its effects. Before their sin, Adam and Eve had the ability not to sin if they so chose, but also the ability to sin. And having sinned once (the woman, the weaker vessel, seducing the man into transgression), they had crossed a bridge of no return. They were punished with expulsion from paradise and with the news that they would die with their bodies. Before this, they had been immortal. Worse, they took with them from paradise the certainty that they and all their offspring for all time would sin again.

Different forces drove Augustine to that doctrine of original sin, his most original and nearly single-handed creation. The high spiritualism of Platonism resonated deeply with him and left him suspicious of body and flesh and the messiness of ordinary human life. That high-mindedness could have kept him out of trouble, except that he was waylaid by the ordinary beliefs of the Christians he fell in among.

Recall the puzzlement he expressed, when he was first back in Africa, at the local habit of baptizing infants.[589] How could this be truly valuable, he wondered, doing this to babies who had no understanding of what was going on? Here he was confronted by anxiety and (worse) logical consistency.

As long as Christianity had been a minority cult, it recruited among adults and offered baptism as an initiation ritual. This baptism was a powerful ritual bath that would take away all sins. The canny adult was one who waited as long as possible before taking baptism, because it was a once-for-all opportunity at wiping the books clean. In the fourth century, it was common for the canniest (including the emperor Constantine) to wait for their deathbed to seize the opportunity and common for non-Christian critics to point to that practice to accuse the Christians of rank immorality. "Sin all you like, as long as you like, then take the saving bath and go to heaven"—that's how the doctrine and practice could appear. But as more and more people became, or were forced to become, Christians and more and more families and communities were imbued with Christian practice across generations, anxiety and logic compelled parents to think that if baptism were truly valuable, indeed were the only way to redemption and heaven, then their infants, who died so easily and so often, were at sad risk. In a world of widespread infant mortality, what was one of make of the tiny babies who came and went so rapidly? Were they all doomed to perdition unbathed? The practice of infant baptism, spreading among Christian communities in the fourth century, arose out of nothing more coherent or doctrinal than this obsessive and logically impeccable anxiety. Augustine the new bishop would find himself compelled to accept (and then compelled to explain, at least to himself) this practice.

The only logical escape was to conclude that the infants themselves carried the stain of sin. The first pages of the *Confessions* contain the famous and emotionally freighted passage in which Augustine infers from the behavior of babies he has seen eyeing each other jealously at the breasts of their wet nurses that the deepest human failings are already present in the most innocent-seeming of infants.[590] From that experience he leapt to imagine a world in which his Platonic skepticism of the body was ratified and underscored by the Christian call to penance and redemption. When he heard that Pelagius had been preaching what he took to be a hearty "take charge of your own life" Christianity, something clicked and he rebelled. For Augustine, his god was all-powerful and all-determining, the human role in redemption at best a cooperation with the inevitable. (The story he had told of himself in the *Confessions*, after all, had portrayed his god as the actor and himself as the object of divine management.) Remember the clunky and disjointed title he gave the book he wrote when he first heard of Pelagius's ideas: *What Sin Deserves; or, Infant Baptism* (*De peccatorum meritis et remissione et de baptismo parvulorum*). From that point on, the doctrine and its associated stories were assured a long future. In books 13 and 14 of *City of God*, a few years later, the story of Adam and Eve would be fully associated with the doctrine.

So human beings were all condemned to sin, and responsible for the sins they committed, for original sin offered no release from culpability. Worse punishment than expulsion from paradise waited for all these sinners. When they died, they would languish in eternal misery. For their souls, though immortal, were subject to pain, spiritual pain, and would feel that pain forever as the punishment for sin. Medieval Christian doctrine would add the further layer of possible punishment of purgatory, and though Augustine says things that are more or less compatible with such a doctrine, he does not enunciate it in any recognizable form.

All this probably sounds familiar to most moderns, too familiar. We need to think of "Glunchism" again, perhaps, to give these ideas a freshness and angularity they probably too readily lack. They certainly had a dissonant ring in the ear of many of Augustine's contemporaries encountering Christianity for the first time, and to many Christians as well. Pelagius and Julian were not madmen and not un-Christian in their dissent. Their exhortations to good moral conduct fell flat by comparison to Augustine's more dramatic portrait of fall, alienation, and redemption that came as a magical and (in the ritual of baptism) visible intervention from outside.

Augustine's doctrine, however, had the effect of reversing and disconnecting important elements of the older Christian teachings. Christianity had taken hold among people for whom the bad news of sin and its consequences came closely followed by the good news of promised redemption. For Augustine the bad news always loomed large. Bodies ache and die, half-controlled sexuality defiles the spirit, and even language comes apart in one's hands as meaning disintegrates. The divine reclamation project has begun here and now, but it has astonishingly little to show for itself. The glass is always half empty, or worse. Christian life here and now loses, in the Augustinian view, much of its charm and certainly loses any flavor of an exclusive club for the smugly redeemed.

And then there was the question of the soul again. Anxiety and logic reinforced each other one more time and left Augustine struggling. If he moved toward the position he took on original sin because of the intersection of old stories, high philosophy, and anxious religious practice, he could not foresee all the logical dilemmas that would face him. The irresolvable one lay in the question of the origin of souls. The question was important because skeptics looking at the doctrine of original sin would ask hard questions about mechanisms of transmission. Just how did the sin of Adam and Eve come to abide in children born thousands of years later?

Well, said Augustine, that's a tough one. He could see four possibilities:

1. God creates a new soul for every human being coming into the world alive. This possibility is the hardest to reconcile with original sin—for how would these new souls have contact with those of their ancestors?
2. God created souls in eternity and then sends them down to bodies as he creates the bodies. The problem is the same.
3. God created souls in eternity but they choose in individual acts of rebellion to "lapse" into bodies. On this view, the move into a body is itself the initial rebellious and sinful act, and so each soul has in fact sinned just by coming to be in bodily form. This view is hardest to reconcile with anything in Christian tradition but quite compatible with Platonic views of spirit, matter, and the fall and rise of spirit. It also emphasizes the responsibility of the individual soul for its own plight.
4. God created a single soul in Adam, gave Eve a piece of it, and all natural reproduction since then has passed down new souls sliced off from old ones. If Adam and Eve sinned and their souls were thus tainted, then all their children—virtuous Abel, wicked Cain, and all to follow—got a soul that had become damaged goods. This view, termed "traducianism" in the theological handbooks, is the most material and the easiest to reconcile with an advancing doctrine of original sin.

Which of these views did Augustine hold? Astonishingly, he never committed himself. The last two have the most to offer for his wider doctrinal positions, but both had disadvantages. One line of modern scholarship has argued that Augustine avoided the easy path of the traducian option because he was really secretly committed to the Platonic theory of the fallen soul.[591] Debate has run heatedly over the last two generations of scholars on this point, with no clear-cut resolution.

The fairest and most accurate conclusion would be that Augustine's indecision was real. He had been driven by his logic to take a public position, and then found himself genuinely torn between parts of his past. Both positions, the Platonic and the traducian, appealed to him, and both were impossible to sustain. The Platonic theory was out of line with the biblical stories, while the traducian interpretation seemed to require a material and corporeal nature of the soul that Augustine abhorred.[592]

He anguished over the issue, ending one long and tortured letter to Jerome (seeking advice from the one figure he would ever ask advice from, though he might not take it) with the passionate hope that he could find "some all-powerful and invincible argument that wouldn't compel us to believe that god could ever damn any soul to hell without justification."[593] The reverse of that hope, the possibility of divine arbitrariness and injustice, the possibility that suffering is arbitrary and release an illusion, is the thing Augustine most fears might be true. We can speculate that fear of an all-powerful father who punishes unjustly and heeds no plea might resonate deeply in the life of Patricius's son, but it had to have a more general force for Augustine to be as persuasive as he was. The intensity of the fear goes a long way to explain the intensity of his arguments against the Pelagians, who seemed to leave the door open to a divine tyrant. Augustine's opponents were the ones who did not share his fear.

Augustine succeeded best in a tactical way in defending the doctrine that led him to this impasse by *not* making up his mind and by having the best, or worst, of both alternatives. If he had chosen one of them, he would have been compelled eventually to recognize its defects. Instead, he managed to espouse a lofty disdain: there must be an answer, but all the answers proposed so far are incomplete, and so by insisting on the four possibilites[594] and making no decision, he could evade responsibility in the end. The passive-aggressive quality to this evasiveness does him little credit. He never addresses the possibility that the dilemma was itself a sign that he and his whole notion of redemption had gone seriously wrong. Augustine had many theological successes, but this one failure cast a long shadow.

When Augustine and Jerome were both dead and gone, someone—we really don't know who—wrote a "letter" that was attributed to Jerome, but was really a dialogue exemplifying the positions of the two powerful figures on the issue of the origin of the soul. "Augustine" and "Jerome" debate back and forth, but the sympathies of the author of this dialogue are with the latter figure. Augustine comes out looking like a chump, unwilling to commit himself on the fundamental issue, not understanding the deeper philosophical issues, and poorly read in the philosophical literature. Although Augustine is a powerful and influential figure in the creation and transmission of western ideas about "soul," to intelligent readers in his own time, he could look like such an amateur.[595]

One more piece of original Christian teaching haunted Augustine's later years. Jesus left no doubt that not all would be saved. Sheep would be separated from goats. How? Why? What would determine which category you fell into? Some early Christians simply could not stand the

thought of an eternal division, and so fell to speaking of the eventual rising again of *all* humankind. On that reading, a preliminary division into
those meriting reward and those meriting punishment would be followed
(after a cleansing period of chastisement) by a blessed reunion of all with
the divine. This position is difficult to sustain in the face of the biblical
texts and like most things identified as heresies may never have been fully
sustained as such by those blamed for it, but the name of Origen, after his
lifetime, was always associated with such optimism.

Augustine was no optimist. And so he wrestled, all his adult life, with
the conflicting data of scripture and experience. In his youth, the
Manichees had enticed him (or so he remembered) by challenging him to
say where evil came from, then offering an answer that flattered human
sensibility. It came from outside humankind and outside the divine, from
a permanent evil principle rooted in the world. Plotinus and Porphyry
persuaded him that the world is a thoroughly good place created by a
thoroughly good god, that evil is only a question of names for things that
are less good than other things, and in the Milan of the 380s that seemed
a satisfactory solution. That phase of his thinking ends in disarray in the
mid-390s, just as he is about to be ordained bishop, when he finds that he
cannot make sense of Paul by reading him this way.

Some well-timed questions from Simplicianus, the elderly priest of
Milan who had nurtured Augustine's conversion and who was about to
succeed Ambrose as bishop there in the late 390s, turned Augustine's
thinking around. The most important and least-read book Augustine ever
wrote was the *Diverse Questions for Simplicianus* of about 396. In those
pages he wrestles with Paul's pessimism and is decisively beaten by it. The
implications were visible almost at once in the story he told of himself in
the *Confessions*, but lay quietly for another fifteen years until drawn out of
him by the questions Marcellinus had to ask on the basis of the teachings
of Pelagius. Two main themes emerge and dominate his thought for the
rest of his life, but they had been a-brewing in him for a long time:

1. God is all-powerful, man is intrinsically weak and further weakened
by sin. Those hankerings (*concupiscentia*) that came from sin are in principle resistible, but in practice no one ever resists them. We suffer an addiction with no known cure. This means that human beings, though
endowed by their creator with freedom, have effectively lost that freedom
through sin and must await the pleasure of their creator in order to be
saved. But since their creator knows all from all eternity, then the creator

himself chose, before ever even Adam sinned, who would be saved and who would not. The act of salvation is divine, not human in origin. This is, in short, the Augustinian doctrine of predestination.

2. Equally important, the *apparent* predestination of the blessed in this life (apparent through outward conversion, baptism, church membership, etc.) is not decisive. For the creator must give two gifts: the gift of conversion and the gift of "perseverance." Human life, even for the baptized, even for the bishop, even for the self-denying monk in the desert, is radically uncertain of its end. The most unlikely candidates can be saved at the last minute, and the most pious can fall by the wayside at any moment.

Every piece of what Augustine says on these topics can be supported from scriptural texts and every piece of what he says can be controverted from scriptural texts. The history of western theology since the fifth century has been marked by a series of outbreaks on this dark theme, most notably that of the sixteenth century, when the reformers took Paul and Augustine as their guides. In every such outbreak, other voices have protested that the loss of human freedom is dispiriting and, worse, imputes to the Christian god himself full responsibility for the condemnation of those whom he chooses not to save. In its extreme form, this anti-Augustinian argument insists that Augustine ultimately makes his god responsible for evil itself.

To understand Augustine's persistence on these central points would be, if we could do it, to understand Augustine himself. Some part is due to personality, some part to continued obsession from his Manichee-beguiled youth, some part to inability to see beyond the literal sense of a few pages of his scriptural texts (with Paul's voice echoing more loudly than Jesus's), and some part sheer pigheadedness.

In the end, there's a deep irony. The two profoundest thinkers of Christian antiquity, Origen and Augustine, ended their careers at the margins of Christian community. Origen would be condemned repeatedly after his lifetime, Augustine rarely so; Origen found the most optimistic Christianity one could imagine, Augustine a far more pessimistic one (though the Manichees found an even *more* pessimistic one). Both were marginalized, respected, read, copied, and evaded for centuries afterwards. The Christianities that emerged in the Greek and Latin worlds were heavily under their influence, and at the same time finally resisted both, settling in a middle ground that was intuitively preferable, though difficult to defend with clarity and coherence. The job of imparting clarity and coherence awaited the coming of the scholastic theologians of the twelfth and thirteenth centuries. The working out of that divine message, by the time it was expressed, had taken a long time, fully fifty generations and more of believers from the time of Jesus till the time of Aquinas.

And even then, the issues have never been genuinely settled among believers.[596]

THE NEVER-ENDING DIVORCE

Ontogeny recapitulates phylogeny, or so they tried to tell us. The biological idea embodied in this confusing phrase has lost its respectability, but the jargony jingle persists as a substitute for thought. It captures, however, something essential about Augustine's thought.

The supposed principle is that the individually lived experience of a given creature (ontogeny) reflects over time the structure and physical form of the evolution of the family to which the individual creature belongs (phylogeny). The notion goes back to a nineteenth-century evolutionary biologist, Ernst Haeckel, who saw what he thought were gills in fetuses and interpreted that as evidence of a transition in the womb through the archaic fishy state of an earlier ancestor of humankind. He was, to put it kindly, wrong; to put it unkindly, dishonest.[597]

But Augustine was there ahead of him. For Augustine, the life of a human being merely retold on a smaller scale the story of all human history. The story of fall and redemption that he constructs into human history matches the story of the individual and explains it, for Augustine can show no awareness that his reading of history is a projection of his reading of human behavior. The closest he comes to that is in the way he interprets the six ages of man, which provided a framework of interpretation for his own life decades earlier. Now he starts to unfold the cosmic pattern of the seven days of creation,[598] finds that sevenfold structure reflected in common ways of speaking about the stages of human life, and then transposes that back onto the biblical/Christian reading of history:

first age: infancy—corresponds to the time from Adam to Noah
second age: boyhood—the time from Noah to Abraham
third age: adolescence—the time from Abraham to David[599]
fourth age: youth—the time from David to the Babylonian
captivity

fifth age: maturity (*gravitas*)—the time from the Babylonian
   captivity to the coming of Christ
sixth age: old age—the time from the first coming of Christ to the
   second coming at the end of time
seventh age: the afterlife, for both individual and society

The most curious and influential part of this pattern was the gloomy res-
ignation implicit in imagining that the present age, ostensibly the time of
redemption and reception of the good news that Jesus represented, is to
be understood as old age, and this in an era when old age was likely to be
premature, brief, and marked by illness, weakness, and decline. To think
of your own time in this way is hardly an inspirational theme for preaching or leadership.

Augustine is ever a willing prisoner of the logical implications of his arguments. Once he has made a connection like this, he must pursue it, and
in this case he finds the opportunity to welcome that pursuit. He had used
the imagery—and it was scarcely more than imagery, hardly an argument—of the ages of man from early in his career as preacher and writer.
When in the 410s he found himself pressed to explain the fate of empires
and the place of his god in human history, the old imagery was pressed into
service. But once that story was told, there remained the ambiguous condition of humankind living divided from itself in multiple ways.

In Augustine's time, the boundary between barbarism and civilization
was the sharpest and clearest one, or so it seemed. In practice the peoples
we learn from Augustine's contemporaries to think of as "barbarians"
were often themselves every bit as "Romanized" as the people with whom
they contested for political influence. The long-stable boundaries of empire and the willingness of Rome to recruit for its military from among
the peoples who lived astride those borders had led to an infusion of barbarian presence within the empire. In Augustine's time, the ascendancy
of the general Stilico at Ravenna from 395 to 408, when he effectively
ruled the Roman west during the childhood of the emperor Honorius, revealed the integration of "barbarian" culture into Roman. But when the
struggle for power led by the German- (and Latin-) speaking general,
Alaric, led to the symbolic sack of Rome in 410, the "barbarian" interpretation struggled to prevail, alongside the "pagan" one, as we have seen.

Augustine deserves credit for resisting both. None of us is likely to believe that the old gods abandoned Rome to its barbarian fate in jealous
anger over yielding place to the Christian god. More moderns have credited the barbarian interpretation, but serious scholarship in the last two

generations has significantly undercut the factual basis of such argument.[600] If barbarian and Roman were truly different from one another by this period, it was by choice and not necessity, and the Roman would pay a price for perpetuating that hostility.

Augustine did not participate in either of those systems of self-delusion. What he had to offer in their place, however, had its own long-term implications and costs. For Augustine saw a deeper and more intimate hostility within humankind, ultimately that which separated Abel and Cain. That sibling rivalry for Augustine is what marked the origin of two communities, two cities. Every "pagan," every "Christian," every "Roman," every "barbarian" belongs to one of those communities. In mortal life, membership is fluid and people can go back and forth, from the city of Abel to that of Cain by their own free will, back in the other direction only by divine intervention. But once death has its way, change is impossible: sides have been taken for all eternity.

The interim ("this time between times"[601]) is the tricky part. Shifting shapes and patterns of the two communities will emerge, struggle with one another, reshape themselves, and go on struggling. The discerning eye (the one gifted with divine grace) will be able to determine which community is which, and thus the true church will be a touchstone of authenticity and safety. But even that church will harbor within itself the insincere, the lukewarm, and those who are at some still unknown future time going to fall away. And the community of the hostile contains within itself many who will yet be saved, though they may yet be among the most hostile. The case of biblical Saul who became Paul is Augustine's assurance of that expectation.

The future this line of thinking leads to is one in which an organized and visible church looms large, managing its own boundaries and denying the right of other such communities to exist. In practice, however, it also means that there will always be competing communities, each questioning the other's *bona fides* and authenticity. Each, moreover, would be able to explain the other's existence precisely in terms of the notion of two rival communities.

At the very least, it might have seemed that such a view of human society and history would be resolutely theocratic, seeing the only basis for human governance in the power of the theologically authorized. All three religions of the book (Judaism, Christianity, and Islam) harbor such tendencies within them and realize them often enough, at least in part. For Augustine, his suspicion of everything that is not spiritual saved him from that extreme of his own opinion. The world of secular affairs was to be left (with an overtone of mild contempt) in the hands of secular governments, and churches were to be devoted to the world of the spirit. That belief might have led to a radical dissociation of the spiritual from the temporal and a pure separation of church and state.

Such was not to be the case. Already in the century since Constantine's conversion (Augustine began his *City of God* almost exactly a century after the battle in which Constantine had a miraculous vision of the Christian god's ability to support his military ambitions), the interpenetration of Roman state and Christian church had gone too far for Augustine's spiritualizing ideals to prevail. Here is where Orosius's misinterpretation of his master's teaching was too easy and too obvious. Church and state *had* coalesced in the Roman empire, and the church depended too heavily on the coercive power and financial resources of empire ever to break free. In the Greek east, empire and church would long work hand in hand, until church outlasted empire after the capture of Constantinople by the Turks in 1453. In the Latin west, the evanescence of imperial forms over the fifth and sixth centuries, as barbarian kingdoms took root in the provinces of Africa, Italy, Gaul, and Spain, might have left church without state and thus triumphant. The eventual rise of the papacy reflected an enthusiasm for such a model. For long centuries, it was even believed that the emperor Constantine had deliberately handed over the western provinces to the popes to govern in the realms of both spiritual and secular affairs. Western attempts to claim an imperial filiation with Rome ended only in 1806, when the last holy Roman emperor yielded to Napoleon's imperial ambitions, leaving Hapsburg Vienna, tsarist St. Petersburg, Ottoman Istanbul, and Manchu Beijing to survive as imperial capitals into the early twentieth century.

But no purely ecclesiastical government ever prevailed over any wide territory or for any duration in Christendom. Instead, Augustine's elevation of the church to a role as embodiment of community put church and state in endless contact and competition with each other. If in the fourth and fifth centuries church and state seemed to many to come together in a divinely ordained unity, what we have seen since is an unending state of separation not unlike that of the modern failed marriage: church and state sharing responsibility for the same population as parents share responsibility for children, both church and state tending to see themselves as parental authorities rather than as instruments or servants, and neither church nor state able to disentangle itself from the other. In one way or another, that pattern still persists in many places.

So Augustine's contribution is of dubious value in two ways. First, he turns the frictions and rivalries of the human condition into cosmic conflict between armies of dubious loyalties, with angels and demons fighting alongside humankind, but then leaves the human participants indistinctly swarming together in a confusing world and left to bicker until the end of time. Second, he offers a theoretical basis for pulling that conflict out of the secular and governmental realm but fails to make his case persuasive enough to have effect in the real world. We live with the results.

THE AUTHORITY OF AUGUSTINE

The Lincoln Memorial is a good place to go to think about Augustine. Nothing we know suggests that Abraham Lincoln was a particularly happy or well-adjusted man. His life was full of failures, personal and professional. His side won a war that it had seized almost every opportunity to lose.

But if you go up those steps and enter that space, you find yourself between two panels of words. One contains his Gettysburg Address, the other his second inaugural address. Those short texts have a fiery power that leaps across a century and a half. Go there of a Sunday afternoon and there will always be a half-dozen people standing or sitting quietly in alcoves, just reading those texts, slowly, carefully, from beginning to end, and going off thoughtfully afterwards.

Embracing seemingly antithetical propositions at the same time is hard, even when both are true. One reaction to such a puzzle is dismissive reductionism. But Lincoln, like Augustine, confounds us. Deeply flawed people, hated and tolerated and reviled and loved in their own times, are surprisingly capable, if rarely enough, of extraordinary achievements, achievements that have their own flaws hidden within them. Augustine the African bishop had one life, but he wrote books that have had multiple lives since his time. They can still sneak up on the unwary and overwhelm them with insights so persuasive and so beautifully expressed as to seem to defeat all debate. And even if the persuasion is resisted, the persuasiveness and the beauty remain undeniable. Accomplishment like that transcends its moment, is rewritten regularly, and persists because of its ability to remake itself. One might as well describe such transcendence as the mark of a classic, but the category of the classic remains elusive.

But there's another life story of Augustine, one that has not yet been written, that started on August 28, 430, and continues to the present. That is the Augustine who has survived and thrived and had his influence, under various guises.[602]

And so what became of him? How did Augustine come to us? Let us look harder.

Holy men often attract a veneration that they would (or should) deprecate. To take an example Augustine could have known, the first paragraph of the *Life of Plotinus* by his chief disciple, Porphyry, records an act of rebellion against the philosopher and offers a measure of the distance between master and disciples. Porphyry recounts a subterfuge by which the students managed to have an artist create a portrait of the philosopher, despite Plotinus's reluctance.[603]

The subterfuge was comical: the painter Carterius attends Plotinus's lectures as if to listen but actually to look, and look hard, at the speaker, then to go out to create just the sort of image that Plotinus abhorred. Though the reluctance to face the painter is soundly based in Plotinus's philosophical ideas,[604] and though his disciples could cite nothing in his doctrines in support of their act, they nonetheless overrode his judgment in order to ensure that he was made a plaster (or pigment) sage according to their preconceptions of the role that was his to play.

We leave our holy men no choice: we insist they be saints. One could as easily cite the veneration accorded Socrates or Francis of Assisi. But they did not write, and Plotinus resisted writing, and wrote with difficulty. Is it different when we deal with a figure like Augustine, who wrote as though his life depended on it? Does he not at least deserve to become a Great Book?

The authority of books—other than the scriptures—plays a small role in what Augustine wrote. Nonbiblical books are rarely quoted, and names of authors are infrequently cited. When they appear, gradually and late, it is to be cited not as individuals of authority but as supporters of a common tradition of agreement.[605] Part of this reticence is literary style of a sort (quotation of anterior texts is relatively infrequent in ancient discursive literature, even when those texts, like the dialogues of Cicero, are pervaded through and through with the ideas and expressions of other older texts). Part of it is a reflection of the specific Christian deference to scripture. Scriptural texts are the waves of the ocean beating on the shore in Augustine's work, while the quotations from the works of the "fathers" are by comparison occasional glasses of tap water.

Part of this reticence should be explained in terms of Augustine's own standing as bishop: for the church in front of him, he was the living authority, and that standing is explicit in works like *Christian Doctrine* and implicit everywhere else. Pope Gregory I still resembled Augustine almost two hundred years later. He was a writer who had read widely and deeply in the Latin theological tradition available to him, but who nevertheless rarely quoted or cited those texts, while designedly allowing the *ipsissima verba* of scripture to permeate his text as fully as they did that of Augustine.

But part of this independence is Augustine himself. It requires no partisanship and not even any approval of a single word he wrote to stand nevertheless in awe of his independence of mind, his freshness of approach, and the novelty of the questions he asked. Each time he takes up the task of writing, he approaches his subject afresh, asking good questions. Where Augustine repeats himself, he becomes the jazz improvisationalist, repeating old themes but never in the same way. Though many themes, expressions, and ideas recur in Augustine, few if any of his works may be dismissed out of hand as simple rehash of something that has gone before. Sermon after sermon and work after work does something he has not done before, asks some new question, presses some new line of argument. He is not dependent on others for the questions that press him, though he exploits the curiosity of others with rare resourcefulness. To read the dossier of correspondence with Marcellinus and Volusianus in the early 410s and then to turn to the *City of God* is to see the extraordinary range and power of thought Augustine could bring to bear on pedestrian lines of inquiry and thoughtless objections. The way in which Augustine continued to ask questions, fresh questions, and to press his inquiries well into late middle age has a moral elegance about it. Even in the gloomy days of whaling away at Julian, a fair reading will show that the strength of mind and the freshness of approach was still there, however the atmosphere had clouded.

And what did people make of him? Many things. In the sixth century, the monk Eugippius, refugee from frontier Noricum (in modern Austria), compiled a thousand-page anthology of Augustine at the monastery of Lucullanum, near Naples. His monastic and literary endeavors were extensive, but he remains little known.[606]

The "authority of Augustine" in Eugippius's collection is limited in an interesting way. He had no idea of producing *The Essential Augustine* with a view to illuminating Augustine's special contributions to Christian thought or his distinctive positions. Rather, the usefulness of Augustine lay in his way of representing a common Christian tradition. What was valuable about Augustine, put another way, was not what was distinctive about him but what he had said that formed a useful part of the common deposit of faith and interpretation. He had acquired his authority not by being unique and brilliant and original, but by accomplishing the common task of interpretation and teaching in a way that others could share wholeheartedly. So we might think that, especially in view of the controversy over grace and free will that had animated Gaul in the last century, a reasonable anthology would have a distinct section of concise excerpts from the anti-Pelagian writings, to make Augustine's position known. Those writings are seriously underrepresented in the collection as a whole, and the few excerpts that do appear come near the end, with no special emphasis. So much had the issues faded from current concern.

Eugippius makes no attempt to represent distinctive Augustinian ideas or works. Passages that we regard as essentially Augustinian are missing, and the organization is at every turn an obstacle to an attempt to see what Augustine thought. The extracts from the *Confessions*, for example, show very little interest in the autobiographical element and reflect rather an interest in passages that modern, post-Romantic readers regard as stolidly theological.

The principle of organization is scriptural. The arrangement of excerpts does not follow the order of Augustine's own works, except incidentally, and does broadly follow the order of the books of scripture. What Augustine has to say that can in one form or another illuminate the Book of Genesis, for example, leads the collection, Old Testament preceding New. The point is again the effacement of the cult of personality and emphasis on the common task of interpreting scripture. Whatever we may think of the relation of theory and practice in Augustine's own writings, Eugippius is an heir of the theory who is determined to put it into practice. The authority of Augustine for Eugippius is what Augustine has that can help the reader come to a better interpretation and fuller understanding of the scriptural text. Augustine's authority, in other words, is derivative and dependent, not a function of his own qualities, his own genius.

But another history can be written here, of the quality of Augustine's readership in late antiquity. Cassiodorus, statesman turned monk, spin doctor turned scholar, in the sixth century, rereads and rewrites Augustine pedantically.[607] Such is his revision of Pelagius's commentary on Paul.[608] Absent a connected commentary on Paul, and in possession of a copy of Pelagius's version of just such a commentary, Cassiodorus thought it would be possible to go through and "purge the poison" by selective and careful editing. A recent study has shown that the revision produces a hybrid artifact with which Augustine himself might have been very little satisfied. Quotations from Augustine have been inserted and the most objectionably "Pelagian" bits omitted for the most part, but the overall structure and approach is still very much true to Pelagius's thought and intent.

The history of Augustine's rise to widespread acclaim in the fifth and sixth centuries accompanies and exemplifies one of the most important developments in the history of Christianity: the emergence in the Latin west of a distinctively Christian body of religious literature. Histories regularly focus on the producers of a high literature, and so too emphasize what can only be called a golden age: the few decades in which Hilary, Marius Victorinus, Ambrose, Prudentius, Ambrosiaster, Jerome, and Cassian, to name only the leading lights along with Augustine, created a body of Latin Christian literature that far outshone all that had come before and that would loom large over all that came after. But in the conditions of a manuscript culture, production was only a part of the story. In their lifetimes, those authors' books had a certain life, but also very pronounced limitations. No Christian libraries or schools preserved or promoted them, no established means of distribution helped them find audiences, and there were not even any systematic means of disseminating the mere fact that a book existed.

So the second essential stage in the making of Latin patristic literary history is the period from roughly Jerome to Cassiodorus, when the fact of the literature's existence imposed itself on the minds of an audience. Gradually a body of supporting literature began to emerge. Augustine's own *Reconsiderations* and Possidius's *Indiculum* are early examples of texts that helped the reader keep track of other texts. Jerome's *De viris illustribus* marks the first major attempt to gather and disseminate in Latin information about Christian writers generally; Augustine's catalogue of *Heresies* (*De haeresibus*) makes an odd, and in a way archaic, counterpoint to it. But in the course of the fifth century we then get a Gallic writer, Gennadius, also writing *Famous Men* (*De viris illustribus*—by now it was particularly important that books had known and named authors if they were to be taken seriously), followed in the early sixth century by the very important "pseudo-Gelasian decretal" specifying which books could be read and which should be rejected. Once attributed to Pope Gelasius (492–96), now it is thought to be north Italian in provenance, but it helped authorize the idea of the Roman church's *Index of Banned Books* centuries later. Eugippius not only collected his anthology, but gathered the works of Augustine and indexed them with chapter headings and so represents another stage in the attempt to gather and control the growing body of literature.[609] Dionysius Exiguus ("Dennis the Short") from Scythia ended up at Rome, where he studied chronology and collected church legal texts, while at Rome we have evidence of the increasing dependence on texts and the consequent organization of texts of the papacy itself: the library of Pope Agapetus (535–36) was only one example. The first compilations of the *Book of the Popes* (*Liber pontificalis*—with short biographies of each pope from Peter onward, kept current, pope by pope) apparently date to the early sixth century. From that period we even have evidence of competing versions of the book of popes being created and disseminated by rival factions in the Laurentian schism that arose from the papal election of 498. That schism also spawned bogus documents from earlier papal history, the so-called Symmachan apocrypha, whose relevance here is that they show that authority by now resided, for the Christians of Rome, in texts brought forth from a bookcase and was no longer controlled by the spoken word of the inspired and anointed leader of the community. By 600, Rome as a city of power had been bled almost dry, but the Roman church had found a way to assure its continuing influence through the written word.

Augustine was not only a bishop and a holy man, but he was the preeminent writer, his works far outrunning in sheer bulk those of any nearest competitor. His office, his holiness, and his orthodoxy were all factors in claiming his place. But had he not written, had he not written so much, and had his works not survived so consistently (we have already seen some reasons why they did), he would never have become the authority figure that he did become. He was the right man in the right place at the right time. He did not have to read his predecessors anxiously and endlessly, but his successors had to read him that way.

AUGUSTINE THE CATHOLIC

I have resisted—some will undoubtedly think perversely—calling Augustine a "catholic" until now, but this is the point for it. One line of development from Augustine respects and reflects the profundity and originality of his thought on high issues of god and the soul, no question. But in one other compelling way he succeeded in being just that half-second ahead of his time that marks the true leaders (or the truly lucky) among the failures, near-misses, and impressive obscurities of history.

The Donatist alternative was one Augustine always rejected. Just why and how he chose the other side and just how he managed to stay on the other side are hard questions to answer. But one essential part of his *argument* against the Donatists was his interpretation of "catholicism." We have seen how the Donatist reading of that word could emphasize a completeness found within the walls of a single African town, but for Augustine it evoked instead a universality of church across the Mediterranean world. To be "catholic" for Augustine meant to be in communion with people one had never seen, people who lived across seas one would never dare to cross. The idea was not original with Augustine, for all that it may be native to Africa and his party in Africa.[610]

But what an idea it was. The Christianities of Augustine's time had an intuition of universality, an idea that they could claim to be true for all places and all times. "Catholicism" in the Latin west made that intuition concrete, and by 600 that notion of "catholicism" had undoubtedly prevailed. The idea antedated but empowered notions of papacy, as that institution created itself and extended its sway beyond Rome in the fifth and sixth centuries, culminating in the figure of Gregory I, still pope in 600, the patron saint of that archaic, premedieval "catholicism." We can watch Gregory in his letters pushing the boundaries of his authority toward the horizons. His colleagues preached the Christian message in Britain while he himself insisted on Roman dominion over rogue churchmen in the Balkans and wheedled Frankish queens and bishops toward a submission that would come only long after his time. That particularly Latin embodiment of the idea of a universal church was not Augustine's to claim for his own; he spoke for it so memorably because he needed the idea to help him win a local war of punishing intensity.

But it was an idea with a future. Augustine supported that future, and that future supported and received and embraced him. His most insurmountable ideas about predestination were harder to grasp and less obviously relevant than the high-concept notion of a church that would reach out to embrace the whole world and so supplant and render functionally obsolete the notion of worldwide empire. That church is an idea that has triumphed, lapsed, and triumphed again in all the centuries since, though the power of the institution and the power of the idea are often out of synch with each other. The Jesuits of the sixteenth century spoke for a vision of universal Christianity that went beyond what the papacy of their own time could tolerate, and the lapse that followed as they were pulled back from China and checkmated in South America begat centuries of narrow community-building. The twentieth century saw another exhilarating movement into openness in the papacy of John XXIII, but popes since have retreated into narrower definitions of community. But no Christianity after Augustine, no Christianity that has learned from Augustine, can avoid the challenge of thinking how a doctrine that descends from Jesus can resist indefinitely the need to think about how its demands can make sense in a world of proliferating and competing cultures. A "catholicism" that enfolds more religious traditions than the ones that claim a home in Jerusalem remains a very Augustinian project, as yet uncompleted. But Augustine continues to live at least in part because of his association with that desire for universal brotherhood that is divinely approved.

Some theologians have all the luck. In that first decade of his baptized religious opinions, much that he thought, said, and did was far more continuous with who and what he had been before than with what he became later. He still held on to the optimism and idealism of ancient high culture and he was still emphatically Augustine the gentleman, or the would-be gentleman, seeking a role for himself based on what he knew of the traditional culture of his world. He escaped that persona without meaning to or knowing quite how.

XII

WHO WAS AUGUSTINE?

DEATH IN HIPPO

When he lay down to die, Augustine wanted to be alone. For ten days in August he lay undisturbed, except when they brought him food and drink, or when the physicians came to check on him. He was seventy-five.

Alone, he stared at the walls where he had made them put up copies of the Psalms of repentance for him to see and read. And so he read the words the Psalmist gave to David when Nathan came to reproach him for his conduct with Bathsheba.

> Have pity on me, god,
> pity to match the greatness of your mercy
> and the multitude of your kindnesses:
> erase my wickedness.
>
> For I know my wickedness
> and my sin stares me ever in the face.
>
> I was conceived in wickedness
> and in sin my mother conceived me.

You have loved the truth
and you have revealed to me the unknown
and hidden sides of your wisdom.

. . . .

God will not turn away a worn and humbled heart.

Once in a crowded church in Carthage, almost twenty years earlier, he had given a sermon on this psalm, competing for the audience's attention with a thronged circus not far away. The circus drew not only "pagans" and Jews and waverers, but also the very people he thought most ought to be in church—the baptized faithful. He preached, as usual, not to the converted so much as to a people in constant need of reconversion.

As he spoke that day, the psalm was not just about a libidinous king and his devious ways: it spoke of every sin and every sinner. The temptations and delights of the flesh, he said, were all of a piece, and sexual transgression stood for all of them. David's fall was meant to remind readers that no one was immune from temptation, from sin, not even kings, surely not bishops. The sermon lasted about forty-five minutes, the preacher savoring each verse, finding material for exhortation and for caution and for fragments of hope, finding his own story in an ancient book.

And so when he faced that familiar text on the wall above his deathbed, the famous bishop approached his end not with satisfaction in a life well lived but in hope that a life badly lived would yet be absolved and redeemed. If his "heart" (the word is always a metaphor at best and one that Augustine did much to make commonplace in western vocabularies[611]) was worn and humbled, then he took it to be the paradoxical sign of a happiness to come. He had spoken memorably in his most famous book of the restlessness of the human heart, and he carried that restlessness with him still.

His first biographer, Possidius, telling us the carefully constructed story of this deathbed, balances the story of psalm reading with a pithy quotation from "a certain wise man," one who probably stood in a Greek rather than Hebrew tradition, offering a model of disdain rather than hope: "You won't be a great man if you think it's a great thing that stones and wood should fall and that mortals should die."[612] Cities and people alike vanish and the wise man remains aloof.

Aloof and alone. In all the books and sermons and letters we have of Augustine's, a consistent pattern emerges. The fundamental human relationship is the solitary individual's relationship with his god. Every other human relationship in Augustine's life that we know of gets rewritten in his books to be a story about him and his god. Over and over, the small and large distances that separate people from one another persist and usually grow larger for Augustine as he intensifies the divine connection, until he ends there, alone with his god, alone.

Until those last days, Augustine had been working quietly on one more lonely book.

THE SECOND INSTALLMENT OF
THE *CONFESSIONS*

Not since the eighteenth century has any publisher (at least any that I know of) gotten Augustine's autobiography right. The last several hundred years have been a great age for readers of the *Confessions*, and translations and editions of that work appear as regularly as a New York subway train, but to read the *Confessions* alone is to fall squarely into one of Augustine's most cunning traps and to miss something of great importance about him. The second half of his autobiography is almost invisible by comparison.

For the *Confessions* tells only part of the story, bringing its narrative up to the author's thirty-third year. Thirty years after he wrote the *Confessions*, Augustine proceeded to bring the story up to date, in the book he called his *Reconsiderations* (*Retractationes*). Because it is, or seems to be, a book about books, and not about events, it is relegated to the status of a curiosity, but when written it was unquestionably a remarkable undertaking.[613] It has been translated into English only once that I know of, thirty years ago, never issued in paperback, and is hardly ever read or studied. In the seventeenth century, at least, the Benedictine editors of Augustine had the sense to put the *Confessions* and the *Reconsiderations* side by side in the same first volume of their great edition of Augustine's complete works—and, indeed, the *Reconsiderations* come first. I often wonder what readers would make of them if the two could be translated in the same volume.

Most readers, I think, are distracted by the performance that the *Reconsiderations* represent. In it we hear the voice of Augustine again, speaking of himself and his life, looking back at all the books he has written since the time of his conversion. He lists those books, one at a time, and offers his "reconsiderations" of them, along with a brief description of the book and how it came to be. Augustine was working on this project in the evenings during his last years, at a time when we've already seen him spending his daylight hours attacking Julian of Eclanum over and over again. The performance is extraordinary: an elderly man going back through a library that holds five million words of his writings, hoping to review all of them: books, letters, sermons. The books alone add up to about three million words, and that is the part of the task he more or less completed. Given the physical demands of ancient reading—dealing with bulky, handwritten manuscripts—we must assume both an intense interest on Augustine's part, not to say self-absorption, and a heroic memory for what he had said and where he had said it.[614]

Read in this way, the individual notes in the *Reconsiderations* are of quite variable interest. In some cases, more often those of his earlier books, he has corrections or amendments to make. He spends the most time and shows the thinnest skin concerning his *Free Choice of the Will* (*De libero arbitrio voluntatis*), inasmuch as Pelagius and others had quoted this work over the years in support of doctrines that Augustine would not now acknowledge.[615] Though he says often, both in the *Reconsiderations* and elsewhere, that he believes that he has learned and progressed as he has grown older ("Whoever reads my books in the order they were written in will likely find out how much progress I have made with my writing"[616]), he is loath to admit that he was ever distinctly *wrong* on a point of substance. We can fairly describe his development by saying that the ideas of *Free Choice of the Will* were brought forth by an Augustine who had not yet settled on his distinctive reading of Paul, and thus on his ideas of grace and predestination. In the *Reconsiderations*, Augustine wants to make it seem as if the ideas that Pelagius is missing were simply irrelevant to the narrow topic of the early book. Few readers not already committed to finding Augustine in the right on every possible point have been persuaded by this.

For the most part, however, the corrections and amendments made in the *Retractations* are of slight import, not of much more interest than the *addenda et corrigenda* slips that publishers sometimes drop into a badly printed volume.

And so the book escapes modern attention. But it has exercised an invisibly powerful influence over our view of Augustine. First of all, by cataloguing and indexing the work of Augustine, even usually giving the *incipit* (or opening words) of each text, this book made it remarkably easy in the middle ages to know what Augustine had written, to identify books that could be found, and to know what books to look for that were not at hand. At or shortly after the time Augustine was working on the *Reconsiderations*, his friend and biographer Possidius compiled a sketchier index of Augustine's works, one including sermons and letters. Together with the *Reconsiderations*, Possidius's work made it easy for those who had heard of Augustine to find their way in a mass of material. The self-presentation that Augustine as writer had been careful to manage was thus perpetuated into later centuries with extraordinary success.

More important, in the *Reconsiderations* we find the place where Augustine invents the story of Augustine the bishop, the story of the dogged controversialist, dragged against his will into one battle with heresy and error after another. That story has remained the armature of every biography written of him since, from Possidius to Lancel, from 430 to 1999. The Augustine who appears here dueled first with Manicheism, then with Donatism, then took on the "pagans," and finally found himself compelled to face the Pelagians, with Arians, Jews, and heretics in various supporting roles.

But this was a man whose own story about himself was that he was at all times on fire to meditate on the law of his god, day and night, nothing more. Indeed, Augustine's sermons offer a far more balanced picture, often, to be sure, flecked with his current controversies, of the pastor seeking to do justice to the spiritual needs of his congregation. But the *Reconsiderations* don't represent Augustine's life in that way—a way that would be both intimate and public at the same time.

That story, the narrative of Augustine's life, is the real message of this book and the real creation. Just as the *Confessions* had built a past for the younger bishop, so now the *Reconsiderations* built a past for Augustine the cleric to take to the afterlife with him, to leave for others to contemplate when he was gone. It replaced the living, breathing, quarreling cleric with Augustine the author, and that is how he has been known ever since. Because the *Reconsiderations* seems *only* to be a work of bibliography, it has received far less scrutiny and skepticism than it deserves, and has been deftly and quietly effective, shaping readers' views in ways they never sense or expect.

AFTER AUGUSTINE

Augustine departed the world as he had chosen to live it, Roman and Christian, disdainful and remorseful and hopeful, hearing in his mind words of dead sages and poets, holding the present at arm's length, thinking of the parents who had conceived him in the midst of their sins.

When he was gone, no shrine and no cloud of miracle stories marked where he had walked. Was this his choice? The only miracle story his biographer tells isn't much. While Augustine was dying, the story goes, a sick man was brought to him and Augustine was asked to lay his hand upon him to make him well. Augustine ventured what, for him, was almost a joke: if he had any power of this sort, he said, he would have used it on himself first. But then the man's friend tells Augustine about a dream he had in which he heard a voice say to him, "Go to Bishop Augustine to have him lay hands on this man and he will recover." When Augustine heard that, he did as he had been asked and the sick man went away healed. A fragment of divine power pushed its way through its (reluctant?) instrument, just that once. And then the performance was over.

By many measures, Augustine died a failure.

The barbarians were at the gates, literally. Invited to Africa by the Roman general Boniface to support his own ambitions, these eighty thousand barbarians (the number may well exaggerate) proved impossible to control. They threatened the whole sweep of Romanized north Africa from the straits of Gibraltar to Carthage and up into the highlands of Numidia. They landed far west of Augustine, in 429, and by the following August they were besieging the city where Augustine neared his end. He escaped to the afterlife before the city surrendered, but surrender it did, not long after. Nine more years passed until, in 439, the Vandal general Gaiseric entered Carthage and seized control of the province. Before Augustine could take to his deathbed, he had had to answer the bishops of his vicinity coming to ask whether they were obliged to stay at their posts as the enemy approached. His answer left them room to flee more or less honorably. The ones whose communities were not much more than fortified farmsteads were likely grateful to do so, while Augustine stayed where he was. His books escaped destruction, we know not how.

The poignancy of that lonely death room, the isolation of the bishop, and the atmosphere of fading future are all carefully constructed by Possidius to achieve an effect. These barbarians offer a powerful narrative resolution to the life story of a saint. We know too easily, again today, what barbarians are and how they give us parts to play in a story larger than ourselves, innocent (because civilized!) victims of historical forces too vast to control. Augustine was not an innocent victim, but he knew a lot about escaping from experience into stories. His own deeds had smoothed the path for those barbarians and his ideas helped make it hard for his contemporaries, and for us, to see the barbarians as anything but bogeymen and heretics.

Boniface, the Roman general in charge of Africa, was pursuing his own ambitions when he invited the Vandal warlord active in Spain to support him in rivalry with the imperial government, which found its own mercenaries to send against him from Italy. Though the warriors who came to Africa on both sides of this conflict were all subjects of long service in the Roman empire, and all professed the Christian religion, contemporaries and moderns alike chose to make much of their barbarian affiliations, but especially in the case of those who fought against the reigning emperor and his forces. Barbarians who fought *for* the emperor were somehow Romanized by that act, at least for the moment, but could be demonized again almost instantly when it suited. When Roman control of the military situation began to fail in the late fourth and early fifth centuries, contemporaries were quick to speak of "barbarian invasions," and our textbooks to this day are illustrated with maps showing brightly colored arrows swooping across sharply drawn borders, then dashing back and forth across Roman territory. The same maps do not usually show the sites of the four serious Roman army rebellions in Africa in Augustine's lifetime, or of the two civil wars that irrupted into Italy, killing one emperor and almost overthrowing another, in the last years of the fourth century. Barbarians make better copy.

Augustine himself had written in his *City of God* an antidote for that way of avoiding thought and responsibility. In its pages, every place was equidistant from eternity, and Rome's privilege turned out to have been a way station on the way to Christianity, not an "empire without end"—the prophetic words from Vergil that Augustine ironically and boldly put on the first page of *City of God*. Possidius's story of Augustine's deathbed under a dark cloud of threatening barbarians reveals how poorly that lesson had penetrated Augustine's own inmost circle.

Throughout his life, Augustine represented himself as the object of forces beyond himself. He succeeded at every level—autobiographically, historically, theologically—in presenting himself in that light. Augustine the agent, Augustine the actor, Augustine the misreader of his times, Augustine the mismaker of African society: he has escaped, until now. Knowing Augustine's failures and keeping them in mind can make it easier to understand who he was, how he lived, what he did, and what was dying when he died.

First, we should not forget the evident disarray all around him, little of it having anything to do with barbarians. In the last twenty years of his life, he had been increasingly preoccupied with a set of ideas and controversies that have marked his reputation ever since, as Vietnam has marked that of Lyndon Johnson. His battle against "Pelagianism" was murky and unnecessary for all that Augustine portrays himself as an unwilling warrior in a fateful struggle. Well-wishers lament that if only that one false step had not been taken, an underlying benign liberalism would be evident. The escape is not that easy.

The burden of his obsession with Pelagius weighs Augustine down. In order to attack and humiliate one or two charismatic and socially lionized rivals, Augustine found himself generalizing and making explicit ideas he had nurtured for years, nurtured without fully understanding where they had come from. Beliefs that had helped him to make sense of and give beautiful expression to the patterns of his own life proved harsh and self-defeating when he proclaimed them dogmatically. Worse, the controversy that ensued divided him from those he would have had as friends, made allies for him of some unsavory characters, and left him to spend his last years in a series of flame wars that pleased and impressed no one. Few could bring themselves to condemn him, but few could truly agree with him, and his intellectual heirs silently sidled away from him in the decades and centuries that came after.

Anti-Pelagianism was of little concern at home in Hippo. It was a cause for big cities and fashionable churches, proclaimed in books and pamphlets sent back and forth across the Mediterranean. But the business of managing the home front—that fractious and venal clergy, that ever-volatile congregation—was at least as preoccupying for him.

Augustine never managed his succession planning very well. In his first years in Africa, he and a few friends had seemed a force for reason, order, and cultural advance in his church, but those friends scattered to take up posts as bishops throughout Africa. Back at Hippo, they were replaced by nonentities, and none of them produced successors anything like themselves. Augustine chose and announced his own successor at Hippo, Eraclius, in a public ceremony, and he carefully kept a transcript of it in his files. Augustine had just returned from a sad trip to Milevis, where he installed the successor of his old and dear friend, the bishop Severus. Severus had not made his choice for a successor publicly known, and there had been awkwardness. Augustine in his turn wanted to avoid all ambiguity. He wanted also to transfer to Eraclius as much as possible of

the administrative work of the church, to free himself to write and meditate on the scriptures. All we know of Eraclius's earlier life is what we've
already seen, that he had funded the construction of a chapel in the basilica at Hippo. No joy or lightheartedness animates Eraclius as he praises
Augustine for combining eloquence with continence, authority with humility, and learning with patience. Eraclius describes his own sermon-
making (and few have disagreed) as a cricket chirping in the presence of
the swan, and he quickly vanished from the stage, perhaps dislodged or
even killed in the upheaval after the barbarians captured Hippo.

There was no one else. Prolific writer, inspired imaginer of divine truths,
powerful controversialist, Augustine was intellectually childless and left behind a deprecated church and community. There had been would-be disciples, like Orosius and Consentius, but they embarrassed the master. The
other defenders of Augustine in the generation after his death were invariably single-minded and unimaginative: Quodvultdeus, Marius Mercator,
and Prosper of Aquitaine spoke up for the master's most controverted ideas,
and did so energetically, but their limitations outweighed their abilities.

The "barbarians" were Augustine's to answer for as well. They came
to Africa at the invitation of a political ally of Augustine's (but Augustine
had gone cool on the alliance and thus weakened it), as pawns in a chess
game that went bad for Augustine's party. They succeeded in destroying
the church to which Augustine had given his career. The catholicism that
Augustine had helped invent and sustain was tossed out bodily by the Arian churchmen the barbarians brought with them. Augustine's own basilica they made their own, and their burials are the ones we find traces of
now. The story we are told by his party is that a hundred years would
lapse until orthodox armies from Constantinople dislodged the African
barbarians and restored the religion that Augustine preached. Restore it,
that is, until the next wave of "barbarians," this time Islamic invaders from
the east, came to uproot it once again in the seventh century, sweeping
back east to west over Augustine's country by about the year 700.

But settled Christianity would not have been so easily overturned and
eventually uprooted in Africa had Augustine himself not led an astonishingly successful ecclesiastical putsch of his own against the well-rooted
native Christian tradition. In the name of catholicism he brought the full
and clumsy might of Roman government to bear on compelling his coreligionists to sing his tune, the government's tune, in his churches. The
mass of believers complied, but the effect was in the long run disastrous.

The anti-Pelagian quarrels were of little importance in comparison with the struggle close to home, in which the state-supported puppet church Augustine represented imposed its name and will on recalcitrant believers. By the end of his life, Augustine had very quietly rewritten his original views about the church to which he belonged in order to find a place where his intellectually ambitious practice could live side by side with a whole raft of behaviors that he had once boldly called "superstition." It was too little, too late.

WHEN SAINTS DIE

Inventing saints took a long time. What began as a courtesy title became eventually a brand name, handed out carefully after only the most rigorous scrutiny. The modern formal process of canonization does not date back before the tenth century and the title depended before that on the spontaneous voice of public acclaim.

In the world of history and humans, though, saints come and go. One generation's paragon may be another's pervert, or fashion may simply shift, as cloistered virgins see their stock drop in value while more worldly figures engage the imagination of later generations. The monopoly on sainthood once carefully managed by churches, moreover, has given way once more to pluralistic and polymorphous bandying of the term, with (to be sure) less claim of assurance of eternity.

And so saints die, in more ways than one. In a sense, the only good saint was a dead one, because people believed, and Christianity had reinforced this belief, that only a happy ending made a life happy or blessed. Whether good cheer or good works are in question, the ride to the finish line is often enough bumpy and unreliable.

But the saint who fades from memory, the saint whose reputation is rewritten to his disadvantage after death, or the saint who turns out not to have existed at all—such saints are only too well known. In an age when traditional churchly structures crumble and when the place of Christianity in the cultural landscape changes dramatically, more saints than ever fade from view.

Augustine of Hippo has long been secure in his claim to the title of saint, too secure. His relics are still in Pavia, whatever we may think of them. Numerous religious communities of men or women following his rule, including some bearing his name, continue to do business around the world, though with fewer numbers than in decades past. Churches in his name are common, though mainly now in older neighborhoods. One such church in Philadelphia, one of the oldest in the city, lost its steeple to a lightning bolt a few years ago. In another age, that omen would have been observed with some concern; now it is a question for historic preservationists.

Augustine has always lived more in his books than otherwise. Jaroslav Pelikan, whose command of the history of Christian doctrine knows no rival, has said, "There has, quite literally, been no century of the sixteen centuries since the conversion of Augustine in which he has not been a major intellectual, spiritual, and cultural force." Edward Gibbon played it both ways: "Augustine possessed a strong, capacious, argumentative mind. He boldly sounded the dark abyss of grace, predestination, free-will, and original sin." And again Gibbon (on *City of God*): "His learning is too often borrowed, and his arguments too often his own." Nietzsche read him and laughed at the pear-theft story, but Heidegger read him with great care and lectured on him to monks.

His sainthood remains alive most visibly in the interest that people give to the way he lived his life. The power of his *Confessions* has assured a lively interest. Contemporary readers who come to Augustine most often take up the *Confessions* first, which is remarkable enough testimony to that work's power. If readers of the last generation pick up even one book *about* Augustine, that first book is almost always a biography, and a particular biography—Peter Brown's classic *Augustine of Hippo* (1967).[617] Brown's book, marvelous, imperfect, and enduring, was the first modern biography and easily outclassed all competitors.

Whatever Augustine taught and did, he is reduced by this preference for life-story-telling to a more ordinary saint than he really is. Having achieved great repute, he is the more readily trivialized. Since he became the first saint known to have his own website (since 1994, when this writer became his webmaster), he has attracted a fairly steady flow of questions and inquiries. Many are quite specific and studious, even scholarly, but the commonest are more superficial. That he was born and lived in Africa leaves many readers, in an age of renewed consciousness of the troubled history of African relations with the developed world, wondering, "Was Augustine black?"[618] No less rooted in contemporary concerns is the commonest doctrinal question, a search for a particular quotation: Did Augustine really say the benevolent ecumenical words recommending "in essentials, unity; in doubtful matters, liberty; in all things, charity"? No, he did not, but many have heard he did and very much hope he did, seeking an august, ancient, and improbable patronage for a contemporary predilection for ecumenism.[619]

What the dying saint thought, what he did, what was of his own doing, what was that of his friends, and what was that of those of us who have read and written of him since—these forces have turned him into a celebrity, known for being known, an object of curiosity, a pawn in our contemporary conversations. He saw us coming, deploring "a tribe eager to know about another man's life, too lazy to amend their own."[620]

Trivialization is not the only risk his future faces. The place of the churches that have been fondest of him is changing in our world, and those churches themselves have been reinventing themselves in ways that need less of him or figures like him. With them or without them, his future begins to shimmer uncertainly.

But leave aside his religion and see him only as a figure of the western past, and he is still threatened with misunderstanding and obscurity, and he is not alone. Fundamental assumptions that he made about humankind, assumptions that undergird everything he wrote even before his religious conversion, are on the brink of a historic challenge. He is an heir and a shaper of a long tradition that takes from the Greco-Roman past assumptions about human beings and how they work. The intellectual revolution of Greek antiquity and the cultural revolution of Christian antiquity both made sense within that underlying tradition. If that tradition now gives way, ideas built on them will find the ground shifting precipitously. Whatever becomes of "soul" will determine what becomes of Augustine.

Augustine writes and worries at length about the nature of the human soul because that soul is central to his understanding of himself, of humankind, and indeed of his god. If "heart" was always metaphor, "soul" was regularly insisted on as standing for something quite real. Augustine's soul is a spiritual creature, somehow both coterminous with the body but immortal, whether destined for heaven or for hell, often torn by emotion and distraction but potentially a serene unity at the heart of human existence. Augustine knows his soul well enough to talk to[621] and sees his life's work to reside in soul management. Body will fail, so soul must be saved. Body and soul will be reunited in resurrected life, soul now to dominate body and its impulses. Augustine could never quite say exactly how this would come about.

But if there is no soul? If there is no soul substitute called "mind" or "personality"? Contemporary cognitive science challenges our deepest western assumptions about human beings and what they are. Attempt af-

ter attempt to locate a mental or spiritual unity in some convincing relation with the brain and body of a mortal human fails, fails increasingly often in our times, to be replaced by a series of competing hypotheses about
the loosely coupled functioning of multiple systems distributed throughout the body. Deeply held personal, political, philosophical, social, and
religious ideas depend on the view of the human person that they share.
Roughly, we all know the broad western view that there exists something
spiritual that we might as well call a soul, something that accompanies humankind through life, explains our differences from the animal kingdom,
is the locus of solace and grief, love and hate, lust and abashment, and is
the object of whatever hopes for a life beyond the visible and the mortal
that we may still cherish.

Augustine threw himself into the collective work of constructing that
broad western view. Even if his theology did not prevail, his psychology
persists. The Augustine of the *Confessions* lends himself easily to post-
Freudian interpretation, and, having made that transition, remains the
voice of a powerful tradition. His body of work about soul and its meaning changed the imaginations of men in his own time and remained influential long after. Late-antique controversies about "soul" were lively
and often renewed, when writer after writer felt he had to define what no
one had ever seen. Augustine was no exception, and he was far more persuasive than most, even though—and this is the truly curious feature of
his teaching—he was unable to resolve a fundamental question (where
does soul come from?) or the paradoxes into which he was thrust by that
uncertainty. Bodiless, eternal, dispassionate, and even unchanging, soul in
union with body, moreover, was shot through with aberrancy: change,
passion, illness, death. The successful soul was the one that transcended
ordinary human experience in ways difficult to imagine.

That Augustine, the Augustine who imagined his own self so persuasively in ways that seem so traditional to us even if they were innovative
in his own time, is the Augustine most at risk now of dying. If his view of
the human person and his narrative account of the inner life is supplanted
by better science, then all that he has been to centuries of devout and not
so devout heirs could crumble very quickly into irrelevance.

What can history do for such a man? Can he be rescued from his sainthood before he dies completely a second time?

He achieved much, and now he risks much. That paradox makes him
a promising object for historical study, for study, that is, that defamiliar-
izes the famous and sees for the first time what we might think is already

well enough known. Augustine comes weighed down with the assumptions, expectations, and conventional narratives of many generations. But he is complex, well documented, and knowable in a way only a tiny handful of other ancient figures are knowable. To reduce him to a familiar story is to do him and ourselves an injustice. Can he be set free?

WHAT'S LEFT?

Augustine lived and died a long time ago. Most of our contemporaries will make it through their lives without hearing his name, and many of those who do will be cheerfully ignorant or decisively misinformed about his deeds and words. Those who will know that he made a difference to our world will accordingly remain few. For those connoisseurs—including all readers of this book, by definition—the question at the end is, what remains? What is left to us from him?

Let me suggest just a few things that are part of our world that either would not be here or would not be so strongly marked here had he not played a part in our history.

First, the idea that wisdom, critically necessary wisdom, lies in the pages of a book. Antiquity invented the written word, but it was late antiquity that gave the written word its particular place of prominence. The idea that a given book would embody all that you needed to know in order to build a building or govern a state or save your soul, that is an idea that was born in his time and that perhaps today is dying, but it has been undeniably an immensely powerful shaping idea in all the time between. To "canonize" something as "scripture" is a distinctly postclassical move shared by Judaism, Christianity, and Islam, and we live with the results of all three of those choices today. As late as the nineteenth century it could be argued that social transformation would come from the man who wrote the next book: Spencer perhaps, Schopenhauer perhaps, Nietzsche more likely, Marx definitely, Freud certainly. But their times are already over, or ending, and the expectations with which they were greeted seem already overblown and preposterous. In our own time there can be no serious expectation of a new book that will reveal all, transform all, save all: but our bookstores are full of books that claim to do just that. Pop stars seem particularly well suited to discovering such texts and proclaiming their transient worth. But in the parody is a sketch of the thing parodied. The notion of the book-as-guide was a devastatingly powerful one, one that we have so far naturalized that it will take us another generation at least to recover from it. Augustine helped give the notion roots.

His god is with us still. Listen attentively to people talking about "god" (or God or G-d or Allah) and observe how remarkably predictable the divine has become across religious traditions. The late-antique Christian mélange of biblical and Platonic qualities is perhaps the most powerful and lasting cultural creation in history. He may have died a hundred or more years ago, but he is with us still, the undead deity for whom the zealots of many cultures compete. The jury is still out on the profit/loss assessment of this god's impact on history.

But his god is forbearing in one important way: he keeps a bit of distance from politics. He doesn't stay *out* of politics exactly, but he doesn't try to run things either. The closest Christianity ever came to theocracy was probably in Byzantine Constantinople, but even there you could always tell the difference between emperor and patriarch. Popes may have tried to set the rules for politics in Catholic domains, but they have a long history of defeat and retrenchment and defeat again. Christianity meddles in politics but does not supplant government.

But Augustine is also associated with the *seriousness* with which we take religion. Many people, of course, take their religion lightly, but know that somehow they shouldn't. Religious festivals may even be uproarious from time to time, but they are always in some way serious because in the Christian, which is to say late-antique, disposition they always have something to do not only with the here and now but with the high and sublime. There are no trickster gods in Christianity, no Saturnalian festivals of reversal (even if Mardi Gras rather snuck in the back door in some neighborhoods). Religion is solemn and serious business, arising out of the deep inner experience of some, a deep inner experience that is eerily aligned with the most stringent rules and regulations of mass religion. The raptures and virtues of the few justify the rigors and discipline and guilty consciences of the many. That's Augustine all over.

And his religion goes well beyond negotiating with gods. We are a culture blithe in our praise for freedom and our missionary zeal to share freedom with others, but at the same time obsessed with a series of discourses—political, ethical, medical—about the conflicts and limits of freedom, the illusory sense of control and responsibility that seems indispensable (otherwise how is society to control the impulses of the restless) but at the same time philosophically not quite defensible. We act as though we are free, but we beg off the consequences of our actions by pleading incapacity. The conflict between the ethical (you can be good, therefore you should) and the therapeutic (you can't really be good, therefore you are not responsible and it is the responsibility of others to heal you) runs deep in contemporary society. It is, I suspect, the Freudian turn from the Augustinian pastoral to the psychological-therapeutic vocabulary that shields our Augustinian and religious past from attack when that conflict heats up. Within Christianity the divide separates right (ethical) from left (pastoral) in ways that often elude debate precisely because they run such deep roots.

And finally, sex. A student's mother introduced on a street corner, hearing that I write about Augustine, exclaims, "Oh, yes, he's the one who got it all wrong about sex!" On that charge, Augustine can quite plausibly mount a strong and persuasive defense. But if as a culture we think more about sex and are more divided about its expression and more inclined to paint the colors of sexual experience in chiaroscuros and colors both muted and strong at the same time, then we are adding pages, unknowingly, to the collected works of Augustine. It is easy to be ungrateful for that heritage, but I am not so sure that he did not do us at least some favors. If the alternative was Julian of Eclanum, for whom obeying the straightforward moral dictates of conventional biblical ethics was simple, easy, and obvious, then I think we are better off with the frustrations and the possibilities Augustine represents. But however we may think of him, we think *with* him more often than we know, even (or rather especially) when we disagree with him.

WE ARE NOT WHO
WE THINK WE ARE

The Socratic philosopher's task was always to know himself.[622] The idea was fresh and unsettling to those who found themselves and their fellows transparent, who observed the public man and inferred that they knew the man they observed. Nothing is more characteristic of the literary and philosophical culture of Greco-Roman antiquity than the exhilarating discovery that the inner self, standing ironically apart from the public man, knows itself better than anyone else can know. Ancient man has learned to talk to himself and to find meaning and direction in an inner space of the mind. Augustine stands near the head of the line of those who found meaning in the more intimate metaphor of the "heart," the most private space, the most important space, the stage on which the real drama of a person's life is played. The *Confessions* had begun with that restless heart.

But that phrase contains by implication the revolution Augustine represents. Augustine is not the final authority on Augustine. "I had become a mystery to myself."[623] The mystery has an authorized solution: "What happens when we hear about ourselves from you? [i.e., god]? We come to know ourselves."[624]

Borrowed from the Hebrew tradition, the god who knows the heart and the kidneys (Psalms 7.10) becomes the authoritative source of self-knowledge, and with him the spirituality of Christianity is defined. Not any longer the Platonist seeking to find fullness in knowledge of the eternally remote One, the Christian is a fallen mortal who seeks to hide from the sight of his god (Genesis 3.8). That post-Edenic stage of personal confrontation and self-abasement is where Augustine lives and moves. Original sin is a cultural creation of the first order, a geological upheaval that raises mountains where none were suspected before. We are all unreliable narrators of our own lives, none of us authorities on the things we know most intimately. That sense of the contingency of human existence is a creation of him and his culture that will long outlive any formal association with his expressed doctrines.

Not that we have not tried to escape it. The modern move, much discussed regarding Augustine in his relationship to the thought of Descartes in recent years,[625] restores self-knowledge to the primacy of place, as the intimately knowing god withdraws to a higher and more remote judgment seat. It is only in late-modern and postmodern times that the self has been dethroned from self-knowledge and others reinstated. The biographical tradition embodies that arrogance of the other, empowered by trains of thought for which Freud can stand as the patron saint. The analyst, the biographer, the journalist—by now, anyone at all is presumptively a better authority on the innermost thoughts and motivations of the object of public attention. Only the other can surmise the hidden springs, plumb the subconscious motivations, and see the patterns the self is too close to see. Pirandello's *Right You Are (If You Think You Are)* ends on a refusal to determine identity that leaves people playing different roles to different audiences, and for good reason.

We know how to live in that world. We think we recognize it in Augustine, when he surrenders the quest for self-knowledge in book 10 of the *Confessions* after pressing it as hard and far as he could. He would agree with us that we are not who we think we are, and in that way he is easy for us to understand. But he would beg to differ when it came to saying what we really are, and how we might come to know what we are. He offers us no easy solutions, and that is kind of him.

PURSUING AUGUSTINE FURTHER

Students of Augustine's life are like Nabokovian butterfly hunters, trying always to snare the marvelous creature in their nets, pin him to their corkboards, and sketch his anatomy with elaborate care (with particular attention, still metaphorically speaking, to the genitalia). And yet he escapes.

Without the *Confessions*, a work so preternaturally designed to survive the decay and rebirth of several cycles of western cultural imagination since his lifetime, perhaps he would not be so elusive. Other writers of Christian late antiquity can be found who have in their works as much poetry and imagination and passion as Augustine does. John Chrysostom, Gregory the Great, and the fathers of the Greek *Philocalia* all have their followers and devout readers today, and even the impassioned John Cassian has pages that inspire. Gregory Nazianzen's poem "On His Own Life" is nearly contemporaneous with Augustine and tells a story outwardly similar to the *Confessions* and is barely known. But all those writers impose themselves in the first instance on readers who have already chosen to make themselves open to Christian claims. Augustine reaches a broader readership. Readers will persist with him for their own reasons and choose the links they please to spin together a web between him, his books, and their own concerns.

But reading him is far from a simple business. Here are a few words of guidance for Augustine hunters.

The translations that bring us Augustine come out of an artless tradition, which assumes the conventional is accurate. Augustine today too often reads like an old-fashioned preacher man, and he can still be found full of *thee*s and *thou*s, reminding us of a long tradition of establishment religion. Nobody in his own time heard or read him that way. When he wanted to sound like a traditionalist, he made himself sound like a classical writer, so imagine him writing sonatas after the style of Brahms. And when he wanted to depart from that mode and when he sought to infuse his style with the Christian vocabulary and scriptural resonance, he sounded to many of his contemporaries dissonant and "modern," so imagine him producing short pieces of uncertain genre in the manner of Schoenberg or Shostakovich. Finding translations of Augustine that give him the directness of his voice, the modernity and freshness of his style, is hard. Garry Wills's *Saint Augustine* and his translations of individual books of the *Confessions*[626] have some fresh and vivid versions of the passages he quotes. In what I quote in this book, I have tried to capture freshness of voice and accuracy of tone (often sacrificing the elegance of long, balanced periodic sentences in the process), but I cannot conceal how extraordinarily difficult it is to translate an author who is separated from us by such a long period of respectability, familiarity, and drearification. If every banker and every politician of the last century had written in painfully unimaginative imitation of Emily Dickinson's verse, her own work would be far harder to hear fairly and carefully and far less likely to knock us off our chairs. You have not heard Augustine properly if he has not made you hang on to the armrests of your chair for dear life now and then.

But make the effort. Think of Augustine as a great literary artist, and ask how you can read him best. The obvious way to begin is to read his most distinctive and most successful works, and those are the easiest to find. The *Confessions* have been translated interminably (to give that work a decent rendering is no small task: this writer has been wrestling with Augustine over this for more than a decade, and Augustine is still winning easily). On balance, the recent Vintage paperback by Maria Boulding has the accuracy of the old J. K. Ryan translation (but Ryan's is very devout and old-fashioned in style) and at least something of the fluency of the Pine-Coffin version in the Penguin paperback series. Pine-Coffin is still very readable and fluent, achieving this by blithe paraphrase, which will annoy the attentive and serious reader. A good *City of God* is by Bettenhouse, and *On Christian Doctrine* is well approached either through D. W. Robertson's older translation or the newer version of R.P.H. Green.

Reading that trio of works will introduce Augustine's characteristic high styles, orient the reader to his human-centered, text-mediated view of the world and its fundamental story of redemption, and leave a vivid sense of the ubiquity and pervasiveness of scriptural texts in Augustine's thinking and writing. Mostly missing from those books is the atmosphere of Augustine's Africa. They were written (at least for us) by "Saint Augustine" and not "Augustine of Hippo." To capture some of that other flavor, you might start instead with his *Letters*.[627] Arranged by editors in chronological order (except for the juicy new ones discovered in the last decades), they plunge you into his African life. The letters we have are a selection and were doubtless meant to represent him well, but even so, they give a more fully fleshed sense of the man and his anxieties than his more official and artful products.

Another place to lie in wait for him is in his church on Sunday morning. The hundreds of sermons we have capture a rather different public man from the one who wrote the books for tasteful intellectuals, and they are simply so abundant that they inevitably reveal things he keeps out of his other books. These are now more abundantly available (see below) in English than ever before, and there is already a translation of the recently discovered Dolbeau sermons.[628]

Letters and sermons are familiar kinds of products, and we know how they plunge us into their author's world. The truly venturesome, even daring, reader would be the one who insisted on starting someplace even more particular and remote. Why not choose the Manichee-hater or the Donatist-basher or the Pelagius-hounder and throw yourself into his waters? The books will be harder to find and will require more notes for the novice reader, but you will be starting with an Augustine better known to many of his contemporaries than the calculated author of *Confessions* or *City of God*. To see him first quarrelsome and then to reach out for his calmer self-presentations can be a revelation.

Every reader of Augustine must make one more decision: What to do about his Bible? Everything we have from him plays off against the texts of his scriptures. To hear him expound the Gospels or Paul or Genesis or the Psalms will sound plausible enough if you have an ordinary awareness of those books. But if you would really challenge him, you would demand that he stand alongside the best modern interpreters of those books and allow his assertions to be confronted with theirs. His Bible, which is to him a fascinating and inexhaustible resource, will turn out to be a far more contentious and dubious place, and the conclusions he draws from its study far less obvious. He gave to all those he read (including, most notably, Jerome) the homage of intense examination and disagreement. The Augustine that emerges when we pay him the same homage is yet another avatar of the protean figure we have been tracing.

How to find him? Much of Augustine has been translated into English, but not all. The old series of *Fathers of the Church* and *Ancient Christian Writers* are found in many serious libraries and have much of him, while the new series *Augustine for the Twenty-first Century* published by New City Press has the great advantage of having the sermons, and many more works are appearing rapidly. In Italy, the Nuova Biblioteca Agostiniana is rapidly filling its shelves with handsome and readable editions that give both Latin text and Italian translation (and most of what it produces is freely available on its admirable website: www.augustinus.it), while in France, the Bibliothèque Augustinienne has a distinguished history going back half a century, again with Latin texts with translation on facing pages and abundant notes.

To pursue reading and investigation further, the encyclopedic *Augustine Through the Ages* (A. Fitzgerald, ed.; Grand Rapids, 1999) is a valuable guide; the more ambitious multilingual *Augustinus-Lexikon* (Basel, 1986ff), is only part of the way through its alphabet and is more for scholars than general readers. Many introductions to Augustine's thought have been written, more often recently by philosophers (look for titles by Christopher Kirwan and John Rist). For a good reading of Augustine's career as theologian, it's necessary to go back to E. TeSelle, *Augustine the Theologian* (New York, 1970).

On Augustine's influence in after ages, no satisfactory and consistent study has been done. J. J. Pelikan's magisterial history of Christian doctrine, *The Christian Tradition* (Chicago, 1971–85) returns to the theme repeatedly and is the best guide, but a wonderful book deserves to be written if only the erudition can be found to make it possible.

Augustine was the first saint to have his own home page on the World Wide Web, www.georgetown.edu/faculty/jod/augustine, and that page points to many more translations and texts available in electronic form. What may become of him in the age of cyberspace is matter (already) for another volume.[629]

ABBREVIATIONS FOR WORKS CITED

Augustine's surviving works are catalogued and briefly described in my
Augustine (Boston 1985). For further information, see Augustine's home
page, www.georgetown.edu/faculty/jod/augustine.

Ad Don. p. coll. = *Ad Donatistas post collationem (To the Donatists,
After the Conference)*

An. et. or. = *De anima et eius origine (The Soul and Its Origin)*

B. coniug. = *De bono coniugii (The Good in Marriage)*

Beata v. = *De beata vita (The Happy Life)*

C. Acad. = *Contra Academicos (Against the Academic [Philosophers])*

C. Cresc. = *Contra Cresconius (Against Cresconius [the Donatist])*

C. ep. Pel. = *Contra duas epistulas Pelagianorum (Against Two Letters
by the Pelagians)*

C. Faust. = *Contra Faustum (Against Faustus [the Manichee])*

C. Fort. = *Contra Fortunatum (Against Fortunatus [the Manichee])*

C. Gaud. = *Contra Gaudentium (Against Gaudentius [the Donatist])*

C. Iul. = *Contra Iulianum (Against Julian)*

C. Iul. imp. = *Contra Iulianum opus imperfectum (Incomplete Work
Against Julian)*

C. litt. Pet. = *Contra litteras Petiliani (Against a Letter by Petilian
[the Donatist])*

C. Prisc. et Orig. = *Contra Priscillianistas et Origenistas* (*Against the Followers of Priscillian and of Origen*)

Cat. rud. = *De catechizandis rudibus* (*Training the Beginners*)

Civ. = *De civitate dei* (*City of God*)

Coll. Carth. = *Collatio Carthaginiensis* (*Conference of Carthage* [stenographic transcript])

Conf. = *Confessiones* (*Confessions*)

Cura mort. = *De cura mortuorum* (*Looking After the Dead*)

De fide (*Faith*)

Div. daem. = *De divinatione daemonum* (*Conjuring Up Spirits*)

Div. qu. Simp. = *De diversis quaestionibus ad Simplicianum* (*Various Questions, for Simplicianus*)

Doctr. chr. = *De doctrina christiana* (*Christian Teaching*)

Duab. an. = *De duabus animabus* (*Two Souls*)

En. Ps. = *Enarrationes in Psalmos* (*Interpretations of the Psalms*)

Ench. = *Enchiridion* (*Handbook*)

Ep., Epp.: Epistula(e) (*Letter[s]*). Where the letter number is marked by an asterisk (*) the reference is to the new series of letters discovered by Johannes Divjak and published at Vienna in 1981. *Ep. Sec.* denotes the letter of Secundinus that appears as a preamble to Augustine's *Contra Secundinum* (*Against Secundinus*)

F. et op. = *De fide et operibus* (*Faith and Works*)

Gest. Pel. = *De gestis Pelagii* (*The Proceedings Regarding Pelagius*)

Gn. c. man. = *De Genesi contra Manichaeos* (*Genesis: Against the Manichees*)

Gn. litt. = *De Genesi ad litteram* (*Genesis Taken Literally*)

Gr. Chr. = *De gratia Christi* (*The Grace of Christ*)

Haer. = *De haeresibus* (*Heresies*)

Io. ep. tr. = *In Iohannis epistulam tractatus* (*Homilies on the First Letter of John*)

Io. ev. tr. = *In Iohannis evangelium tractatus* (*Homilies on John's Gospel*)

Lib. arb. = *De libero arbitrio voluntatis* (*Free Choice of the Will*)

Loc. hept. = *Locutiones in Heptateuchum* (*Passages from the Heptateuch*)

Mend. = *De mendacio* (*Lying*)

Mor. = *De moribus Manichaeorum et de moribus ecclesiae catholicae* (*Lifestyles of the Manichees and of the Catholic Church*)

Op. mon. = *De opere monachorum* (*The Work of Monks*)
Ord. = *De ordine* (*Order*)
Persev. = *De perseverantia* (*Perseverance*)
Ps. c. Don. = *Psalmus contra Donatistas* (*Psalm Against the Donatists*)
Qu. Dulc. = *De octo quaestionibus ad Dulcitium* (*Eight Questions for Dulcitius*)
Qu. hept. = *Quaestiones in Heptateuchum* (*Questions Regarding the Heptateuch*)
Quant. an. = *De quantitate animae* (*The Size of the Soul*)
Retr. = *Retractationes* (*Reconsiderations*)
Rom. exp. inch. = *Epistolae ad Romanos inchoata expositio* (*Unfinished Treatise on the Epistle to the Romans*)
S., SS. = *Sermo(nes)* (*Sermon[s]*). Some sermons are further identified by the name of the scholar who discovered them or the place where they were found, e.g., *S. Denis, S. Dolbeau, S. Frang., S. Guelf., S. Morin.*
Sol. = *Soliloquia* (*Soliloquies*)
Util. cred. = *De utilitate credendi* (*The Usefulness of Belief*)
Vera rel. = *De vera religione* (*True Religion*)

Other ancient works cited in brief form include:

Amb. *De off.* = Ambrose, *De officiis* (*Duties*)
Ammianus Marcellinus = Ammianus Marcellinus, *Res gestae* (*History*)
Breviarium Hipponense
CTh. = *Codex Theodosianus*
Ep. Jer. = *Letters of Jerome*
Ep. Paul. = *Letters of Paulinus of Nola*
Gennadius *Vir. ill.* = Gennadius, *De viris illustribus* (*Famous Men*)
Juvenal *Sat.* = Juvenal, *Satires*
Orosius *Apologeticum* (*In Self-Defense*)
Paulinus *Vita Ambrosii* (*Life of Ambrose*)
Pelagius *Libellus fidei* (*Pamphlet: What I Believe*)
Porphyry *Life of Plotinus*
Possid. *Indic.* = Possidius, *Indiculum* (*Index [of Augustine's Works]*)
Possidius *Vita* = Possidius, *Life of Augustine*
Rule of the Master
Sidonius Apollinaris *Ep.* = Sidonius Apollinaris, *Letters*

Symmachus *Ep.* = Symmachus, *Letters*
Symmachus *Rel.* = Symmachus, *Relationes (Reports)*
Victor Vit. = Victor of Vita, *Historia persecutionis Africanae ecclesiae*
    (History of the Persecution of the African Church)
Vita Melan. iun. vers. grec. = *Vita Melaniae iunioris (versio Graeca)*
    (Life of Melanie the Younger [Greek version])
Zosimus = Zosimus, *Historia nova (New History)*

I quote the Christian Bible with translations adjusted to match the text
Augustine himself knew, which is often at some variance with all modern
versions.

Scholarly works quoted in abbreviated form:

Aug.-Lex. = *Augustinus-Lexikon* (Basel, 1984ff)
Brown = Peter Brown, *Augustine of Hippo* (Berkeley, 1967; 2nd ed.
    with supplementary essay, 2000)
Courcelle, *Recherches* = Pierre Courcelle, *Recherches sur les*
    Confessions de saint Augustin (Paris, 1950; 2nd ed., 1968)
Frend = W.H.C. Frend, *The Donatist Church* (Oxford, 1951, and
    later reprintings)
Lancel = S. Lancel, *Saint Augustin* (Paris, 1999)
Van Der Meer = F. Van Der Meer, *Augustine the Bishop* (London,
    1961)
Lössl = J. Lössl, *Julian von Aeclanum* (Leiden, 2001)
McLynn = Neil McLynn, *Ambrose of Milan* (Berkeley, 1994)
PL = *Patrologia Latina* (Paris, 1844ff)
Vössing = K. Vössing, *Schule und Bildung im Nordafrika der*
    römischen Kaiserzeit (Brussells, 1997)
Wermelinger = O. Wermelinger, *Rom und Pelagius* (Stuttgart,
    1975)
Wills = Garry Wills, *Saint Augustine* (New York, 1999)

NOTES

1. *S.* 4.9.9.

2. "Aurelius" suggests that his ancestors received Roman citizenship 150 years before his birth under the generosity of the emperor Caracalla, who made universal what had hitherto been a special privilege. "Augustinus" suggests, as we shall see later, a social aspiration of his immediate family. The modern English rendition of his name, Augustine, is variously pronounced AW-gus-teen and a-GUS-tin; both are as correct as any such can be.

3. The honorific he acquired from custom, having lived, died, and been venerated long before the age when churchmen began to manage a process of canonization to determine the right to the title.

4. *Conf.* 1.1.1.

5. The city's name probably combines a word of Punic origin for "bay" or "gulf" and a Latin marker that it took from the time of the Numidian kings, that is, about the time of the late Roman republic. In the seventeenth century, the Augustine-zealots of the abbey of Port-Royal outside Paris chose to interpret "Hippo" as "port" and to see an accidental but pleasing coincidence between the name of Augustine's city and their own landlocked headquarters (Lancel 690). Under colonial rule, the city was called Bône, but natives tended to say "Buna." Its name today is Annaba, and it is still a provincial commercial harbor, but now looks west to Algiers, while in Augustine's day its senior rival was Carthage (near modern Tunis) to the east.

6. *Ep.* 7.3.6—"but the flavor of strawberries and cherries we could not imagine until we tasted them in Italy."

7. *Civ.* 22.24.5—"in the great spectacle when the sea dresses itself in all its colors: green—all sorts of green—and purple and sky blue. . . ."

8. *Ep.* 55.8.14 compares pilots of ships to travelers in the desert—both are in trackless wastes and relying on the stars to navigate.

9. Roman law texts and many modern scholars speak of such individuals as ones who flee their tax burden and civic service to join the clergy, but because we have a report of his spiritual development from Augustine, few say that of him. If the laws had been effective, they would have seriously impeded the clergy from recruiting among the upper classes. The failure of these laws sped the success of Christianity.

10. *Ep.* 126.7. Augustine spoke in the presence of Pinian, one of the richest men in the world, and may have been inclined to deprecate his own wealth by comparison.

11. *Ep.* 259. That the letter's recipient was Romanianus is highly probable but not certain.

12. The proconsul was a connection to the wider world of power and prestige. The three predecessors of the distinguished physician Vindicianus, who crowned Augustine, had all been family members or intimates of Ausonius of Bordeaux, at that moment virtually "prime minister" in the imperial government at Milan. By 393, when Augustine was presbyter in the church at Hippo, one of his former students, Flaccianus, had assumed the office.

13. *Conf.* 6.11.19.

14. Possidius *Vita* 3. Possidius was a junior colleague of Augustine and bishop of Calama, near Hippo.

15. *Mor.* 1.31.65ff, esp. 1.33.70, display a knowledge of contemporary monasticism that Augustine could have easily linked to his own activities, but didn't.

16. The two fifth-century writers from generations after Augustine who most distinguished themselves for their writing stood notably outside the Christian literary community. Macrobius's *Saturnalia* imitated Cicero's dialogues to show contemporary wealth and learning at leisure discussing traditional notions of literature (especially Vergil) and religion, while Martianus Capella's *Marriage of Philology and Mercury* combined mythology and learning in a flamboyant display implicitly exhorting readers to pursue similarly deep studies.

17. See Van Der Meer 18–19 on the scene.

18. At least a Punic one, and probably a Roman one. A nineteenth-century basilica dedicated to Augustine now claims the space for a more modern god.

19. Van Der Meer 23. Imagine a modern cult setting up for services in the food court of a shopping mall.

20. *Ep.* 29.11.

21. P. Horden and N. Purcell, *The Corrupting Sea* (Oxford, 2000), explores the ancient Mediterranean and ancient and modern attempts to understand it.

22. *Civ.* 2.4, 2.26. It's not clear whether Augustine knew that he was seeing the last days of the worship of Tanit/Astarte and of Cybele, gods modern west-

erners have heard of in their original Near Eastern form, later imported to Carthage by Phoenician colonizers, later Latinized by the Romans.

23. *S.* 355.1.2.

24. From Possidius's version of these events (*Vita* 3–4) it's clear that the man was already Christian and the "winning" had entirely to do with persuading him to leave behind the imperial career as "special agent" and enter a religious community.

25. The Latin word *presbyter* is generally translated "priest," but the role is not the same as the modern cleric of that name: a *presbyter* was more subordinate to a bishop and not generally found serving as an independent pastor. Many "bishops" in this period indeed had responsibilities more like those of parish pastors in modern times.

26. Possidius reports that Augustine burst into tears on his selection, which some took as a sign of disappointment that it was only the rank of priest and not of bishop that was offered him. They tried to console him that promotion would soon be his. In telling the story, Augustine said his tears arose from a sense of the burdens of office and his own unworthiness. (Forced ordination was not unheard of in Augustine's time, as in the case of Ambrose of Milan, as we shall see shortly.)

27. The fundamental social line separated the somebodies (*honestiores*) from the little people (*humiliores*). Clergy were on the safe side of that line and thus had various legal protections. Possidius *Vita* 24 emphasizes Augustine's neglect of matters financial: just the sort of neglect that only the comfortably-off can afford, but it got him in some trouble in the end.

28. *C. Acad.* 2.2.6.

29. *Epp.* 156–57.

30. *Conf.* 10.36.59ff.

31. Augustine was always the one asked to give the sermon and seems rarely to have sat through anyone else's. He professed to be wearied by his popularity (*S.* 94), as celebrities often are.

32. *Ep.* 23.3.

33. Van Der Meer 629 (n1) itemizes chalices, hanging lamps, and candelabra; on the wealth of churches, see Dominic Janes, *God and Gold in Late Antiquity* (Cambridge, 1998).

34. *Ep.* 33.5; *S.* 137.14.

35. *Ep.* 113–16; cf. also *Ep.* 8*.

36. *Aug.-Lex.* 1.514–15.

37. *Io. ev. tr.* 6.25.

38. Possidius *Vita* 24.31. For the household outlined here, see Vössing 231.

39. *Ep.* 10*.6.

40. *Ep.* 24* is addressed to Eustochius, who seems to serve in this capacity.

41. See Richard Klein, *Die Sklaverei in der Sicht der Bischöfe Ambrosius und Augustinus* (Stuttgart, 1988) esp. 133–63; R. MacMullen, *Changes in the Roman Empire* (Princeton, 1990) 240–41.

42. The laws of the time make it clear that clergy *could* own slaves (*CTh.* 16.2.8; 4.7.1 of 321 C.E. assumes that clergy may be freeing slaves in their wills). C. Sotinel, "Le personnel épiscopal," in *L'évêque dans la cité du IVe au Ve siècle: image et autorité*, E. Rebillard, C. Sotinel, eds. (Rome, 1998) 105–26, finds that both Paulinus of Nola and Ambrose owned slaves, but argues these were holdovers from their former social status, not part of their episcopal life. This conclusion does not address the question of how episcopal households were constituted. H. C. Teitler, *Notarii and exceptores* (Amsterdam, 1985) 91, reports fourth-century Greek bishops whose *notarii* were slaves but finds that the task was increasingly shifted to junior members of the clergy.

43. *S.* 356.6, and 356.3–7 generally.

44. Slavery stories: *Ep.* 10*.6, 10*.8.

45. *Ep.* 21.6.

46. *CTh.* 7.13.22 (428).

47. P. Brown, *Power and Persuasion in Late Antiquity* (Madison, Wisconsin, 1992); see also H. A. Drake, *Constantine and the Bishops: The Politics of Intolerance* (Baltimore, 2000).

48. *Ep.* 208.2.

49. *Breviarium Hipponense* 11.

50. Adeodatus had benefited from Augustine's change in fortunes. At Milan, Augustine's mother had been trying to make him a good career-building marriage. If it had gone through, Adeodatus's status as son of a dismissed second-class wife would have been questionable at least and he would almost certainly not have stood in line to inherit all that Augustine had.

51. See *Ep.* 126.7, where the precise time implied for the "abandonment of my father's few paltry acres" is ambiguous, but associated with the *end* of his time in Tagaste. Just as his family had followed him to Milan to ride on the coattails of Augustine's worldly career prospects, so too when he moved to Hippo did they follow him there. Augustine's sister came to lead a community of religious women (see *Ep.* 211) and his brother, Navigius, seems to have sent children as well, daughters to live in the sister's "convent" and a son, Patricius, who was perhaps a subdeacon or perhaps satisfied with a lower clerical status (G. Madec, *Revue des études augustiniennes* 39[1993] 149–53).

52. *Ep.* 21.

53. *Ep.* 22.9.

54. *Conf.* 10.43.70.

55. Paulinus, *Vita Ambrosii* 7.

56. McLynn, *Ambrose of Milan* (Berkeley, 1994) chapter 1, especially 44–52, explores these events and is highly skeptical, thinking the resistance all staged for effect.

57. Amb. *De off.* 1.4. This paradox of teaching with no time to learn echoes a famous passage in the *Confessions* (6.3.3) where Augustine sees Ambrose reading silently and fails to strike up a meaningful conversation with him. Ambrose did not "invent" the practice of silent reading (many think otherwise, but see P. Saenger, *Space Between Words* [Stanford, 1997]).

58. Possidius, *Vita* 8.

59. Augustine reports and tries to defuse the embarrassment at *C. Cresc.* 3.80.92, *C. litt. Pet.* 3.19.

60. Visits to neighboring cities, including Thubursicu, Cirta, and Thiava (*Epp.* 38, 43, 44; and cf. Possid. *Indic.* 6.29) occur almost immediately after Augustine's ordination.

61. We get this image in *Conf.* 6.6.9: Augustine spots a drunken beggar and observes to his friends that the beggar would achieve happiness more surely and sooner than they.

62. Professor Mark Vessey points out to me that there is not much Latin preaching on scripture before Augustine, and it's not clear just how familiar the sight of a bishop explaining scripture would have been to an African churchgoer first hearing Augustine.

63. Ramsay MacMullen, "The Preacher's Audience," *Journal of Theological Studies* 40(1989) 503–11.

64. *S. Dolbeau* 2.2.

65. *Gr. Chr.* 1.1, written in 426.

66. *Civ.* 21.4. At home, Augustine was normally vegetarian (so Possidius *Vita* 22—meat was only for guests and the sick).

67. *Ep.* 38.1

68. Gathered in the Latin text with discussion in *Vingt-six sermons au peuple d'Afrique* (Paris, 2001), Englished as: Augustine, *Newly Discovered Sermons*, trans. E. Hill (Brooklyn, New York, 1997).

69. My interpretations of the *Confessions* are much more fully presented in my three-volume edition of and commentary on the *Confessions* (Oxford, 1991, also available in full at www.georgetown.edu/faculty/jod/conf).

70. *Conf.* 10.27.38.

71. A recently discovered sermon adds vivid detail to the allusion in *Conf.* 3.3.5: *S. Dolbeau* 2.5—"I as a lad used to attend vigils when I was a student in this city, and I kept vigil like that, where the women were mixed in and subject to the impudent advances of men, which no doubt on many occasions put the virtue of even chaste people at risk." Think again how crowded those church buildings were and thus how it made sense for men and women to be separated for the service itself.

72. *Conf.* 8.7.17.

73. *B. coniug.* 5.5 talks about the hypothetical case of a couple who live together, have a child, then separate because the man seeks a better marriage while the woman goes off to live chastely and unmarried—exactly the situation of Augustine and his wife. At that moment (in the 400s) Augustine is harsh enough on himself (calling the man in that case an adulterer) and generous enough to the woman (declining to accuse her of the same sin).

74. J. Gaarder, *That Same Flower* (New York, 1998).

75. S.N.C. Lieu, *Manichaeism in the Later Roman Empire and Mediaeval China* (Manchester, U.K., 1985; rev. ed. Tübingen, 1992), is the best history of the sect. Much important research continues.

76. Augustine regularly assumes that landowners will take sexual advantage of their slaves: *S.* 224.3, 152.5.6, 9.2–4, 132.4, 392.2; *Io. ev. tr.* 4ff; *Io. ep. tr.* 7.8; *S. Denis* 7.3, 21.4.

77. *En. Ps.* 36.s.3.19 makes it clear that not everyone believed him.

78. *C. Fort.* 1.1.

79. *Lib. arb.* 1.11.22, with a similar passage at *Lib. arb.* 3.18.52–3.19.53.

80. There were even earlier "confessions" in Augustine's works, e.g., the short narrative written just before his move to Hippo in 391 in *Util. cred.* 8.20 (the purpose there is to defend his past against *Manichee* critics).

81. *Retr.* 2.10.36.

82. This is a nicely aimed shot. Hortensius was a famous Roman orator who figured in a now-lost dialogue of Cicero. The purpose of the dialogue was to persuade the reader to enter a life of philosophical reflection, and in it Hortensius played the part of the unpersuaded worldly man. Augustine tells us in *Conf.* 3.4.7 that this particular book of Cicero set him on fire, drove him to look for truth in Christian scripture, and then, on the rebound, sent him into the arms of the Manichees. Augustine would use Hortensius against Julian of Eclanum years later, with similar stinging effect (*C. Iul.* 4.13.72).

83. *Ep. Sec.* 1.

84. *Ep.* 93.13.51.

85. R. Cameron and A. J. Dewey, trans., *The Cologne Mani Codex* (Missoula, Montana, 1979).

86. See again S.N.C. Lieu, *Manichaeism in the Later Roman Empire and Mediaeval China* and cf. J. BeDuhn, *The Manichean Body* (Baltimore, 2000).

87. In China, Manicheans escaped attention by speaking of their spiritual guide as the "Buddha of light" and at least one temple that enshrines that figure survives in southeastern China.

88. Imagine if *all* we knew of modern Marxism came from Whittaker Chambers. In the ancient world, Epicureanism suffered a similar loss of definition to hostile stereotype.

89. This was the view of Augustine's acquaintance Faustus (quoted in *C. Faust.* 15.1).

90. *Conf.* 4.1.1.

91. *Mor.* 2.19.68–72 records tales from his Carthage days of the Manichee "elect" and their hypocrisy that capture something of his state of mind then. Among the Manichees he was himself both prig and hypocrite (for his relationship with his wife).

92. *C. Iul. imp.* 3.136–37; on the text Julian discovered, see Aalders, "L'Épitre à Menoch attribuée à Mani," *Vigiliae Christianae* 14(1960) 245–49, and Brown 370.

93. *C. Iul. imp.* 6.41, which concludes thus: "But when you deny that evil things are evil and don't connect their origins to the sin of the first humans, you don't succeed in making them not evil, but rather you make them, because their *nature* is evil, coeternal with eternal goodness. In that way in your detestable

blindness you support the Manichees, and your accusations are empty because you're really helping them abominably."

94. *Conf.* 5.14.25. "Catechumen" was the term for a "trainee" Christian, someone affiliated with the church and taking instruction but not yet baptized.

95. See below on the religious history of Tagaste implied here.

96. Garry Wills, in his biography and subsequent translations from the *Confessions*, calls the work *The Testimony* on just these grounds.

97. In Ambrose's case, the opposition was the imperially sponsored "homoean" form of Christianity, one that Ambrose would condemn as fundamentally equivalent with the Arian heresy. See R.P.C. Hanson, *The Search for the Christian Doctrine of God* (Edinburgh, 1988).

98. W. Achelis, *Die Deutung Augustins* (Prien-am-Chiemsee, 1921). The essays in "psychobiography" that have approached Augustine have been too little skeptical (taking the narrative of the *Confessions* at face value) and too little ambitious (failing to exploit the riches of, to take one example, Augustine's sermons, a treasure trove of the images, themes, and preoccupations that followed him all his life). From time to time, opaque passages of the *Confessions* are taken as suggesting that Augustine was gay. There is no persuasive argument in favor of that proposition, and indeed proponents seldom point to the same passages.

99. *Conf.* 9.3.4–9.5.13.

100. One of Augustine's students there that winter later wrote a poem, part of which (translation from Wills 49) catches the atmosphere: "Could Dawn, with happy chariot / Wheel back to me the past, / When we prolonged our wise retreat / 'Neath Alpine shadows cast, / No frost would now repel my feet / With firmness planted fast, / No storms or winds beat off return / Of friendships meant to last." Not all that winter's friendships lasted very long.

101. *Beata v.* 4.35.

102. *Conf.* 8.2.2, where the phrase captures the relationship between Ambrose and his own baptizer, Simplicianus.

103. Literally "given by god"—the translation here I owe to Wills's biography. Augustine shows off his son with remembered and mournful pride in *The Teacher*, a dialogue between doting father and precocious adolescent son.

104. *C. Iul. imp.* 6.22.

105. *Conf.* 7.20.26.

106. *Conf.* 9.6.14.

107. Pierre Courcelle's *Recherches sur les Confessions de saint Augustin* (Paris, 1950) worked a revolution in modern readings of this book by pressing the question of its historicity in a way that was both hard and fair.

108. *Conf.* 9.6.14.

109. P. Courcelle, *"Les Confessions" de saint Augustin dans la tradition littéraire* (Paris, 1963) traced the history of this readership.

110. More traditionally (E. B. Pusey in the last century): "Great art thou, O Lord, and greatly to be praised; great is thy power, and thy wisdom infinite."

111. *Conf.* 1.6.7.

112. To be fair, some moderns have thought to unravel the mysteries of the book's composition by arguing that it originally broke off after book 9 and was completed only sometime later. This would have given at least some early readers the experience of ending narrative and book simultaneously, but all the readers we know of had the more complex experience that we do.

113. 1 John 2.16. "Hankerings" here is my rendition for Augustine's use of Latin *concupiscentia*, more commonly rendered in English through the desiccated theological jargonism "concupiscence," with a sexual overtone that derives from but goes beyond Augustine's own practice.

114. *Conf.* 10.30.41ff.

115. In that passage of *Conf.*, Augustine works through all five senses in order to show how sinful he can be. He is unpersuasive in arguing that he can be led astray by smell, and when it comes to music, the middle-aged bishop can only allow that sometimes he gets a little distracted by fine church music and forgets why he's supposed to be listening to it.

116. For this link between 1 John and the temptations of Jesus, see Aug. *Vera rel.* 38.71, *En. Ps.* 8.13, and *S.* 284.5: see my commentary on *Conf.* 10.30.41.

117. *Conf.* 1.20.31, with my commentary. Pleasure points to the third divine person, exaltation the first, and truth the second.

118. *Conf.* 3.1.1. Eliot, "The Waste Land" lines 307–11, alludes to the passage and overplays the already fervid spirit of the passage.

119. That Augustine accuses himself of curiosity as a vice does not demonstrate that he was by nature a curious and inquisitive man. What curiosity Augustine shows is focused on texts, historical and philosophical (and the combination of the two that is scriptural). But of the world around him he takes little notice. His travels have little or no effect on him, and his ignorance of many things he might reasonably have wanted to know is notable. His best prose has psychological vividness about people but little painterliness about the world.

120. *Conf.* 4.7.12.

121. *Conf.* 8.11.29–30.

122. Romans 13.13.

123. That is how Augustine and others would take Romans 6.3—"Know ye not, that so many of us as were baptized into Jesus Christ were baptized into his death?"

124. *Civ.* 11.1.1.

125. *Conf.* 10.27.38.

126. This description of the bishop at work picks up Ambrose's idea of the bishop as a Ciceronian orator. In trying to write his book *Christian Doctrine*, Augustine elaborated a theory of Christian Ciceronianism; in writing the *Confessions*, he shows the theory in action.

127. *Conf.* 11.1.1.

128. Courcelle, *Recherches* 23–26.

129. Brown 99–102; see Lancel 142–43, doing the same thing for only a bit more than half a page.

130. John 1.47–48.

131. *Conf.* 7.21.27.

132. It may even be that Augustine came back to the book he had been reading and read literally the *next* passage on the page. But many doubt whether this scene could have happened in just this way. Paul looms small in the Augustinian corpus for almost ten years after the event, and when the particular passage Augustine quotes as deciding his fate first appears, it is late, unremarked, and unremarkable.

133. *Conf.* 8.12.29.

134. On this theme, see G. Madec, *Saint Ambroise et la philosophie* (Paris, 1974).

135. MacMullen, *Christianizing the Roman Empire* (New Haven, 1984) unsettled this tradition.

136. Quoted at *C. Iul. imp.* 2.7.20. Ambrose himself was a notable praiser of virginity, and at least one other would-be convert in Augustine's circle, the schoolmaster Verecundus, seemed to think that he had to renounce sexual activity (and in his case his wife, or at least the conventional life of matrimony) in order to be baptized (*Conf.* 9.3.5).

137. *Sol.* 1.10.17.

138. P. Brown, *Body and Society* (New York, 1988), 341–65.

139. *Mor.* 2.65. He accuses the Manichees of knowing and encouraging the "rhythm method" of monthly abstinence for the permanent avoidance of pregnancy, which he polemically interprets as meaning that the Manichees prefer marriage for lust to marriage for children. By the 1950s the Vatican was recommending the method that Augustine condemned.

140. I. Hadot, *Arts libéraux et philosophie dans la pensée de l'antiquité tardive* (Paris, 1984).

141. Robert Markus, *Conversion and Disenchantment* (Villanova, Pennsylvania, 1989).

142. *Conf.* 10.1.1–10.3.3.

143. *Various Questions for Simplicianus* (*De diversis quaestionibus ad Simplicianum*).

144. Peter Brown, "A Servant of God at the End of Time," *University Publishing* 9(1980) 3.

145. *Conf.* 9.10.24–25.

146. The history of "soul" has not been written, but the books of Jan N. Bremmer, *The Early Greek Concept of the Soul* (Princeton, 1983) and *The Rise and Fall of the Afterlife* (New York, 2002), survey the ancient part of the story.

147. *S. Dolbeau* 21.6.

148. In the philosophical language of the time, he puns by asking what the "efficient cause" of evil may be and insisting that the cause is not "efficient" but "deficient." The pun travels badly.

149. *Civ.* 12.7, ending with quotation of Psalms 18.13.

150. *Conf.* 13.38.53.

151. M. Gleason, "Visiting and News: Gossip and Reputation Management

in the Desert," *Journal of Early Christian Studies* 6(1998) 501–21, explores this point.

152. Women took to the ascetic life as quickly as men: see S. Elm, *Virgins of God* (Oxford, 1994).

153. One surviving manuscript, now in St. Petersburg (Russia), is sometimes argued to have come directly from Augustine's library, out of hundreds he owned.

154. Symmachus *Ep.* 9.51.

155. *Conf.* 5.13.23.

156. *Epp.* 130–31.

157. Ammianus Marcellinus 30.5.4–10; Zosimus 6.7.

158. *Ep.* 150; Lindsay Thompson, "Ecclesial Virginity: A Cultural Analysis of Roman Origins" (dissertation, Classics, Johns Hopkins University, 2001), explores the prestige which that one generation of Roman aristocrats assigned to their daughters' permanent virginity and how it arose in part from the still-flourishing (in the late fourth century) practice of devoting daughters as Vestal virgins.

159. *Ep.* 96.1.

160. *Epp.* 191, 192, 194: to Sixtus and Caelestinus.

161. *Ep.* 200, sending his book *Marriage and Desire* (*De nuptiis et concupiscentiis*) to Valerius, who had been approached otherwise by Augustine and Alypius already.

162. *Ep.* 187.

163. Sidonius Apollinaris *Ep.* 5.9.1.

164. Dennis Trout, *Paulinus of Nola* (Berkeley, 1999).

165. The correspondence has attracted endless specialist study, e.g., R. Hennings, *Der Briefwechsel zwischen Augustinus und Hieronymus* (Leiden, 1994). See J.N.D. Kelly, *Jerome* (London, 1975), though Kelly takes Jerome a little too much at his own word.

166. M. Vessey, "Jerome's Origen: The Making of a Christian Literary Persona," *Studia Patristica* 28(1993) 135–45.

167. A non-Christian gentleman observed at the time that the position of bishop of Rome was profitable enough to be worth turning Christian for.

168. *Ep. Jer.* 105.

169. *Ep. Jer.* 102.2 (to Aug.) sees exactly what the younger man is doing: "it's boyish crowing, the stuff teenagers like to do, to seek fame for yourself by attacking famous men" ("puerilis esse iactantiae, quod olim adolescentuli facere consueverant, accusando illustres viros, suo nomini famam quaerere"). (Augustine picks up that phrase to deny it at *Ep.* 82.1.2.)

170. That's an odd selection. We have to wonder if somebody sent Jerome Augustine's psalm sermons precisely so the old professional would be scandalized by Augustine's complete ignorance of Hebrew, feeble knowledge of Greek, and lack of contact with the existing serious Christian literature on the subject.

171. The Greek theologian Origen had died 150 years earlier, but his writ-

ings remained influential and controversial. Around 400 a firestorm of recriminations erupted among Latin theologians, all seeking to avoid being accused of
having been influenced by the most interesting and influential of Christian theologians. See E. Clark, *The Origenist Controversy* (Princeton, 1992).

172. *Ep.* 81.

173. *Ep.* 82.1.2.

174. See *Ep.* 31.3, noodling in the common style with Paulinus and commenting on the way biblical language was a *shared* language in more ways than
one.

175. P. Courcelle, *Les Confessions de saint Augustin dans la tradition littéraire*
(Paris, 1963) 559–607, reconstructs the correspondence and its missing items.

176. *Persev.* 20.53.

177. *Ep. Paul.* 4.2 (= Aug. *Ep.* 25.2).

178. A flattering reference to a collection of five of Augustine's works that
he had sent to Paulinus.

179. The field repays further study; see J. Ebbeler, *Pedants in the Apparel of
Heroes* (dissertation, Classical Studies, University of Pennsylvania, 2001); cf.
C. Conybeare, *Paulinus Noster: Self and Symbols in the Letters of Paulinus of Nola*
(Oxford, 2000).

180. We have substantial collections, most running to many hundreds of
pages, from (in rough chronological order) Ausonius, Paulinus, Symmachus,
Ambrose, Jerome, Augustine, the so-called *Collectio Avellana* (mainly papal and
imperial letters), Pope Leo, Sidonius Apollinaris, Salvian, Rusticus, Caesarius
of Arles, Ruricius of Limoges, Ennodius, Avitus, Cassiodorus, and Pope Gregory I, to say nothing of Greek writers.

181. *Epp.* 27.2, 27.5, and 31.2 show Augustine reading aloud letters in the
presence of his own community, to general approval. Such readings were
doubtless even more entertaining when the content was a misdirected or boot-
leg copy of a letter.

182. *Ep.* 201 (419).

183. See my *Avatars of the Word: From Papyrus to Cyberspace* (Cambridge,
Massachusetts, 1998).

184. C. H. Roberts, *The Birth of the Codex* (London, 1987); see also Frances
Young, *Biblical Exegesis and the Formation of Christian Culture* (Cambridge, U.K.,
1997).

185. *Ep.* 109.

186. *Ep.* 84.1.

187. *Ep.* 109. The reader may reasonably want to take a deep breath after
this passionate and vivid prose. I have followed the text and metaphor carefully,
except that where I say "essence" or "innermost essence," the Latin word is
even more physical and graphic: *viscera* ("inner bodily organs"). Augustine's
breasts are stripped of their very skin so that Severus can more directly get at
the nourishing, delighting substance within.

188. *Conf.* 4.8.13.

189. *Ep.* 98.8.

190. E.g., *Epp.* 149, 162.

191. Augustine once spoke (*Ep.* 73.3.10) of the consolation he finds from throwing himself upon the kindness of his friends when he is wearied by the scandals of the world, and he explains his relief as arising from the presence of his god in those friends. What he trusts in his friends is his god.

192. *C. Iul. imp.* 1.42, 3.35.

193. *Ep.* 44.3.

194. *Ep.* 125; see below for the story.

195. See my commentary on *Conf.* 9.4.7.

196. Quoted in full in a letter of Augustine: *Ep.* 15*.

197. *Conf.* 1.11.17.

198. *Conf.* 5.9.16.

199. *Conf.* 9.2.4, 9.4.12.

200. *Ep.* 38.1.

201. Evidence of his health in 410: *Epp.* 109.3, 118.5.34, 119.1, 122.1, 124.2.

202. *Civ.* 22 is the best summary of Augustine's views on resurrection, and see M. Miles, *Augustine on the Body* (Missoula, Montana, 1979); see also C. Bynum, *The Resurrection of the Body in Western Christianity* (New York, 1995).

203. *Duab. an.* 9.11.

204. Henry Chadwick, *Priscillian of Avila* (Oxford, 1976) esp. 132–38; V. Burrus, *The Making of a Heretic* (Berkeley, 1995).

205. See "Augustine in Parody," page 285, for this fragment of Augustine's "influence."

206. Greg Woolf, *Becoming Roman: The Origins of Provincial Civilization in Gaul* (Cambridge, 1998); Ramsay MacMullen, *Romanization in the Time of Augustus* (New Haven, 2000).

207. The one great surprise on the linguistic map is the persistence of Romanian—an offshoot of Latin in a province that Rome held only for a few decades in the second century C.E. There is no convincing explanation for how this happened.

208. See J. N. Adams, "Latin and Punic in Contact? The Case of Bu Njem Ostraca," *Journal of Roman Studies* 84(1994) 87–112; and "The Poets of Bu Njem: Language, Culture and the Centurionate," *Journal of Roman Studies* 89(1999) 109–34.

209. W.H.C. Frend, "A Note on the Berber Background in the Life of Saint Augustine," *Journal of Theological Studies* 43(1942) 188–91. "Adeodatus" translates *Iatanbaal* ("gift of [the god] Baal"), and "Monnica" recalls the goddess Mon.

210. "Patricius" and "Augustus" were titles of high Roman honor.

211. Lepelley in *Atti: Congresso internazionale su S. Agostino nel XVI centenario della conversione, Roma, 15–20 settembre 1986* (Rome 1987) 1.103.

212. See J. N. Adams, *Bilingualism and the Latin Language* (Cambridge, 2002) 237–40, which brings sociolinguistics and philology together in a learned

synthesis. See also Vössing 243–44 and Lancel, "La fin et la survie de la Latinité en Afrique du nord: État des questions," *Revue des études latines* 59(1981) 269–97.

213. *Epp.* 16–17.

214. They thought they were descended from Punic ancestors: *Rom. exp. inch.* 13 reports how Bishop Valerius, the Greek-speaker, overheard a discussion among peasants, who, when asked what *salus* (Latin for "health, salvation") meant in Punic, said "three." (The bishop took this as evidence for the doctrine of the Trinity.) These same *rustici* call themselves *Chanani*, that is, Canaanites, which is what the Hebrew scriptures call the Phoenicians.

215. *Ord.* 2.17.45.

216. *Doctr. chr.* 4.10.24.

217. *Ps. c. Don.* 1–11.

218. *S.* 180.5.5.

219. Brown 153.

220. The likeliest candidate is Mallius Theodorus, who was a senior government minister at Milan and then retired to a life of Christian philosophy about the time Augustine arrived there. By the time of the *Confessions*, Theodorus had plunged back into public life, and Augustine may have disapproved of his decision.

221. The same prestige of Paul the visionary would lead to the creation of a set of texts a century or more after Augustine attributed to Paul's acquaintance "Dionysius the Areopagite," texts of mystical vision and ascent drawing their authority from the presumed connection with Paul.

222. *Vera rel.* 3.3.

223. The Hebrew texts, moreover, had been translated twice, first into Greek, then Latin: Augustine did not much like Jerome's project of translating the Hebrew scriptures freshly into Latin.

224. M. Vessey, *"Opus Imperfectum*: Augustine and His Readers, 426–435 A.D.," *Vigiliae Christianae* 52(1998) 264–85.

225. *Conf.* 1.13.20.

226. *Epp.* 117–18.

227. The books we do hear of coming into Augustine's house were religious books, including apocrypha and other dubious texts—see, e.g., *Ep.* 237.2–9, on a "Priscillianist" hymn supposedly sung by Christ but nowhere to be found in scripture.

228. *En. Ps.* 36.1.2.

229. *Conf.* 9.4.8, 9.12.31.

230. *Ep.* 82.1.3.

231. Augustine gives his list most explicitly in *Doctr. chr.* 2.8.12–13. The common list had come into being gradually over the two centuries and more preceding Augustine, but by his time differences of opinion about what to include were mainly a thing of the past. The list importantly includes books of the Jewish/Greek Septuagint that some later Christians exclude.

232. *S. Dolbeau* 5.14.

233. Literally the Hebrew might be taken: "For the man in charge [of the music]. A poem of David."

234. *En. Ps.* 51.1.

235. *En. Ps.* 51.4.

236. Jerome, in his *Hebrew Names* (a collection of these etymologies) would have it that the name means "my father, king."

237. *En. Ps.* 51.5.

238. These words echo Psalms 118.85, but are not marked by Augustine in the delivery as biblical echoes. No modern edition fails to mark them, but we are thus misled. The audience for the spoken sermon will have heard them unmarked, some recognizing perhaps, others not, some just feeling a certain resonance. Augustine was a master of those pedal effects.

239. Psalms 33.9: this time the echo is marked, but not pedantically.

240. Matthew 21.19. This time the marking is even slighter: "*that* fig tree," like "*that* woman."

241. *En. Ps.* 51.18.

242. Christian liturgy was always hidden from prying and infidel eyes in antiquity. The fourth century still had the ambiguous class of unbaptized belongers (the catechumens) who were part of the community but expelled from the core of the liturgical service. When infant baptism became more or less universal during and after Augustine's time, the obsessive exclusion of the unbaptized began to fade from practice.

243. Henri De Lubac, *Medieval Exegesis* (Grand Rapids, Michigan, 1988ff, a translation of four volumes originally published as *Exégèse Médiévale* [Paris, 1959–64]), is a classic exposition of this style and its history by a partisan; David Dawson, *Allegorical Readers and Cultural Revision in Alexandria* (Berkeley, 1992), sets the early practice in Hellenistic Alexandria in a more complicated context.

244. E.g., *Doctr. chr.* 3.27.38.

245. Elizabeth Clark, *The Origenist Controversy* 238, cites the example of Vincentius Victor: although Augustine himself is agnostic with regard to the origin of the soul, and although the subject does not arise in the core creeds, when Vincentius holds in favor of a material origin and nature of the soul, Augustine is immovably hostile.

246. Possidius *Vita* 18.

247. *Ep.* 23a*.3. Ancient scribes had ways of measuring prose in artificially standard units that equated with lines of poetry for purposes of calculation, and we assume that payment was often related to quantity in this way.

248. C.E.V. Nixon and B. S. Rodgers, *In Praise of Later Roman Emperors* (Berkeley, 1994), translate and annotate these remarkable orations.

249. There's one exception, a talk he was invited to give to other clerics under his bishop's auspices, handed down to us as the pamphlet *Faith* (*De fide*).

250. The only warning of what lay in store is hidden in the pages of *Diverse Questions for Simplicianus*, where Augustine set out to reply to some queries

from his old Milan mentor and found himself suddenly at sea in Paul's ideas, grasping, as it happened, for the new ideas that would define his view of the human person and free will for decades to come. Few of his contemporaries would have seen that work, and it was really only in the last century that scholars recognized the importance of this more obscure work in giving Augustine the theories that made both the *Confessions* and his later theological polemics possible.

251. *Gn. c. man.* 1.1.

252. *Ep.* 2*.3.

253. *Ep.* 12*.1

254. Sisela Bok, *Lying* (New York, 1978), surveys the history of mendacity and emphasizes Augustine's extremism.

255. *Ep.* 11*.

256. Van Der Meer 317–46 describes what occurred; for the background, see T. Klauser, *A Short History of the Western Liturgy* (London, 1969). The assimilation of Christian liturgical practice to traditional rituals of sacrifice and secrecy is a striking departure from what a reader of the New Testament texts might predict.

257. *Ep.* 55.18.34: "The Donatists criticize us because we sing the divine songs of the prophets modestly in church, when they inflame their drunkenness, singing songs made up by human minds as if they were battle trumpets."

258. P. Jackson, "Eucharist," in Fitzgerald, ed., *Augustine Through the Ages* (Grand Rapids, Michigan, 1999) 330–34.

259. *F. et op.* 6.9.

260. *An. et. or.* 3.9.12.

261. *S.* 47.10.17 introduces us to a man who seems sincere, but *S. Morin.* 1.2–3 offers a more dubious character.

262. *Conf.* 8.2.4.

263. *Ep.* 227.

264. *En. Ps.* 125.14.

265. For the atmosphere, cf. Rebecca West, *Black Lamb and Grey Falcon* (New York, 1943) 765, which recalls a scene in an Orthodox cemetery in Macedonia in the 1930s: "I saw a peasant woman sitting on a grave under the trees with a dish of wheat and milk on her lap, the sunlight dappling the white kerchief on her head. Another peasant woman came by, who must have been from another village, for her dress was different. I think they were total strangers. They greeted each other, and the woman with the dish held it out to the newcomer and gave her a spoon, and she took some sups of it. To me it was an enchantment; for when St. Monica came to Milan over fifteen hundred years ago . . . [t]hat protocol-loving saint, Ambrose, had forbidden the practice because it was too like picknicking for his type of mind. To see these women gently munching to the glory of God was like finding that I could walk into the past as into another room."

266. *Mor.* 1.34.75.

267. *Ep.* 29.

268. Feast days still remained a time of some hullaballoo: Lancel 227 and 692; for events around the feast of Cyprian, see S. 311.5, En. Ps. 32.2.1, S. Dolbeau 2.5 (all from the early 400s).

269. See Frend, The Donatist Church 175, on Donatist carousing.

270. Rule of the Master 48.

271. Ench. 15.58, C. Prisc. et Orig. 11.14.

272. See first Ep. 9.3 (to Nebridius), then Div. daem. 5.9, and then Retr. 2.30.

273. Conf. 10.30.41.

274. Epp. 46–47 (Publicola's queries and Augustine's reply); see C. Lepelley, "Diabolisation du paganisme et ses conséquences psychologiques: les angoisses de Publicola, correspondant de saint Augustin," in L. Mary and M. Sot, Impies et païens entre Antiquité et Moyen Age (Paris, 2002) 81–96.

275. S. Dolbeau 7.

276. The phrase is common in Paul—e.g., Romans 2.11.

277. "Faithful" in Augustine (fidelis) is regular language for "baptized Christian"—accepting baptism is the exact and necessary and sufficient mark of fidelity for him.

278. Io. ep. tr. 9.5–8.

279. The Latin here is castus, which is the origin of English "chaste." Its "purity" is both moral and sexual and has at least some slight overtone of religious obligation, even in classical Latin.

280. Ep. 263.

281. S. 180.14.

282. S. 340.1.

283. I owe this argument to P. Rousseau, in Howard-Johnson and Hayward, The Cult of Saints in Late Antiquity and the Middle Ages (Oxford 1999) 57–58.

284. L. Stone, The Family, Sex and Marriage in England 1500–1800 (New York, 1979 [abridged edition]) 109–13.

285. Epp. 122, 124.

286. Ep. 268.

287. The right of sanctuary was often exercised: Ep. 113–15, 151.3.11, and 268; for the legal right, see CTh. 9.45.1–3 (all from the 390s).

288. En. ps. 147.8.

289. For these prayer practices, see Civ. 22.8.9 and 22.8.13, Io. ev. tr. 3.21, Cura mort. 5.7, and S. 311.13, 90.9.

290 En. ps. 72.34.

291. S. 302.19–21.

292. Ep. 36.

293. Ep. 98.3; there's a strikingly similar story 150 years earlier in Cyprian (De lapsis 25): the eucharistic wine simply refused to stay in the polluted stomach.

294. Retr. 2.11.

295. Haer. 87.

296. En. Ps. 48.s.1.13.

297. *S. Morin* 1.2–3.

298. *Ep.* 250.

299. *Ep.* 242.

300. *Mor.* 1.32.69.

301. *Mor.* 1.34.75 and *Ep.* 21.2.

302. *CTh.* 16.2.32.

303. See R. A. Markus, *Gregory the Great and His World* (Cambridge, 1997).

304. Augustine's *The Work of Monks* was written to make just this case in 401 at the behest of Bishop Aurelius of Carthage; cf. *Op. mon.* 22, 25, 26.

305. The sources are *Ep.* 213 and *S.* 356.

306. Possidius *Vita* 24 and *Ep.* 126.9 make his inattention clear, as do the remarks in *SS.* 355–56, recounted on the opening pages of this book.

307. *Ep.* 26*.1.13.

308. Lancel 503.

309. *Ep.* 84.

310. *Ep.* 208.

311. *Ep.* 65.

312. *Ep.* 78.3.

313. *Ep.* 35.

314. *Ep.* 64.3.

315. *Ep.* 211.

316. *Ep.* 211.14.

317. *Ep.* 211.6.

318. *Ep.* 211.9.

319. *S.* 355.2ff.

320. Juvenal *Sat.* 6.347–48.

321. *PL* 33.1095–98.

322. I deliberately chose not to follow Gibbon's path in imagining Islamic hegemony over western Europe, but his words (shocking in his time) are worth recalling for their insinuations: "A victorious line of march had been prolonged above a thousand miles from the rock of Gibraltar to the banks of the Loire; the repetition of an equal space would have carried the Saracens to the confines of Poland and the Highlands of Scotland; the Rhine is not more impassable than the Nile or Euphrates, and the Arabian fleet might have sailed without a naval combat into the mouth of the Thames. Perhaps the interpretation of the Koran would now be taught in the schools of Oxford, and her pulpits might demonstrate to a circumcised people the sanctity and truth of the revelation of Mahomet" (*Decline and Fall*, chapter 52 [ed. Womersley (London, 1994) 3.336]).

323. Harold Stone, *Saint Augustine's Bones: a Microhistory* (Amherst, 2002), tells the story of the pamphlet wars that erupted in early modern times in Pavia when the remains were "rediscovered."

324. Augustine on the passing of the age of miracles: *Vera rel.* 25.47; even earlier and more skeptical: *Ord.* 2.9.27; explaining away the skepticism of *Vera rel.* late in life: *Retr.* 1.13.7. The discovery of Protasius and Gervasius is recounted at *Conf.* 9.7.16 and recalled otherwise at *Civ.* 22.8.2 and *S.* 286.5.

325. The rich material does not yet have a full study; the best treatment is Josef Martin, "Die revelatio S. Stephani und Verwandtes," *Historisches Jahrbuch* 77(1957) 418–33.

326. These texts are collected in *PL* 41.

327. See e.g., *Ep.* 212, where Augustine commends a mother and daughter to their bishop as they return home with a little bit of Stephen for the bishop to venerate.

328. See S. Bradbury, *Severus of Minorca: Letter on the Conversion of the Jews* (Oxford, 1996), a good study of the surviving contemporary account.

329. *Ep.* 52.2.

330. H.-J. Diesner, *Kirche und Staat im spätrömischen Reich* (Berlin, 1964) 79; for more modern examples of similar flourishing of new cults around old sites in the U.S.-Mexican borderlands, see J. Griffiths, *Beliefs and Holy Places* (Tucson, 1992).

331. The bills were paid by Eraclius (*S.* 356.6), the deacon later to be Augustine's successor-designate.

332. *S.* 316.5.5.

333. *S.* 319.8.7.

334. *S.* 317.1.1.

335. *S.* 323.3.4.

336. *See Loc. hept.* 1.14 on Genesis 6.6.

337. *C. Iul.* 3.10.22.

338. *Conf.* 10.5.7.

339. See *Ep.* 93.7.22–23 for the alternate view. R. S. Eno, "The Work of Optatus," *The Thomist* 37(1973) 668–95, attributes the development of the familiar later idea of catholicity to Optatus, a mid-fourth-century member of Augustine's community.

340. *S.* 22.4.

341. *S.* 359.8.

342. *Ep.* 50.

343. *S.* 62.13. On the 399 outbreaks as reflected in Augustine's writings, see Lancel 231, and cf. *Ep.* 232.3.

344. *En. Ps.* 73.25, *S.* 361.6.

345. *Cat. rud.* 25.48, *SS.* 250.3, 252.4, *En. Ps.* 30.2.

346. *S. Denis* 17.7.

347. *En. Ps.* 88.s.2.14.

348. Lancel 452: admitted at *S.* 196.4, *S. Morin.* 1.4, *S. Frang.* 8.5, defended at *C. Faust.* 20.4.

349. *Io. ev. tr.* 7.6.

350. *Ep.* 90.

351. *Ep.* 91.

352. Either Nectarius or his father was consulted in 397 on the succession of bishops when Megalius of Calama died (*Ep.* 38).

353. Maud Gleason, "Festive Satire: Julian's Misopogon and the New Year at Antioch," *Journal of Roman Studies* 76(1986) 106–19, shows how closely

Christian celebration could resemble traditional rites, the priggish and self-consciously anti-Christian emperor Julian being turned into the butt of jokes with a very "pagan" cast—despite the fact that they came from professed Christians who hated the emperor's policy.

354. *Ep.* 103.

355. *Ep.* 104.

356. Sometime in these same years Augustine had gotten a similar letter written on behalf of the whole town council of Madauros, addressing him as "father" and wishing him "salvation in the lord," but defending the traditional rites. His response (*Ep.* 232) was no more tactful or, apparently, successful.

357. *Civ.* 18.46 and *C. Faust.* 16.21.

358. *Ep.* 8*.

359. *C. Faust.* 12.

360. A fresh telling of the story awaits P. Fredriksen's forthcoming *Augustine and the Jews*.

361. See my "The Demise of Paganism," *Traditio* 35(1979) 45–88. The nostalgia of Samuel Dill's *Roman Society in the Last Century of the Western Empire* (1899) survives in Pierre Chuvin's *Chronicle of the Last Pagans*, trans. B. A. Archer (Cambridge, Massachesetts, 1990). A fresh exploration and account of the sociology of religions in Augustine's time is needed.

362. *Conf.* 3.4.7.

363. Peter Brown, *Cult of the Saints* (Chicago, 1981) 17–22, dates this phenomenon precisely to the eighteenth century and puts it no further back than Hume, even while deploring it. Brown argues that the two-tier theory is a *modern* interpretative escape, to help avoid reconciling the conflict of styles.

364. In other times, this syncretism would have been spoken of as bridging Christianity and Hellenism, but to make that connection requires us to think that Christianity had a fundamental existence apart from the culture in which it lived and that then a negotiation of sorts occurred. Better to see that the "Christianity" we receive is a representation of traditions and practices of various kinds and that the dividing line is not so much in matters of intellect and text as in matters of class and practice.

365. Donatism, had it prevailed and become the Christianity of the middle ages, would have been far more like Islam.

366. See E. Pagels, *Beyond Belief* (New York, 2003), for an evocation of the Christianities these texts make possible and a discussion of the current state of scholarship.

367. W. Bauer, *Orthodoxy and Heresy in Earliest Christianity* (orig. ed. 1934; trans., Philadelphia, 1971), was the watershed study that changed the way we have to think about the multitude of earliest Christianities.

368. H. A. Drake, *Constantine and the Bishops: The Politics of Intolerance* (Baltimore, 2000).

369. On these survivals, see R. MacMullen, *Christianity and Paganism in the Fourth to Eighth Centuries* (New Haven, 1997).

370. Seth Schwartz, *Imperialism and Jewish Society, 200 B.C.E. to 640 C.E.*

(Princeton, 2001), in a way reviving ideas advanced by J. Parkes, *The Conflict of Church and Synagogue* (London, 1934). P. Fredriksen, "What 'Parting of the Ways'? Jews and Gentiles in the Ancient Mediterranean City," in *The Ways That Never Parted: Jews and Christians in Late Antiquity and the Early Middle Ages*, ed. A. H. Becker, and A. Yoshiko Reed (Tübingen 2003) 1–28, pushes further beyond conventional ideas.

371. This theme has been explored in two beautifully learned and eloquent books by Robert Markus: *Saeculum: History and Society in the Theology of Saint Augustine* (Cambridge, 1969) and *The End of Ancient Christianity* (Cambridge, 1990).

372. The present archbishop of Canterbury, for example, has explored this process in the case of Arius: R. Williams, *Arius: Heresy and Tradition* (London, 1987). On the great enemy of "Arianism," see T. D. Barnes, *Athanasius and Constantius* (Cambridge, Massachusetts, 1993).

373. Histories of this period are generally written retrospectively. Though the councils of Nicea (325) and Constantinople (381) ruled in one (eventually prevalent) direction, majority opinion between and even at those dates was subtly different, though rarely "Arian" in the way their rivals claimed.

374. Everyone agreed that Jesus was the meeting place of divinity and humanity. Did this make him two things in one body or was he somehow a unique mixture of elements? Monophysites held for the mixture, Nestorians for rigid separation. The orthodox party (that is, the victors, defined as such by their acceptance of Chalcedon's decrees) took a middle ground and believed in one "person" with two "natures."

375. Brown, *Power and Persuasion in Late Antiquity*.

376. J. Pelikan and V. Hotchkiss, *Creeds and Confessions of the Faith in the Christian Tradition* (New Haven, 2003).

377. Augustine tells the story in his *Doctr. chr.* 2.15.22.

378. The real story of the Greek translation of the Jewish writings and its influence is more complicated: see M. Hengel, *The Septuagint as Christian Scripture* (Edinburgh, 2002).

379. The Donatists didn't suffer this disadvantage, and other minority Christian sects have found it one of the pleasures of a minority position to be hounded—occasionally—to death. It can be argued that more Christians were persecuted *after* the conversion of Constantine than before.

380. *Quant. an.* 80.

381. G. Bonner, "*Baptismus parvulorum*," *Aug.-Lex.* 1.592–602; the practice was seen in Africa in the time of Cyprian, a century before Augustine was born.

382. There is unsuspected irony, then, in Jerome's fulsome praise to Augustine (Aug. *Ep.* 195 = *Ep. Jer.* 56.2); "catholici te conditorem antiquae rursus fidei venerantur atque suscipiunt" ("the world accepts and venerates you as the one who refounded the ancient faith").

383. Cf., among many Augustinian passages expressing the preference sketched here, *Ep.* 120.1.4, where the humble can achieve the heights of con-

templation but the educated are more likely to be scandalized by Christ cruci-fied and so fall away in the end. Augustine always believes this, but the work-ing out of his pastoral practice over the years would give it increasingly substantial meaning.

384. About the best he can do is *Doctr. chr.* 2.20.31 (best if delivered with the rhythms of Groucho Marx): "So it's a fine saying they report of Cato, who was asked one day whether it was a *monstrum* [an omen or portent] that his slip-pers were being gnawed on by the mice. Cato said that wasn't a *monstrum*, but it really would be a *monstrum* if the mice were being gnawed on by the slippers."

385. C.L.R. James in *Beyond a Boundary* recounts how Thackeray's *Vanity Fair* was that kind of scripture to him as a boy growing up in the West Indies, measuring the ways in which he was and was not "English."

386. Augustine himself had resisted Christian scripture at first on just these grounds: *Conf.* 3.5.9.

387. Literally this phrase should suggest an abstract entity characterized by order and intelligibility (*ratio*) embedded in created things in the manner of a seed (*semen*): "seedly patterns/models." Some modern readers have tried to connect this Augustinian notion to the arguments of evolutionary biologists.

388. J. J. Pelikan, *The Emergence of the Christian Tradition 100–600* (Chicago, 1971) 318–31 treats the Council of Orange as a victory for Augus-tinianism, but the cost is made clear as well.

389. Even more remarkably, this Christianity was willing to make the same claim for the pre-Christian stories of the Jews, whose literal truth or falsehood has been an immense stumbling block for many over the centuries. That choice to adopt and privilege the Jewish stories was a conscious one, fought out in con-troversy with many different communites of Christians, starting at least as early as those led by Marcion, within three generations of Jesus's lifetime.

390. For the story of Donatism, see W.H.C. Frend, *The Donatist Church* (Oxford, 1951; later editions reprint the original text with addenda and updated bibliography). Frend, "Donatus paene totam Africam cepit," *Journal of Ecclesi-astical History* 48(1997) 611–27, and R. A. Markus, "Africa and the *orbis ter-rarum*: the theological problem," in Fux/Roessli/Wermelinger, eds., *Augustinus Afer* (Fribourg, 2003) 321–27, have made explicit some of what was only im-plicit in their work earlier, especially the importance of remembering how differently people in late antiquity could view the competing brands of Chris-tianity they knew and how strong a claim Donatism had to being the normal form of Christianity in Africa.

391. *Mend.* 13.23.

392. Frend, *The Donatist Church*.

393. *Epp.* 56–57.

394. *Ep.* 139.

395. *Ep.* 58.

396. This is how I read *Ep.* 112 (to Donatus) and *Ep.* 89 (to Festus).

397. *Ep.* 66, see *C. litt. Petil.* 2.83.184.

398. *Ep.* 52.

399. *Mor.* 1.1.1, 1.34.75; cf. from the same period, *Ep.* 21.2.

400. So in *Ep.* 10.2 he speaks favorably for himself and Nebridius of "becoming gods [godlike] in retirement" by contrast to the busy distraction of clergy.

401. Julian has not yet found a suitably skeptical biographer. The best scholarly study is G. Bowersock, *Julian the Apostate* (Cambridge, Massachusetts, 1978), but Gore Vidal's novel *Julian* (Boston, 1964) is a very responsible, if partisan, attempt to do justice to the facts of his career.

402. *C. litt. Pet.* 2.83.184.

403. The word denotes a woman uprooted from her family and social situation to a committed life of celibate religious observance. "Nun" is the closest English equivalent.

404. *Ep.* 35.4.

405. *Ep.* 44.5.12.

406. *Ep.* 93.5.17. On Augustine's attitudes, see P. Brown, "Saint Augustine's Attitude to Religious Coercion," *Journal of Roman Studies* 54(1964) 107–16; R. A. Markus, *Saeculum* 133–53.

407. *Ep.* 185.8.33.

408. *Epp.* 33, 34, 35.

409. *Ep.* 108.5.14.

410. *Ep.* 108.6.18.

411. *En. Ps.* 54.20.

412. *S.* 46.15.

413. *Ep.* 185.1.1.

414. *Ep.* 44.5.6.

415. *Ep.* 93.5.17.

416. *Ep.* 185.9.35, *Io. ev. tr.* 6.25, where Augustine is very disingenuous in claiming to have no interest in property. He makes the argument there that since property was given to the *church* (when it was given to a Donatist bishop), it is appropriate for the *true* church to take it over.

417. *Ep.* 20.3 (to a layman, Antoninus): probably the first mention of Donatism in Augustine's surviving works.

418. *Ep.* 23.

419. That particular Donatist, Maximinus of Siniti, may be identical with a Maximinus who turns up in *Ep.* 105.4 around the year 407 or later, converted to Caecilianism.

420. *Ep.* 33.2.

421. *C. litt. Pet.* 2.38.90.

422. *En. Ps.* 21.s.2.31.

423. *Epp.* 43–44.

424. *Ep.* 53.

425. Brown 405 is keen-eyed on this difference between the law of 405 and the later, more successfully coercive, decision of 411. If any one of these failed

attempts at suppression had been the last, we would now inherit a history of heroic persistence and victory over cruel government persecutors.

426. *Ep.* 185.27 quoted; cf. *C. Cresc.* 3.43.47.

427. One modern reader suggests this was a dungheap, but perhaps he was too mindful of the similar landing place for persecuted officials in the "defenestration of Prague" of 1618.

428. *Ep.* 105.2.3–4.

429. Frend 269–74.

430. Augustine and Possidius mention the event repeatedly: *S. Guelf.* 28.7–8, *Ench.* 17, Possidius *Vita* 12.2; recently discovered: *S. Dolbeau* 26.45. Usually dated to about 410, with the new Dolbeau sermon it may more likely be placed in 403 (see Lancel 407).

431. *Coll. Carth.* 1.142.

432. *S.* 359.

433. *Ep.* 173.1 4.

434. *S. Guelf.* 28.

435. *Ep.* 185.3.12.

436. Ibid.

437. Brown 420, Frend 296; *Ep.* 204 to Dulcitius.

438. *Ep.* 204.5–6, instancing 2 Maccabees 14.37–46.

439. Augustine makes a point of bringing up the same biblical story to refute in *C. Gaud.* Religious suicide had its practitioners and apologists then as now, e.g., religious women who killed themselves to avoid rape at the sack of Rome and were praised for it: *Civ.* 1.16–23.

440. Unpublished work on Possidius by E. Hermanowicz wil elucidate the events of this year in remarkable ways; I am grateful to the author for allowing me an advance view.

441. E. Diehl, *Inscriptiones Latinae Christianae Veteres* (Berlin, 1925) 1.2052, from Ad Miliaria in western Mauretania.

442. German "Arianism" is deceptive. The earliest German converts to Christianity were made by a bishop of their own nationality named Ulfilas, who translated scripture into Gothic and traveled among peoples in the Balkans in the mid-300s, representing the brand of Christianity dominant in Constantinople at that time. By the time those doctrines were rejected and labeled as "Arian," Ulfilas's conversion efforts had borne great fruit. For hundreds of years, this would make Germanic-speaking newcomers easy to reject as heretics.

443. *Ep.* 151.

444. McLynn, *Ambrose of Milan* 315–30.

445. Brown 337 observes the shift to flattering generals.

446. *Ep.* 220.

447. *Ep.* 230.

448. *Ep.* 231.6.

449. *Ep.* 231.7.

450. Already suggested by Brown 423.

451. *Ep. Jer.* 126.2.2.

452. *Ep.* 111.1–7.

453. Ammianus Marcellinus 14.6.19.

454. *Civ.* 1.32.

455. *Ep. Jer.* 50 gives a fleeting vignette of a rival from Jerome's time in Rome whom some scholars identify as Pelagius.

456. The word is that of Robert Markus, *Conversion and Disenchantment.*

457. They did correspond, and Augustine later had to defend with some embarrassment just how polite he had been. See Aug. *Ep.* 146 (to be compared now with *S.* 348a, expanded by Dolbeau's discoveries), explained at *Gest. Pel.* 26.51.

458. Melanie is interesting for far more than her encounter with Augustine. Her story was told in a life whose Greek version survives (Gerontius, *Vita Melaniae Iunioris*, ed. D. Gorce [Paris, 1972]; Eng. trans. by E. Clark [Lewiston, Maine, 1985]).

459. Such huge sell-offs were disruptive at many levels. Even slaves feared what would happen to them and regarded their pious masters as self-indulgent profligates: see A. Giardina, "Carità eversiva: Le donazioni di Melanie La Giovane e gli equilibri della società tardoromana," *Studi storici* 29(1988) 127–42.

460. *Vita Melan. iun.* 21.

461. *Ep.* 126. Augustine also had to apologize to Alypius for appearing to be poaching on a "development prospect" that Alypius had found for himself.

462. Brown 300.

463. For the events of these three days and what led up to them, we have the stenographic transcript, approved by the parties, best available with Latin text and French translation in S. Lancel, ed., *Actes de la Conférence de Carthage en 411* (Paris, 1972–91).

464. The precise claim of the Caecilianists (*Coll. Carth.* 1.18) is that they were in the majority except in *Numidia consularis*—the heartland of the prosperous olive-growing high country. The implicit acknowledgment of their focus of weakness is important and gives credibility to the overall claim.

465. On these machinations, see Brent Shaw, "African Christianity: Disputes, Definitions, and 'Donatists,' " in M. R. Greenshields and T. A. Robinson, eds., *Orthodoxy and Heresy in Religious Movements* (Lewiston, Maine, 1992) 4–34; reprinted in Shaw, *Rulers, Nomads, and Christians in Roman North Africa* (London, 1995). This article fundamentally changes the terms in which we can speak of fourth-century Christianity in Africa and underlies my approach to Donatism and Caecilianism.

466. *Ep.* 87.

467. The facts are likely to be more complicated. "Bishop" was the title of the senior cleric of a community, and in many places in Africa, quite small communities—sometimes amounting to just the residents of a great man's estate—

would have bishops. The Caecilianists had certainly been seeking to inflate their numbers, but they likely did have communities to support them.

468. Milevis was a substantial see, where Augustine's old friend Severus was bishop against the Adeodatus quoted here. The quarrel is over a village in the neighborhood where Severian has made himself secure.

469. *Coll. Carth.* 1.133–34.

470. *Coll. Carth.* 1.181.

471. *Coll. Carth.* 3.75.

472. *Coll. Carth.* 3.258.

473. *Coll. Carth.* 3.99.

474. *Coll. Carth.* 3.258.

475. *Coll. Carth.* 3.279 the first time, 3.420 the second.

476. The surviving documents have been compiled, translated, and annoted in J.-L. Maier, *Le dossier du Donatisme* (Berlin, 1987–89).

477. *Ad Don. p. coll.* 35.58.

478. S. Lancel, "Le sort des évêques et des communautés donatistes après la Conférence de Cathage en 411," *Internationales Symposion 1987*, 149–67; see also Frend 299, reporting half a century ago that there was still no convincing evidence that any Donatist church outside a city in Africa had ever been transformed into a catholic one.

479. See *Death Comes for the Archbishop* (book 5, chapter 1; p. 172 of the Library of America edition), which tells of a corrupt priest at Taos, New Mexico, and the episcopal deliberations on how to deal with him.

480. *Ep.* 209.2.

481. We know the story from *Ep.* 209, *Ep.* 20*, and *S. Guelf.* 32 (esp. 32.9), preached at Antoninus's ordination.

482. *Ep.* 20*.15.

483. *Epp.* 20.1, 20.33.

484. He mentions the atrocity at *Epp.* 133.1, 134.2, and 139.1.

485. Volusianus's father, Ceionius Rufius Albinus, is generally said to have been a "pagan," but in fact there is no evidence for his religious affinities; *his* father, Volusianus's grandfather, had been involved in traditional religious practices.

486. Volusianus received an imperial rescript in 418 and published his own edict in compliance, banning Pelagius's putative chief disciple, Caelestius, from the city and vicinity of Rome (printed in the so-called *Collectio Quesneliana* at *PL* 56.500); see Wermelinger 198, 204–6.

487. *Ep.* 132.

488. Robert Wilken, *The Christians as the Romans Saw Them* (New Haven, 2003; 2nd ed.), explores the Greek tradition. Porphyry's book was reputedly the best, but it survives only in fragments.

489. There are other connections back to Augustine's own case, not least that he mentions Volusianus's predecessor as proconsul, the physician Vindicianus, who had succeeded in turning Augustine away from giving credence to astrologers in an episode retold in *Conf.* 4.

490. *Ep.* 154.2. Possidius in his biography (*Vita* 20) quotes this passage the way publishers snatch blurbs from positive reviews from the right sort of critic.

491. *Civ.* 22.28 suggests that Augustine consciously meant to reply to both Plato and Cicero. The best study of *City of God* is G.J.P. O'Daly, *Augustine's "City of God": A Reader's Guide* (Oxford, 1999).

492. *Civ.* 4.4; "Remota itaque justitia, quid sunt regna, nisi magna latrocinia?"

493. Orosius is still studied more for his words than his deeds, an unfortunate limitation in my opinion. The standard study is B. Lacroix, *Orose et ses idées* (Montreal, 1965).

494. *Civ.* 5.24–26.

495. R. A. Markus *Saeculum*, is the best study of Augustine on history and society.

496. Ephesians 5.27.

497. Herodotus, *Histories* 1.32.

498. R. A. Markus in A. Sommerstein, *Religion and Superstition in Latin Literature* (Bari, 1996) 79; "there never was a 'paganism' until the generation of Christians contemporary with Augustine created one."

499. That controversy in many ways created the community—importantly including Latins in a dispute about Greek Christianity—that would reform in slightly altered way to fight the "Pelagian" battles, and Jerome was central both times. Both controversies centered on issues of the soul's origin and the will's freedom, and both were more than tangentially concerned with the very practical question (to which I return in the following chapter) of determining the nature of ascetic practice and theory that would prevail in the Latin church.

500. *Ep.* 22*.5–11.

501. The dismissive gesture evokes one of Augustine's most famous maxims: "Dilige et quodvis fac" (*Io. ep. tr.* 7.8.)—"Love and do whatever you like." The maxim implies that authentic love will inevitably beget right action, but a high episcopal disdain is unmistakable in both.

502. In other words: the bishop who was imposed on the Donatists of Cherchell and Augustine are of one accord in both wooing and warning Emeritus at this point. The risk for Deuterius was real: if Emeritus reconciled, then he would presumably become the senior bishop of Cherchell and his junior colleague, Deuterius, would have to share power.

503. *Caterva* is the Latin word. The phenomenon is something of a puzzle, but something similar survives in the running of the bulls at Pamplona, or the running of the football thugs in Britain—violent outbursts confined by custom to a ritual function and mostly forgotten the morning after.

504. The three goals of an orator, Augustine taught in *Christian Doctrine* 4, were to inform (with the humble style), to delight (with the middle style), and to persuade (with the grand style).

505. *Doctr. chr.* 4.24.53.

506. *Civ.* 19.7.

507. *Qu. hept.* 1.167.

508. Augustine and "just war": see R. A. Markus, "Saint Augustine's Views on the 'Just War,' " in W. J. Shells, ed., *The Church and War* (Oxford, 1983) 1–13, and on the growth of the theme, F. Russell, *The Just War in the Middle Ages* (Cambridge, 1975).

509. Contrast Aristotle, "All men by nature desire to know" (*Metaphysics* 1.1). For Augustine, that would be "curiosity," hence problematic.

510. One of Augustine's first surviving works in his *Order (De ordine)*. He finds order in stasis, making it in the world of matter at best an epiphenomenon.

511. *Civ.* 19.12–13.

512. Orosius, *Apologeticum* 3; see Wermelinger, 57–70, 87–89.

513. *S. Dolbeau* 30.5–7.

514. *Conf.* 10.30.40ff.

515. *Persev.* 20.53. The official Roman church would later agree with Pelagius against Augustine on just this text: see L. Kolakowski, *God Owes Us Nothing* (Chicago, 1995) 3–110. The story of official Latin Christianity's long and gradual drawing back from assent to the extremes of Augustine's position, while always asserting his authority, has yet to be written in any detail. Arguably it began as soon as he died and continues to this day.

516. The best narrative of Augustine's history with Pelagius is Wermelinger.

517. Lancel 465 shrewdly suggests that Marcellinus was likely in some sympathy with Pelagius, who was just the sort of chaplain and role model the pious layman liked.

518. Pelagius's best and canniest statement, dating from 417, is his *Libellus fidei* (PL 48.488–91).

519. Y.-M. Duval, "Pélage en son temps," *Studia Patristica* 38(2001) 95–118.

520. *Ep.* 168.

521. *Ep.* 186. Paulinus never fell out with *any* of his friends, even though many of them hated each other.

522. *Ep.* 217. The list of teachings Augustine wanted Vitalis to subscribe to is a usefully concise statement of what really mattered to him at this point: infants have no merits of their own but inherit the "contagion of primordial death" and are justly damned unless reborn through grace in Christ. God's grace is not given according to merits, for it goes to the unworthy as well as to the virtuous, given for single acts and for whole lifetimes of persistence, without regard to merit. But the one who benefits from grace and believes in god is doing so entirely of his own free will. Prayer for unbelievers is virtuous, and rejoicing and thanksgiving when they convert is equally praiseworthy. In giving his grace, the divine giver is always acting justly, and he is equally just when he withholds the grace from others. Infant baptism is effective and necessary: unbaptized babies go to hell. (Even in Augustine's time, this was the most scan-

dalous thing he said in his critics' eyes, and the medieval doctrine of limbo, un-satisfactory on all counts, is the face-saving compromise that resulted.)

523. Much theological discussion has focused on a sentence in Augustine's *S*. 131 of September 417, in which he says, "Rome has spoken: the matter is set-tled." The context is often neglected by those who take it as a support for pa-pal authority, for it came at a moment when Zosimus, the new bishop of Rome, was refusing to support what his predecessor had decided. The true meaning of the sentence is something like "Rome has *already* decided in the person of In-nocentius, so the matter is settled and no other *Roman* decision is appropriate" (Lössl 264).

524. Augustine quotes this maxim at *Civ*. 10.29 and 12.26, attributing it to a now-lost work of Porphyry and expressing reservations about the conclusions the Platonists draw. Compare the first words of Porphyry's *Life of Plotinus*: "Plotinus, the philosopher born among us, was like a man ashamed of being in a body."

525. Peter Brown, *Body and Society*, is indebted to conversations with Michel Foucault, whose idiosyncratic *History of Sexuality* has been published only up to the threshhold of his discussion of late antiquity; more was written but may never be published.

526. A. Rousselle, *Porneia* (Oxford, 1988) 24–46, is pointed and effective on the way that dependence on texts means we know very little about women's bodies and their care in antiquity, because most such lore was orally transmit-ted among women; what male doctors in antiquity say is often vitiated by the writer never having actually examined a female body medically.

527. *S*. 224.3.3.

528. S. Treggiari, *Roman Marriage* (1991), the standard study, does not broach the subject.

529. *Conf.* 9.9.19 has a highly ambiguous passage that most take to refer to wife-beating (of Monnica by Patricius), but that is at least as likely to be a neg-ative portrait of ordinary marital sexuality.

530. The classic statement of that history is D. J. Chitty, *The Desert a City: An Introduction to the Study of Egyptian and Palestinian Monasticism under the Christian Empire* (Oxford, 1966); Susanna Elm's *Virgins of God* (Berkeley, 1994) is a refreshing counterbalance and suggests how open all the main historical questions about this subject are. See also D. Brakke, *Athanasius and the Politics of Asceticism* (Oxford, 1995).

531. John Wilkinson, *Egeria's Travels* (London, 1971), translates and docu-ments this vivid account.

532. *Conf.* 8.6.14–15, 8.12.29.

533. See K. Cooper, "Insinuations of Womanly Influence: An Aspect of the Christianization of the Roman Aristocracy," *Journal of Roman Studies* 82 (1992) 150–64, on ancient and modern ideas about the role of women in the "Chris-tianization" of the Roman aristocracy.

534. If Professor Henry Chadwick's speculation is correct, history has its comic retribution here, for Priscillian's grave may have been the one misread in

later centuries as that of the apostle James and forming the heart of the shrine of Santiago de Compostela (Chadwick, *Priscillian of Avila* [Oxford, 1976] 233).

535. See page 144 on the letter of the Balearic idiot Consentius (published as Aug. *Ep.* 11*), taking the side of the easily beguiled.

536. Trout, *Paulinus of Nola,* tells his story.

537. Trout 75 makes this shrewd surmise.

538. See Trout 133: "Paulinus recognized and honored the complex practical and emotional obstacles facing men and women of elite background." An unkinder biographer would say he toadied to his rich parishioners. His church building demonstrated his good citizenship and incidentally filled the need for a basilica suitable for dignified congregants to be seen in.

539. *New York Times,* 17 July 2003, "The Patron Saint of Sore Shoulders," recounts the hundredth year of annual celebration and street fair that joins Paulinus with Our Lady of Mt. Carmel. The website www.olmcfeast.com proclaims the revels.

540. *Ep. Jer.* 48.20; "I praise virginity to the skies, not because I have it, but because I admire it all the more for not having it."

541. K. Cooper, *The Virgin and the Bride* (Cambridge, Massachusetts, 1996) 92–115.

542. Consider Augustine's *Ep. 13*.1* for a story of a clergyman's embarrassment. What was he to do in his innocence when a woman came to where he was sleeping and lay down beside him to tell him her troubles? Embarrass her by sending her away, or hope (in vain, as it happened) that the awkward-appearing episode would escape notice?

543. In the course of his work, Augustine had seen it all: one of his letters is addressed to a deacon who was sorry he had vowed his daughter to virginity: *Ep. 3*.*

544. *C. ep. Pel.* 3.5.14.

545. *Civ.* 14.26.

546. Milton's imagination was not so chaste: *Paradise Lost* 4.740ff.

547. Julian was also the sort of prosperous gentleman bishop to sell off farm property he owned in order to buy food to relieve a famine: Gennadius *Vir. ill.* 45.

548. C. Stewart, *Cassian the Monk* (Oxford, 1998).

549. *Epp.* 214–16 give the material for this story.

550. The Augustinian "rule," cobbled together from letters of guidance he wrote, is relatively unspecific and suits well to communities living without the strict structure, enclosure, and austerity of Benedict's house. It is thus the most popular rule among Roman church orders to this day, but that popularity is a late-come thing. See G. Lawless, *Augustine of Hippo and His Monastic Rule* (Oxford, 1987).

551. *Conf.* 3.1.1: "Awash in conceit, I postured to be polished and sophisticated." He doesn't see, when writing the *Confessions,* that *this* set of traits did not disappear in Milan. They vanished, if they ever did, in Hippo.

552. Orosius *Apologeticum* 26.

553. Romans 7.22–23.

554. M.-F. Berrouard, *Recherches augustiniennes* 16(1981) 101–96: Augustine was probably wrong in his later view. J. Gager, *Reinventing Paul* (Oxford, 2000), explores the contentious readings of Paul that started with the Book of Acts, preceded and followed Augustine, and continue to the present day.

555. T. De Bruyn, *Pelagius's Commentary on St Paul's Epistle to the Romans* (Oxford, 1993) 103–5, esp. 105; "This shows that he is speaking in the person of someone else, not in his own person."

556. Esp. Romans 5.12, where Augustine reads an ambiguous Latin translation in a way that turns the phrase "because all have sinned" (the reading of most modern translations) into "[Adam] in whom all have sinned."

557. Augustine's contemporary, John Chrysostom of Antioch, later bishop of Constantinople, was an eloquent and undismayed Pauline partisan. His very un-Augustinian approach (and a sense of the possibilities that Latin Christianity has missed) can be seen in the elegant study of Margaret M. Mitchell, *The Heavenly Trumpet: John Chrysostom and the Art of Pauline Interpretation* (Tübingen, 2000; Louisville and London, 2002), esp. 411–23, where Augustine and Chrysostom are compared.

558. *Gest. Pel.* 3.10, quoting Pelagius: "and if anybody believes differently, he's an Origenist."

559. Christians drew near to classical Epicureans in this regard. Both expressed a disdain for the high politics of the great world, and both emphasized the individual: the Epicureans set him in a world of divine absence, the Christians in a world of presence. The link was not ignored, e.g., by Tertullian in *De pallio* 5.4, which quotes as an old saw, "No man is born for another who is destined to die for himself" and acknowledges its force.

560. On Gregory, see C. Straw, *Gregory the Great* (Berkeley, 1988), and R. A. Markus, *Gregory the Great and His World* (Cambridge, 1997).

561. On this tribe and its predilections, see M. Salzman, *The Making of a Christian Aristocracy* (Cambridge, Massachusetts, 2002).

562. *Ep.* 101.4–5.

563. One can compare, from just a few years before, the learned and witty *epithalamium* of Ausonius in honor of a secular wedding—more frankly sexual, but every bit as elegant and tasteful.

564. See Brown 383 ("Julian devoted himself to ridiculing the ideas of his elders") and G. Bonner, *Saint Augustine: Life and Controversies* (London, 1963) 347 ("an arrogance of a most unattractive nature").

565. After long playing second banana in the last act of stories about Augustine, Julian has finally gotten his own story told by a clear-eyed critic: Lössl. His view, "History has justified Julian" (xiii), has much to be said for it, for the way later generations abandoned all the harshest positions Augustine fought so hard for.

566. *C. Iul. imp.* 4.46; cf. *C. Iul. imp.* 2.15, quoting Julian, who accuses Augustine of promoting immorality: "There's one thing we can't deny: the crowds

really love it when you blame the defects of character on the filth of nature. By defaming the seed we spring from, you justify the most heedless behavior. The result is that no one needs try to change."

567. *C. Iul. imp.* 5.26: Julian had visited Carthage and there encountered Honoratus, who may be the ex-Manichee dedicatee of *Util. cred.*; Lancel 579 dates that visit to 410–11 and matches it with *Ep.* 140.83 to Honoratus (412) warning him against Pelagians living chaste lives who are nevertheless fundamentally wrong about key issues—and of course an ex-Manichee is going to put a high value on continence. It's not at all clear, however, that Julian would have been marked as "Pelagian" at so early a date.

568. Julian as reader of *Conf.: C. Iul. imp.* 1.25, 2.147.

569. One cannot help but suspect that the loyalty of Augustine and his faction to Ravenna's chosen generals, displayed in the battles with the Donatists, earned him the favor of support against Pelagius.

570. See the narrative in Brown 361 70.

571. The steep indignation of Julian and Augustine's delight in his discomfiture can veil the way in which the decrees of Rome were a defeat for Augustine. Rome attacked men, not ideas—Pelagius and Caelestius, not the "Pelagianism" Augustine reviled. Augustine's Italian spin doctor Marius Mercator (*Commentarius de nomine Caelestii* 36) claims that Julian had been ordained by Innocentius and so went along with the condemnation as long as his patron was alive. See Lössl 259 60.

572. *Ep.* 224.2 reveals Augustine working day and night in his last years, by day attacking Julian, by night working on the catalogue of *Retr.*

573. Lössl, esp. 250–329, on the chronology

574. *Libellus fidei* 3.19 (PL 48.523: see E. Clark, *The Origenist Controversy* 220 [n220]).

575. On this theme: P. Fredriksen, "Beyond the Body/Soul Dichotomy: Augustine on Paul Against the Manichees and Pelagians," *Recherches augustiniennes* 23(1988) 87–114.

576. F. Gori, *Il Praedestinatus di Arnobio il giovane* (Rome, 1999).

577. See www.bardstown.com/~brchrys/Trinity.html (recorded on 3 June 2002).

578. See H.-I. Marrou in his *Christiana tempora* (Rome, 1978) 401–413. For modern misreadings, try Sting's "Saint Augustine in Hell," or Bob Dylan's "I Dreamed I Saw Saint Augustine."

579. Bert States, *The Shape of Paradox* (Berkeley, 1978), 1–4.

580. C. Kirwan, *Augustine* (London, 1989), and J. Rist, *Augustine: Ancient Thought Baptized* (New York, 1994), are the best surveys reflecting recent work; in briefer compass, Henry Chadwick, *Augustine* (Oxford, 1986), is very effective.

581. E. TeSelle, *Augustine the Theologian* (New York, 1970).

582. *Sol.* 1.2.7.

583. *Conf.* 1.4.4.

584. On the tradition of "negative theology," see now D. Carabine, *The Unknown God: Negative Theology in the Platonic Tradition (Plato to Eriugena)* (Louvain, 1995).

585. *Conf.* 3.7.12.

586. *Conf.* 6.4.6.

587. Symmachus *Rel.* 3.10; "uno itinere non potest perveniri ad tam grande secretum."

588. See *Sol.* 1.13.23; "sed non ad eam [sapientiam] una via pervenitur," regretted at *Retr.* 1.4.3, though *Vera rel.* 28.51 echoes the same phrase of Symmachus.

589. *Quant. an. 80.*

590. *Conf.* 1.7.11.

591. R. J. O'Connell, *The Origin of the Soul in St. Augustine's Later Works* (New York, 1987). Augustine was not the first Christian to frame his thoughts gingerly in Platonic terms. On Origen's similar tendencies (but firmly preferring Platonic to traducian), see Henry Chadwick, *Early Christian Thought and the Classical Tradition* (New York, 1966) 111–16.

592. See *Ep.* 190.4.15 on traducian corporeality. Such ideas were all around him: his own friend Evodius, bishop of Uzalis, tended that way (*Epp.* 157, 161, 163) and the fine lady Italica (*Ep.* 92) had been hearing such ideas as well. Evodius had a point: how the inner man could be so affected by the outer without material contact is hard to imagine, and he represented vividly the struggles of the inner (*Ep.* 158.4): "As long as we are in a body, we have this inner sense on constant watch, as alert as we can be. It is ever more eager and vigilant insofar as we struggle to make it so, but it still seems like the soul is dragged back by the body. Who can say all the ways in which the body imposes itself on the mind? In all this crowd of troubling ideas coming from the impressions, the temptations, and the needs of the body, the mind hangs on to its strength, resisting, winning out—and yet sometimes being beaten."

593. *Ep.* 166.8.26.

594. Jerome saw five: see his letter (*Ep. Jer.* 126) to Augustine's friend Marcellinus, sharing Augustine's dislike for all the possibilities.

595. The Jerome-Augustine dialogue is printed at *PL* 30.261C–271C: see E. Clark, *The Origenist Controversy* (Princeton, 1992) 243.

596. Augustine still has his defenders: E. Stump makes the attempt in "Augustine on Free Will" in Stump and Kretzmann, eds., *The Cambridge Companion to Augustine* (Cambridge, 2001) 124–47.

597. S. J. Gould, *Ontogeny and Phylogeny* (Cambridge, Massachusetts, 1977).

598. Augustine never took the seven days of creation as literally as a modern fundamentalist would, for he acknowledged the metaphorical language underlying the Genesis text.

599. In a human life, this *adolescentia* runs from about age fifteen to about age thirty.

600. See, e.g., H. Wolfram, *The Roman Empire and Its Germanic Peoples* (Berkeley, 1997).

601. "Hoc interim saeculum" (*Civ.* 11.1.1).

602. In "The Authority of Augustine," *Augustinian Studies* 22(1991) 7–35, I sketch the issues, but a serious study remains to be written.

603. Porphyry, *Life of Plotinus* 1 (trans., Armstrong); "Why really, is it not enough to have to carry the image in which nature has encased us, without your requesting me to agree to leave behind me a longer-lasting image of the image, as if it were something genuinely worth looking at?"

604. E.g., *ibid.* 1.2.7: "For it is to [the gods], not to good men, that we are to be made like. Likeness to good men is the likeness of two pictures of the same subject to each other; but likeness to the gods is likeness to the model, a being of a different kind to ourselves."

605. E. Rebillard, "A New Style of Argument in Christian Polemic: Augustine and the Use of Patristic Citations," *Journal of Early Christian Studies* 8(2000) 559–78.

606. His work has been rediscovered in the last generation by Michael Gorman: see his *The Manuscript Traditions of the Works of St. Augustine* (Florence, 2001).

607. See my *Cassiodorus* (Berkeley, 1979; or: www.georgetown.edu/faculty/jod/cassbook/toc.html).

608. D. W. Johnson, "The Myth of the Augustinian Synthesis," *Lutheran Quarterly* 5.2 (Summer 1991), 157–69, shows how Cassiodorus's version of Augustine was not so much unfaithful as simply incoherent, an incoherency arising from the difficulty of the issues and the imperfection of Cassiodorus's own grasp of the positions taken by both Augustine and Pelagius.

609. See M. Gorman, "Eugippius and the Origins of the Manuscript Tradition of St Augustine's 'De Genesi ad Litteram,'" *Revue Bénédictine* 93(1983) 7–30, reprinted in his *The Manuscript Tradition of the Works of St. Augustine* (cited above).

610. See above, note 339 (citing Eno).

611. E. de la Peza, *El significado de 'cor' en San Agustin* (Paris, 1962).

612. Possidius *Vita* 28–31.

613. In antiquity, only the doctor Galen attempted something similar, cataloguing the 250 books he had written.

614. There are signs that his management of and control over his own works was always very close and complete. When a man named Dulcitius wrote him with eight large "questions," his reply (*De octo quaestionibus Dulcitii*) consists of extracts from earlier works, plucked from the library: *F. et op.*, *Ench.*, *Cura mort.*, *En. Ps.*, *Div. qu. Simp.*, *C. Faust.*, and *Gn. litt.*—only one answer is fresh.

615. Cf. *Epp.* 143.5 and 143.7 for indications that it was *specifically* the *De libero arbitrio* and its later use by people Augustine disagreed with that inspired him to pick up the pen for the *Reconsiderations*.

616. *Retr.* prol. 3.

617. First edition, Berkeley and London, 1967; reprinted with substantial epilogue summarizing recent research, Berkeley and London, 2000.

618. The question is anachronistic but should be answered with a mild negative. Augustine's skin was doubtless dark enough to earn the bigotry of many pale and obtuse moderns, but he lived in a time when both extremes of light and dark were thought remote from civilization, and he speaks of "Ethiopians" as "black" (see his *En. Ps.* 73.16, commenting on Psalms 73.14), while his richer contemporaries were busy importing Saxon captives—blond hair, blue eyes, great natural athletes by all repute, but not showing great mental prowess—to fight as gladiators in their arenas (the practice was dying out, for reasons we do not really know, late in Augustine's lifetime). Of greater urgency than Augustine's "blackness" should be Augustine's Berber connections and the modern survival of Berber consciousness in Algeria, but few outside that country understand the issues that keep a province there seething and insurrectious.

619. At www.georgetown.edu/faculty/jod/augustine/quote.html.

620. *Conf.* 10.3.3.

621. *Conf.* 4.11.16.

622. A theme with a long history: P. Courcelle, *Connais-toi toi-même: de Socrate à saint Bernard* (Paris, 1974–75; 3 volumes).

623. *Conf.* 4.4.9.

624. *Conf.* 10.3.3.

625. See, e.g., Gareth Matthews, *Thought's Ego in Augustine and Descartes* (Ithaca, New York, 1992), and now the "radical orthodoxy" of Michael Hanby, *Augustine and Modernity* (London, 2003).

626. *Saint Augustine's Childhood* (New York, 2001: book 1, with translation of *The Teacher* in appendix); *Saint Augustine's Memory* (New York, 2002: book 10, with translation of book 11 in appendix); *Saint Augustine's Sin* (New York, 2003: book 2); and *Saint Augustine's Conversion* (New York, 2004: book 8); Wills intends to publish a complete translation in due course.

627. The only complete English translation is in the series *Fathers of the Church* (Washington, D.C., Catholic University of America Press) and out of print, but New City Press (www.newcitypress.com) has published a first volume comprising letters 1–99 and will carry the project forward. There is also a selection available in the Loeb Classical Library (Harvard University Press).

628. Sermons translated by E. Hill (Hyde Park, New York; 11 volumes). For the impact of the new discoveries on our understanding of Augustine, see the epilogue to the 2000 reprinting of Brown 441–520.

629. See my *Avatars of the Word* (Cambridge, Massachusetts, 1998).

AUTHOR'S NOTE

I have been reading Augustine for thirty-five years, for many reasons, different ones at different times, and by now he's learned to put up with me. I'm glad that John Adams and Bob Hollander, who sent me this way, and John Fleming, who gave me, among other things, a book, have been friends with whom to share such things. Without Nico Knauer, exemplar before he was colleague and friend for half a lifetime, this book could never have come about. Similarly, Jary Pelikan had more to do with making this possible than either of us realized. Robert Markus gave a lecture in Dublin once and another in Philadelphia a few years later, and the conversation has flourished ever since, most memorably amid the ruins of Augustine's Hippo. Some of what is here formed part of the Charles Beebe Martin Classical Lectures at Oberlin College in 2001, and I am sorry not to have given my friends there the slender volume of lectures they wanted: I hope they enjoy this one. The universities in which I have been at home these years (Penn and Georgetown) have supported me in various ways, but Yale also gave me a visiting perch at a crucial time. Professors Paula Fredriksen, Patout Burns, Mark Vessey, and Jen Ebbeler read an early version of the manuscript and made the later versions much better in the process. John Brockman and Katinka Matson saw possibilities, while Dan Halpern, Jason Epstein, and Lisa Chase cleared away a lot of underbrush, and Ed Cohen did peerlessly accurate and intelligent copyediting. To add one more name at this point in the list of thanks would compel me, in fairness, to add hundreds, of colleagues and students over many years, and would remind me that I have been fortunate beyond measure. If it were not for Ann, there would not be a life-sized fiberglass donkey in my office and my life would be infinitely poorer in ways I scarcely dare imagine. It's really her book but we agreed that the dedication should present these pages to people we specially cherish.

INDEX